First Edition

November 2000

Second Edition

February 2001

FROM THE GHETTO TO THE MAIN:

—

The Story of the Jews of Montreal

by Joe King

Edited by Johanne Schumann

with an introduction
by Historian Graeme Decarie

Published by
the Montreal Jewish Publication Society
Montreal – February 2001

This book is dedicated
to my children
Howard and Gail
Barbara and Michael
Norman and Lucile
and to my children's children
Jessica
Erin
Ilana
Joelle
and to my dear wife
Shandle Lipkus King

It is a fabled City that I seek,
It stands in Space's vapour's and Time's haze,
Thence comes my sadness in remembered joy
Constrictive on the throat,
Hence do I hear, as heard by a Jewboy,
The Hebrew Violins,
Delighting in the sobbed Oriental note.

Abraham Moses Klein (1909-72)
"Rocking Chair"

CONTENTS

X

XI

PART FOUR
The New Jerusalem

CHAI = LIFE
The number 18 has special significance among Jews. It is called "Chai," meaning "Life" in Hebrew. Gifts to charities or individuals often are made in multiples of 18 as a way of wishing good luck. Mazel Tov!

Montreal Jewish Publication Society

Preface

It is my pleasant task to introduce you to the first official publication of the Montreal Jewish Publication Society. I say "official" because the core group associated with the publication of this History of Montreal Jewry was also involved in the preparation of "Architect of a Community," the biography of Manuel G. Batshaw, in 1998. It was the presentation of the Batshaw book, and the warm welcome it received, that convinced us we should establish a Publication Society. After some consideration, the Society Executive determined that a comprehensive, detailed history of this great community was our first priority.

We are now privileged to submit this history to the public, fully aware that we are providing readers with the most extensive volume of its kind. The author, Joe King, has exhausted research sources in an all-out effort to ensure three things:

- that the book is a completely accurate chronicle of Montreal Jewish History;
- that the story is told in a most readable manner;
- that the history is comprehensive and reaches into dusty corners of our past heretofore left virtually unrevealed.

I recommend that you read this book, pass it on to others and retain copies for future generations. It is also important that this Society, conceived almost two-and-a-half centuries after the community was born, continues to provide the public with publications that reflect the past while recording the present.

I wish to thank all those who helped make this history a reality.

Lawrence M. Bessner

Lawrence M. Bessner, F.C.A.   July 10, 2000
President

C/O JOE KING – HAMILTON HOUSE, 5501 ADALBERT, SUITE 1520, CÔTE ST-LUC, QUÉBEC H4W 2B1

TEL.: (514) 481-8801 • FAX: (514) 933-9606 • E-MAIL: lbessner@cyberglobe.net

Montreal Jewish Publication Society

Executive Committee

Chairman: Lawrence Bessner, F.C.A.
Vice-Chairs: Sylvain Abitbol
Monty Berger
Anne Joseph
Joseph Paperman

Members: Babette Barkoff
Pearl Grubert
Ethel Kesler
Debbie Newpol
Barry Pascal
Advisor: Robert A. Kleinman, F.C.A.
Executive Secretary: Joe King

Honorary Editorial Committee

Hy Adelman
Manuel G. Batshaw, O.Q.
Charles Bedzow
Hillel Becker
Lavy Becker
Monty Berger
Neri J. Bloomfield
Charles R. Bronfman, C.C.
Marjorie Bronfman, M.S.W., LL.D.
Bernice Brownstein
Morty Brownstein
Miriam Charron
Barry Clamen, FCA
Marvin Corber, FCA
Norma Cummings
Steven Cummings
Professor Ben Zion Dalfen
Melvin Dobrin
Leonard Ellen
Senator Sheila Finestone
Marc Gold
Dr. Phil Gold, C.C., O.Q., MD, PhD, Dsc, FRCP(C),
  FRSC, MACP
Dr. Victor Goldbloom, O.C., O.Q., MD, LL.D.,Litt.D.
Sheila Goldbloom, C.M., BA, MSW
Yoine J. Goldstein
Rosalind Goodman
Harry Hopmeyer
Lily Ivanier
Paul Ivanier
Rabbi Howard Joseph
Norma Joseph
Naim Kattan, O.C.
Joel King
Sheila Golden Kussner, O.C., BA, LL.D.
Milly Lande, C.M.

Rabbi Leigh Lerner
Professor Loren Lerner
Harvey Levenson
Boris G. Levine, FCA
Steve Lipper
Dr. Frederick Lowy
Sam Luft
Mr. Justice Herbert Marx, BA., MA,
  LL.L., LL.M.
Eva Marx
Herb Paperman
Stanley Plotnick
Dorothy Reitman, C.M.
Oscar Respitz, C.R.
Diane Sassoon
Evelyn Schachter
Manuel Schachter, Q.C.
Judge Barbara Seal, C.M.
Judge Donald Seal
Dr. Bernard Shapiro
Herbert E. Siblin, FCA
Dr. Harvey Sigman
Dr. Maxine Sigman
Gerald Soiferman
Professor Blema Steinberg, PhD
Professor Jim Torczyner, D.S.W.
Lillian Vineberg
Robert S. Vineberg
Ben Weider
Reg Weiser
Jonathan Wener
Ike Wenger
Professor Ruth Wisse
Harvey Wolfe
Edward B. Wolkove, C.A.
Sheila Zittrer

The Society is most appreciative of the support given to it by the following contributors to this History project:

Grand Patrons

Sylvain Abitbol
Lawrence Bergman, MNA
Lawrence M. Bessner, FCA
Edward M. Bronfman Family Foundation
Gerald and Marjorie Bronfman Foundation
Federation/CJA of Montreal
Gouvernement du Québec;
　La ministre de la Culture et
　des Communications
Jewish Community Foundation
Paperman and Sons
Barry Pascal

Patrons

Harvey Adelman
Elliott Aintabi
David Azrieli, C.M.
Charles Bedzow
Albert Bensadoun
Joe Brott
Bernice and Gordon Brown Foundation
Russell Copeman, MNA
Cummings Family
Joel King
The Sandra and Leo Kolber Foundation
Dr. Marvin Kwitko
Sam Luft
Lewis C. Smith Foundation
Rhoda and Robert Vineberg
Faigie and Rubin Zimmerman

Sponsors

Babette Barkoff
Mitzi and Hillel Becker
Robert Benson
Stephen R. Bronfman
Howard B. Hoppenheim
Marbilosu Corporation
Cyril & Dorothy, Joel and Jill
　Reitman Family Foundation
Miriam Roland
Libero Rossini
Rose Marie Segal
Ruth and Micky Smolkin
Mireille and Murray;
　Blema and Arnold Steinberg

Benefactors

Monty Berger
Hyman Bloom
Mitzi and Mel Dobrin Family
Foundation
Linda Migicovsky and Norman
Jaskolka
Sheila and Marvyn Kussner
Boris G. Levine, F.C.A.
PharmaScience Inc.
Sara and Irwin Tauben

Members

David Abracen and Ann Lambert
Gershon Adelman
Ruth and Manuel G. Batshaw
Raphael Bessner
Freda and Irwin Browns
Arthur Diamond
La Fondation Divco
Rosetta Elkin
David Kirsch Forwarders Ltd.
Goldstein, Flanz & Fishman
Granofsky Holdings Company
Ernest Guter
Harry and Steffi Halton
Sheva and David Honig Foundation
Stanley Hyman
George Itzkovitz
Rabbi Leigh Lerner
Edward Levinson
Mrs. Gerry Lisser
Eva and Mr. Justice Herbert Marx
M.E. Fashion Imports
Milgro Investments
Debby and Matt Newpol
Optica Westmount
Mrs. Frances Pascal
Sydney & Miriam Pinchuk
Sally Raicek
Susan, Adam and John A. Rothschild
Roy Salomon
Donald W. Seal
Barry H. Shapiro
Roz and Max Shrier
Alex U. Soyka
Sport Collection
Rita Tenenbaum
Two Roads Investments Inc.
Jonathan Wener

Acknowledgments

The following Libraries and archives
were consulted in the preparation of this history:

Archives, Ville de Montréal
Atwater Library
Canadian Jewish Congress National Archives
Canadian Jewish News Library and picture archives
Cote St. Luc Public Library
Libraries of Concordia University
   Georges P. Vanier Library
   R. Howard Webster Library
Dawson College Library
Federation/CJA picture archives
Fraser Hickson Institute
Jewish People's and Peretz Schools Library
Jewish Public Library and Archives
McCord Museum
   The Notman Collection
   The Museum Library
McGill University's Libraries
   Humanities and Social Sciences Library
   Lawrence Lande Canadiana Collection
   Rare Books and Special Collections
National Archives of Canada
Town of Mount Royal Library
Ontario Jewish Archives
Ottawa Civic Library
Pointe-Claire Public Library
Suburban Newspaper photographic archives
Westmount Public Library

INTRODUCTION
by Professor Graeme Decarie
Concordia University Historian

My father pushed open the glass door for me. That's what fathers do when you're 11 years old. They push open doors for you, and they can push open the most wonderful doors.

We were on Park Avenue, just south of Bernard, and it was my very first visit to the big world beyond the streets of my home in Villeray District. The sign over the door said "Benny's". I entered, and sat at the longest, shiniest counter I had ever seen. Then my father talked to a big man all in white, and he talked to another big man with a big knife, and soon I had—oh, how can I describe it?

Now, I was just a kid, you know. I'd been in restaurants before. Well, once before, when I'd had a hot dog and a Coke actually served in a glass. But this before me was something else. My father told me it was called a smoked meat sandwich, and it had fries and a pickle—and a napkin. Then, when it was over, my father casually put a quarter on the counter—just as though money meant nothing at all. And that was my introduction to Montreal's Jewish community.

It had begun just weeks earlier when my father decided I should travel to Outremont to join a scout troop. In Villeray, he thought, I'd just meet a low class of bum; but in Outremont, I'd meet a much higher class of bum. In the years that followed, I never did much warm to Outremont but, oh, I just loved Park and Bernard and Fairmount and everything east to St. Laurent.

I hung out with boys who belonged to a B'nai Brith Club called Dovers. I developed intellectual curiosity I had never dreamed of at Bonder's Book Store. (Owner Abe Bonder was a delightful treasure of that period of my life.) And, whenever I could scrape together a quarter, there was the delight of Benny's. The whole district was an area of extraordinary intellectual excitement, full of ideas and attitudes I never knew existed. And it was, in a word that gets much overused, a real community.

The people of that community had no more money than we did in Villeray—which is to say they had none at all. But what a difference in attitude!

Back in Villeray, the height of ambition was to finish grade 9—maybe grade 11 for a real bookworm—and then to find a job. The very pinnacle of achievement was to become a clerk at the Bell because that was steady. But in that Jewish district, they thought like Westmounters. Their children would be doctors and lawyers and engineers—just as if that were natural.

Nor was it just to make money, though making money was important. But their children would also know theatre and painting and music and books. (Listening to a friend's father reading "Juno and the Paycock" to us in an accent flecked with Yiddishisms remains one of the enduring memories of my childhood.)

It wasn't that the parents in Villeray didn't care about their children, because they most certainly did. But we were raised mindful of our station in life and of our limitations. In the Jewish community, there were no limitations. Go for it, kid. Go for it, and your station in life will be whatever you want it to be.

Everything was geared to that. The boys in Dovers, then club secretaries and treasurers, were learning to be the hospital directors and school commissioners and politicians and community leaders that, in fact, they did become. Still today, I meet with discussion groups that still learn with friends as they have been meeting and reading and discussing regularly since their teens.

Some of it even rubbed off on me. It was along Park Avenue I learned you didn't have to vote for the party your father and grandfather voted for. There were other possibilities, even radically different possibilities. That made me a bit of a suspicious figure back home, but it has served me pretty well over the years as a political commentator.

It was a hard-nosed community, as dismissive of sentiment as the punch line of a Yiddish joke. Friendship was friendship. Business was business. It was, I guess, like that in Villeray, too. The difference was that in Villeray, we pretended it wasn't so; we were sneakier. Along Park Avenue, it was right up front. As well, along Park Avenue, it was softened by a warmth and caring that ran all through family and community. It was all very—how can I put this in an introduction to a history of the Jewish community? It was all very—Christian.

That Jewish community was the product of the history sketched in this book and, in its turn, part of the history of a community that remains as vibrant now as it was then. Forgive me for using this introduction for rambling on about my own limited experience of that history. But it was such a pleasure.

Graeme Decarie

"A people's memory is history; and as a man without a memory, so a people without a history cannot grow wiser, better."

Isaac Leibush Peretz (1851-1915) Yiddish novelist, critic and poet. Poland. From his book *"Vegn Geshitche,"* 1890.

FOREWORD

This book is the story of one of the world's greatest Jewish Communities. The story of the community has been, in many ways, that of Jewish people over countless centuries. Since 70 C.E. (A.D.), with the Roman destruction of Jerusalem, Jews began what seemed an endless search for freedom and safety. They wandered the earth, searching for sanctuary. Sometimes they found one, only to have it taken away in a year, or a generation or a century.

The waves of Jews reaching the New World were often escaping religious or nationalistic frenzy...the Roman Catholic Inquisition in Spain and Portugal in the 15th century...The state-directed persecution, poverty and pogroms of 19th-century Russia...the 20th-century Nazi crimes against humanity.

Jews who came to Canada, beginning two-and-a-half centuries ago, brought with them their history, their traditions and their culture. They also brought with them their memories of hate and hostility, of abandoned homes and ancestral graves.

In Quebec, after centuries of wandering, the Jews found opportunity and relative freedom...a new Promised Land. And in Montreal, they helped create a New Jerusalem. But it was in the context of a Christian nation, periodically misunderstanding, and even mistreating, this non-Christian minority. As former Prime Minister Pierre Elliot Trudeau, who represented the largely Jewish constituency of Mount Royal throughout his political career, put it,"a democracy is judged by the way that the majority treats the minority." And Quebec was that strange slice of the Canadian pie assembled from minorities—the English who were a minority in Quebec; the French, a minority in Canada, and the Jews, a minority everywhere but in their own neighbourhoods.

If we go back to the very beginning of the Jewish Community—to Aaron Hart in 1760 —we can see how a determined and capable individual can serve the nation while retaining his deep commitment to the Jewish people. Jews worked loyally and assiduously to help build the country that had provided them with a home. At the same time, they remained committed to their people, their culture and their traditions.

From the period in the late 19th century when they began to count their numbers in the thousands, rather than in the hundreds, Jews did what they traditionally did—they formed a community. "Join a community, by which alone your work can be made universal and eternal in its results," S.R. Hirsch wrote in 1836. Jews formed their own distinct society—positioned geographically along the vibrant St. Lawrence Boulevard, "The Main," with the bulk of francophones to the east, and most of the anglophones to the west.

Denied equal opportunity in the marketplace, they created their own commercial and industrial world, poured into the professions and provided leadership in the development of their city, their province and their country.

Jews left their mark on the land out of all proportion to their small numbers. In the military, they were officers and soldiers on both sides in the battle for New France. And they were prominent on the battlefield in all the conflicts following the Conquest. Jews were founders of Canada's merchant marine. They were leaders in building the first Canadian railway, the first telegraphic service, the first banks, the first waterworks system, the first gas supply system, the first street cars and the first electric light system in a Canadian city. Turned away from established industries, they were receptive to invention and innovation, and helped keep the nation at the cutting edge of science and technology.

Jews were and are prominent in the arts—in music, painting, sculpture, poetry. And they have been generous supporters of all the arts. They were and are distinguished academics and scientists, lawyers and doctors.

The Jewish community per se has thrived, proudly developing and maintaining the finest network of human services in Montreal. From birth to death, in sickness and in health, the community serves its constituents brilliantly. One of the most important words in Jewish philosophy is "Tzedakah", Hebrew for social justice. Helping those in need is not a matter of choice. It is an obligation.

The title of this history encapsulated the great saga of the Jewish people, beginning with the word "ghetto," a term first used in 1516 when the Jews of Venice were expelled to an island within the city which contained an iron foundry. The Old Venetian word "geto," meaning foundry, became the term for areas where Jews were compelled to live, and this confinement later was decreed by Papal Bull in 1555. Ghettoes disappeared, in western Europe, in the 19th century, but the Germans and Italians renewed the concept during World War Two. Ghetto meant confinement, denial of liberty, restrictions. The ghetto was a harsh reality, a cruel memory, for almost all Montrealers or their ancestors. Therefore, the word had special, even emotional, meaning for Jews, for nearly five centuries.

The word "Main" was used to underscore the importance of St. Lawrence Boulevard, or The Main, a neighbourhood which harboured the bulk of the Jewish community for nearly a century, and because the word also suggests mainstream, emphasizing the ascendency of Jews from cold-water flats on St. Urbain Street and The Esplanade, moving into the mainstream of the nation.

The Main, moreover, was a ghetto—but one without walls, a throbbing, vital Jewish neighbourhood, in the midst of the French and English of Montreal. It was a ghetto by definition, even though newcomers, by choice, sought to live there, with kith and kin, because of the area's familiar foods, familiar sounds and familiar people.

It was the funnel into which immigrants poured from steamship piers and downtown railway stations, starting their Canadian adventure. As they persevered and prospered, they moved up the ladder of streets, emerging from the slums in triumph.

This area of a few square blocks was the breeding ground for a remarkable number of critically important Canadians—icons of the 20th and 21st centuries—poets and politicians; artists and actors; judges and journalists; architects and academics; merchants and musicians. Sculptor Stanley Lewis says, "This area was like Florence during the Renaissance." From these few blocks came novelist Saul Bellow, writer Mordecai Richler, poets A.M. Klein, J.I. Segal, Irving Layton and Leonard Cohen, Mr. Justice Herbert Marx, actor William Shatner, painter Moses Reinblatt, politician David Lewis, medical researcher Phil Gold, conductor-composer Alexander Brott, and a bevy of barristers and businessmen. From this narrow strip, often the progeny of penniless immigrants, came some of Canada's most influential figures.

Jewish immigrants provided Canadians with a variety of exotic foods, but especially Montreal smoked meat, lovingly hand-rubbing spices and herbs into briskets, and the unique Montreal bagel, baked to perfection in wood-fired ovens.

On the lower Main, the Pascal, Reitman and Steinberg families got their start as glaziers, tailors and operators of a corner store, on the road to developing huge, successful retail chains.

"From the Ghetto to the Main", therefore was researched and written to make people aware of the exceptional role played by Montreal Jews in the growth and development of Canada. Despite what they accomplished, Jews are rarely singled out for appropriate recognition in Canadian history books. Abraham Gradis saved New France from starvation in 1752 but search in vain for his name and contribution in Canadian histories. Aaron Hart, in the 18th century, was one of the most successful fur-traders and businessmen in early Canada, but where the McTavish and McGill families are noted, Hart's name and accomplishments are neglected. Sir Mortimer B. Davis, head of Imperial Tobacco, was a major figure in the important tobacco business. But he is rarely acknowledged in books dealing with the industry. Jewish developers were and are among the foremost property developers in the city, conceiving and constructing soaring skyscrapers and constructing a multiplicity of shopping facilities. Montreal was and is a great city in significant measure because it was privileged to accommodate a visionary, venturesome, versatile and vibrant Jewry. They were frequently in the vanguard of much of what made and makes Montreal great.

I hope this volume will help illuminate a neglected portion of Canadian history.

One of this book's most important aspects is the building of lists of some of the earliest families. Many Montrealers will be able to spot the name of an ancestor who came here in the 18th or 19th century and some of those names are still prominent in 21st-century Montreal.

In this book are many stories, some amusing, some tragic. These vignettes of the famous and not-so-famous are often presented without names because they mirror the experiences of many.

We have borrowed freely from the work of great Montreal Jewish artists—including the poetry of A.M. Klein, Leonard Cohen and Irving Layton; the prose of Mordecai Richler and Saul Bellow; the artwork of Ernst Newman, Moses Reinblatt and Stanley Lewis— all gifted, all Montrealers. Artist Sydney Berne put aside his pallet and brushes to draw our map of The Main.

Finally, I have to single out those people who helped greatly to make this history a reality—Professor Lawrence M. Bessner FCA, who has been my partner in many successful community efforts, Professor Graeme Decarie of Concordia University, who provided guidance in the shaping of this story, McGill University's Professor Morton Weinfeld, who was an adviser, and, above all, Johanne C. Schumann, the book's editor, who applied her immense skills, with enthusiasm and genuine interest, to the development of the manuscript. Our frequent editorial consultations were aided by the consumption of endless briskets of smoked meat, dozens of bagels (cream cheese optional), pounds of gefilte fish and gallons of tea with lemon (served in a glass, of course). And long editorial conferences tried the patience of waitresses from the Brown Derby to Wilensky's.

I ALSO OWE SPECIAL THANKS TO
Archivist Janice Rosen and her assistant Hélène Vallée of the National Archives of Canadian Jewish Congress; Eiran Harris and Ronald Finegold of the Jewish Public Library; Eleanor London and her reference staff at the Cote St. Luc Public Library; Gary Tynski at McGill University's Rare Books and Special Collections Division; Charles Shahar of Federation/CJA, for his detailed information on the community; Geneviève Boutry for helping with translations, and on the technical side, to Frank Panarello and Trilogix, and computer consultant Bruce Tirer. Hy Becker, and his Graphique CDS, is owed special thanks for his customary, exceptional assistance.

Thanks too to Elaine Shatenstein for patient proofreading and more.

Finally, I must express particular appreciation to my wife, Shandle Lipkus King, for her endless patience while I toiled over this manuscript.

Joe King, Montreal, July 10, 2000.

Not sole was I born, but entire genesis:
For to the fathers that begat me, this
Body is residence. Corpuscular,
They dwell in my veins, they eavesdrop at my ear,
They circle, as with Torahs, round my skull,
In exit and in entrance all day pull
The latches of my heart, descend and rise —
And there look generations through my eyes.
Abraham Moses Klein (1909-72)
Psalm XXXVI
"A Psalm touching geneology" 1944

PART ONE

JEWS IN A NEW WORLD
The Pioneer Years

Jewish history in America began with the expulsion of Jews from the Iberian nations in the fifteenth century. Denied a homeland for 20 centuries, persecuted and impoverished in Europe, they boldly followed on the heels of the explorers of the New World in their quest for a safe abode. With musket and cannon, they fought on both sides in the war for New France, but it was the British victory that opened Canada's doors to Jews. Pioneers braved the harsh climate and the difficulties of a frontier town, building a strong community and living in harmony with their neighbours. Quebec granted its Jewish citizens full civil and political liberties a generation before Britain followed suit. In their first century, the Jews of Montreal followed the path of trade and commerce to prominence, prestige, and prosperity.

CHAPTER ONE

WANDERING IN THE WILDERNESS
The Search for The Lost Tribes

He journeyed across vast stretches of lowlands and forests along the shores of the lakes and tributaries of the great St. Lawrence River, from one Indian encampment to another, squatting on the ground while he listened intently to the natives to hear if some of their words were, indeed, from Hebrew! Though not a Jew, Marc Lescarbot, the first historian of New France, subscribed to the widely held belief that the North American Indians were descendants of the Ten Lost Tribes of Israel. Lescarbot, making notes on sheets of thick hand-made paper, began his search for cultural and linguistic ties to the ancient Jewish language almost from the moment he stepped ashore, in 1608, at the small wooden Habitation built that year by Samuel de Champlain at Quebec.

Historian, diplomat, playwright and poet, Marc Lescarbot was also a lawyer, who came to the French colony on the invitation of one of his clients, Jean de Biencourt de Poutrincourt, with the intention of glorifying 100 years of French exploration and discovery. As was common for a well-educated Renaissance man of the seventeenth century, Lescarbot studied many classical languages, including Hebrew. In his books, he showed a deep knowledge of Judaism, writing some passages in Hebrew, and

TIMELINE—THE 17TH CENTURY
1600. King Henry IV grants a group of French Merchants exclusive rights to fur trading in the Gulf of St. Lawrence.
1608. Quebec City founded by Samuel de Champlain.
1627. Cardinal Richelieu bans non-Catholics from the colony.
1642. Paul de Chomedy, Sieur de Maisonneuve, founds the colony of Ville Marie.
1663. Quebec is made a Royal Province.
1666. Canada's first census records 668 families living in Quebec—3,215 individuals. Indians were not counted. Officially, there were no Jews.

The search for the legendary **Ten Lost Tribes** began after the conquest of the Northern Kingdom of Israel, in 722 Before Common Era (or B.C.). Assyria attacked and destroyed much of Israel, leaving only two tribes confined to the southern Kingdom of Judah (whence came the word Jew). The remaining ten tribes were taken captive. Their ultimate fate is not known. (For 27 centuries, the search has continued. Periodically, there are reports that some remnants of the tribes have been discovered.)

THE SEPHARAD SEARCH FOR FREEDOM

When Christopher Columbus sailed from the port of Palos, Spain, in 1492, his fleet of three ships passed numerous vessels crammed with desperate Jews, fleeing religious persecution, notably the Inquisition. In Spain and Portugal, secret trials and torture were used to identify and punish those who did not adhere to the teachings of the Church; penalties ranged from flogging and imprisonment to *auto-de-fe*, burning at the stake. The Spanish monarchs, Queen Isabella and King Ferdinand, serving as reluctant agents of the religious hierarchy, ordered all Jews to convert to Catholicism or be banished. (Jews had earlier been expelled from England in the thirteenth century and from France in the fourteenth century.) Of the estimated 150,000 Spanish Jews, known as **Sephardim** (*Sepharad* is the Hebrew word for Spain), many of whose families had lived in the Iberian peninsula for five centuries, 100,000 were dispersed across western Asia, north Africa and Europe. One-third reluctantly converted to Christianity, and of those, many continued to practice Judaism in secret. Some of Columbus' crew were Jews who had become "New Christians," or *conversos*. The Spanish called them *marranos*, meaning swine.

making frequent references to the **Talmud**, the body of oral Jewish law, that supplements the Torah or Old Testament. And so it came to be that the Word — the written Hebrew language — was used and documented in New France long before history recorded the arrival of the first Jew!

THE SEARCH FOR THE LOST ISRAELITES

Lescarbot spent a great deal of time with the natives, seated among groups of lean and sinewy warriors — noting what they said, striving to detect similarities with the ancient Israelites. He transcribed, as best he could, their chants. Did their songs have any similarity to traditional Jewish prayers? He found none. His wanderings included visits to the Micmac, Huron and Algonquin Indians, chatting with both braves and chiefs, and occasionally eating with them in their bark-covered lodges. Was there anything Jewish about their diet? Nothing that he could identify. In fact, Lescarbot failed to find anything Judaic among the diverse tribes — whether in language, custom, food, or tradition.

Lescarbot's "Histoire de la Nouvelle-France," published in France in 1609, succeeded —with its eye-witness accounts of "the province's Moral, Natural and Geographic History"— in arousing European interest in the distant colony. Early accounts of exploration, such as those by Lescarbot and authorized by royalty, were intended to promote interest in France's overseas possessions and in so doing inspired countless Jews to consider sanctuary in the New World, and to renew the dream of a Promised Land.

FIRST JEWS IN THE NEW WORLD

The theory that the Indians might be descendants of early Jews was widely held. When Christopher Columbus arrived in the New World, the first European to step onto American soil was a

Indians greeting settlers in 17th century New France. Many believed the natives were descendants of the Ten Lost Tribes of Israel. (Historic drawing by C.W. Jefferys, National Archives of Canada, negative C73423)

Jew. Luis de Torres, a translator and interpreter for the Columbus expedition, had been nominally baptized the day before he set sail for the Caribbean. The multilingual de Torres shared Columbus's belief that the natives were related to the Lost Tribes, and he tried communicating with them in Hebrew and Arabic — with no success. Exploration of North America, however, opened the door to new possibilities for European Jews in exile. In the words of the Jewish poet Emma Lazarus, it served "**to unlock the golden gates of sunset and bequeath a Continent to freedom.**"

The first significant movement of Jews to North America took place in 1654 when 23 Jews arrived in New Amsterdam, a Dutch colonial outpost, later New York. These Jews were mostly descendants of those expelled from Portugal in 1497, who had re-settled in the Netherlands, and later Brazil. They were sailing back to Holland when pirates seized their vessel. Later, a French privateer vessel attacked and captured the pirate ship. The Jews were rescued and transported to the nearest port, where they unwittingly became the pioneers of Jewish settlement in North America. These Sephardim, or Spanish Jews, regarded themselves as aristocrats of New World Jewry, and looked upon their sailing ship as the Jewish version of the Mayflower, the ship in which the Pilgrims sailed to America.

> They left behind the grape, the olive, and the fig; the vines they planted, the corn they sowed, the garden-cities of Andalusia and Aragon, Estremadura and La Mancha, of Granada and Castile; the altar, the hearth, and the grave of their fathers.
>
> Emma Lazarus
> (1849-1887)

JEWS IN QUEBEC

In the frantic search for freedom and opportunity, unknown numbers of Jews began the long, perilous voyage across the North Atlantic. New France until the late 1660s was almost entirely a wilderness outpost, with three small fortified towns—Quebec City, Trois-Rivières and Montreal—controlled by fur-trading companies. Discouraged by the long harsh winters and remoteness, adventurers did not settle, staying one or two years, only long enough to make their fortune. A Royal Proclamation (1627) prohibited the settlement of non-Catholics. France's powerful Cardinal Richelieu, Chief Minister to King Louis XIII, imposed the ban, when he formed the Company of New France. The Company was intended to build the population of the colony, but with the pledge to maintain the exclusivity of the Catholic Church. Jews who entered the colony did so covertly.

JEWISH NAMES APPEAR IN COLONIAL RECORDS

Seventeenth-century records in Montreal and Quebec City include names of men of obvious Jewish lineage. Some bore

Champlain's "Habitation", founded in 1608 by French explorer Samuel de Champlain. It was from outposts like this that Canada's first historian, Marc Lescarbot, wrote his books, with passages in Hebrew and Talmudic references. (Historic drawing by C.W. Jefferys, National Archives of Canada, negative C73448)

The Spanish Edict expelling the Jews, signed by Queen Isabella and King Ferdinand and dated March 31, 1492.

names derived from their city of origin: Toledano (from Toledo), Valenis (from Valencia), Amereydos and several names linked to the Spanish city of Bejar. In Montreal, a creditor of the colonial government was referred to as Joseph de Silva, the "so-called Portuguese." Documents of the time refer to such names as Maranda (possibly a distortion of Miranda), and Joseph Coste (possibly a corruption of Costa). Similarly, the names of some early Jesuit priests and missionaries indicate they were of Jewish descent.

Accordingly, descendants of the exiled Spanish and Portuguese Sephardim turn up in many parts of the New World, including Canada. For those who reached Montreal in its earliest days, their wandering had lasted nearly 300 years.

From the time of the Spanish Inquisition, many individuals of Jewish origin concealed their religious and cultural expressions, maintaining secret identities in order to 'pass' in the majority culture. Known as conversos or crypto-Jews, they created hybrid private/public personas merging Hispanic, Catholic and Jewish elements. In the modern era, many Jews have paralleled the converso experience of 'hidden-ness' and 'emergence.' For some, explicit manifestations of Jewish identity are seldom expressed in public life, and Jewishness is relegated to the private sphere. Recently, a number have returned to more active and public identification as Jews.

From the Council of Jewish Museums
Annual Conference, 2000

CHAPTER TWO

"I AM JEWISH!"
The Story of Esther, The Defiant Jewess

The Quebec port authorities spotted her right away. She was dressed in the baggy garb of a sailor and was stepping onto a jetty from the merchant ship 'Saint-Michel' when the discovery was made. Actually, it was the medical officer who noticed what a ship's crew had failed to recognize during the entire six weeks at sea. That this handsome 'boy' was, in reality, a woman! Worse, when interrogated, she disclosed that she was Jewish! Officials were outraged that a Jew dared defy a Royal Edict by stepping onto the holy soil of New France. The Intendant was notified, and a report was drafted, the first of many, to be sent directly to the King.

The year was 1738. For more than a century, France had barred immigration to its oversea colony, New France, by non-Catholics, particularly Protestant Huguenots, but the ban applied to Jews, too. Despite this, an unknown number of Jews, or people of Jewish ancestry, seeking adventure or opportunity, tried to slip into the French colony unnoticed but—insofar as we know—they were all detected and given a choice: convert or be deported. Records are sparse. However, there are two documented cases of Jews who converted: George Hart in 1740, and Marianne Perious from France in 1749. The only recorded exception: a defiant young girl named Esther Brandeau, who withstood a year-long, intensive effort to convert her.

On September 15th, 1738, the Quebec Marine Commissioner, in his report on an interview with the girl, wrote: "This day, before the undersigned, appeared Esther Brandeau, aged about 20 years, who embarked at La Rochelle, dressed in boy's clothes, under the name Jacques La Fargue...she declared her name to be Esther Brandeau and that she is of the Jewish religion." Brandeau

THE "ROYAL PROVINCE"
Canada (from the Huron-Iroquois word *Kanata*, meaning a village or community) evolved in sharp contrast with the English colonies to the south. While Roman Catholicism was the only faith permitted in New France, the American colonies were settled by Protestants and Catholics fleeing religious intolerance in their own lands, and seeking the right to worship as they pleased. In addition, there were Puritans and other dissenters. The earliest law in history granting full equality to citizens—regardless of their religion—was the Virginia Bill for Establishing Religious Freedom, passed in 1785. Under English law, the settlers in America also enjoyed a large measure of self-government. The first General Assembly in America occurred in 1619 in Virginia. By contrast, Court appointees ruled Quebec. The French

colony's domination by a single religion, with a feudal, seigneurial land-holding system, was to prevail until long after British Conquest in 1759. Other than subsistence agriculture, virtually the only economic activity in French Canada was fur trading—in contrast with the vigorous growth of commerce and industry in the burgeoning English colonies, where the climate was more moderate. By 1760, the British colonies in North America had more than one million inhabitants, including 3,000 Jews.
Between 1608—when Champlain founded Quebec City—and 1760, when that city was lost to the English, only 10,000 immigrants came to Quebec: 3,500 soldiers, 1,100 women, 1,000 prisoners and 4,400 settlers—three-quarters of whom were indentured servants. Almost all these people were from France, sent by the crown. In addition, the population included slaves—African Blacks and Indians. After Conquest, few immigrants to Canada were from France. In 1760, Quebec's population was estimated at 65,000. Officially, there were no Jews.

readily acknowledged that she was "daughter of David Brandeau, a Jew, trader of St. Esprit, diocese of Daxe, near Bayonne."

She was turned over to nuns at Quebec Hospital where they hurried to sew her more appropriate clothes to replace the sailor's outfit she wore on arrival. They provided her with a coarse homespun skirt, a bonnet, and other garments.

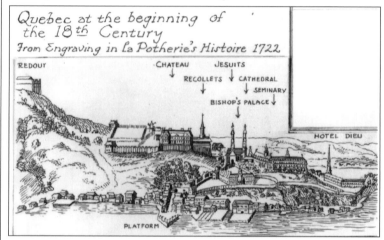

Quebec City at the time of the visit of Esther Brandeau, the Jewish girl who posed as a man and refused to convert when discovered. (From an 18th century engraving, National Archives of Canada, negative C69134)

TO ENJOY THE SAME FREEDOM AS CHRISTIANS

In interviews with the clerics, the young woman told her story: Five years earlier—when she was fifteen years old—her family had sent her by ship to stay with her brother and an aunt in Amsterdam, Holland. However, the vessel was wrecked on the French coast, and a member of the crew rescued her. A woman from Biarritz named Catherine Churiau gave her shelter and fed her pork and other kinds of meat forbidden to Jews. Apparently, Brandeau was from an observant home, and having violated the laws of **Kashrut** (kosher food) believed she was unable to return to the family. According to an official summary, "she decided not to return to her parents but instead to enjoy the same freedom as Christians." For more than a year, she drifted about, often dressed as a male, finding occasional employment as a ship's cook, a tailor's assistant and, ironically, as a servant in a Recollet convent, before leaving France. The captain of the 'Saint-Michel,' Sieur de la Sallaberi (sic), claims to have had no idea his crew had included a woman.

In Quebec, this young woman—alone, openly Jewish, and defiant of the establishment—became a subject of speculation
among the aristocrats running the colony, including the governor,
the intendant, the commander of the armed forces and the
bishop. The Intendant (or manager of the colony), M. Hocquart,
was responsible for periodic reports to His Most Christian
Majesty King Louis XV.

"Since her arrival at Quebec," he wrote "her conduct has been fair-
ly restrained." And he added: "She appears desirous of being
converted to Catholicism." Nuns and priests had begun a series of
frequent discussions aimed at convincing her to accept baptism.

Brandeau remained in Quebec City for about a year, extending
her stay by periodically hinting that she might convert.
Brandeau appears to have toyed with the religious people; otherwise, they never would have allowed her to linger for that length
of time. Apparently, she was not a prisoner, as she was housed in
a number of private homes during her stay and had a lot of freedom to move about the fortified town, known as the Citadel.
From the battlement on the heights, she could look down on the
bustling harbourfront and Lower Town.

Quebec City in the 1700s was a well-established military base
and administrative centre—with outpost districts in Trois-
Rivières and Montreal—and a population of about 7,000, which
included a military garrison, fur-traders, tradesmen, farmers, and
a handful of merchants. The fur trade was still active in the
colony, despite its being unprofitable due to repeated Indian
wars. Mostly, the purpose of the colony had become military: to
sustain a threat to England, tying up British troops in North
America so as to be unavailable to fight in Europe.

SOCIAL ACCEPTANCE BY CONVERSION

To maintain order in the colony, and loyalty among the Indians,
the Crown tolerated the presence of a powerful church hierarchy
consisting of a small number of fervent religious. On at least one
occasion the Bishop was known to have defied the King. Having
passed through a series of religious wars, France prohibited other
religions as they could provide a nucleus of opposition.

A conversion was a cause for celebration, sometimes on a
grand scale. On one occasion, when a would-be Jewish colonist
agreed during the sea passage to convert, an elaborate ceremony
was held in Fortress Louisbourg, with high-ranking senior officials from Acadia in attendance. Conversion, it would appear,
was more than religious; it meant admission to society.

After a year of vain efforts to convince Brandeau to become a Catholic, the authorities lost patience. "She is so fickle," Hocquart wrote on September 27, 1739, "that at times she has been as much receptive as hostile to the instructions that zealous ecclesiastics have attempted to give her." And he added: "I have no alternative but to send her away."

A question arose as to who would pay her passage back to France. In a letter, King Louis XV indicated he would pay for her return trip out of his personal account. Her departure was confirmed in a formal letter from the intendant to the Admiral of France, dated January 25, 1740: "My cousin the Sieur Hocquart...has embarked at Quebec on the ship 'Comte de Matignon' of La Rochelle the so-called Esther Brandeau, a Jewess whom he had to send back to France in execution of my orders." In the end, they weren't even sure if she had given them her right name.

After that, no more is heard of Esther Brandeau.

Two and a half centuries, and the story of the defiant Jewess remains an enigma. She never explained why she disguised herself as a man and undertook the long and dangerous voyage to New France. Writer Max Bookman (in the Canadian Jewish Reference Book of 1963) suggested "it is interesting to speculate that her real reason for her sojourn to the New World could have been romance. The object of her affection could have been a Marrano, of whom there is ample evidence that these refugees from the Inquisition settled in Canada outwardly Catholics but secretly loyal to the Jewish faith." If that was the goal of her trip, she probably met with him. However, it is equally possible that Esther, despite what she had been told by society, understood a fundamental truth—she was deserving of the same opportunities and civil liberties as enjoyed by Christian men. While her true motives may never be known, what is apparent is that Esther Brandeau was a determined and courageous individual, who said "I am Jewish" and dared to defy the Establishment.

Jewishness is far more than religion; it is an inextricable mixture of faith, nationhood and culture. It is an order of being perhaps more than of believing. Being Jewish is feeling the past in one's bones and living all out in the present; it is Job's 'Chutzpah' as well as his submission to God; it is the lingering melancholy which the 17th century writer Judah Halevi called 'the aching heart of nations' and it is sharp humour, often directed at oneself. For all his changes, the American Jew has not lost these qualities; in fact he is making them, more than ever, a gift to the world."

Essay, Time Magazine, 1968

CHAPTER THREE

THE ADVENTUROUS HOUSE OF GRADIS
The Family that Helped Emancipate
The Jews of France

The year was 1752, and the colonists of New France were star-ving. There had been another crop failure; the colony was unable to feed itself and remained dependent on the mother country for periodic supplies. France, immersed in the fifth costly war with England in 137 years, was mired in court intrigue and corrup-tion. The commander of the Quebec troops wrote to his mother that the peasants were beginning to eat grass. The very existence of the colony was in danger. However, the townspeople became excited and hopeful when word sped through the military outpost and nearby farms that the masts and sails of a merchant vessel had been spotted, moving up the St. Lawrence River. They crowded to the ramparts of the Citadel and cheered wildly when the vessel, with the blue and white flag of France flapping at its mainmast, dropped anchor near the waterfront. Aboard the 'Benjamin,' with its life-saving cargo of wheat and "other foodstuffs," was the ship-owner, a Jewish merchant from Bordeaux, Abraham Gradis, who would prove to be one of the greatest friends of New France. Yet, after enduring the six-week-long perilous voyage on the rolling and pitching North Atlantic, Gradis did not leave the bridge of his ship. He was not permitted to step onto the land, because he was a Jew.

TIMELINE—THE 18TH CENTURY
1713. The Treaty of Utrecht confirms British possession of Hudson Bay, Newfoundland and Acadia (Nova Scotia without Cape Breton Island).
1748. Gradis founds the "Society of Canada" to promote trade between France and French colonies in Canada.
1752. The 'Benjamin', owned by Jewish merchant Abraham Gradis of Bordeaux, France, arrives at Quebec City with wheat for a starving city.

Abraham Gradis, successful French-speaking merchant and strong supporter of efforts to develop overseas colonies, repeatedly risked his tubby merchant ships and cargoes on seas dominated by the men-of-war and frigates of the powerful British Navy. Why would someone risk his entire fortune, endanger his own life and continue to do everything in his power to help a colony where he was not welcome? The answer lies in the family history. The Gradis family was Jewish Portuguese, originally. Their Sephardic ancestors were respected and even admired in the Golden Age of Iberian nations. They were leading figures in society—philosophers, scientists, doctors, high government officials, map-makers—before they were expelled from the peninsula in the late fifteenth century. Forced to abandon centuries of history, and to look for new homes, some Jews went to England, the Netherlands, North Africa, and in considerable numbers, to Turkey. The Gradis family was accepted by France, where they did their utmost to serve their adopted nation, despite limitations on their civil liberties. They deeply appreciated that they had found a place where they were able to live and prosper. They believed that—in due time—France would grant them full citizenship. And they were right!

The French port of Bordeaux in the late 18th century, base of operations for the Jewish House of Gradis, which strove to save the colony of New France through the provision of food, supplies and even soldiers. (Copper plate engraving by Thomas Allom)

David Gradis, the patriarch, formed the House of Gradis, an assemblage of highly successful merchant bankers, who at one time controlled a fleet of 14 sailing ships, many of them bearing Biblical names. He developed trade between France and its North American colony, thereby establishing the French merchant marine. His son, Abraham, took up passionately the cause of New France. He formed, in 1748, the "Society of Canada," to promote trade with the colony, ensure availability of colonial resources, and guarantee France's self-sufficiency during wartime.

With resources earmarked for wars in Europe, France did little to help its isolated, often snowbound, colony and left merchants to provide for its overseas possessions. The cost of maintaining a military presence in New France was enormous. Paris had to defend the colony from the burgeoning New England colonies, and from Indian raiders, particularly the Iroquois confederation. Furthermore, French nobility was not interested in Canada. "Canada is useful only to provide me with furs," sniffed Madame Pompadour, mistress to King Louis XV. "I think France can do very well without Quebec," declared the influential French writer, Voltaire.

The outbreak of the Seven Years' War (1756-1763) quickly put New France in a desperate condition. The government entrusted Abraham Gradis with the task of supplying the colony using fleets he would organize. Gradis was named Agent of the King's Navy, positioning him as the second-highest authority in French naval matters. He assembled and armed a fleet that included his finest vessel, the 'Robust,' which had done well in earlier escapades involving the British Navy. Gradis convinced a relative, David Alexander of Bayonne, to add his vessel, the 'Prince Noir.'

Repeatedly, the House of Gradis sent shiploads of food, supplies, weapons, gunpowder and even soldiers to Quebec City, and other destinations.

A Jewish merchant in 18th century France.
(original engraving)

MONTCALM'S DEPENDENCE ON THE HOUSE OF GRADIS

The commander of troops in New France, the Marquis Louis-Joseph de Montcalm, became increasingly dependent on help from Abraham Gradis and his associates. Montcalm makes many references to Gradis in his journal. His entry on June 9, 1757, notes the arrival of the 'David' and the 'Jason,' two of Gradis' ships: "The most important news for us...is that we have received food, powder, soldiers and all that we have latterly requested."

While Gradis worked with Montcalm to save Quebec, their efforts were undermined by interference from the Governor, M. Vaudreuil, and the corruption of the Intendant, François Bigot. Paris had appointed no fewer than three leaders in its tiny colony, (the third was the Bishop) and the lines of authority between and among them, were not clear. This fragmentation of leadership meant confusion and inefficiency. History would prove it the undoing of French control in Canada.

While the *habitant* went hungry, Bigot lived in luxury and accumulated a fortune through the illegal sale of goods that Gradis had shipped to New France for the welfare of the colonists. The people in Quebec City and Montreal made no secret of their disdain for the Intendant. They openly labelled Bigot's warehouses la friponne, the cheat. While Bigot held lavish dinners and colourful balls, General Montcalm and his troops were on short rations.

In 1757, Montcalm wrote his mother, the Marquise de St. Veran, at her home in France: "M. de la Porte, Chief Clerk of the Navy Office is so neglectful that I must ask you not to write through him any more, but through M. Gradis at Bordeaux." Apparently, Montcalm had more faith in the reliability of Gradis than that of French naval officials.

ELUDING THE BRITISH BLOCKADE

Besides supplies, the Jewish supporters of Montcalm recruited and transported 400 soldiers to the New World. In this effort, Gradis lost his ship 'David' on the return leg of the journey. As the war progressed, Gradis lost more merchant ships and cargoes through interception by British warships. On July 6, 1757, Montcalm noted in his journal: "My supplies from Montpelier and from Bordeaux were sent by several ships, three (of which) have come in. The 'Robuste' was in a hard fight and put back into this port. There is no news of the 'Superbe' and of the 'Renommée'."

Survival of the French presence in North America depended, inexorably, on supplies from the homeland, and Paris had neither the resources nor the will to supplement Gradis' efforts. By the fall of 1758, Gradis was providing the beleaguered French colony with the only help it was receiving. In November, he recognized the precarious situation of the French, when he wrote rather discouragingly: "Nothing has happened for twenty months now, except that we have let our navy be destroyed. We have just lost Isle Royale (Cape Breton Island) and now Canada is threatened. We have only one warship left...and it is impossible to send a single vessel to the colonies."

A LAST-DITCH EFFORT TO SAVE NEW FRANCE

Gradis, well aware of the formidable British Navy patrolling the Gulf, nevertheless made a final effort to supply Montcalm. In July 1759, one of his merchant vessels came across the British and the largest naval flotilla ever assembled. Gradis' skipper, Denis de Vitre, of Quebec City, gawked at the forty English warships— some of them huge men-of-war equipped with more than 100 cannons—maneuvering in the waterway. Gradis' lightly armed merchant ship was intercepted by the entire British invasion fleet, with 27,000 soldiers, bound for Quebec.

It was the first time ships of this size had navigated the St. Lawrence. In a curious twist of fate, the French skipper de Vitre, an expert pilot, was dragooned into working with British Naval Lieutenant James Cook (later of Pacific Ocean exploration fame) to guide the huge sailing ships up the relatively narrow channels of the great river. As the immense fleet passed under the cannon of the Citadel, the Intendant Bigot, under investigation for corruption even as the city came under siege, complained in his journal: "They passed by night as well as by day." The stately procession of sailing craft was several miles long.

In another ironic turn, supplies intended for a beleaguered Montcalm, including gunpowder, went into the holds of the ships of Admiral Charles Saunders. Later they would help propel cannon balls against the walls of Quebec City.

For Gradis, the outcome was painfully clear. He had lost a vessel and its cargo—and France was about to lose its grip on North America. In later years, the House of Gradis continued to transport food and supplies to French colonies in the Caribbean. Again, bureaucrats in Paris failed to compensate them properly.

After the war, the Intendant Bigot was tried for his crimes, in Paris, with Abraham Gradis testifying against him on the personal invitation of the king. Some Quebec historians have suggested that Gradis fabricated the charges against Bigot. However, at the time of the trial, 24 magistrates investigated Bigot and found him guilty of extensive corruption. He narrowly escaped execution. The magistrates seized 354,602 livres from the French official's estate, and compensated Gradis a portion of the money owed to him.

FREEDOM FOR THE JEWS OF FRANCE; HONOURS FOR GRADIS
The Gradis Family's costly and valiant efforts did not go unrecognized. On August 21, 1779, King Louis XVI formally honoured Abraham Gradis—granting his family full and equal rights as citizens of France. Historian Benjamin G. Sack wrote of the Gradis family: "To them France was indebted for her commercial leadership as well as for the founding of her merchant marine and thereby for the defence of her widespread colonial possessions." French historian Camille Jullian wrote that Gradis "appeared to protect and represent France more than royalty itself."

The efforts of the Bordeaux family led, a decade later, in the wake of the French Revolution, to the emancipation of all Jews in France. During a 1789 debate, a revolutionary priest, Abbé Henri Gregoire, rose in the French National Assembly and recalled the sacrificial efforts of Gradis on behalf of France, and particularly the shipment of wheat, saving the colony from starvation. The priest demanded full civil liberties for Jews and told the assembly: "Fifty-thousand Frenchmen arose this morning as slaves. It depends on you whether they shall go to bed as free men." In

Abbé Henri Gregoire, the French clergyman who successfully fought for the emancipation of Jews in the French Revolutonary Assembly in 1790

1791, France passed the Act of Emancipation, giving its 90,000 Jews full citizen rights—the first such proclamation in the world. This momentous decision was made, largely, because of the Gradis family's services to its adopted land. The decision of the French Assembly resonated throughout Western Europe and led to the freedom of Jews in many countries.

Jewish historian B.G. Sack wrote of Abraham Gradis: "His efforts to maintain France's prestige in the New World at a time when her influence was rapidly waning have earned him a particular niche in the history of the French regime in Canada." However, histories of Canada, in French or English, rarely mention him.

What is national freedom if not a people's inner freedom to cultivate its abilities along the beaten path of its history?

Ahad HaAm,
HaShiloah, 1902

CHAPTER FOUR

THE BATTLE FOR NEW FRANCE
The Dramatic Story of A Jewish Naval Captain

Spring 1759. Night on the St. Lawrence River. Visibility poor. Captain Alexander Schomberg, a daring young British naval officer, planned to remain all night on the quarterdeck of his 36-gun frigate 'Diana' as the sailing vessel, amidst some 40 other British warships, slowly pushed its way to where the river narrows at Quebec. All went well, until a small, armed sloop, caught by a sharp breeze, collided with the Jewish officer's warship, driving it hard aground. The 'Diana' lay stranded on a craggy shore— within range of batteries of French cannon. Through the night, Schomberg and his crew laboured to lighten the frigate and haul her off the rocks. They lowered heavy cannon into lighters moored alongside while cannon balls from French positions splashed into the river. At dawn, the French General, Montcalm, arriving to appraise the situation, found two of his gunners swinging from a hastily rigged gallows, punished for failing to destroy the 'Diana.' Across the fast-flowing river, Schomberg's lightly damaged frigate was being towed off the rocks.

TIMELINE—THE 18TH CENTURY

1755. Britain expels the Acadians from Nova Scotia; they migrate to other British colonies in North America.

1756. Formal declaration of war between France and England beginning Seven Years' War.

1759. British forces led by General James Wolfe capture Quebec in a battle on the Plains of Abraham.

1760. French General de Levis almost recaptures Quebec but British naval vessels destroy his supply fleet, and he is forced to retreat.

1760. The first Jews settle in Quebec—Aaron Hart in Trois-Rivières; Samuel Jacobs in Saint-Denis and several in Montreal.

1763. The Treaty of Paris cedes Quebec to the British.

1764. The first Jewish child is born in Canada, David David, son of Phoebe Samuel and Lazarus David.

1768. Shearith Israel, the first synagogue in Canada and the first non-Catholic place of worship, is founded in Montreal.

CONTEST FOR A CONTINENT

The Royal Navy's ability to transport troops and supplies, destroy French warships and supply vessels and blockade enemy ports was the key to British victory in New France during the Seven Years' War, 1756-1763. Schomberg and his warship played an important role as the battle between France and England for control of the New World came to a spectacular showdown at Quebec.

The Jewish captain, who would have had to convert, at least ostensibly, to Christianity before enlisting in the navy at age 23, first showed his mettle during the assault on the strategically important military position of Fortress Louisbourg, which guarded the entrance to the St. Lawrence—and then in the effort to conquer the heart of New France, the Citadel of Quebec.

In 1758, British forces under Colonel James Wolfe attacked Louisbourg, considered by the French to be impregnable because of its $2^1/_2$ miles of 30-foot-high wall. Schomberg's frigate helped cover the landing of 400 seamen in the teeth of French batteries. The Jewish naval officer, along with Wolfe, scrambled ashore under heavy cannon and musket fire, and positioned artillery to batter and break the 12-foot-thick walls. Schomberg was in command of the assault cannon. After the French surrendered, the British commander praised Schomberg in his dispatches and

1768. Moses Hart, eldest son of Aaron Hart, is born in Trois-Rivières.

1768. Uriah Judah is named protonotary of the Superior Court in Trois-Rivières.

1770. Ezekiel Hart, second son of Aaron Hart, is born in Trois-Rivières.

1771. Levy Solomons is named Food Commissioner to His Majesty's forces in Canada.

1774. The Quebec Act guarantees religious freedom for Roman Catholics in Quebec and restores French Civil Law. Jews are not mentioned.

1775. Montreal is captured by American revolutionary forces and held for 188 days.

1775. Lazarus David buys land on St. Janvier Street for first cemetery.

1776. Col. Moses Hazen, a Jewish officer, becomes Military Commander of Montreal for the Americans.

1777. The first synagogue in Canada, Shearith Israel (The Spanish and Portuguese) is erected at the corner of Notre Dame and St. James streets.

1783. The American Revolutionary War ends; a border is marked between Canada and the United States as far west as Lake of the Woods.

1790. John Franks appointed Chief of Fire Brigade in Quebec City.

1791. The Constitutional Act divides Quebec into Upper and Lower Canada.

1792. Montreal is divided into an East Sector and a West Sector at Saint Lawrence Boulevard.

awarded him a gold medal for courage and determination. (Note: The medal was, as of the late nineteenth century, in the possession of his great-grandson, Colonel Herbert St. George Schomberg of the Royal Marines).

THE BRITISH NAVY DOMINATES THE SEAS

With the fall of Louisbourg, the campaign ended for 1758 as winter halted navigation on the waterways. When spring eased ice conditions on the St. Lawrence, the tremendous British fleet, including Schomberg and 'Diana,' moved upstream to confront the French army. It was a remarkable sight. With their great white sails, caught by steady winds, the great men-of-war, mounting as many as 108 guns, proceeded in a stately manner up the river, with the smaller warships, frigates, sloops, and supply vessels crowding the navigable portion of the mostly uncharted river. Schomberg, who had a close rapport with Wolfe—now the general commander of the invasion force—was among those called to a number of essential conferences, where he gave his advice on assault strategy.

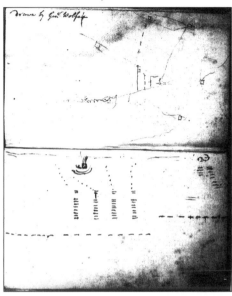

Sketch for attack on Quebec City, 1759, drawn by British forces commander General James Wolfe in the journal of Alexander Schomberg, a Jewish naval officer who was an important strategist for the mission. (From Schomberg's Journal, 1759, held in the "Quebec Box", National Archives of Canada)

Wolfe penciled four pages of comments on preparations for the impending battle and a map, in Schomberg's journal (now held by the National Archives of Canada). Historian B.G. Sack wrote that Schomberg "was frequently consulted by General Wolfe who valued his judgment highly...next to Admiral Saunders, who was in command of the British fleet in Canadian waters, it was he who carried out the operations requiring the greatest daring and enterprise."

TRIAL AT MONTMORENCY FALLS

To test the strength of French defences, Wolfe and his advisers decided to land at Montmorency Falls. As naval beachmaster, Schomberg was the first to set foot on Quebec soil as thousands of redcoats swarmed ashore from assault craft. However, the attack, undertaken in a lashing rainstorm, was a failure; Montcalm's positions were too strong. More than 400 British soldiers were killed. Schomberg was the last to leave—cradling a wounded British Grenadier in his arms—as his boat was rowed away, under musket fire from French positions.

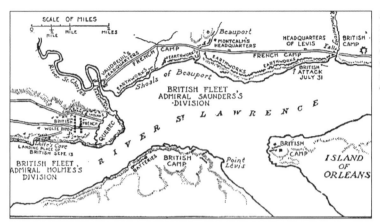

Historically accurate map of the Battle for Quebec City drawn by C.W. Jefferys. (National Archives of Canada)

An 18th-century artist's impression of the British landing at Wolfe's Cove, in 1759. The lead warship covering the landing was commanded by Alexander Schomberg. (etching by Hervey Smyth, National Archives of Canada, negative C788)

CLAMBERING WOLFE'S COVE

The failure of the frontal assault forced the British to seek an alternative approach to Montcalm's defences. They discovered a cove leading up a rugged slope to the Plains of Abraham. Scouts noticed women washing clothes along the riverbank, and later the clothes were seen drying at the top of the cliff. Obviously, there was a path! Montcalm had foreseen the vulnerability of the cove and positioned the Guienne Regiment at the edge of the cliff. However, his orders were countermanded by the Governor, the Marquis de Vaudreuil. A letter from Montcalm, dated July 25, 1759, states: "I swear to you a hundred men posted there would stop their whole army." Vaudreuil replied, "We will review the situation tomorrow." Tomorrow, of course, was too late.

'DIANA' ASSIGNED TO COVER THE LANDING

The landing began at 1:30 a.m., on July 26, 1759. Clutching trees and roots, the squad of 24 handpicked soldiers scaled the cliffs and found a single French soldier on guard.

While the bulk of the fleet sailed up and down the St. Lawrence to confuse the French, Schomberg led the first of three waves of assault troops. Under Schomberg's skillful manoeuvering, the 'Diana' escorted the first landing craft, carrying an invasion force of more than 1,000 soldiers to the beachhead.

Sir Alexander Schomberg, the Jewish naval officer who was an important adviser to General James Wolfe for the attack on Quebec in 1759. (National Archives of Canada - C146753 - from the painting by William Hogarth)

BATTLE ON THE PLAINS OF ABRAHAM

By 6 o'clock in the morning, in the rain and fog, 4,500 British soldiers had scaled the heights and assembled into a thin red line. Wolfe began his attack by bombarding the walled city; Schomberg wrote one line in his journal: "Quebec lower town on fire." Rather than attacking Wolfe's regiments before they were in position, Montcalm, incredulous that the British had scaled the heights, wasted valuable time riding out to see for himself. There before him was not a landing party, but the entire British army, ready for battle. Montcalm then ordered his troops out to face the British on open ground, rather than making a stand behind the fortress walls.

Though matched in numbers, Wolfe's men were mostly well trained, highly disciplined professional soldiers, including a number of Jews, while Montcalm had many insufficiently trained militiamen and volunteer civilians in his ranks. The British line remained firm as the French advanced, firing their muskets. Thick smoke from the gunfire drifted across the battlefield. The red line, on command, fired two volleys—mowing down the French forces. Then, the British—led by highland pipers—charged with fixed bayonets. The battle was brief, and costly; both Wolfe and Montcalm were fatally wounded.

THE COUNTER-ATTACK UNDER DE LÉVIS

Upon the death of Montcalm, the Chevalier François de Lévis (see footnote) assumed command of the French army, and determined to retake Quebec the next spring. Montreal, that winter, became the capital of New France. In the spring of 1760, de Lévis mounted his horse and led 7,260 soldiers, half-starved and in rags—picking up loyal *habitant* volunteers as they advanced—on a ten-day march of more than 160 kilometres, through April slush and mud, to reach the Plains of Abraham. The British commander, General James Murray, knew the French were coming. A few days earlier, a British sentry, stationed on the banks of the St. Lawrence, rescued a French soldier whose boat filled with supplies for the attack had capsized.

The Chevalier de Lévis, a dashing and courageous French officer of Jewish descent; he assumed command of the army in New France after the death of General Montcalm.
(From an 18th century engraving, National Archives of Canada, negative C69304)

De Lévis was named a marshal of France, the country's highest honour for a soldier. He died in 1787, two years before the outbreak of the French Revolution. Many members of his aristocratic family, including his widow Gabrielle Augustine Michel de Tharon, were sent to the guillotine. Two of his three daughters were also executed, but his son survived. De Lévis' grave was defaced.

General Lévis, having dismounted, leads the charge of French troops against the British in 1760. Lévis, of Jewish descent, almost recaptured Quebec City (Drawing by C.W. Jeffreys/National Archives of Canada.) C73436

THE BRITISH OUTNUMBERED AND AILING

Meanwhile, the reduced British garrison huddled behind the broken walls of conquered Quebec. Unaccustomed to the bitter cold Canadian winter, the British, suffering from scurvy and sporadic bloody French militia attacks, were in a bad state. On May 19, 1760, the General Murray wrote to his commanding officer, General Amherst: "We are very low, the Scurvy makes terrib(le) Havock—for God's sake send us up Melasses, and See(d)s which may produce Vegetables—whoever winters here ag(ain) must be better provided with bedding and warm...than we were."

On April 28, 1760, when the French army, with French-Canadian and Indian volunteers, returned to Quebec City, the British formed up on a battlefield where they had been victors less than a year ago. This time, the French won. De Lévis galloped down the French battle-line, waving his hat on the tip of his sword to stir the blood of his soldiers. The bedraggled troops cheered their gallant commanding officer, discharged their muskets at the wavering British line, and then drove the enemy, outnumbered two to one, back behind the battered fortifications. It appeared only a matter of time before the British would surrender. The French were on the verge of recapturing New France.

BRITISH NAVY TURNS THE TIDE

However, the outcome of the battle was decided on water—not on land. De Lévis' lookouts shouted wildly when they saw, at great distance, tips of the masts of approaching warships. Silence fell when they recognized les trois couleurs anglais, the British colours. The warships, including Schomberg and 'Diana,' had made the earliest ascent of the St. Lawrence River ever recorded at that time. 'Diana' and a second Royal Navy warship, 'Vanguard', attacked the French supply fleet, moored beyond the narrows, and destroyed it, driving one frigate onto rocks above Cape Diamond, forcing the second to beach at Point-au-Tremble, where it was set on fire. All other French vessels were either destroyed or seized.

Afterward, a British officer, Captain John Knox, who was on the Quebec waterfront when the victorious squadron anchored, wrote in his journal (his spelling):

"At night-fall came to an anchor in the bason, to the unspeakable joy of the harrassed garrison, the Van-guard ship of war,

Commodore Swanton, with the Diane frigate, Captain Schomberg; our gunners immediately gave the enemy a general discharge of all our artillery, three times repeated, without any return."

Added Knox:

> "**The Honour they have acquired on this occasion should render their names immortal**."

The senior naval officer in North America, Lord Alexander Colvill (sic), in his account, stated:

"At 4 p.m., Captain Deane came on board from above the Town; he acquainted me that Captain Schomberg and him have effectually destroyed all the enemy's ships above the town."

THE FRENCH ABANDON THE FIELD

The French, outnumbered ten to one on the battlefield, with gunpowder and other supplies destroyed, had no choice but to retreat, abandoning 40 cannon and leaving sick and wounded behind. De Lévis retreated to Montreal, where he wanted to fight from the fortifications on St. Helen's Island. However, Governor Pierre de Rigaud Vaudreuil overruled him, again, surrendering on September 8, 1760, without firing a shot. An angry de Lévis, having been denied the right to do battle to the end, burned the regimental flags in the presence of his troops. On September 9, the British formally occupied Montreal with the deployment of an infantry detachment to Place d'Armes. That evening, British drums were heard for the first time on the streets of Montreal. A week later, the defeated troops marched out of town.

Schomberg was assigned to take the news of the victory, with all speed, to the Admiralty in London. General Murray wrote: "It is necessary immediately to dispatch a Frigate with advice to Mr. Pitt (British Prime Minister) of the happy issue of Monsieur de Lévis enterprise." Schomberg was honoured with a number of decorations, and praised in dispatches. Immediately after he participated in the destruction of the French fleet near Quebec in 1760, he received a major promotion to the captaincy of the 64-gun Essex—a ship almost double the size of the frigate he had commanded in the Louisbourg and Quebec campaigns. Schomberg was on the quarterdeck of Essex when the British navy attacked the French at Belle Isle, one of the final engagements of the Seven Years' War.

With drums beating, the British accept the surrender of French forces, commanded by Chevalier de Lévis in Montreal, 1760. (Oil painting by Adam Sherriff Scott, National Archives of Canada, negative C11043)

WHO WANTS CANADA?

The British were not certain they wanted to keep Canada. They wanted to acquire, from France, the Caribbean islands of Guadeloupe and Martinique. Prime Minister William Pitt the Elder told the British House of Commons: "Some are for keeping Canada, some Guadeloupe. Who will tell me what I shall be hanged for not keeping?" Eventually, British sugar merchants won the day. They persuaded a hesitant London to choose Canada because they did not want competition from plantations on the French islands for their own sugar cane.

In Quebec, a significant portion of the population—about 2,000—prepared to return to France. Many of the government officials, some church dignitaries, army officers, nobility, soldiers and merchants, returned to the mother country, where the signing of the Treaty of Paris, in 1763, was celebrated in Paris with grand fireworks displays. King Louis marked the occasion joyously, hosting a magnificent dinner where he noted there would no longer be an alarming drain on his treasury. Writer Voltaire congratulated his Highness for having "rid himself of those fifteen thousand arpents de neige."

Apparently, Schomberg liked the New World, and requested a senior posting in the American colonies. The famous English actor, David Garrick, supported his application with a poem including the lines:

> "Send him where oft he fought and bled,
> Again to cross the Atlantic sea.
> To tomahawk and wampum bred,
> He's more than half a Cherokee."

THE JEWS OF ENGLAND
In 1290, King Edward I expelled Jews from Britain. Around 1640, during the reign of Oliver Cromwell, they began drifting back into England without fanfare. Cromwell's reign as Protector signaled a period of religious tolerance in England after almost 200 years of conflict between Anglicans and Roman Catholics. Jews surfaced legally in 1654, when marranos in London petitioned King Charles II for the right to worship openly.

Schomberg, however, was never assigned to a North American naval base. He was active in convoy duty to the Caribbean and in patrols in the Bay of Biscay, off the French Atlantic Coast. In 1771, he was appointed to command the Irish viceroy's yacht, 'Dorset,' despite the objections of Lord Sandwich, head of the Admiralty, who wanted the position of honour for one of his friends. Lord Sandwich later spitefully prevented Schomberg from being named an Admiral. Consequently, the Jewish officer became the oldest captain on the Admiralty's list and was denied the opportunity of leading naval forces during the American Revolution. Eighteen years after the fall of Quebec, Alexander Schomberg was knighted by the Lord Lieutenant.

THE SCHOMBERG FAMILY

William Hogarth painted Sir Alexander, and Gainsborough painted a full-length portrait of his brother Ralph. These towering figures in eighteenth-century British art only painted subjects they felt worthy of their skill. In his canvas entitled *A naval officer*, Hogarth used Schomberg to model qualities representative of officers of the Royal Navy. Other Schombergs preceding Alexander had been outstanding officers in the Royal Navy. One became a Vice-Admiral. Schomberg's two sons both became decorated naval officers: Alexander Wilmot Schomberg became a full Admiral, and Charles March Schomberg was Lieutenant Governor of Dominica, and Commodore and Commander-in-chief of the British naval forces at the Cape of Good Hope. Both sons, like their father, were knighted.

The Schomberg family also had a reputation in medicine. Schomberg's father was Dr. Meyer Low, a German-born physician who moved to London in 1720 and became one of Britain's leading physicians. Members of his family were prominent Hebraic scholars and physicians. He was a Fellow of the Royal Society in 1726, and was appointed physician to the Great Synagogue. He built up what journals of the time referred to as a "fashionable clientele."

Alexander Schomberg died in Dublin on March 19, 1804, aged 84. Although he never lived in Canada, he was a key figure in the success of the British Conquest. British control over Canada ended French colonial rule in the province and, for the first time, opened the doors of the colony to Jews.

THE HOUSE OF LÉVI
The memory of two distinguished French leaders, of Jewish descent, is honoured in Quebec by place names: "Pointe de Lévy" and the city of "Lévis."

The first member of the ancient and aristocratic House of Lévi to become prominent in the affairs of New France was Henry de Lévi, Duke of Ventadour. He was the French Court's Viceroy to the Colony from 1625 to 1627. French explorer Samuel de Champlain referred to the "Cap de Lévy," in his report on a 1629 voyage to New France. That promontory is now called "Pointe de Lévy." The Lévi coat of arms incorporates three symbols resembling the **Mogen David** (Star of David). The city of Lévis, located across the St. Lawrence River from Quebec City, honours one of New France's most courageous military figures, Chevalier François de Lévis, a descendent of the Duke. Following the death of Viscount Montcalm in 1759, the Chevalier succeeded to command of the French army, in New France. De Lévis organized and gallantly led a counter-attack against the British in Quebec City, and almost recaptured Québec.

CHAPTER FIVE

KOSHER IN THE CANOE
Aaron Hart and Canadian Jewry's First Family

The neighbours were accustomed to the Friday night ritual at the residence of Aaron Hart, the home of the only Jews in Three Rivers, a town of 800. The mother and her daughters, their heads covered with shawls, went through the routine of lighting candles and saying prayers. Passersby could see the flickering candles on the table—five pairs of candlesticks, two for each of the women present. Aaron, the first "legal" Jew to settle openly in Quebec, sat at the head of the table, flanked by his four sons and four daughters, glorying in the 3,000-year-old ritual of Shabbat, or Sabbath prayer.

When the commander of the English forces, General Sir Jeffrey Amherst, rode triumphantly through the gates of the walled city of Montreal on September 8, 1760, Aaron Hart, 36, at the General's request—rode at his side. With the occupation of Montreal, New France ceased to exist, and the colony became part of British North America. Jews, barred from settlement under the French Regime, now were cordially invited to make their home in British Quebec. Those first pioneer years in the new colony heralded significant "firsts" for Jews—the first families, the first places of worship, the first synagogue, the first community, and the rise of a first wave of successful Jews, the first merchant class. From a modest beginning trading furs, Aaron Hart became one of the richest men in the British Empire, outside Britain, and the first to create a permanent Jewish presence in Canada. For this latter achievement he is widely regarded as the founding father of the Jewish community.

Born in London, in 1724, Hart served in the British Army in the so-called German Legion, and journeyed to Jamaica before visiting the American colonies, in 1752, with General Sir Frederick

Aaron Hart, accepted as the first Jew to settle openly in Quebec.
(Canadian Jewish Congress National Archives, Montreal)

Haldimand and Colonel Bouquet. He settled in New York. At the outbreak of war with France, Hart re-enlisted in the British Army, where he was responsible for maintaining the army in the field through supplies of food and ammunition. With difficulty, he succeeded in recruiting a battalion of 600 men, which became part of the 60th Royal American Regiment of New York. Many names in the regimental rosters indicate they were of Jewish descent, for example, Hananiel Garcia, Emanuel de Cordova, Isaac de Miranda, Lazarus David, Uriel Moresco, Jacob de Maurera, and Abraham Franks. In appreciation of his achievement in recruiting and supplying troops during the Seven Years' War, Amherst promised Hart the rank of Brigadier, with command of a full regiment. However, the newly crowned King George III refused to honour the commitment, and Hart settled for the role of commissary officer to Amherst's troops.

TRADERS AND ADVENTURERS WANTED

Five days after French surrender, in the midst of chaos ensuing from the changeover to British rule, General Amherst issued a broad invitation for merchants to come to Quebec. They were urgently needed to provide food and other supplies for the expanding population, and the British army of occupation. Amherst sent his invitation to governors in three neighbouring colonies: New Hampshire, Massachusetts and New York, urging "traders and adventurers to transport themselves hither and to Quebec with quantities of molasses, salt, wines, teas, sugars and all kinds of grocery, as likewise sheep and everything else that may occur to them to be useful for the benefit of a population that

---

THE PIONEER JEWS OF QUEBEC

The following Jews were living in Quebec in the first years after Conquest. Most of the names appear in the business transactions of Aaron Hart and Samuel Jacobs, in the official dispatches and correspondence of Generals Monkton, Amherst and Gage, and Colonel Bouquet, and others are found in the extant records of the Spanish and Portuguese synagogue:

Chapman Abraham	Moses Hart	Barnett Lyons
Joseph Bindona	Andrew Hays	Jacob de Maurera
Emanuel de Cordova	Pines Heineman	Emmanuel Manuel
Lazarus David (first Jew to settle in Montreal)	Samuel Jacobs	Meyer Michaels
Judah Elvada	Isaac Judah	Isaac de Miranda
Fernandez de Fonseca	Joseph Judah	Uriel Morosco
Abraham (or Abram) Franks	Samuel Judah	Hyam Myers
David Salisbury (or Salesby) Franks	Uriah Judah	Elias Salomon
Jacob Franks	David Lazarus	Elias Seixas
John Franks	Eleazor Levy	Levy Simons
Moses Franks	Gershom Levy	Ezekiel Solomons
Hananiel Garcia	Isaac Levy	Levy Solomons
Manuel Gomez	Simon Levy	Meyer Solomons
Aaron Hart	Benjamin Lyons	

had been cut off from trade with France for two years." A similar invitation was extended to merchants in Britain.

A dozen Jews, both American and British, almost all veterans of the war to conquer Canada, were among the approximately 100 merchants of English and Scottish ancestry, who decided to seek their fortune in the northern colony. About two dozen Jews arrived in Quebec from the British Isles and the American colonies, sometimes in transit from other European nations, such as Germany. The Jewish merchants, like Hart, had capital with them and valuable ties with family and friends in England and America. The Jews also spoke English and found themselves living in a largely rural society among approximately 65,000 French-speaking Catholics and 400 Protestants. They quickly became aware of widespread antagonism from the French, who were shattered that their dreams lay in ruin, that the English (and Protestants!) had defeated their army. Also, les canadiens were determined to retain their distinctiveness. Consequently, the few score English, Scots and Jews became supportive of each other. The major commercial activities were the fur trade, supplying the population and provisioning the armed forces. Jewish merchants won large contracts to supply the British garrison. They diversified their interests—importing goods, exporting wheat, setting up industries, lending money and building fleets of ships to carry their own cargoes or merchandise for others.

Montreal in 1762, two years after the city surrendered to the British Army, and Jews were allowed to settle openly in Quebec.
(Etching by P. Canot, from the drawing by Thomas Patten - from the McCord Museum of Canadian History, Montreal)

NAVIGATING THE WILDERNESS

Aaron Hart, after retirement from the army, settled in Three Rivers (Trois-Rivières), apparently at the request of his friend Haldimand, governor of the town. He became active in the fur trade, an industry he quickly dominated. Determined to remain Jewish, Hart journeyed to London, England, to marry his cousin Dorothy Judah—a trip that took months. Her brother Samuel Judah and his wife also settled in Canada, close to the Harts. Aaron and Dorothy had a large family—eight children who lived. Hart recorded their names, in Yiddish, in his prayer book. A deeply religious man, Hart created over the years a com-

A frontier shop in the late 18th century. Pioneer Jews often traded merchandise, including muskets, for furs in trading posts like this.
(C.W. Jefferys drawing/National Archives of Canada)

THE FIRST JEW TO SETTLE IN QUEBEC
Aaron Hart was actually preceded in Quebec by Samuel Jacobs, who with his schooner 'Betsey' boldly followed the British fleet as it sailed up the St. Lawrence River for the siege of Quebec City. As early as January 1758, Jacobs was supplying British troops at Fort Cumberland, in what is now New Brunswick. He settled in Saint-Denis, near Montreal, and prospered, but he married a French-Canadian woman and his five children were Catholics. He remained Jewish himself—insisting on swearing on the Hebrew Bible when appearing in court. The merchant kept a curious business diary (preserved in the National Archives, Ottawa) written in a mixture of phonetic English, Yiddish and French. He signed many of his letters, even to non-Jews, with his Hebrew name "Shmuel," in Ashkenazic Hebrew script. Jacobs was not the only Quebec Jew to marry out of the faith. For example, his brother Thomas also married a Catholic.
It was difficult for pioneer bachelors to find a suitable mate; the nearest Jewish women were in the American colonies, a long, even dangerous journey through interminable wilderness. After years of isolation, some pioneer Jews abandoned their religion to marry non-Jewish women close at hand. Joseph Bindona, who arrived in Montreal in 1767 from England, married a non-Jewish girl in Christ Church. Sergeant-Major Jacob de Maurera, who arrived with British troops in 1760, also married a Catholic in the same church in 1768.

munity on his own, including a (private) place of worship, and two family cemeteries. Each Jewish holiday was celebrated. As was customary at the time, the Harts sent their four sons—but not their daughters—to live with friends in New York and Philadelphia, to obtain a Jewish education. And he urged his children to remain faithful to Judaism. When it appeared difficult for one son to return home for the Passover holiday, Hart sent him (using the variable English spelling of the time) cautionary fatherly advice:

> **"I hope you will not risk in any danger if you find that you cane not be hear Pesah (Passover). You will acarding to my instrucktions go to New Yark and keep Pesah...You will say as leetle as passable about your businiss to any of the Jues in New Yark nore to you Unkils too. You must remain Pesah in a Jues house."**

Hart carried kosher food in his birch bark canoe when he ventured into the wilderness to trade with the Indians. Considering the general hardships and privations of late eighteenth-century Quebec, Hart and other early Jewish pioneers went to considerable effort to prepare animal meat in a ritual manner. Kosher butchering, called *shehitah*, involves the slaughtering, by ritual, of "any animal that has cloved hoofs and is cleft-footed and chews the cud—such may you eat." (Leviticus 11:3) Slaughtered animals must be drained of blood, as the Bible forbids the enjoyment of blood.

A FLOURISHING BUSINESS

Hart hired some of the ablest voyageurs, and they helped build his successful trade with the Indians. After years of insufficient supplies, the Indians were eager to obtain a new source of manufactured goods, such as cutlery, kettles, handkerchiefs, shoes, nets, muskets, ammunition, tobacco, liquor, blankets, wool cloth and other textiles, fish hooks and ornaments.

Fur-trade merchants sent out "brigades," a convoy of usually four large canoes, each capable of carrying three to four tons, with crews of eight to ten men. Each May, the fleets set out from Lachine, Quebec, for rendezvous with trappers at the head of Lake Superior. After trading with the Indians, the crew loaded canoes with furs and began the long journey home. Many Jewish merchants, such as Hart, undertook these journeys until the business expanded or they could find a trustworthy supplier.

In Three Rivers, Hart established the first general store in the area, and imported merchandise, such as arms, clothing, furniture and other goods, from Europe and the southern colonies.

The Hart family's close ties with the Levys and Judahs in New York and Liverpool, England, facilitated a trade network. Customers paid using a wide variety of coinage—everything from Spanish silver dollars to French half-crowns—or barter, namely fur. The Hart family did considerable business with the new United States, but the Republic apparently was a poor payer. In 1831, President Andrew Jackson wrote the Harts with embarrassment that Washington could only pay $15,000 of the $60,000 they owed.

The license to permit Aaron Hart to operate a "common Ale-House, or victualling house" in Trois-Rivières, in the late eighteenth century.

Hart purchased immense amounts of property, much of it from impoverished French seigneurs. He acquired seven seigneuries, of which Becancour was the largest and most important. As Seigneur of Becancour, he recruited a battalion called "Hart's Regiment Militia."

GENERAL MURRAY DISLIKES THE MERCHANTS

Quebec's first British governor after Conquest, General James Murray, was not enthusiastic about the merchants arriving in Quebec. He referred to them as "licentious fanaticks" who were, in his words, "Quakers, Puritans, Anabaptists, Presbyterians, Atheists, Infidels and even Jews." General Murray resented the merchants for many reasons, namely that they were mostly republicans or Yankee traders, who were accustomed to a great deal of freedom and did not like to function within the restrictions of the new colony. The merchants led the demand for greater self-government, going so far as to petition London to recall Murray. The petition includes the signature of Eleazor Levy.

A NEW SPECIES OF MAN IN POST-CONQUEST QUEBEC

Quebec society was completely changed by the outburst of revolutionary entrepreneurial activities by British and Jewish immigrant merchants. According to B.K. Sandwell, editor of Saturday Night magazine: "It was a transition from an economy in which money and credit were unimportant, and a feudal relationship existed between the tillers of the soil and the lords of the manor, to an economy in which everything was regulated by market price. The lords had no skill in this sort of economy and were speedily worsted by the 'business men'—among whom the few Jews then in America were pre-eminent for their exceptional energy, judgement and cash resources."

HART SONS MAKE THEIR MARK

"He who is survived by a son devoted to Torah is as though he has not died."

Simeon B. Yohai

Aaron's two eldest sons, Moses and Ezekial, stayed in Trois-Rivières and were active in family businesses (Moses brewed beer and Ezekiel continued in the fur trade); the two youngest boys, Benjamin and Alexander, eventually moved to Montreal.

In 1817, **Moses Hart** helped found the Bank of Montreal. He invested in Canadian banks and, in 1837, established his own bank in Trois-Rivières, which issued its own currency—Hart bank notes. When he was forced to close its doors because he lacked the necessary permits, he bought back all the money issued by the short-lived institution. While his business reputation remained, his personal life differed greatly from his father or brothers. He eloped with Sarah (Sally) Judah, despite her father's objections. Moses was an unfaithful husband, and 15 years later Sarah left him citing "poor conduct." However, he was said to have been a good father—providing for all his children—legitimate and illegitimate. Moses also became involved in steam navigation—launching two vessels, the "Hart" and the "Toronto." In this effort an adopted son, Alexander Thomas Hart, and a nephew, Ira Craig Hart, supported him. Moses was also an important importer-exporter. He lived to be 83 years old. **Benjamin Hart** moved to Montreal several years after his father's death in 1800. Besides leadership activity in community affairs, he was one of the founders of the Montreal General Hospital. Benjamin had three sons: Wellington, who became colonel of a Michigan regiment; Frederick, who became adjutant-general of Louisiana, and Aaron Philip Hart, the only son to remain in Montreal. He became a distinguished lawyer, was active in politics, and raised a company of loyalist militia during the rebellion of 1837-1838.

THE HART DAUGHTERS
Three of the Hart daughters married: Catherine married Dr. Bernard Samuel Judah of New York (their son, Samuel Judah, became attorney general of Indiana); Charlotte married Moses David of Montreal; Sarah married Samuel David of Montreal. Oddly, at a time of woman shortage, Elizabeth remained single. Hart left each daughter an inheritance of £1,000.

The French seigneurial class was ill-prepared for the rapid change. In a Petition in 1766, three years after the colony came under British rule, the Seigneurs voiced their displeasure: "A crowd of people have come in, in the wake of the army, who as clerks and managers for London merchants, merit no preference, either by their conduct or by their lack of education...people of no birth, without education, incapable of proper feelings, soldiers demobilized from the French army, barbers, serving men...even Jews...who have not hesitated to raise themselves above the new subjects, to whom this species of man was hitherto unknown."

HART FAMILY'S IMPORTANT ROLE

Hart did much for the local economy of Three Rivers, where a street is named in his honour. As an indication of status and influence, the family home in Three Rivers became the second post office in Canada, and Hart became paymaster for British troops stationed in the area. Hart's support for the wider community, particularly donations to churches, earned him the local title of "the pope of Canada." At the time of his death, on Dec. 28, 1800, he was immensely wealthy. Two events underscore Aaron Hart's wealth and prominence: In 1791, Edward, Duke of Kent, visited the Harts during a visit to the colony. Also, records show that Hart bought a woman slave "on the block" in Montreal for the princely sum of 45 pounds.

Canadian historian B.G. Sack in his "History of the Jews in Canada" states that Hart "was reputed to be the wealthiest man in the British Empire outside the British Isles." Historian Erna Paris, in her "Jews: Their Experience in Canada," conservatively suggests that Hart "became the wealthiest landowner in the British Empire outside Britain." Despite his financial success, Hart is not included in historical references to influential merchants of the era, such as McTavish and McGill.

Hart, a pious Jew with great concern for the continuity of the Jewish people, helped settle many new immigrants, particularly from his own family. For example, he invited his sister's sons, the Joseph brothers, to Canada in 1792. He also helped provision the movement of United Empire Loyalists from New York to British North America, including some Jewish loyalists who settled in the Eastern Townships.

CHAPTER SIX

THE PIONEER JEWS OF MONTREAL
Building the First Synagogue
and Jewish Community

Behold, how good and how pleasant it is for brethren to
dwell together in unity.

The Bible, Ps. 133.1

*It was a cold late afternoon in February. The small group of
Montreal-area Jews, warming themselves over a wood fire, were
dismayed that only eight men had turned up for evening prayers.
A **minyan** of at least ten men was required. The **parnas** (president) directed members of the small congregation to scatter to
nearby homes and businesses to gather together the required
minimum to doven **mincha** (the evening prayer). The
Congregation Shearith Israel (Remnant of Israel) had been formed
only a few months before, on December 10, 1768, and gathered for
their services in a room at 86 St. James Street. Within a few
minutes, the summons had brought together the required ten congregants. And, with their heads piously covered with **yarmulkes**
(skull caps), they began the centuries-old prayers of the Jewish
people, before the first star ushered in the night.*

As soon as their numbers permitted, the pioneering Jews of
Quebec (about 15 to 20 men and women) banded together to form
a congregation and took the first step toward establishing an
organized community. In 1777, a synagogue was built on the corner of Notre Dame and St. Lambert (St. Lawrence) Streets. (This
location is marked by a tablet erected by the Numismatic and
Antiquarian Society of Montreal.) Co-founded by five community leaders—Lazarus David, Uriel Moresco, Abraham Franks,
Simon Levy and Fernandez du Tosco—the Shearith Israel
Synagogue, the only synagogue in Montreal, and, for almost 80

years, in Canada, was more than a place of worship. For Jews living in nearby villages, the synagogue became a gathering place for cradle-to-grave rites of passage, for **simchas** or celebrations, such as weddings, bar mitzvahs and the **bris** (circumcision of a baby boy). The synagogue became a focus of social activity, a community centre helping to unite Jews and strengthen Jewish life in Montreal, a city that in the eighteenth century remained a frontier town dominated by Christianity. The Shearith Israel—**the first non-Catholic place of worship in Quebec**—was instrumental in helping the early Jews maintain their Jewishness, and it helped create the first organized Jewish presence in the city!

Engraving of the Spanish and Portugese Synagogue on Chenneville Street from Hochelaga Depicta, 1839. This was the second building constructed by the congregation, completed shortly before this engraving was made.

THE TWO RITES OF JUDAISM
The two major rites in the Jewish religion are the **Sephardic**, related to descendents of Jews expelled from Spain and Portugal in the 15th century, and the **Ashkenazi**, representing traditions of Jews from central and Eastern Europe. Both names come from Biblical references. Sepharad is the name of a land in the Bible (Obadiah 20). The term Ashkenaz applies to a people named in Genesis 10.3.

IN THE BEGINNING
Before there was a building, or even a rabbi, the congregation had to decide which ritual of Judaism to follow—the Ashkenazi, or European rite, or the Sephardic in the tradition of Spanish and Portuguese Jews. Despite the fact that most of the Jews forming the new congregation were Ashkenazim (European Jews), they decided to follow the Sephardic ritual and call Shearith Israel the "Spanish and Portuguese Synagogue". This decision was made because there were, at that time, no Ashkenazi synagogues in the New World. Earlier congregations—in New York, Savannah, Philadelphia, Charleston and Newport—were all Sephardi, and if the fledgling group in Montreal wanted to receive co-operation and financial support, such as donations of special prayer books for the holidays, they had to follow the same rite. In addition, many of the congregants had come to Montreal via England or the American states, and some had ties with the great Sephardic synagogue in London, Bevis Marks, founded in 1657.

The naming of the synagogue paid off immediately insofar as the London connection went. The Bevis Marks synagogue presented the new congregation with two Torah scrolls, already "counted as being very old," according to the 1916 Jewish Encyclopedia.

Neither of these precious scrolls is in use now. Recently, they were removed from the synagogue because of wear and tear. The one in best condition was presented to the Canadian Museum of Civilization while the second, according to custom, was buried in an unmarked location in the congregation cemetery on Mount Royal.

The congregation's first spiritual leader was the Reverend Raphael Cohen, brought from England, to act in a multiple capacity as Shochet (to ensure animals are slaughtered according to Jewish ritual), Hazan (cantor to lead the singing of prayers), Teacher and Reader.

A memorial erected at the cemetery "to commemorate the founding families of this synagogue and the Jewish community of Montreal," lists the following:

Chapman Abrahams	David David	Lazarus David
Moses Eleazor David	Samuel David	Abraham Franks
David Salisby Franks	Jacob Franks	
Alexander Hart	Benjamin Hart	Moses Hart
Andrew Hays	Moses Judah Hays	Samuel Jacobs
Henry Joseph	Abraham Judah	Isaac Judah
Uriah Judah	Eliezer Levy	Simon Levy
Benjamin Lions	Levy Michaels	Myer Michaels
Hyam Myers	Myer Myers	Joseph Pines
Ezekiel Solomons	Levy Solomons	

Many of these people obviously were not involved in the actual formation of the congregation. Benjamin Hart, for example, listed as a founder, was only born in 1779—two years after the synagogue was constructed. An interesting footnote: Despite extensive business and social relationships with Montreal Jews, community patriarch Aaron Hart and his family worshipped on their own.

THE PIONEER FAMILIES

Montreal in the late eighteenth century was still a small forest town hacked out of the wilderness. The population began to grow as revolutionary sentiment in the southern colonies encouraged Loyalists to flee the Thirteen Colonies. As an entry port for cargoes bound for new settlements to the west, Montreal's population and commercial activity grew. The city became larger and more important than Quebec City. With the influx of more immigrants, particularly Loyalist families, the number of British (i.e. English, Scottish, Irish and Welsh) began to grow rapidly, and Montreal's French-speaking population majority began to decline.

When Aaron Hart felt more Jews would be welcome and would likely do well, he encouraged members of his own family to join him. Hart's sister had married Naphtali Joseph in England, and Aaron invited some of her sons to Canada. In 1792, Judah,

Jews included among the signators of petitions to the King seeking a degree of self-government in the Colony of Quebec, 1763, 1770, 1773 and 1774:
Isaac Abrams
David David
Lazarus David
David Salesbury
  (or Salesby) Franks
John Franks
Abraham Hart
Ezekiel Hart
Moses Hart
Andrew Hays
David Jacobs
Samuel Jacobs
Isaac Judah
Uriah Judah
Eleazor Levy
Simon Levy
Hyam Myers
Elias Solomons
Ezekiel Solomons
Levy Solomons

Abraham and Henry Joseph arrived to seek their fortunes. Henry Joseph settled in Berthier (now Berthierville), in the Eastern Townships, and developed one of the largest chains of trading posts in the colony. Other pioneer families included the Franks, Davids, Judahs, Hays, Solomons, Mayers, Lyons and Abrahams. Their names, and those of their descendants, begin to appear in colonial and business records. Almost without exception, they became part of the Spanish and Portuguese congregation.

The pioneer of the David family, Lazarus David, accompanied by his wife Phoebe, arrived in Montreal from Swansea, Wales, in 1763. He established a successful general store, became one of the first landowners. Their son, David David, was the first Jewish baby born in Montreal, and in Lower Canada.

LAND FOR THE FIRST CEMETERY

The first Jewish landowners in Montreal (according to municipal records) were Lazarus David and Levy Simon—both listed in the 1767 register of property owners. David bought property on St. Janvier Street, "to serve in perpetuity as a cemetery for individuals of the Jewish faith who may die in the Montreal district." The cemetery is arguably the first Jewish cemetery in North America, and where, by chance, David was the first to be buried, upon his death in 1776. Ezekial Solomons became a property owner in 1780. In 1782, Solomon Levy was indicated in the records to be the biggest Jewish landowner in the city.

After Lazarus David's death, his widow apparently fell on hard times. In 1780 Phoebe David petitioned Governor Frederick Haldimand for relief, citing the difficulty of getting by "out of the profits of a small shop." Five years later, a merchant named Robert Hunter had tea with her, and reported (in his journal) that she remained in good spirits. She was "really a very sensible clever old woman and very entertaining in her conversation." He added: "Her son showed us the synagogue, which is a very neat one for so small a congregation."

David David followed in his merchant father's footsteps, maintaining a wholesale and retail store at 15 rue Notre-Dame. By 1804 he had prospered enough to pay £999—a substantial price in those days—for a house. In 1817, he was accepted as a member of the prestigious Beaver Club, an annual gathering of fur traders with wilderness experience. His eligibility indicates he made at least one trip, lasting a winter, in the wilderness, David David died unmarried, aged 60, in 1824.

THE RANSOM

In the summer of 1763, Ezekial Solomons, a bold experienced fur-trader, who previously ventured far afield into what is now Ontario and Michigan, was taken prisoner at his trading post in Mackinac (Michigan) by a renegade band of former French soldiers and Indians—and held for ransom. Jewish merchants in Montreal raised money to obtain Solomons's release. On August 14, 1763, Solomons (who sometimes spelled his name without an 's') made the following affidavit before the town mayor of Montreal: *"I, Ezekial Solomon (sic), resident in the Fort of Michilimackinac at the time was surprised by the savages, declare that on the 2nd day of June, a Frenchman, Mons. Cote, entered my house several times and carried from thence several parcels of goods, my property. And also an Indian named Sanpear (St. Pierre?), carried the peltry from the house to the house of Aimable Denviere in whose garret I was then concealed."* Solomons apparently knew his attackers. He and his associates were fortunate to survive the attack; a few days earlier, this same band had slaughtered a garrison of British soldiers.

A SECOND BUILDING

With the death of David David, the land on which the first synagogue was built reverted to his heirs. The 47-year-old building was demolished and work began on raising money for a second structure in another location. However, 14 years passed before it became a reality. Land was acquired in 1835, and the new synagogue on Chenneville Street was dedicated in 1838. In the meantime, services were held in a building near the home of Benjamin Hart.

The largest gift toward the cost of the new building was £575 ($1,000) from Mrs. Frances Michaels, widow of David Michaels. A further $1,000 came in the form of a $400 legacy from David David and $600 from the sale of the site for the first synagogue. The campaign raised a total of $4,000.

(The congregation is now in its third century and functions today as "the Spanish and Portuguese Synagogue." It is located on St. Kevin Street in Snowdon.)

The first Jew born in Montreal, David David, lived to be 60. He never married.
(Canadian Jewish Congress National Archives)

CHAPTER SEVEN

HERO OR TRAITOR JEW
The American Revolution in Canada;
A Lesson in Divided Loyalties

The French habitant found Montreal district Justice of the Peace Moses Hazen going over his farm accounts. Breathlessly, he told Hazen that American troops were marching toward their town, Saint Jean. Hazen, a retired British Army lieutenant, mounted his horse and, riding hard, covered 130 miles in 2½ days in search of the governor. Though he did not know it, Hazen, a prominent citizen of American Jewish descent, was riding into history. He was the first to advise his old comrade-in-arms, Sir Guy Carleton, governor of Canada, that American troops, revolting against British rule, were slogging their way north in a bid to draw Quebec into the revolution, and make Canada a fourteenth colony. He had given the British an extra 24 hours' notice of the invasion; the official courier did not reach the Quebec Citadel for another day. But almost immediately, Hazen—a native of Massachusetts—began to have second thoughts.

Revolutionary forces were advancing along the Lake Champlain route. With them were a raggedy group of Vermont militia led by Ethan Allen. Allen made the first ill-judged thrust at Montreal, but musket fire decimated his forces. Allen was captured and spent the rest of the war in a London prison. The main American force had better luck. Governor Carleton, with insufficient troops to defend both Montreal and Quebec City, fell back on the larger capital city, leaving the small frontier town of Montreal to the mercy of the invaders. Carleton left 12 merchants—six British and six French—to negotiate surrender of the town. Two days after the British withdrew, on November 13, 1775, the Americans marched through the first snow flurries of the season and entered the Recollets gate.

Montreal became part of the United States of America for seven months and seven days in 1775-76. The invasion of Canada, coupled with the early success of American arms, tested the loyalty of the population, particularly members of the Jewish community. Many Quebec Jews, such as Hazen, had migrated from New England, and they expected the same degree of freedom they had experienced in the Thirteen Colonies. Many resented their inability to participate in the administration of the colony, which was ruled entirely by a governor and council appointed by the King. Furthermore, the Quebec Act of 1774, a policy aimed at winning the loyalty of the French-Canadians, aroused resentment because it denied an assembly and granted favours to seigneurs and clergy. On the other hand, many had prospered under the British crown. Hazen, with his success in farming and business, was well established and could lose everything.   Merchants feared losing their trade. French-Canadians feared losing their language in a merger with the English-speaking colonies. Who would join the Revolution and who would remain loyal to the Empire? The only Canadian Jews who changed allegiance— Moses Hazen and David Salisbury Franks—became controversial figures; hailed as heroes on one side, and as traitors on the other. Both were prominent in the Revolutionary efforts to win Quebec; both were charged with treason; both were eventually cleared of charges and, in time, were honoured by the newly created United States of America.

MOSES HAZEN: LOYALIST OR TRAITOR?

Moses Hazen was born on June 1, 1733, in Haverhill, Massachusetts, where his Sephardic father was a merchant. Hazen became a tanner but preferred military service. He enlisted in the colonial militia and fought alongside British forces at Louisbourg, in 1758, as a lieutenant in Captain McCurdie's Company of Rangers, where General Wolfe singled him out as a

---

After the fall of Louisbourg in 1758, General James Wolfe, frustrated when winter denied him the opportunity of moving his army against Quebec City, and angered by attacks on his men by French-speaking Acadians, ordered Hazen to eradicate the attacker's base at St. Ann's (now Fredericton, N.B.). Hazen carried out the attack with exceptional brutality, even for those times, killing and scalping inhabitants, taking women and children prisoner, killing livestock and levelling the community. The raid earned Hazen his captaincy.

"good soldier." When McCurdie was killed, Hazen was promoted to command the Rangers, thereafter known as "Hazen's Own," and was named commander of Fort Frederic (later Saint John, N.B.). Hazen's Rangers took part in the Battle of Quebec in 1759, and Hazen was seriously wounded in the Battle of Ste-Foy (1760).

After Conquest, Hazen bought, as was the custom of the time, a commission in the British Army and became a lieutenant in the 44th Regiment. Two years later, he retired on half pay, purchased a farm on the Richelieu River, near St. Jean, and settled down. He married Charlotte de La Susssaye in Montreal in 1770. (They had no children.) As he prospered, he added sawmills, a forge, and a "potash house" to his property. For 12 years, Hazen busied himself with his farm and other interests. Then, in the historic year 1775, in the wake of disturbing reports of revolutionary ferment in the Thirteen Colonies, Hazen learned of the American invasion.

Fearing an attack from British Quebec, the rebel American colonials were anxious for Canadians to join the Revolution. Despite what spies in Montreal and Quebec City told them, French-Canadians were not interested. Firstly, they regarded the conflict as a battle between mainly Protestants—no business of a Catholic *habitant*. Secondly, the British in Quebec, in a bid to win the confidence of the French-speaking majority, had granted the 65,000 French the right to retain their language, religion and much of their form of law. The Roman Catholic hierarchy, satisfied the peasants would remain French and Catholic, warned parishioners not to side with the Americans. Recognizing the limitations of living in a feudal society without the unfettered opportunities he had enjoyed as a British citizen in the States, Hazen was ready to sacrifice everything.

THE AMERICANS OCCUPY MONTREAL

Bearing a flag of their own design, the revolutionaries marched into Montreal to the sound of drums beating, and made their headquarters in the former governor's residence, Chateau de Ramezay. In the short space of 25 years, three

The Chateau Ramezay, built in 1705 as the residence for the Governor of Montreal, served as headquarters for the American Army of Occupation, 1775-1776. Among those who stayed in the Chateau was Col. Moses Hazen, for a time military commander of Montreal. (**Lithography by Montreal Jewish artist Ernst Newman;** *from the Atara and Murray Marmor collection of art*)

The kitchen of the Chateau de Ramezay as it was when Hazen stayed during the winter of 1775-76.

different flags had flown over Montreal—the fleur de lys, the Union Jack and the American Continental Congress, an early version of the Stars and Stripes. One of the first delegations to contact the occupation authorities represented anxious fur traders, and included a number of Jewish merchants. They asked for the right to continue trading with the Indians, and were accommodated temporarily, until the military commander in Montreal, Brigadier General David Wooster, withdrew the concession. He despised Canadians, did not trust merchants and suspected fur-traders would use their canoes for supplying and spying for the British. Caught between conflicting forces, Hazen was accused of being a spy and was arrested, on separate occasions, by both sides.

HAZEN ASKED TO RECRUIT CANADIANS

The Americans, with most of their resources locked into the Revolutionary War, found it difficult to provide reinforcements to expand their hold in Canada. They therefore sought to recruit two regiments from among the Canadians, and Moses Hazen, now openly committed to the invaders, was promoted Colonel and asked to form one of the units. The Public Crier in Montreal read Hazen's proclamation, inviting Canadians to "enlist for one year or the duration of the war." Volunteers were to receive a bonus of 40 livres, or eight dollars, and be paid a similar amount for each month in American uniform. Hazen was commissioned on January 22, 1776, as Colonel of the 2nd Canadian Regiment, known as "Congress' Own" and also as "Hazen's Own."

The appeal met with little success; the French-Canadians were ready to sell what they could to the Americans, provided they paid in gold, but they would not fight for them. Moreover, the Americans hurt their cause by seizing supplies without payment—General Benedict Arnold looted the storehouses of Montreal merchants—or offering paper money, which the habitant believed to be worthless. General George Washington had hoped that Hazen's regiment and the companion unit would each number 1,000 at full strength. However, Hazen's formation never numbered more than 250. Many of his recruits were former French soldiers, described in contemporary accounts as "riff-raff."

An American militiaman in the late 18th century; Moses Hazen and his colonial troops would have been dressed like this. (National Archives of Canada - Neg. C6208)

THE AMERICAN ATTACK ON QUEBEC CITY FAILS AND HAZEN BECOMES COMMANDER OF MONTREAL

On New Year's Eve 1775, the Canadian-American regiments, including Hazen's, marched in a blinding snow storm and launched an unsuccessful attack on Quebec City. Nevertheless the siege continued, as the invaders stayed until spring. After Brigadier-General Wooster replaced a wounded general, **Hazen was named Military Commander of Montreal, assuming control of the city on April 1, 1776**. At this time, Colonel Hazen wrote to the overall commander, General Schuyler, asking him to send "immediately to Canada able Generals, a respectable army, a Committee of Congress, a suitable supply of hard cash, and a printer." The urgency of the letter shows Hazen understood the precariousness of the American hold on Montreal. He needed reinforcements. Unfortunately, with New Englanders barely holding their own against the British forces, the general could provide little of what Hazen requested, but he did send a prestigious committee of revolutionary leaders, including Benjamin Franklin.

Printer Fleury Mesplet, brought to Montreal by Col. Moses Hazen prints a newsletter aimed at encouraging French Canadians to join the American Revolution.

BENJAMIN FRANKLIN GUEST OF HAZEN

Benjamin Franklin—scientist, printer and politician—was one of the most outstanding Revolutionary leaders, and the fact that Congress would send such a senior statesman to Montreal indicates the importance they attached to the effort to draw Quebec into the American Revolution. Franklin helped draft the American Declaration of Independence and the U.S. Constitution.

After a difficult three-day crossing of Lake Champlain, with its ice floes, Franklin's party stayed two nights at Colonel Hazen's house in St. Jean. But the home had been thoroughly pillaged—all the doors and windows were missing—and the distinguished Congressional Committee, including the 70-year-old Franklin, had to sleep on the floor, where biting winter winds added to their discomfort. In Montreal, the committee was unable to persuade the wary Canadians to join the Revolution. Franklin and his associates had their first cold reception when, at breakfast, they tried to pay for a meal with "Continental" paper money which the tavern-keeper refused to accept.

HAZEN PLANS THE RETREAT AND LEADS HIS REGIMENT INTO EXILE

The arrival of a British fleet sailing up the St. Lawrence River in May 1776, and other British offensives, forced the Americans to retreat. Hazen's next assignment was to plan the retreat, and take command of the forts at St. Jean and Chambly. A letter by Franklin dated May 6, 1776, Montreal, notes that the Commander of American Forces, General Benedict Arnold, thought "the publick (sic) interest would be better promoted by appointing Colonel Hazen to command at St. John's and Chambly...Colonel Hazen speaking the French language, and having a considerable influence over the people in the neighborhood." This assignment was painful for Hazen; his properties were nearby and now would be lost to him. In fact, Hazen torched his own seigneury, as ordered, and watched years of hard work burn to the ground.

Approximately 8,000 took part in the retreat, including Hazen's 'congressiste' battalion (124 men and their families), American soldiers, and sympathetic French-Canadians. Of this number, 2,000 were said to be sick; the route through forests was strewn with the bodies of those who perished from smallpox, exposure, or starvation. The flight from Canada represented the largest exodus of French-Canadians since the expulsion of the Acadians.

Back in New England, Hazen hoped the Americans would make another bid to capture Canada, therefore he continued to recruit men for his 2nd Canadian Regiment. In 1777, France declared war on Britain, and the American Revolutionaries got a much-needed ally. The French General, the Marquis de Lafayette was keen to undertake the re-conquest of "New France." He specifically asked Colonel Hazen to lead his troops and help plan a Franco-American invasion. Hazen, accompanied by a number of French-Canadians and four Indians, marked out an invasion route from Vermont into Quebec—called Hazen's Road. But the offensive never materialized. Six years later, General Washington sent Hazen a long list of questions on how another attempt on Canada might be undertaken. However, Washington decided against a second invasion.

HAZEN'S CANADIANS FIGHT ON AMERICAN SOIL

"Hazen's Own" continued to fight for the Americans; the unit took part in the Staten Island campaign, in the battles of Germantown and Brandywine, and finally, in the defeat of the British at Yorktown—the battle effectively ending the Revolutionary War. Hazen was named Brigadier-General by Congress on June 29, 1781—taking command of a brigade in General Lafayette's Light Infantry Division—and, when the war was over, he resigned. He and his men were given land grants in Vermont, and Congress eventually compensated him, in part, for his losses. He died in Troy, New York, on February 3, 1803. His widow was unable to collect $42,000 in claims against Congress. Allan S. Everest, writing in the Dictionary of Canadian Biography (1983), declared:

"As a soldier, Moses Hazen displayed extraordinary leadership qualities. A combative man, he was happiest in action. Courageous and impetuous, he was also throughout his life restless, frustrated by obstacles, stubborn and hypersensitive about his honour."

DAVID SALISBURY FRANKS, PAYMASTER TO THE AMERICANS

When the Americans pulled out, British authorities posted a list of 17 "traitors." In addition to Hazen, the list included the name David Salisbury Franks, the only other Jew to have sided, despite great personal cost, with the Americans. The entire Jewish community of about two dozen, with two exceptions, had remained loyal to the British crown. Salisbury, who migrated to Montreal with his father as early as 1767, was a prominent leader in the community, and had made a fortune in trade. He had been parnas (president) of the Shearith Israel. During the American occupation, Franks, an outspoken campaigner for greater self-government for Quebec, joined the Revolutionary cause—despite the angry opposition of his father. When a bust of King George III was defaced, Franks was jailed a few days for his hostile remarks about the monarchy.

As paymaster for the Revolutionary troops, Franks overextended himself loaning the Americans money. Frequently, he used his own savings to pay the rebels. Congress later acknowledged it was in debt to Franks for $3,748.84, but years later, still owed him $2,148.84. When General Arnold ordered the retreat from Quebec, Franks was forced to abandon everything. He later wrote: "My good offices and purse were ever open to them, at a time when they had neither friend nor money."

Col. David S. Franks, Parnas (President) of Shearith Israel Synagogue, who changed loyalties during the 1775 American invasion of Quebec, and became a hero of the Revolution. (Canadian Jewish Congress National Archives, Montreal)

FRANKS HONOURED

In time, the Americans recognized Franks for his efforts. He was assigned to West Point military base and served under General Arnold as adjutant and secretary. When Arnold was found guilty of collaborating with the British, the Jewish officer was automatically court-martialled. Arnold wrote General Washington stating that Franks had no knowledge of his treasonous activities. Eventually Franks was cleared of wrongdoing and promoted colonel. He was later appointed to the staff of General

The Revolution drove out many Americans loyal to the British crown. The United Empire Loyalists; 20,000 (English) came to Quebec, bringing the population to 160,000 in 1791. A number of Jews were included in the great migration.

Washington. And for a time, he served in a militia unit in Charleston, South Carolina, known as the "Jew's Company." In 1783, the Treaty of Versailles, which recognized the new United States of America and re-drew boundary lines, ended the Revolutionary War. Congress sent Franks to France, where he was later appointed American vice-consul at Marseilles. **In 1789, when George Washington was inaugurated as President, his friend David Salisbury Franks stood at his side. Franks was one of the marshals who inaugurated the first President of the United States of America**.

GREATER FREEDOM FOR CANADIANS

Moses Hazen, David Salisbury Franks, and their associates were remarkable for their courage to choose according to conscience, despite great personal cost. The American Revolution triggered demands in Canada for greater freedom. In 1784, a petition for reform was submitted to King George III. Twenty-five Jews, including Aaron Hart, Jacob Kuhn, Moses Hart, Ezekiel Hart and David David, were among hundreds who signed the petition. The Act of 1791, creating legislatures in Upper and Lower Canada, met some of these demands for greater justice and constitutional liberties.

A STRANGER HANGS AROUND

When he appeared, as if out of nowhere, in Quebec province in May 1797, the well-dressed stranger gave his name as Jacob Felt. He intimated he was Jewish, but his behavior was very suspicious. He later claimed he was Monsieur Audet, a French general sent by the French Ambassador in Washington to encourage unrest in Quebec as part of an effort to restore the province to France. Felt was arrested and identified as David McLane, an American. He confessed that he was in the British Colony to cause unrest. He was sentenced to death and executed a few days later.

Jewish historians have paid little or no attention to the role of Moses Hazen in Canadian history, and more specifically in the story of Montreal.

This obviously stemmed from the fact they did not know he was Jewish or of Jewish descent.

One of the most important historians of Canada, Francis Parkman, dismissed Moses Hazen as a "renegade" and suggest that identifying him as a Jew was erroneous; rather, Parkman suggests he was a Puritan.

Parkman was wrong in his off-hand observation; there are numerous references, in a variety of publications, to Hazen's Jewish background, and no Hazen family is listed in the comprensive records of Puritan settlers in New England.

Many References to Hazen's Jewish roots

References to Hazen as being Jewish, of Jewish parentage, or son of a Jewish merchant may be found in the Dictionary of American Biography, The Cyclopedia of American Biography, the Dictionary of Canadian Biography (1936), the Dictionary of Canadian Biography (1945), the MacMillan Dictionary of Canadian Biography (1963), the Encyclopedia of the American Revolution (1966), Harrison Bird's "Attack on Quebec"

(1968), the 1978 Edition of the Macmillan Dictionary of Canadian Biography, and The American Revolution 1775-1783, An Encyclopedia (1993).

George F. Stanley, in his "Canada Invaded, 1775-76," writes:

"The Governor of Canada first learned on May 20th from Moses Hazen, an American of Jewish extraction who had served under Wolfe during the Seven Years' War..."

Not listed in Puritan documents

Was Hazen a Puritan as Parkman claimed? Elsdon C. Smith in "American Surnames" states "the name Hazen identifies the Spaniard who served as a cantor in the synagogue."

Puritan families are identified in massive documentation collected by proud descendants or scholars. No book identifies a Hazen family in the lists of Puritan emigrés, nor can the name "Hazen" be found in the passenger lists of vessels which brought them to the New World. Edmund S. Morgan in his "Puritan Family" (1944) does not identify a Hazen family nor do many other books listing Puritan Families in New England, including "The Founders of New England," published in Boston in 1860 after three years of research in British Archives, and John Adair's "Founding Fathers, The Puritans in England and America," published in 1982 by J.M. Dent & Sons Ltd. Furthermore, a careful examination of the lists of passengers conveyed to New England in the seventeenth century, and they are remarkably comprehensive, lists no one named Hazen.

Of Portuguese origin

Most likely, the Hazens were of Portuguese or Spanish Jewish origin— driven from the Iberian peninsula at the time of Columbus' first voyage to the New World. They could have been among the early settlers of New Amsterdam (now New York), moving to a town established by English Puritans to do business there. In the early years of the Colonies, Jews were not allowed in Massachusetts, where Moses Hazen was born, but there are numerous references to Jews in documents so the ban apparently was not complete. One reference is on the arrest of a Jew for peddling in the state. Moses Hazen did not remain Jewish. After taking part in the Seven Years' War, he married Charlotte de La Saussaye in Montreal in 1770. They had no children. His younger brother, William, and some cousins, moved to New Brunswick—not then a separate province—in 1771 and established a Canadian (and Christian) branch of the Hazen family. One of them was knighted and became premier of the province.

Copy of the Register of British subjects professing the Jewish Religion, above the age of 21 years, according to the records of the Prothonotary of the Superior Court in Montreal, as of September 11, 1832:

Name	Age	Occupation	Residence
1. Henry Joseph Senior	55	Merchant	Berthier
2. Alexander Hart	48	Gentleman	Montreal
3. Benjamin Hart	51	Merchant	Montreal
4. Isaac Valentine	43	Gentleman	Montreal
5. M.J. Hays	32	Gentleman	Montreal
6. H. Solomon	42	Furrier	Montreal
7. M. Davis	28	Furrier	Montreal
8. Samuel Davis	40	Furrier	Montreal
9. M. Hart	62	Merchant	Montreal
10. Esdaile P. Cohen	32	Merchant	Montreal
11. Jacob Jacobs	33	Merchant	Montreal
12. Isaac Aaron	39	Merchant	Montreal
13. Samuel Joseph	29	Merchant	Berthier
14. E.D. David	21	Student-at-law	Montreal
15. A.P. Hart	21 and over	Advocate	Montreal
16. A.H. David	25	Physician	Montreal
17. Jacob H. Joseph	22	Merchant	Montreal
18. Samuel Hart	21	Merchant	Montreal
19. Theodore Hart	21	Merchant	Montreal
20. Henry Bernstein	47	Teacher	Montreal
21. Moses Samuel David	81	Gentleman	Montreal
22. David Piza	22	Minister (Rabbi)	Montreal

—Additions to the list made in 1839—

Name	Age	Occupation	Residence
23. Jesse Joseph	22	Merchant	Montreal
24. Myer Solomons	23	Student	Montreal
25. Lewis Lyons	42	Merchant	Montreal
26. Lambert A. Phillips	37	Merchant	Montreal
27. Itzic David	31	Trader	Montreal

—Names added in 1842—

Name	Age	Occupation	Residence
28. Aaron S. Solomons	22	Gentleman	Montreal
29. A. Saltiel Frederics	26		Montreal
30. Solomon Isaacs	25	Gentleman	Montreal
31. Samuel C. Benjamin	29	Merchant	Montreal
32. P. Solomon	42	Merchant	Montreal
33. M. Moses	32	Merchant	Montreal
34. Abraham Prince	32	Optician	Montreal
35. M.E. David	29	Gentleman	Montreal
36. William Benjamin	26	Merchant	Montreal
37. Isaac Sanguietti	31	Merchant	Montreal
38. M. Binley	21	Student-at-law	Montreal
39. G. Joseph	21	Student-at-law	Montreal
40. Moss	28	Merchant	Montreal
41. B. Hart Jr.	22	Gentleman	Montreal
42. Barnett Harris	32	Merchant Tailor	Montreal
43. Abraham Lyons	23	Merchant Tailor	Montreal
44. Edward Moss	24		Montreal
45. Lawrence Moss	28	Merchant	Montreal
46. Thomas H. Rosing	22	Dyer	Montreal
47. J. Joseph	42	Merchant	Montreal

CHAPTER EIGHT

EQUALITY UNDER THE LAW
Ezekiel Hart and The Charter of Emancipation

There was a problem right away. Ezekiel Hart, the first Jew elected to a legislative body in Quebec, was to be sworn in and he insisted on using his Jewish bible, the Old Testament, during the ceremony! Others had always taken their oath on a Christian bible. Then the newly elected member, whose candidacy local clergy in Trois-Rivières had endorsed, insisted that his head be covered with a yarmulke. Finally, Hart wanted the words of the oath changed. After all, how could a Jew—and the son of the pious Aaron Hart, no less—take an oath "as a Christian gentleman?" When Hart tried to take his seat, he was blocked by angry French members of the Quebec Legislative Assembly, and ejected. After being barred from taking his seat because he could not take the oath, as required, his friends and associates pressed him to run again the following year. In 1808, the constituents of Trois-Rivières re-elected Hart in defiance of the council. This time, he sat in the legislature for nine days before being ejected. He was urged to run a third time, but declined.

TIMELINE—1800-1849

1800. Aaron Hart donates land for a Jewish cemetery in Trois-Rivières.

1801. Henry Joseph inaugurates shipping services between Canada and England.

1801. Aaron Hart dies.

1804. Sidewalks are constructed on St. Lawrence Boulevard.

1805. Joseph Franks builds Canada's first saw and grist mil.

1806. Jewish population 100 (250,000 French; 20,000 English).

1807. Ezekiel Hart elected to Legislative Assembly but is refused his seat as he is not a Christian.

1809. The Governor of Canada, Sir James Craig, acts as godfather to the son of Ezekiel Hart.

1812. Britain and the United States go to war and the Americans again fail to capture Canada.

1818. David David is elected a director of the newly established Bank of Montreal, and is joined by Henry Joseph and Moses Judah Hays as charter members.

WAR OF 1812
The question of rights was set aside when war broke out between England (and by default, Canada) and the United States. A number of Jews served with valour when Lt.-Col. Charles de Salaberry led Canadian forces to victory over a much larger American force on October 25, 1813, at a battle on the Chateauguay River. Among those in uniform were the following Jews: Ezekiel Hart and his brothers, Benjamin and Alexander, Henry Joseph, Jacob Franks, Isaac Phineas, Myer Michaels and Joseph Hersh. Three Jewish officers were promoted to the rank of Colonel. David David commanded an English-speaking regiment, and Samuel David was a major, given command of the Second Montreal battalion.

Before the war, Benjamin Hart had applied for a commission in the militia. He did not receive an answer to his request for more than a year, and then the commander-in-chief turned him down. "Christian soldiers," declared the colonel, "would not tolerate a Jew in their midst." However, it was politics, not religion that prompted the colonel's ire. Twice, he had lost Trois-Rivières elections to Benjamin's brother, Ezekiel. Nevertheless, Benjamin Hart enlisted as a private in Captain Ogilvy's Company of Light Infantry and participated in the battle at Chateauguay. When the Canadian garrisons at Fort William Henry (now Sorel) lacked funds for supplies, Hart loaned them money. Eight years later, Hart became a lieutenant in the First Battalion of the Montreal Militia.

TORONTO'S FIRST JEW
The first Jew to settle in Toronto was a Montrealer. Arthur Wellington Hart reached the Queen City in 1832. He was the grandson of Aaron Hart, the founding pioneer of the Canadian Jewish community.

The denial of Ezekiel Hart's right to sit in the Legislative Assembly touched off a 25-year-long struggle to achieve full civil and political rights for Jews in Canada; and was one phase in the fight for responsible government in Quebec. The push for more independence from British rule began even before Canada formally became part of Britain in 1763. The first petition seeking the right to elect a legislative assembly was submitted to London in 1762, a year before the pact making Quebec British. Among those signing it was a Jew named Eleazor Levy. In 1784, Canadians tried again to win a degree of self-government; another petition (with the names of 25 Jews) submitted to the English Parliament demanded the framing of a constitution and the granting of responsible government. The pressures on London increased. The United States proclaimed its Bill of Rights (1791), including guarantees of freedom of worship, of speech, of the press, of assembly and the right to petition the government. In the wake of the American Revolution, immigration to Canada rapidly increased as thousands loyal to the British crown fled or were driven out of the new United States. The Loyalists flooded into Canada, resulting in the creation of New Brunswick and what is now Ontario. In response to the demands of the newcomers, a Constitutional Act created Upper and Lower Canada. Upper Canada (Ontario) was largely Protestant and English-speaking while Lower Canada (Quebec) was mainly Roman Catholic and French-speaking.

TIMELINE—1800-1849
1818. The 49th parallel is accepted as the border between Canada and the U.S.
1824. Aaron Ezekiel Hart and T.S. Jacobs are the first Jewish lawyers.
1829. Legislation is passed allowing incorporation of a Jewish religious corporation, with the right to keep registers of births, marriages and deaths.
1831. The Jewish population of Canada is 107.
1832. Legislation is passed granting Jews equal civil and political rights.
1832. Moses Judah Hays sets up the first waterworks system in Montreal.
1835. Frank Hart is the first Jew to obtain a medical degree from McGill University.
1835. Moses Judah Hays and Benjamin Hart become the first Jewish magistrates in Canada.
1836. The Joseph brothers help establish Canada's first railway.
1837. William Lyon Mackenzie and Louis-Joseph Papineau lead rebellions in Upper and Lower Canada.
1839. Lord Durham's Report recommends the establishment of responsible government in a united Canada; the union of Lower and Upper Canada is recommended.
1841. The Jewish population of Canada numbers 154.
1845. Moses Judah Hays becomes Montreal Police Chief; he served until 1861.

ANTI-ENGLISH NOT ANTI-SEMITIC

Ezekiel Hart's difficulties did not relate to his faith, but rather reflected anti-English sentiment. Many of the French-speaking members felt Hart would vote pro-English. They used his Jewishness as a pretext for preventing him from taking his seat. A French-Canadian, Amable de Bonne, who regularly voted with the English, was also deprived of his seat—confirming that the Quebec Assembly was more anti-English than anti-Semitic.

The expulsion of Ezekiel Hart from the Quebec Assembly was not legal, and the committee that made that decision knew they were contravening the law. In 1740, some 67 years before Hart, the British House of Commons had passed the "Uniform Naturalization Act." The Act granted aliens—a term meaning non-Protestants, Roman Catholics and Jews—exemption from taking the oath "upon the true faith of a Christian." Hart drew attention to this legislation, but a review committee rejected his protest. Hart argued that the Statute of 31st George III permitted the manner in which he wished to take the oath—with his hand on the Old Testament, and his head covered. His expulsion was in violation of the Statute of the 13th, George II, Chap. VII. However, Hart would have found it difficult and expensive to take advantage of the rarely used 1740 legislation. Not only did it require passage of an Act of Parliament, in London, but also Hart needed a certificate provided by the British Home Secretary stating that the applicant was "of good character." The immense costs of the application would have included hiring a lawyer in Britain.

JEWS IN LOWER CANADA ONLY

Other than a few enterprising fur traders, Jews lived entirely in Lower Canada. In 1806, there were only 100 Jews in Canada—almost all in Quebec and living harmoniously with the 250,000 French and 20,000 English. In contrast, Upper Canada denied Jews the right to settle until well into the nineteenth century; Toronto had only 12 Jews in 1846, and the 1861 census listed four Jews in Ottawa.

Ezekiel Hart (1770-1843), twice elected to the Quebec Legislative Assembly and twice rejected because he could not take the oath "as a Christian gentleman."

MONTREAL'S JEWISH CHIEF OF POLICE

Moses Judah Hayes, a leader in business and innovator of the Montreal waterworks, is best known as the first Jew to head the Montreal constabulary. He was the son of Andrew Hayes (or Hays), a Montreal pioneer Jew. Moses, a talented military engineer, who retired with the rank of captain, created The Montreal Water Works in 1832. Before the reservoir on Notre Dame Street was built, households were supplied with water from wells or water peddlers, who drew river water around Montreal Island and delivered it in barrels and other receptacles. Montrealers were very proud of the Hayes' installation. In "Hochelaga Depicta" (1839), historian Newton Bosworth wrote "with the exception of Philadelphia, Montreal has the best water supply of any city on the continent." In 1843, the city of Montreal bought the waterworks, and Hayes expanded into real estate.

TIMELINE—1800-1849

1846. A charter is granted to a German-Polish Ashkenazi Synagogue (Shaar Hashomayim).

1847. Rabbi Abraham de Sola is named to the Chair in Hebrew and Rabbinical Literature at McGill University.

1848. Moses Judah Hays erects the first theatre in Montreal.

1849. Samuel Benjamin is the first Jew elected alderman to Montreal City Council.

1849. The Jewish population in Montreal is 181; in Quebec City it is 40.

Captain Hayes, and Benjamin Hart, were appointed magistrates in Montreal, in 1837—the first Jews to hold that position in the British Empire. Hayes was a Judge in the Court of Special Sessions. In the period 1846-1847, he built the "Hayes Block" on one side of Dalhousie Square. It included a hotel and a theatre. In April 1849, a riotous mob burned down Parliament House in Montreal to protest a bill that would give compensation to those who had suffered losses during the 1837-38 Rebellion. After helping to restore order in the city, Hayes offered his theatre to parliamentarians for the remainder of their session. (Shortly after the fire, the decision was taken to move the national capital from Montreal.) Three years later, on a hot July day, a fire that eventually destroyed 1,100 buildings swept through his property. He lost nearly everything.

In 1854, a sympathetic city administrator offered him the position of Police Chief of Montreal. It was not an easy job. Given a tiny budget to recruit officers—less than a dollar a day—Hayes occasionally had to hire petty criminals who had been jailed the night before for minor offences. If someone appeared suitable, the chief would provide him with a uniform and put him to work. During Hayes' tenure, the city hall, jail and police departments were all housed in the Bonsecours Market. Hayes remained head of the constabulary until his death, in 1861.

In 1819, Thomas Doige published "An Alphabetical List of the Merchants, Traders and Housekeepers" of Montreal. The list includes nine Jews: Jacob Franks, fur merchant; Solomons and Company; Levi and Benjamin S., tobacconists and chocolate manufacturers; Henry Solomons, furrier; Ja-

A general store, about 1820.
(Drawing by C.W. Jefferys, from the collection in the National Archives of Canada)

cob Jacobs, watchmaker; Moses Hayes, engineer; Benjamin Hart, Commission merchant; Samuel and David David, merchants; and Lewis Blumhart, dry goods merchants. The official census of 1831 recorded a Jewish population of 107 in Lower Canada.

QUEBEC GRANTS FULL CIVIL AND POLITICAL RIGHTS TO JEWS

In 1823, a group of Jews petitioned Quebec City to grant their community the right to keep an official register of marriages, births and burials. Six years later, parliament granted the request. A Bill to grant Jews emancipation in Quebec was submitted to the Legislative Assembly. It received the support of the influential Speaker of the House, Louis Joseph Papineau, and quick approval. The measure was signed into law on **January 13, 1831. Quebec became the first part of the British Empire to grant Jews full civil and political rights.** (Britain granted voting rights to Jews in 1832, but did not permit them to stand for parliament until 1858. British Prime Minister Benjamin Disraeli had converted before he was elected to the British House of Commons in 1837.) When the Charter of Emancipation became law, Ezekiel Hart invited Papineau and his associates to a celebratory dinner in his home.

REBELLION OF 1837-38

Demands for greater measures of self-government reached a crisis in 1837, when Upper Canada (under William Lyon Mackenzie) and Lower Canada (under Louis J. Papineau) revolted. Lower Canada Jews were in an uncomfortable situation, forced to choose sides. They favoured, and had lent their names to petitions calling for, self-government in the colony, so they understood the impatience of *les patriotes*, the French-Canadian nationalists. The Jews also had great respect for Papineau, the man who had championed their individual rights. Two Jewish leaders, Moses Hart and Henry Judah, were sympathetic to the rebel cause and outspoken in their support. When some rebels were arrested, Jewish lawyer Adolph Mordechai Hart defended them in court.

However, when actual fighting broke out between the rebels and the British colonial government, almost the entire community rallied to the Union Jack. There were 20 to 25 Jewish families— about 120 individuals—in Lower Canada at this time, and almost every family had one or more members active in the ranks of the Loyalists.

One of the fervent supporters of Papineau's rebellion was Louis Marchand, whose real name was Levi Koopman. He was a Jewish immigrant from Holland who took up the rebel cause passionately and fled Canada when the rebellion failed. With the promise of amnesty, in 1838, he returned to Montreal and became a leader in the nationalistic St. Jean Baptiste Society. A co-founder of the Society was Joseph Olivier Joseph, a descendant of a pioneer Jewish family.

CAP. LVII.

An Act to declare persons professing the Jewish Religion entitled to all the rights and privileges of the other subjects of His Majesty in this Province.

31st March, 1831 —Presented for His Majesty's Assent and reserved "for the 'signification of His Majesty's pleasure thereon."
12th April, 1832,—Assented to by His Majesty in His Council.
5th June, 1832,—The Royal Assent signified by the proclamation of His Excellency the Governor in Chief.

WHEREAS doubts have arisen whether persons professing the Jewish Religion are by law entitled to many of the privileges enjoyed by the other subjects of His Majesty within this Province: Be it therefore declared and enacted by the King's Most Excellent Majesty, by and with the advice and consent of the Legislative Council and Assembly of the Province of Lower Canada, constituted and assembled by virtue of and under the authority of an Act passed in the Parliament of Great Britain, intituled, "An Act to repeal certain parts of an Act passed in " the fourteenth year of His Majesty's Reign, intituled, "*An Act for making* " *more effectual provision for the Government of the Province of Quebec, in North* " *America,*" and to make further provision for the Government of the said " Province of Quebec in North America;" And it is hereby declared and enacted by the authority aforesaid, that all persons professing the Jewish Religion being natural born British subjects inhabiting and residing in this Province, are entitled and shall be deemed, adjudged and taken to be entitled to the full rights and privileges of the other subjects of His Majesty, his Heirs or Successors, to all intents, constructions and purposes whatsoever. and capable of taking, having or enjoying any office or place of trust whatsoever, within this Province.

The Act granting Quebec Jews political and civil rights (1832), the first such freedom granted the Jewish people anywhere in the British Empire.

QUEBEC JEWS BEGIN TO ENTER THE PROFESSIONS

Over the period that Jews and the small community were fighting for political acceptance and respect, changes were afoot in society. In the early nineteenth century, Jews were few in number and they mingled freely with non-Jews, mostly the English because of strong ties with either America or the British Isles. Jews and English attended the same social events, belonged to the same sleighing and snowshoeing clubs and were partners in businesses. A spirit of openness permeated society, and Jews responded; they began slowly moving beyond commerce and into the professions. For example, in 1833, Aaron Hart David received the degree of Doctor of Medicine from the Royal College of Physicians and Surgeons, in Edinburgh. After practicing for some years in Montreal, he became Dean of the Faculty of Medicine at Bishop's college in Lennoxville, Quebec. He retained that position until his death. In addition, he served as general secretary of the Canadian Medical Association, and was a co-founder of the Canada Medical Journal. In 1835, the first graduating class in medicine at McGill University included a Jew—Frank N. Hart.

In Montreal, Jews socialized with the anglophone establishment; for example, Jacob Henry Joseph, an important railway and shipping investor, was extended membership in the prestigious Royal Montreal Golf Club.

Outside Montreal, Jews did much of their business in French. Abraham Joseph, in his diary, noted on April 3, 1840: "Rose at 7. Took my first lesson in French." On February 27, 1841, he wrote of a visit to a cousin's store in Trois-Rivières, where he found "a number of (French) Canadians smoking and drinking with Adolphus (Joseph) and Sam Hart— talking politics." By the middle of the nineteenth century, however, the easy relation between Jew and non-Jew began to change. Newton Bosworth, in his 1839 Hochelaga Depicta or the Early History of Montreal, noted: "the privileges of 'caste' are more jealously maintained, and the lines of demarcation more distinctly drawn in Montreal, than in other cities." However relations remained good with the few wealthy, anglicized Jews.

On May 15, 1843, an era ended in Trois-Rivières, a community well aware of its debt to the Hart family, when Ezekiel Hart died. "During the funeral service," the newspapers reported, "most of the stores were closed and a feeling of gloom seemed to be cast over the inhabitants of the town." In 1870, historian Joseph Tassé wrote: "Ezekiel Hart lived long enough to see the Bill (Charter of Emancipation)

An important social note: In 1834, Mrs. Henry Joseph entertained the Governor of Lower Canada, Lord Aylmer, and Lady Aylmer, in Montreal.

In 1849, Samuel Benjamin became **the first Jew elected to Montreal City Council for Centre Ward**. His brothers Goodman and William were also prominent in communal affairs in the period 1849-1860.

adopted, and to witness just how far thinking had progressed since the days when parliament had closed its doors in his face, and forced him to withdraw from political life. By granting political emancipation to Jews, Canada moved far ahead of England in matters of justice and liberality; in fact, in 1847, 1850, 1857 and 1858, the question of whether to grant Jews political rights was still being discussed at Westminister." Through the efforts of Ezekiel Hart and other Jews, the community began making progress toward official recognition and equality.

Rabbi Abraham de Sola, spiritual leader of the Spanish and Portugese Synagogue—the first Jew in the British Empire to be awarded an Honorary Degree (McGill University)
(From "The Jew in Canada")

RABBI ABRAHAM DE SOLA: A JEWISH SCHOLAR OF GREAT DISTINCTION

Abraham de Sola was born in London, England, on September 18, 1825. His father, David Aaron de Sola, had been invited from Amsterdam by Portuguese Jews of the British capital to serve as senior minister. His mother was the daughter of Dr. Raphael Meldola, Chief Rabbi of the Spanish-Jewish congregations of Britain. The Meldolas had provided Chief Rabbis to European congregations for 12 generations.

After being turned down for a more coveted post in England, Rabbi Abraham de Sola came to Montreal and became spiritual leader of the Spanish and Portuguese Synagogue in 1846 when he was only 21. As grandson of Rabbi Raphael Meldola, **the hakkam** or spiritual leader of the Sephardi Congregation in London, his ambition was to succeed to that chair. Quite possibly, London Jews believed he was too young to head up their celebrated congregation. When the selection committee passed him over, he accepted the position in Montreal—a decision that would prove beneficial to Montreal Jewry for decades. De Sola served with distinction for 35 years. In 1852, he married Esther Joseph, youngest daughter of Henry Joseph—one of the pioneers of the Jewish community.

Soon after his arrival, he was invited to lecture at McGill University and in 1853, he was appointed professor of Hebrew and Oriental literature. **He was the first Jew appointed to a university position in Canada**. In 1858, the university awarded him an honourary degree, making him the first Jew with this distinction in the British Empire! Dr. de Sola was active in the wider

SHAAR HASHOMAYIM— A SECOND CONGREGATION IS FORMED
After almost 80 years, Montreal acquired its second synagogue, but not without angering some members of the original congregation. In 1846, German and Polish Ashkenazim established the Congregation Shaar Hashomayim (pronounced shar-show -my-am). Land was purchased for a synagogue on de Bullion at Craig Street; however construction did not begin until 1858, 12 years later. The spiritual leader of the Spanish and Portuguese Synagogue, the Sephardic congregation, refused to take part in a cornerstone-laying ceremony. "Montreal Jewry," declared Rabbi Abraham de Sola stiffly, "did not require a second synagogue." He felt the Jewish population was not large enough to support two congregations. Indeed, the Shaar Hashomayim drew a significant number of worshippers from the Spanish and Portuguese. [In 1841, there were only 30 Jewish families (about 100 individuals) in Montreal. Ten years later, there were only 181 Jews in Montreal and 40 in Quebec City. These figures were to change dramatically in the next few years.] A second building was erected in 1886 on McGill College Avenue.

community. He served for many years as president of Montreal's Natural History Society, and he was the author of a remarkable number and variety of articles on religion and history, and was published throughout North America and Britain. He was Chair of Hebrew at the Montreal Presbyterian College and was appointed lecturer in Spanish literature at McGill University. **In 1872, President Ulysses S. Grant invited Rabbi de Sola to offer the prayer at the opening of the United States Congress—the first time such an honour had been given a non-American and a non-Christian**. He served his congregation with great distinction until his death on June 5, 1882 at age 57, and was succeeded by his son, Aaron David Meldola de Sola—the first Canadian-born Jew appointed to the Rabbinate. Aaron de Sola remained rabbi until his death in 1918.

A list of "ladies and gentlement's seats" in the new Spanish and Portuguese Synagogue, taken from a letter of October 14, 1833, from Benjamin Hart to Isaac Valentine:

Ladies	Gentlemen
Mrs. C. Solomons	Moses I. Hays
Joseph	Myer Solomons
David	Henry Solomons
B. Hart	Dr. David
A.M. Hart	S. Davids
H. Solomons	B. Hart
Asher	J. Hart
S. Benjamin	A.M. Hart
G. Benjamin	Jacob Joseph
W. Benjamin	I.M. Joseph
Levy	C. Joseph
Hart	A. Joseph
Miss Davids	A.E. Hart
S. Davids	Z.C. Hart
Hart	
Jesse Solomons	M.E. Davids
R. Joseph	S. Benjamins
S. Joseph	G. Benjamins
E. Joseph	W. Benjamins
Solomons	Asher
Solomons	A young lad
Valentine	Levey
Roshin (?)	Hart
Hays	M. Hays
Hays	Hays
	Hays
	Hays
	Moses Hays
	A. Cohen

CHAPTER NINE

IN THE COMPANY OF JEWS
The Joseph Family, and Others,
Help Build the Economy of Quebec

*Jesse Joseph, a prominent Jewish businessman and founder of The
Montreal Street Railway Company, beamed with delight as he
inaugurated Montreal's first public transit service in 1861.
Montrealers were pleased and excited as they boarded the horse-
drawn trams—the city's first street railway. The directors of the
company, along with Joseph were on hand in 1864 to approve the
extension of the service to St. Lawrence Boulevard. However, the
horses had difficulty cresting the hill at Sherbrooke Street. Extra
horses were added to make the grade. It was an excellent, frequent
service with cars running every eight minutes during most of the
day, and every 16 minutes in the early morning and after 7 in the
evening. There were no set stops. The driver pulled the reins anywhere along the route to pick up or let off passengers.
Accommodating drivers would stop for brief shopping expedi-
tions. The fare was five cents.*

TIMELINE—1851-1900

1863. Founding of the Young Men's Hebrew Benevolent Society to aid
refugees.

1867. Confederation; British North America Act becomes basis for founding the Dominion of Canada.

1870. Education Act passed by Quebec legislature permitted Jewish tax-
payers to pay their school taxes either to the Protestant or the
Catholic School Boards.

1875. Montreal's Jewish population reaches 500.

1880. The Montefiore Club is established.

1881. The first B'nai Brith Lodge is established in Montreal.

1882. Quebec's Jewish population reaches 989 with the arrival of refugee
Jews from Eastern Europe.

1882. Montreal's first Reform Congregation, Temple Emanu-El, is established.

1888. Jules Helbronner, an Alsatian Jew, is named editor-in-chief of La
Presse and holds the post until 1896.

Winter transit service in Montreal.
From Canadan Illustrated News, 1873

LEADERSHIP IN COMMERCE

Despite their small number, Jews made an exceptional contribution to the growth and development of Quebec and Canada. The introduction of new technology, such as the steam engine, revolutionized the technical and economic development of first, Britain, and then the world, and made possible steamships, trains, telegraphic lines, and sewing machines. It was a time of massive change and massive opportunity. Montreal Jewry, in particular, kept abreast of innovations and helped initiate a new industrial era, in which machinery and manufacturing first challenged, and then surpassed, agriculture in importance. A number of resourceful Jews recognized the opportunities in developing railroads and other transportation facilities, in creating heavy industries and installing utilities. Jews founded Canada's merchant marine, established the first telegraphic service, and helped launch the Canadian banking system. They installed the city's first waterworks and gas systems, public transit service, and electric streetlights. Jews invested in the new canal systems, which offered Canada full advantage of the great waterways penetrating the continent. As Montreal began to grow into a prosperous port city, peddlers who had originally settled in the hinterland migrated to the city. The Jews were on the move.

PROMINENCE OF THE JOSEPH FAMILY

The Canadian Josephs were descended from Naphtali Joseph, a member of an Anglo-Jewish family from the Netherlands. He married Aaron Hart's sister, and his brother-in-law invited his

Silhouette of Henry Joseph (1775-1832)

1890. The Young Men's Hebrew Benevolent Society changes its name to Baron de Hirsch Institute in recognition and appreciation of the generosity of the Austrian Baron and Baroness.

1891. The Jewish population is 6,503.

1891. Inauguration of the Baron de Hirsch Institute on St. Elizabeth Street.

1896. First Talmud Torah School founded.

1897. The *Canadian Jewish Times* is created, in Montreal, the first Jewish newspaper in the country.

1898. Canada's first Zionist organization, Agudath Zion, is founded in Montreal with Dr. David A. Hart as President.

1899. Nearly 3,000 immigrants—most of them from Romania—arrive in Montreal.

three sons to seek their fortune in Canada. From the time Judah, Henry and Abraham Joseph arrived in Quebec in 1792, the Joseph family has figured prominently in the Jewish community.

Henry Joseph married Rachel Solomons in 1803 and they had 13 children, three of whom died in childhood.

Henry Joseph and three of his sons, Jacob Henry, Jesse and Gershom Henry, were instrumental in introducing the latest technology to Quebec.

Born in London in 1775, Henry Joseph, the first to arrive in Canada, became associated with the commissariat of the garrison at Fort William Henry, at the mouth of the Richelieu River, not far from Hart's property. After settling in Berthier, east of Montreal, he developed one of the largest chains of trading posts in the colony. An important figure in the development of Canadian commerce, **Henry Joseph was the first to build and charter Canadian ships for transatlantic trade, and is recognized as the father of Canada's merchant marine**. Later in Montreal, he became an active supporter of the Spanish and Portuguese Synagogue, and numerous non-sectarian institutions. Henry Joseph's brothers, Abraham and Judah, followed their brother to Canada. Both did well, and Judah, after amassing considerable wealth, returned to England. In 1882, Henry Joseph and his eldest son, Samuel, contracted cholera and died.

Jacob Henry, another son, was born in Berthier, Quebec, and moved to Montreal in 1830. He was a partner in the Newfoundland Telegraph Company, which organized the first telegraphic link between Canada and the United Kingdom; and he was involved in organizing the first telegraphic link between Canada and the United States. Jacob helped found three banks— the Union, the Ontario, and the Provident Savings. For many years, he was president and controlling stockholder of the Montreal Elevator Company.

Jesse Joseph was born in Berthier in 1817. The records show that Jesse (pronounced Jess not Jessie) Joseph was living in Montreal by 1838, when he would have been 21 years old. He attended the laying of the cornerstone that year for the new Chenneville synagogue. He helped organize the Montreal Gas Company (later the Light and Heat Power Company) and was appointed director in 1864, and president of the firm in 1887. In addition, he set up the Montreal Telegraph Company. He was involved in a number of telegraph companies and financial institutions. In 1893, he became president of the Spanish and Portuguese Synagogue. He was also a governor of the Montreal

Jesse Joseph, a leading figure in the industrialization of Canada in the latter half of the nineteenth century. (Canadian Jewish Congress National Archives)

General Hospital, and was active with a number of other charitable organizations.

The Steamboat wharf in Montreal, in 1832. Jews were major investors in transportation, including the new steam vessels.

Jesse Joseph developed the first direct steamship line between Canada and Belgium and, in 1850, was appointed the Belgian consul general in Canada. The Belgian king twice decorated him for his initiatives in strengthening trade relations between Canada and Belgium. Joseph also was active in promoting trade with England. Interestingly, Jesse's uncle Abraham continued the family tradition of aggressive entrepreneurship; he was president of the Stadaconda Bank, director of the Banque Nationale, helped form and manage The District Bank of Quebec, was president of the Quebec Board of Trade, and a member of the Quebec City council. He maintained the family's close ties with Belgium, serving as that country's consul to Quebec for almost 30 years.

An interesting footnote: Jesse Joseph, who helped found the City Passenger Railway, was first elected director of that company in 1877, and became president in 1884 for 30 years, until his death at age 87. When the question of electrifying the street railway came up, Chairman Joseph was outraged. "No self-respecting person would ride in a horseless street car," he told the board of directors. However, the proposal for modernization submitted by Louis J. Forget was accepted despite Jesse's objections.

The youngest son of Henry Joseph was Gershom, born in 1820. He studied jurisprudence at the University of Toronto. He practised law in Montreal, but abandoned the profession in 1849 to search for gold in California. He returned to Montreal in 1863 and resumed his law practice. He became a Queen's Counsel in 1892—the first Jew with this honour.

The "Dorchester", first locomotive in Lower Canada, 1836. Two of the Joseph brothers were key players in establishing the LaPrairie Railway —Canada's first.
(Drawing by C.W. Jefferys, from National Archives of Canada)

ESTABLISHING CANADA'S FIRST RAILWAY

Jacob and Jesse Joseph worked together to help establish the first railroad in Canada, the St. Lawrence and Champlain, in 1836. The first train, with a locomotive named Dorchester, pulled two coaches from La Prairie to St. Jean (known as Dorchester from 1815-1835), at an average speed of 14.5 miles per hour, on a wooden track! A small locomotive pulled the first two cars; a team of horses pulled the third. The 16-mile (23 kilometres) route was Canada's only steam railway for

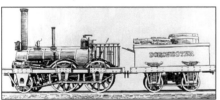

ten years. Before construction of railways, travel was uncomfortable and enormously time-consuming. Large canoes, rafts, horse-drawn wagons, and springless coaches were used to move people and goods. As there were few bridges, stagecoaches were built without doors that would leak during river crossings. Passengers had to clamber through the stagecoach windows. Nineteenth-century roads consisted of a crisscross of logs. Travel over the roads became almost impossible especially during the spring and fall. British government engineer John Mactaggart, in an 1826 report, made these comments on the roads citizens had to use:

"The jolting corduroy roads are a disgrace. Many roads over swamps and gullies are of round logs of wood, or trees, averaging a foot in diameter, laid close by one another and the spaces in between unfilled. These turnpikes are fancied to resemble that famous King's cloth, called Corduroy—hence their name. In a wagon, the poor human frame is jolted to pieces." Nevertheless, before the enterprising Joseph family, there were few alternatives to transport passengers and freight.

Since nearly all communities, of any size, were located on waterways, it was logical for Canadians to take advantage of the great systems of rivers and lakes. As construction of railways involved great capital expenditures, canal building made sense. The first real canal to be completed was the Lachine Canal, bypassing the turbulent rapids on the St. Lawrence River, upstream of Montreal. Jewish investors joined others in underwriting the cost of the waterway. It was started in 1821 and completed four years later.

The earliest known photograph of a Jewish Montrealer, taken in 1859; he is a "herb doctor", selling herbs and spices on the street.
(from the Notman Photographic Archives, McCord Museum of Canadian History, N-0000.5.19)

FORMER PEDDLERS MOVE TO MONTREAL

In the late 1800s, pioneer Jews who had settled in isolated communities along the shore of the St. Lawrence River in Upper Canada—starting as peddlers—began migrating to the city. They would journey to Montreal to mark the High Holidays, but that was not enough. Many had married and wanted their children to have a religious education. Noah Friedman had been the first Lithuanian Jewish immigrant, arriving in 1857, and settling in Lancaster, Ontario. Other immigrants followed—the Kellerts and the Levinsons—from Lithuania and Poland. They eventually sold

Jewish peddlers were a familiar sight in backwoods Quebec for decades. Many lugged, in backpacks, as much as 100 pounds of merchandise and, in the beginning, traveled by foot to isolated farmhouses, logging camps and hamlets. They carried a wide selection of merchandise in their packs to isolated areas, where there were no stores. They lugged everything from cloth to tools and tinware. After a time, some could afford a horse and wagon. Often with paltry French, they became a fixture in households doing personal shopping for everything from makeup to sheet music. When they had built up some capital, they opened stores. Some Montreal companies, until recent times, catered to peddlers, providing them with their first inventory on credit. A newspaper story recalling conditions in the 1870s stated that, at the time, "Jews lived by trade, in small stores. There were several large Jewish firms and two Jewish cigar manufacturers. After coming to Canada, they would spend the first several years peddling in the countryside."

general stores they had founded, from Lancaster to Sudbury, and settled in Montreal in the late nineteenth century. The newcomers included Moses Vineberg, Abraham Jacobs and Lazarus Cohen, among others, and they provided Montreal with a new pool of exceptional leadership. Many of their descendants remained prominent members of the community a century-and-a-half later. For example, Lazarus Cohen, another eastern Ontario settler in Montreal, went into the lumber business, built a brass foundry, developed a dredging company, and was a major coal distributor. Harris Vineberg and Solomon Levinson became clothing manufacturers.

Two enterprising families of note—the Jacobs and Davis—provide a legacy that exceeds success in business. The Jacobs family provided the community with one of its greatest political figures, Samuel W. Jacobs. The Davis family provided Canada with two of its greatest industrial barons, Samuel and his son Mortimer. The latter became one of the burgeoning Jewish community's most important financial philanthropists, and Canada's first Jewish knight.

JACOBS' LADDER

William Jacobs arrived in Lancaster (Ontario) in the early 1860s from Lithuania. In 1867, to marry Hannah Aronson, Jacobs journeyed to Montreal for the ceremony, conducted by Rabbi Abraham de Sola at the Spanish and Portuguese Synagogue. Jacobs set himself up as a dealer in horses in Lancaster, and frequently travelled to Montreal, where he met Jesse Joseph and became the exclusive supplier of horses for the tramway service—an important contract. The couple had eight children—six sons and two daughters. Their second son, Samuel, became an outstanding member of Parliament. The family travelled to Montreal every year to mark the High Holy Days, and in 1881, they moved to the city and William Jacobs set up his business at 16 Hanover Street (now University Street), as "horse dealer, exporter and livestock shipper."

THE DAVIS FAMILY

One of the pioneers of the tobacco industry in Canada was Samuel Davis, an important leader in the evolution of the Jewish community.

Davis was born in London, England in 1834—son of David Davis, a gentleman farmer. As a young man he moved to New York and went into the tobacco business. In 1862, in Montreal, he became a manufacturer of small tobacco products, such as snuff, chewing tobacco and hand-rolled cigars. By 1874, he employed 75 cigar-makers, brought three of his sons into the business, and helped make Montreal the "cigar capital of Canada." In 1888, Davis was the largest manufacturer of tobacco products in the city with 457 employees. His closest competitor had 275 workers. Employees numbered 600 by the time a new seven-storey factory, equipped with steam elevators and an internal telephone system, was built.

Davis was an exceptionally charitable man. He set aside 10 per cent of his profits for philanthropy. He was also active with organizations assisting the underprivileged—Jewish and non-Jewish. When Russian immigrants poured into the city in the 1880s, he personally saw to accommodations for 80 families. He paid university fees for poor scholars, endowed a chair in Hebrew at McGill, and paid the licenses of Jewish peddlers. Davis joined

Cohen and Lopez's Cigar Store, Place d'Armes, Montreal
(From Canadian Illustrated News, Feb. 4 1871

the Spanish and Portuguese Synagogue, and was its president for 17 years. However, he became interested in the reform movement and in 1882, he was one of the founders of Temple Emanu-El. He assumed presidency of the temple for nine years.

BANKING APPEARS IN CANADA

Fur traders dominated commerce during the first years of British control of Canada. However, with industrialization, and the development of a prosperous merchant class, the need for more sophisticated institutions, including banks and insurance companies, grew. Canada's first bank, the Bank of Montreal, was inaugurated in 1817, with three Jewish charter members: Henry Joseph, Moses Hays and David David. David David was elected one of 13 directors of the institution, and he retained that position until his death, in 1824.

The bank was quartered in a building on St. Paul Street, between St. Nicholas and St. Francois Xavier streets. Initial capital was $1 million.

On Oct. 1, 1817, the Bank began to circulate the first bank notes issued in Canada, supported by deposits of gold and silver. However, the directors spent a greal deal of time determining how to issue currency for circulation without making each stock-

CANADA'S FIRST JEWISH ENGINEER
Sigismund Mohr, a German-born electrical engineer, developed hydropower in Canada and installed the first telephone and electric light systems. Mohr settled in Quebec City in 1871. He was an associate of Alexander Graham Bell, inventor of the telephone. As a result, Mohr introduced telephone service in Quebec City only four years after the device was created and tested in 1876. As electricity became commercially viable in the 1880s, Mohr harnessed power from the Montmorency Falls and in 1885 gave the city its first electric light system. Electricity reached Sherbrooke, Quebec, in 1896 and Montreal, two years later. He died in Quebec City in 1893, aged 66.

BATTLING THE BOERS
A number of Jews were among the 8,300 Canadian volunteers who journeyed to South Africa to fight for the British Empire against the two Dutch Boer republics in the Boer War (1899-1902). At least 242 Canadians lost their lives. Among those who served with the Canadian contingent was Captain Hyman Lightsone. Dr. J. Alton Harris enlisted in the British Army.
In 1913, Canada's Minister of Militia, Colonel Sam Hughes, spoke to the Montreal YMHA, paying tribute to Jews for their "loyalty and devotion to the British flag in all parts of the Empire," and he recalled "with admiration" Jews with whom he came in contact during the South African fighting.
After the war, Martin Wolff, a British volunteer, visited Montreal on vacation. During his stay, he met and then married Irene Joseph, a direct descendent of Henry Joseph (1775-1832), one of the pioneer Jews of Quebec. They had six daughters—Fanny, Sarah (Orkin), Annette, Rachel (Esar), Rosetta (Elkin), and Esther (Blaustein).

holder personally liable for its payment. Finally, they agreed to this wording:

"The President and Directors of the Bank of Montreal promise to pay AS.B. or bearer, the sum of five dollars (or other amount) out of the joint funds of the Association, and no other."

However, *habitants* for many years were reluctant to accept paper money. They were accustomed to using gold and silver coins, from many countries, all of them acceptable because they contained precious metals. The coins in widest circulation at that time, all silver, were Spanish dollars, French half-crowns, piastreens valued at one shilling, and seven-pence, half-penny pieces. The prejudice against "paper" money in Quebec stemmed from the fact that most peasants could not read, and many had been defrauded by the previous government. In its latter days, when the French colonial government had run out of coins, it had issued playing cards as interim currency and then refused to honour them after the colony fell to the British.

Nineteenth-century banks were different from those we know. They did not accept deposits. Their partners invested capital, and this money was loaned to merchants of good repute.

Where did people keep their money? Until the mid-1850s, they squirreled their savings away in the bottom of old chests or in other hiding places at home or in their businesses. In any case, very little real money was in circulation in the first half of the nineteenth-century. Merchants accepted in payment everything from bushels of wheat to sides of beef.

As the economy grew and became more sophisticated, more banks appeared on the scene. Abraham Joseph assisted in the establishment of La Banque Nationale, in 1858, and served as one of seven directors from 1860 to 1874. Joseph also helped form and manage the District Bank of Quebec.

List of Jews 21 years of age and over who "have taken the oath and are British subjects"

1874

Name:	Age:	Occupation:
Meldola de Sola	21	Broker and Commission Merchant
Lyon Silverman	30	Jeweller
Levi Abrahams	34	Tobacconist
Morris Teichman	54	Tavern
M. Sternberg	26	Merchant
J. Sternberg	23	Merchant
W.B. Garcia	29	Merchant
Israel Rubenstein	28	Silver Plater
A. Edward Cohen	33	Merchant
Sullivan David	29	Merchant
Joseph Moss	29	Merchant
Jacob E. Moss	31	Merchant

1876

Alfred D. Benjamin	28	Merchant
Samuel Roman	36	Merchant
J. (unreadable)	45	Furrier
Henry Roman	34	Merchant
Noah Friedman	49	Merchant
Julius Scherman	45	Trader
Jacob Hirsch	47	Merchant
Moses Vineberg	30	Merchant
Isaac Vineberg	25	Merchant

1881

Louis Albert	65	Printer and Ker (?)
A. Goldstein	47	Merchant
Jacob Lawrence Moss, J.P.	35	Merchant
Bernard Goldstein	23	Merchant
Hyam David Moss	35	Merchant
Isaac Kaufman	35	Merchant
Salman Fox	31	Hatter and Furrier
D. Golberg	23	Pawnbroker
Rev. Hyman Goldberg	59	Ryby (presumably "Rabbi")

Jews make up less than 1.5% of Canada's population, yet their contributions to the economic and cultural life of this country have far exceeded their proportionate numerical strength...Their contribution to industrial development is evident in the number of Canadian industries that found their beginnings in Jewish enterprises. Initially, Jews were especially active in the founding of the Canadian merchant marine and in the field of railway construction all across the country, in the production of hydro electricity and telephone service.

(From a 1970s Canadian government pamphlet on ethnic communities).

THE BUSINESS AND PROFESSIONAL JEWS OF 1851

An 1851 city directory records the names, business addresses, and activities of a number of Jews. Dr. A.H. David was an officer of the College of Physicians and Surgeons of Lower Canada and is the only professional Jew listed in the directory. Dr. David practised at 48 1/2 Craig St., and was treasurer of the Medico Chirurgical Society. Jesse Joseph, at the corner of St. Helen and Recollet sts., is listed twice—as Consul for Belgium in Montreal and as "importer and general merchant." ➜

(continued)

J.H. Joseph was second vice-president of the Natural History Society and Rabbi Abraham de Sola was third vice-president.

Alexander Levy was described as "importer of and wholesale and retail dealer in china, glass and earthenware, corner of Notre Dame and St. Gabriel sts. —a very superior stock constantly on hand."

Benjamin and Theodore Hart were listed as "general Commission merchants" doing business at 6 St. Sacrement St.

Three Jewish merchants were listed in the category "Hatters and Furriers"—Henry Samuel at 109 St. Paul St. "country merchants are invited to call and examine"; Mark Samuel, 130 Notre Dame St., "opposite the English Church—hats, caps and furs of all kinds constantly for sale at low prices" and Wolfe Sternberg, 197 Notre Dame St.—furs, hats, caps, umbrellas, etc., of all kinds for sale cheap."

William Benjamin, at 131 1/2 Notre Dame St. operated a business of "merchant tailors, clothiers and general outfitters."

Finally, two Jewish merchants operated tobacco and cigar stores. H. Joseph and Co. were at 144 St. Paul St., and they described themselves as "importers, manufacturers and wholesale dealers in tobacco, cigars, snuff, etc., etc." And John Levey at 115 Notre Dame St. was listed as "importer, manufacturer, and wholesale and retail dealer in tobacco, cigars, snuff, pipes, fancy articles, etc."

This list does not take note of the considerable activity of Jewish residents in such fields as banking, transportation, utilities, and public services.

A gathering of the Joseph family in 1882. Jesse Joseph is seated in the alcove with two women while Abraham Joseph is the bearded gentleman seated at the table covered with a throw. (Notman Photographic Archives II-65768.0. McCord Museum)

**We are the dawn and the dusk,
the challenge and the test.**
Abraham J. Heschel
American theologian
"The Earth is the Lord's" 1950

PART TWO

FROM THE SHTETL TO THE MAIN
The Developmental Years

Tens of thousands of Jews pour into Montreal becoming the first non-Christian community in Quebec. They settle in their early impoverished years along a thoroughfare bisecting the island of Montreal, the St. Lawrence Boulevard-Main. They create a vibrant Jewish life in an ethnic enclave positioned between much of the English community to the west and the French residing to the east. The newcomers, largely Yiddish-speaking, flourish commercially, industrially and socially—encountering and overcoming a multitude of obstacles. They create an international reputation for the city with Montreal smoked meat and bagels. They dominate new industries, particularly the manufacture of clothing where Jewish factory owners exploit Jewish immigrant workers in deplorable conditions, a phenomena that gives rise to the Jewish trade union movement in Quebec and has a profound impact on labour standards. Immigrant entrepreneurs break economic boundaries and garner fabulous fortunes. To care for each other, Montreal Jews form fraternal organizations, burial societies, synagogues, libraries, and social and health facilities. In the midst of World War I, they form Canada's first federation of social service agencies.

CHAPTER TEN

THE GREAT JEWISH MIGRATION
The Uptowners learn to cope

"Thou shalt not harden thy heart nor shut thy hand from thy poor brother."

Deuteronomy 15:7

The invitation was sent out to bachelors only, inviting them on July 23, 1863, to a meeting in a room over Mr. Wright's store on Great St. James Street, to consider the desirability of forming some association to assist their needy or unfortunate co-religionists. The wharves were filled with a steady flow of destitute Jewish immigrants, many diseased, arriving in the city from Eastern Europe. And local poor needed coal or Passover food but many were too proud to ask for help. Lawrence L. Levy, an established businessman, in calling the meeting to order, suggested that the proposed organization should be under the entire supervision and control of the young unmarried men of the city, and be "the means of making the Jewish young men of Montreal better known to each other." The men responded enthusiastically. That night they agreed to form the Young Men's Hebrew Benevolent Society—the community's first organized social service.

TIMELINE/1890-1899

1890. The Young Men's Hebrew Benevolent Society changes its name to Baron de Hirsch Institute in recognition and appreciation of the generosity of the Austrian Baron and Baroness.

1891. The Jewish population is 6,503.

1891. Inauguration of the Baron de Hirsch Institute on St. Elizabeth Street.

1896. First Talmud Torah School founded.

1897. The Canadian Jewish Times is created in Montreal, the first Jewish newspaper in the country.

1898. Canada's first Zionist organization, Agudath Zion, is founded in Montreal with Dr. David A. Hart as President.

1899. Nearly 3,000 immigrants—most of them from Romania—arrive in Montreal.

There is no word for "charity" in Hebrew. The closest word to the concept is Tzedakah, which means "social justice." Tzedakah is one of the most important words in the Jewish lexicon. It suggests that everyone has the RIGHT to enough resources to live with dignity. It is the DUTY of those with more to assist those with less. In the Old Country, some synagogues had a room in the back entered one-by-one by the congregation where, on a table, was a plate. Those who could afford to put in a coin. Those in need took a coin. No one ever knew who gave or who took.

Lawrence Levy; he was the first President of the Young Men's Hebrew Benevolent Society when it was founded in 1863—the first Jewish social service agency in Canada

Russian Jews crowded aboard a vessel, 1892. Many continued on to Montreal.
(London Illustrated News)

Lawrence Levy, Founding President of the Benevolent Society, could not have known at that historic meeting of bachelors that his community was about to be inundated with wretched masses of poor Jews—the largest migration in Jewish history, beginning in the 1880s and continuing unabated until the First World War. Driven out of Europe by brutal pogroms and regimes intent on converting or condemning them to destitution or death, 1.2 million Jews fled Russia, Poland, Romania, and Lithuania in a 10-year period from 1900 until 1910, and 67,000 of them came to Canada. The vast majority settled in Montreal or transited the city. While the number of immigrants arriving in Canada was manageable at first, by the turn of the century, the river of desperate refugees pouring into Montreal overwhelmed the small Jewish community. In 1871, after 111 years in Quebec, there were only 518 Jews living in the city. They comprised the Uptowners—about 40 families who had evolved into something of a well-to-do Jewish aristocracy. They were established, anglicized Jews living mostly in Westmount, Outremont, and points west of St. Lawrence Main. By 1901 the Montreal Jewish population had expanded to almost 7,000 and consisted of predominantly poor, Yiddish-speaking immigrants, known as the Downtowners. Many Uptowners were shocked by the destitution and embarrassed by the Old Country customs and clothing. However, they were serious—albeit patronizing—in their responsibility for their co-religionists. What followed was a period of transition as the Uptowners learned to cope with the cultural, economic and linguistic divide. Their seminal efforts led to the eventual development of a comprehensive network of human services unparalleled in Canada—The Federation of Jewish Philanthropies.

AN OVERWHELMING RIVER OF PEOPLE

The civilized world was shocked by the official terrorism and massive atrocities perpetrated against the Jews of Czarist Russia in the late nineteenth century. The Procurator of the Holy Synod, Pobyedonostzev, announced:

The wharves of Montreal in 1872, as they appeared to thousands of Jewish immigrants in the late years of the 19th century.
McCord Museum of Canadian History, Montreal
(From the Notman Photographic Archives 1-77117.7)

"One third of the Jews of Russia would be forced to emigrate, another third to accept baptism, and the remainder would be brought to the verge of starvation."

Protests around the world had no effect on the Russian government. Consequently, hundreds of thousands of Jews fled, hoping to reach "America." Few made the distinction between the United States and Canada—it was all *goldene medinah,* the golden land.

After generations of forcible confinement in shtetls—isolated shantytowns and villages—Jews were leaving their ancestral homes. Often they left parents, relatives, and friends behind. There was not enough money to allow more than a few to escape. Under appalling conditions, immigrants were crammed into converted cattle boats. Their only consolation during the insufferable weeks at sea was that they were sailing towards freedom and opportunity. Many immigrants who reached the United States discovered to their dismay that the streets were not, as claimed, paved with gold. Many moved on to Canada.

The flow of needy migrants quickly overwhelmed the Benevolent Society. In need of funds, it opened its membership to married men in 1869. The Society was incorporated in 1870, and a Ladies' Hebrew Benevolent Society was formed in 1877. Interestingly, the Benevolent Society represented the first joint effort of members of both synagogues—Shearith Israel and the Shaar Hashomayim. Occasionally non-Jews helped. For example, the Montreal City and District Savings Bank made an annual contribution for years. However, it was not enough. Before long, the organization was compelled to seek help overseas. Some response came from the Russo-Jewish Relief Committee in London, and the Alliance Israelite Universelle, in Paris.

WOLFF, Martin, and Miss Irene Joseph, eldest daughter of Mr. and Mrs. Montefiore Joseph, of Quebec City, were married by Rabbi Meldola de Sola, of Montreal, last Thurs., at the home of the bride's father, 113 Grand Allee. The bridesmaids were: Miss Rosetta Joseph, the bride's sister and Miss Rachel Wolff, the bridegroom's sister. At 4 p.m., Mr. and Mrs. Wolff left for England, via Halifax (2 April 1909, 12, 16)

The Canadian Jewish Times
Apr. 2, 1909

The north side of St. James Street, Montreal, 1870. (From the Leon Jacobson Collection, National Archives, C-065428). Note "S. Davis" sign—tobacco shop of Samuel Davis.

THE UPTOWNERS OBJECT

By 1880, many immigrants were funneled through London, where the well-organized community of

BENEVOLENT SOCIETY'S
FIRST EXECUTIVE
Lawrence L. Levy,
Isidore G. Ascher, Tucker
David, Charles Levey,
M. Gutman, Lawrence
Cohen, Samuel Moss
and Moise Schwob.

MRS. DE SOLA IS PRE-
SENTED TO ROYALTY
One of the outstanding
women community
volunteers at the turn
of the century was Mrs.
Clarence de Sola, wife
of the founding presi-
dent of the Canadian
Zionist Federation, and
daughter-in-law of Rab-
bi Abraham de Sola.
Mrs. de Sola founded
the Friendly League of
Jewish Women and the
Welcome Club for
Jewish working girls. In
addition, she served as
honorary president of
the Canadian Women's
Press Club.
In 1918, King Albert
of Belgium decorated
her in recognition and
appreciation of her
efforts on behalf of
Belgians during the
First World War. In
1923, she was presented
to the King and Queen
in London.

65,000 English Jews did what they could to help, but focussed on encouraging as many as possible to continue their journey to the New World. In New York, there were already 60,000 Jews. Some refugees were driven from place to place. Consequently, many of the new immigrants reaching Montreal arrived from the United States.

In Montreal, the Society began to pressure London to send only immigrants with at least a little capital. In 1875, the Society wrote two London newspapers, *Jewish World* and *Jewish Chronicle*, asking them to discourage Jewish organizations in Britain from sending "too many destitute and helpless Israelites" to Canada. The *Chronicle*, in an editorial in October 1875, commented "Our transatlantic brethren object—and we confess very properly so....to being burdened with the poor and unskillful Jews who are assisted to emigrate from Europe to the United States and Canada."

As part of the entrepreneurial class, the Uptowners had been integrated for generations with the English elite. As they were not distinctive in appearance or manners, they mingled freely and did not experience significant discrimination. Jews and English attended the same social events, belonged to the same clubs, and were partners in business enterprises. However, late in the nineteenth century, warm ties between the Jews and elite cooled. The majority began to identify the Jewish community in terms of the newly arrived ghetto Jews. While they all spoke two or more European tongues, the newcomers spoke neither English nor French; their common language was Yiddish. They had been oppressed for generations in isolated, primitive communities. The Uptowners were understandably dismayed by the impact of so many unsophisticated, impoverished brethren. The Uptowners had to adjust to the presence of a big community with a large working class.

RABBI DE SOLA'S MISSION

Two years after the public letter campaign, London organizations were still sending too many Jews "in a state of destitution and generally incapable of self-help." Finally, Rabbi Abraham de Sola was sent to the Jewish Emigration Society in London to protest. On his return, the Rabbi cautiously suggested that "the statements of the immigrants that they had been sent by the Jewish Emigration Society should not always be accepted."

By this time, the Benevolent Society recognized the need for action and recruited some of the community's leading personalities, such as Harris Vineberg and Lazarus Cohen.

MASS MEETING OF MONTREALERS

In 1886, a mass meeting of all Montrealers was called, with Anglican Bishop William Bennett Bond presiding. To accommodate the destitute immigrants, three warehouses on St. Peter Street were converted into dormitories and dining halls. Volunteers were recruited to provide food and clothing. The Benevolent Society wrote the Federal government for help. The Agriculture Department responded: "The government has no vote from which such assistance can be afforded...If there are not means at the disposal of the Jewish Community to take care of further arrivals of the same class of immigrant it would be wise to cable the parties on the other side to discontinue sending them."

BARON DE HIRSCH HELPS

For six more years, the Society struggled to make ends meet with $5 annual membership subscriptions, and a few larger gifts. By 1890, the Society recognized it was in crisis. An urgent meeting was held and Treasurer Jacob Goldstein was instructed to write the great Jewish Philanthropist Baron Maurice de Hirsch in Brussels, Belgium. At this time, more refugees were arriving in Montreal than in New York City. To stress the importance of the

THE YOUNG MEN'S HEBREW BENEVOLENT SOCIETY,
OF MONTREAL.

FOUNDED, 1863.   INCORPORATED, 1870.

THE PRESIDENT AND BOARD OF DIRECTORS,

request the honor of the presence of

W L Rubenstein

at the Official Opening by his Worship the Mayor,

OF THE

BARON DE HIRSCH INSTITUTE,

7 ELIZABETH STREET,

on Wednesday, 3rd June, 1891, at 2 p.m.

SAM. W JACOBS, Hon.-Sec'y

Jewish Public Library Archives

request, the letter was co-signed by the mayor of Montreal, James McShane, and the consular representatives of Mexico, Austria, Germany, and France. The letter read in part:

> "We undersigned unfortunately expelled Israelites of Russia do hereby asked your Honour to sign our petition."

Of the 76 signatures on the document, 59 were in Yiddish.

The Baron responded immediately and generously. Within three weeks, a cheque for the immense sum of $20,000 came from the Baron with a promise to provide more funding, if required. In

"HUMANITY IS MY HEIR"
The Baron Maurice de Hirsch (1831-1890) was a member of a distinguished family of Jewish landowners and bankers. His grandfather Jacob von Hirsch was the first Jewish landowner in Bavaria. He was ennobled in

appreciation for his efforts during the Napoleonic wars on behalf of Bavaria.

Maurice's father, a banker with the Bavarian court, was named a Baron in 1869. Maurice de Hirsch was born in Munich in 1831 and studied at Jewish schools in Brussels. In 1851, he joined the banking firm of Bischoffsheim and Goldschmid. He branched out from banking into copper and sugar, established his own bank in Belgium, and became prominent in railroad construction. When his only son Lucien died in 1887, the Baron declared "My son I may have lost but not my heir; Humanity is my heir." He strove to assist Jews in distress, particularly those in Russia. He established the Jewish Colonization Association to resettle Jews in the New World—buying land in South America, mainly Argentina, the United States and Canada. Although thousands were settled in these colonies, most left after a few years. As shtetl Jews had not been allowed to own land in Europe, few were farmers or wanted to be. In 1890, his fortune was estimated at $100 million.

The Baron expressed his views on philanthropy in these words:

"It is my utmost conviction that I must consider myself as only the temporary administrator of the wealth I have amassed, and that it is my duty to contribute in my way to the relief of the suffering of those who are pressed by fate."

recognition and appreciation of the Baron's generosity, the Benevolent Society changed its name to the Baron de Hirsch Institute. In 1891, part of the money was used to purchase a large store at 7 Elizabeth Street. It was renovated and officially dedicated on June 17 as the "Baron de Hirsch Institute." The building included a free school for orphans and a home for both immigrants and orphans.

The first Baron de Hirsch School, founded in 1900. Hundreds of immigrant children learned their first lessons as Canadians here. (Allan Raymond Collection, Jewish Public Archives).

MISSIONS TO THE JEWS

The drive to convert Jews to Christianity began in an organized fashion in 1892. By 1898 a "Universal Week of Prayer" was organized with one day—Saturday—set aside for conversion of Jews. Organizers of the conversion effort prayed that "God's ancient people may be brought into the fold of Christianity." In that same year, visiting American evangelist Dwight L. Moody suggested that a school be established for immigrant Jewish children. The most effective way to reach Jews, it was felt, was through the testimony of converts. Accordingly, in 1901, the Protestant Ministerial Association brought three converted Jews to Montreal to preach to their brethren. They had little success. In that same year, the Church of England Missionary Society established its first Montreal Mission and, in 1913, the Presbyterians followed suit.

One technique for proselytizing Jewish girls was through the organization of sewing classes with a suitable educational component. The Jewish community countered, in 1902, by organizing the Jewish Endeavour Sewing Schools of Montreal. Christian missions offered athletic programs to Jewish boys, and medical services. The Jewish community, in response, set up boxing lessons. In 1907 the Ladies' Auxiliary of the King Edward Benefit Association established the Herzl Dispensary and recruited a group of Jewish doctors.

BEQUEST FROM THE BARONESS

In 1900, the Baroness de Hirsch died in Paris. In her will, she left a bequest of 600,000 francs ($89,000) to the Benevolent Society. In appreciation, the Society officially changed its name to the Baron de Hirsch Institute and Hebrew Benevolent Society of Montreal. As it was typical, at that time, to recognize men's contributions and leadership while ignoring women's efforts, the Baroness' name was not included in the title.

According to the annual report for 1900, the Institute aided, among others, 1 Turk, 2 French, 3 Poles, 10 Galicians, 19 Syrians, 27 Austrians, 29 Germans, 36 English, and 426 Russians.

In March 1900, the Institute was incorporated, and its charter read, in part:

"The said corporation is empowered to grant relief to sick and indigent persons of the Hebrew faith, to establish a home or refuge for the distressed, aged and orphans of the said faith, to provide a burial ground for the internment of their dead poor, to conduct schools for general instruction and manual training of the needy of said faith."

In 1901, the cornerstone of a new Baron de Hirsch building was laid on Bleury Street. This was an important development; the new building became the first central address for the community. As there were no professional social workers, community leaders volunteered their time.

The Baron de Hirsch Institute building on Bleury Street, built in 1901.

Every Sunday morning, an Uptowner in bowler hat and tailored suit would stand on the steps of the Baron de Hirsch Institute and hand out dollar bills to anyone who asked. Men almost never came. They were too proud to ask for charity. But the women had children to feed. And a dollar went a long way.

By 1910, Montreal had a Jewish population of 28,000; in nine years, the Jewish population had quadrupled. A hodge-podge of organizations had sprung up to meet real and perceived needs, largely among destitute newcomers, and some sense of order was required. By this time, American Jews—beginning in Boston in the

---

JACOBS, S.W., in the Quebec Recorder's Court, successfully defended several Jewish bakers, Messrs. Richstone, Schachter and Jacobson, whose van drivers were charged with illegally delivering bread on Sun. Dec. 19, 1909. Rabbi Hirsch Cohen testified to the court about the inability of Jewish bakers to carry on business, if the right to deliver bread on Sun. was taken from them. "He stated that for many years Sunday delivery was the custom among Jews, and this was recognized by the authorities, who in no way interfered with the trade until recently

*Dec. 24, 1909
The Canadian
Jewish Times*

MONTEFIORE CLUB
An important development in the latter part of the nineteenth century was the creation of the Montefiore Club. Sir Moses Montefiore, a great English philanthropist, agreed to lend his name to the new organization. The Club began as an association of young people interested in drama. In 1880, 11 Jews in their teens and early 20s gathered to form, with the encouragement of their parents, the "Montefiore Social and Dramatic Club." The young people mounted shows to benefit charities and their beneficiaries ranged from the Montreal General Hospital to the building fund of the Shaar Hashomayim Synagogue. On March 28, 1881, members of the Club presented a program to benefit the "Ladies Hebrew Benevolent Society" and the "Young Men's Hebrew Benevolent Society."
As the membership grew older and increasingly prominent in community affairs, the group changed its name to the Montefiore Club.
New members had to demonstrate that they were making an appropriate contribution to Jewish institutions. In the late 1920s, when the capital campaign was launched for the Jewish General Hospital, the Club noted proudly that "over ninety per cent of its members took an active and useful part." By 1930, when the Club was marking its half-century, it could boast that members were contributing "over two thirds of the annual income of the Fede-

ration of Jewish Philanthropies."

The Club had become, and remains, a social centre for leaders of the community and many historic communal meetings have been held in its dignified premises on Guy Street. The original building was constructed in 1906 and, since then, additions have been made to the structure.

The most dramatic event in the Club's history occurred on Feb. 15, 1918, when the convent across the street caught fire. The nuns cared for vulnerable people, including infants and the aged. Isaac Friedman, Vice-President of the Montefiore Club, realized that the nuns would require immediate assistance, and he offered the club's facilities as a shelter. On stretchers and in wheelchairs, volunteers carried or pushed nunnery residents through snowdrifts across Guy Street. The club's official history records that "the entire ground floor became covered with bed-ridden men and women, some of whom had not seen the outside of their institution for *a score of years*." Rows of babies were placed on billiard tables.

The Montreal Star, in its edition of Feb. 16, 1918, reported "The Sisters of Charity of the Grey Nunnery gave out a statement last night expressing their warmest thanks to those who assisted them in the work of rescue. Special mention is made of Mr. Friedman and the Montefiore Club."

Jan. 8, 1909
The Canadian
Jewish Times

KAUFFMAN, Officer, of the Montreal police force, is seeking Thomas Morris, a Jewish negro, charged with having committed a serious offence in New York. "The communication received states that Morris is a full-blooded negro...and that he speaks no other tongue except Yiddish. Officer Kauffman after ransacking the seventh and eighth wards has failed to find any trace of this black-faced Israelite."

late nineteenth century—had organized more than a dozen federations. Montreal followed suit and in 1917, Canada's first federation of community services was established—The Federation of Jewish Philanthropies.

While the newcomers endured much to reach Montreal, and most lived in abject poverty for years, they nevertheless could, for the first time their lives, feel like human beings. In Europe, they had been ghettoized, humiliated, persecuted, and driven from their homes. In Montreal, they found themselves free to practice their religion—or not—and strive, without restriction, to better themselves.

MARKING A CENTENARY

On the Baron de Hirsch Institute centenary (1963), longtime Executive-Director David Weiss wrote:

"The Institute is a living expression of the ageless Jewish precepts of Mitzvah (good deeds) and Tzedakah (social justice), of Jeremiah's injunction to seek the welfare of the city in which one's own welfare is achieved."

The Ornstein Family of Roberval, Quebec, out for a drive in 1917.
(Canadian Jewish Congress National Archives)

ZIONISTS IN CANADA

Zionism, the movement to re-establish the Jewish State of Israel, captured the imagination of Canadian Jewry and prompted the organization of several local Zionist groups. Theodor Herzl, in

Basle, Switzerland organized the First Zionist Congress, in 1897, and Montreal Jews organized their first Zionist organization that same year. A branch of Chovevei (Lovers of Zion) was founded by Alexander Harkavy, who later achieved great prominence as a Yiddish lexicographer. In 1902, a second group, Shavei Zion, was established and immediately moved to Palestine. They set up a farming community at Hauran, now in Jordan. (Britain created the Kingdom of Jordan out of its Palestinian Mandate in 1922, to help meet its commitments to the Hashemites, royal family of Jordan, in return for their support of Lawrence of Arabia in the First World War campaign against the Turks.) However, the farm project was a failure. Though still committed to Zionism, the disappointed settlers returned to Montreal.

The first Canadian to settle permanently in Palestine was Ya'akov Pruzhansky, who arrived in the Holy Land in 1913. As it was customary to Hebraicize names, Pruzhansky changed his to Ahvah..

THE ZIONISTS FORM A NATIONAL ORGANIZATION

In 1898, one year after the Basle Congress, Zionists formed Canada's first national Jewish organization. The founding leader was Clarence de Sola, third son of Montreal's eminent scholar and Rabbi Abraham de Sola. He remained in office for 22 years, until shortly before his death in 1919. The organization he built was impressive. Herzl's adviser, Jacob de Haas, after visiting Zionist organizations in the United States and Canada, wrote: "The movement (in Canada) appears to be stronger and more solid than in the United States."

Clarence de Sola, pioneer and longtime head of the Zionist organization in Canada.

Reform congregations were not enthusiastic about Zionism, and—while there were many Reform congregations in the U.S.— there was, in Montreal, only one. Zionist-related organizations sprang up quickly in Canada. The Jewish National Fund appeared in 1903; the Po'ale Zion Labour Party in 1905; Mizrachi was formed in 1907; the Farband Labour Zionist Fraternal Order in 1909; Young Judea in 1910, and Hadassah in 1916.

THE BALFOUR DECLARATION

Britain's Foreign Secretary, Lord Balfour, visited Ottawa early in 1917. He invited Clarence de Sola, as leader of the Zionist movement, to meet with him in Ottawa. At that meeting, the British cabinet minister disclosed plans for the announcement, later that same year, of what has come to be known as the Balfour Declaration. The Declaration stated that "His Majesty's

Government views with favour the establishment in Palestine of a national home for the Jewish people." For Jews, this was an incredibly important policy statement, but the only story on the meeting was carried in *The Canadian Jewish Chronicle* of Nov. 23, 1917. De Sola disclosed that Lord Balfour had told him "...we can be the instrument of fulfilling the Biblical prophecy of restoring the Jewish people to Zion. I can assure you that I can tell my colleagues in the cabinet that the Zionist ideals harmonize perfectly with the English policy of the Foreign Affairs regarding Palestine."

Around the world official release of the Balfour Declaration touched off wild celebrations among Jews. When Joe Ain, a future president of the Montreal Federation, was five years old, his father carried him on his shoulders and danced around the room of their Latvian home, declaring "tomorrow we will be in Palestine!"

RAISING MONEY FOR ISRAEL
Zionist President Clarence de Sola saw the role of Canadian Jews as fundraisers to assist in making a future Jewish State a reality. "The Zionist movement," he declared, "aims at securing a home for Jewish living in countries where they are suffering oppression." In 1920, Keren Hayesod—the organization for raising funds for a Jewish State—was formed. And, in 1926, rounding out the coterie of organizations supporting the idea of a Jewish state, Pioneer Women (now called Na'amat) was founded. All of the Canadian organizations focussed on two aspects of Zionism—helping endangered or oppressed Jews settle in Israel, and building the organizational framework for the state-to-be. One example of this effort was the work of the Jewish National Fund (JNF), giving priority to planting millions of trees in the Holy Land. The JNF was a presence in virtually every Jewish home in Montreal. Little blue boxes, to accept coins as donations for trees, were scattered throughout Jewish Montreal. Children were encouraged, immediately before the Sabbath, to deposit a coin in the blue box.

PAULINE DONALDA—A CANADIAN PRIMA DONNA
The London Daily Mail, in 1906, reviewed an exciting performance of Verdi's "Rigoletto" by an impressive Canadian newcomer: "The honours were not altogether with Caruso. Mlle Donalda shared them equally." The paper was referring to the performance by a Montreal Jewish woman, Pauline Donalda, who sang opposite the greatest tenor in the world, Enrico Caruso. To be

Madame Donalda (Pauline Lightstone), the Montreal-born Jewish opera star. (Jewish Public library Archives)

cast in an opera opposite Caruso was the highest possible honour for a singer. For the 24-year-old Donalda, it was undoubtedly one of the greatest moments of her career. "Her singing in the part of Gilda was so wonderfully fine," the newspaper continued, "that the house rose for her. Donalda is going to be a great name at Covent Garden."

Pauline Donalda was born in Montreal, in 1882. She was the daughter of Fanny and Michael Lightstone, eastern European immigrants. Pauline adopted the surname Donalda in tribute to her patron, Sir Donald A. Smith (later Lord Strathcona). Smith underwrote her studies at the Paris Conservatory.

Donalda made her debut as a grand opera singer, in 1904, as Manon in Nice. It was the beginning of an extraordinary career, in which the Montreal singer was paired with some of the greatest names in early 20th-century opera. In May 1905, she was invited twice to sing for the King and Queen at Covent Garden in London, and at the Monnaise Opera House in Brussels.

In 1906, Oscar Hammerstein opened the Manhattan Opera House in New York and booked Madame Donalda for the entire season. She returned to Montreal to form the Montreal Opera Guild, which promoted the first Canadian productions of a number of major operas. She was on a concert tour of Canada in 1914 when the First World War broke out. Donalda left her career to assist in the war effort. She raised large sums of money for patriotic charities through benefit concert performances to sold out crowds.

Pauline Donalda married twice—both times to singers. Her first husband was baritone Paul Seveilhac and the second a famous Danish tenor, Mischa Leon.

In 1967, she was named an Officer of the Order of Canada for "her contribution to the arts, especially opera, as a singer and founder of the Opera Guild in Montreal." She died in Montreal in 1970.

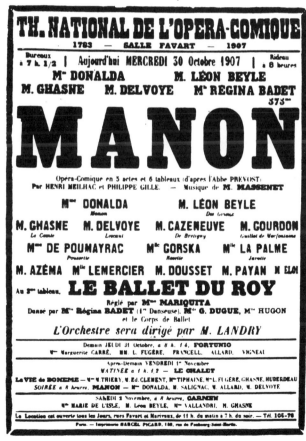

Playbill for a 1907 performance by Madame Donalda (Pauline Lightstone), l'Opéra Comique, Paris. (Jewish Public Library Archives)

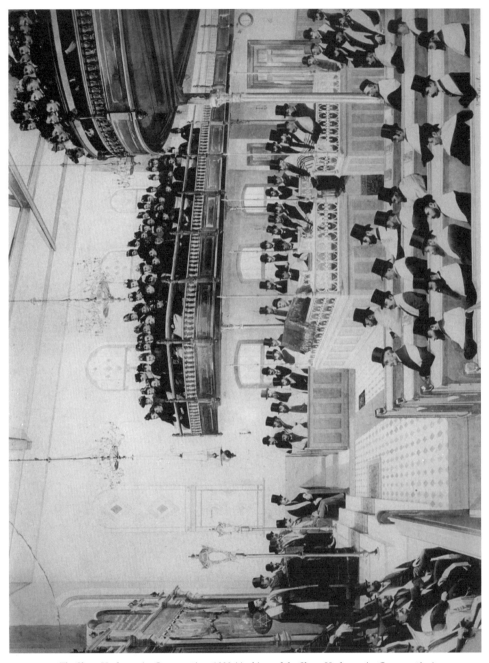

The Shaar Hashomayim Congregation, 1890 (Archives of the Shaar Hashomayim Congregation)

GENTLEMEN

62. Hyam David Moss
63. Rabbi Elias Friedlander
64. John Edward Moss
65. Philip Levy
66. Samuel Myers
67. Isaac Rubinovich
68. Moses Bilsky
69. Joseph Youngheart
70. Edward Youngheart
71. Mr. Mendal
72. Harris Vineberg
73. William Jacobs
74. Moses Greenberg
75. A. Rosenthal
76. Abel Bernstein
77. David S. Friedman
78. B. Wolovich
79. Lyon Cohen
80. Max L. Schloman
81. Abraham M. Vineberg
82. Adolph Goldstein
83. Robert Moss
83a. Edward Moss
84. Hiram Cohen
85. Moses J. Glickman
86. Michael Lighstone
87. Kalman Freeman
88. Moses Vineberg
89. Louis Holstein
90. Arthur Moss
91. Jacob Hirsch
92. Moses Lasser
93. Harris Kellert

94. Michael Hirsch
95. Samuel Roman
96. Louis Kellert
97. Charles L. Friedman
98. Abraham Jacobs
99. Lyon Silverman
100. Henry Jacobs
101. Jack L. Moss
102. Julius Sherman
103. Jacob Cohen
104. Fischel Ship
105. Louis Lewis
106. Lazarus Cohen
107. A. Rogalsky
108. Henry Roman
109. E. Forcimmer
110. Myer Blumenthal
111. Louis Ship
112. Isaac Workman
113. Solomon Levinson
114. Abraham Solomon
115. J.S. Leo
116. Lewis Hart
117. Israel Vineberg
118. Harris Albert
119. Hiram Freedman
120. Myer Lightstone
121. Saul Solomon
122. Abraham Workman
123. Hyman Vineberg
124. Barnett Freedman
125. Boruch Bloomfield
126. A. Kutner

LADIES

1. Mrs. Lyon Silverman
2. Mrs. Abe Workman
3. Miss Annie Friedlander
4. Mrs. Abraham Jacobs
5. Mrs. Louis Kellert
6. Miss Moss
7. Mrs. Michael Hirsch
8. Mrs. Samuel Roman
9. Mrs. Solomon Levinson
10. Mrs. Harris Kellert
11. Mrs. E. Solomon
12. Mrs. Jacob Hirsch
13. Mrs. Louis Ship
14. Mrs. Elias Friedlander
15. Miss Moss
16. Miss Beatrice Moss
17. Mrs. Hyam David Moss
18. Miss Florence Moss
19. Miss Moss
20. Miss Moss
21. Mrs. John L. Moss
22. Mrs. Louis Holstein
23. Mrs. Jack L. Moss
24. Mrs. Max Goldberg
25. Miss Sadie Vineberg
26. Mrs. Noah Friedman
27. Miss Edith Moss
28. Miss Clara Moss
29. Mrs. Samuel Myers
30. Mrs. Kutner
31. Mrs. M. L. Schloman

32. Mrs. Greenberg
33. Mrs. Henry Jacobs
34. Mrs. B. Bloomfield
35. Miss Rebecca Freedman
36. Mrs. Hiram Cohen
37. Mrs. Harris Vineberg
38. Mrs. Moses Vineberg
39.
40.
41. Mrs. Israel Vineberg
42. Miss D. Roman
43. Mrs. Moses Greenberg
44. Mrs. Rosand
45. Miss Sophia Hirsch
46. Miss Bertha Roman
47. Mrs. Jacob Cohen
48. Mrs. Lazarus Cohen
49. Mrs. Fischel Ship
50. Mrs. Kalman Freeman
51. Mrs. Michael Lightstone
52. Mrs. Archie Jacobs
53. Mrs. Moses Lesser
54. Mrs. William Jacobs
55. Mrs. Adolph Goldstein
56. Miss Ray Friedman
57. Miss Mary W. Jacobs
58. Miss Mary Jacobs
59. Mrs. Louis Lewis
60. Mrs. Charles Sisenwain
61. Mrs. M. Blumenthal

A SOUND IDEA

A Jewish immigrant invented the gramophone, in Montreal, but took it to the United States to market it. The inventor was Emile Berliner (1851-1929), who was born in Hanover, Germany, but emigrated to the United States when he was 19. He studied electricity and acoustics at Cooper Union, and began experimenting with the telephone. In 1877, a year after Alexander Graham Bell invented the telephone, Berliner was granted a patent on his idea for an improved telephone transmitter. Bell Telephone bought the patent; the early telephone left much to be desired. Bell also hired Berliner. The inventor was paid $50,000, and he used the money to underwrite further research.

By 1887, he was working in Montreal where he received a patent for the gramophone. Berliner's device used a flat disc to record and play back sound. Until then, the only recording and playback device was the phonogragh, invented by Thomas Alva Edison, using cylinders, with the stylus moving vertically. The weight of the stylus ensured poor recording quality. Berliner's disc had less distortion because the stylus moved horizontally.

In essence, Berliner created the modern record industry. He founded the Gramophone Company of England (now EMI), the E. Berliner Gramophone Company of Montreal (now part of RCA) and a number of other companies to produce records and manufacture record players and, in time, radios.

He patented the gramophone in Montreal and, in 1900, began manufacturing his device, recording discs and distributing his products. His company used Victor records and equipment, and was the first to use the famous trademark "His Master's Voice." It shows a fox terrier cocking his ear to the huge horn of an old-fashioned gramophone. British artist Francis Barraud painted the picture in 1899. Berliner bought the painting, but had the artist paint over the Edison machine, used in the original, and substitute his E. Berliner Model A Gram-o-phone.

The Victor Talking Machine Company bought the patent. And Berliner moved back to the United States to promote and sell the machine. Berliner went on inventing. In 1908, he designed an airplane engine. And, working with his son Henry, he designed three helicopters, the first of which flew successfully in 1919. Finally, in 1925, he developed acoustic tiles for soundproofing; they were used in auditoriums and concert halls.

Emile Berliner still has a following in Montreal. There is a small "Emile Berliner Sound Wave Museum", located at 1050 Lacasse de Richelieu, in the St. Henri district of Montreal. It is entirely staffed by volunteers and is open only three hours three afternoons a week.

CHAPTER ELEVEN

THE YIDDISH
Landsmanshaft in the Goldene Medinah

"It is a grave responsibility this—to be a Jew; and you can't escape from it, even if you choose to ignore it. Ethically or religiously, we Jews can be and do nothing light-heartedly. Ten bad Jews may help to damn us; ten good Jews may help to save us. Which 'minyan' will you join?"

C.G. Montefiore, 1897

When the boy first saw Montreal, he burst into tears. He had left his beautiful St. Petersburg for this city without sidewalks! His first job was demeaning too.

In Russia, only thieves sold newspapers on the street. Skinny, shivering in his ragged clothing, he would turn up in the basement of the Yiddish newspaper, the Keneder Adler, at Ontario and Main streets. He would buy a dozen newspapers for eight cents and sell them, for a penny apiece, in the hustle and bustle of factories on Notre Dame Street. After working for eight months, he deposited $2 with a steamship company as a down payment on tickets to bring his mother and sister from the Old Country.

The boy was one of thousands who had escaped the isolation and deprivation of European city ghettos and village shtetls and had found refuge in the Golden Land. The Canadian Prime Minister Sir Wilfrid Laurier won the hearts of the Jewish community when, at a meeting in Ottawa to

Z. Fineberg's store at 1159 Ontario Street, in 1903. His son, Joseph, stands on the left with G.H. Beaulieu, a store employee. (Canadian Jewish Congress National Archives)

protest Russian pogroms, he declared: "We cannot bring all the survivors here, but whoever chooses to come will be sure of a hearty welcome." Under the Liberal administration, the doors to immigration were flung wide open. Canada was in a period of tremendous expansion. The population increased 30 per cent in the decade from 1901 to 1911, and employment was plentiful—in factories, railways, and on the street. Immigrant families herded together in low-rental areas around St. Lawrence Main, and worked together. And their wider family was the landsmanshaft, fraternal organizations where they could socialize with people of similar backgrounds and interests from the Old Country. Hungry for recognition and status, they were eager to transcend their menial, oppressive jobs through participation in clubs and activities, where among their own kind they were respected human beings. Support came from the organized community as it grew steadily in scope and effectiveness. However, if the newcomers needed a service and it did not exist, they created it themselves— librairies, schools, medical clinics, and synagogues. They helped create a plethora of new organizations that enriched the modern

TIMELINE/1900-1909

1900. First Canadian Zionist convention held in Montreal.

1900. Montefiore Joseph elected President of the Quebec Board of Trade.

1901. The Jewish population of Quebec reaches 7,607.

1901. The cornerstone is laid for the new Baron de Hirsch building on Bleury Street. Gov. Gen. Lord Minto opens the building.

1902. 2,692 immigrants arrive at Halifax aboard the steamer 'Bulgaria'— the largest single boatload of immigrants Canada had ever known. Most of the immigrants are Jewish, Ukrainian, Italian, and German.

1902. Rabbi Herman Abromowitz becomes spiritual leader of Congregation Shaar Hashomayim, serving 45 years.

1902. The Jewish Endeavour Sewing School of Montreal is organized to counter Christian proselytizers.

1903. The Jewish Library is founded at 68 St. Lawrence Blvd, in premises occupied by the Zionist organization.

1903. Montreal Talmud Torah incorporated as the Montreal Hebrew Free School, and a building purchased at 143 St. Urbain Street.

1903. A Montreal Jew, Max Kirt, is tried three times for murder; an anti-Semitic prosecutor refuses to accept verdicts of not guilty.

1904. Dr. Edward Elkan is first Jew in Canada to graduate as a dentist from a Canadian university (Bishop's College).

1905. First Yiddish Public Library in Canada opens in Montreal in a rented room.

1907. The *Keneder Adler* (Canadian Eagle) Yiddish daily newspaper is established.

1907. A group of physicians establish the Herzl Dispensary.

1908. The Montreal Jewish population is estimated at 30,000.

1908. Young Men's Hebrew Association (Y.M.H.A) is founded in Montreal.

1909. The Montreal Hebrew Orphans' Home is founded.

Jewish community. In so doing, they transformed Montreal into one of the greatest centres of Yiddish culture in the world.

LINGUA FRANCA

The newcomers came predominantly from Imperial Russia, Poland and Romania, and most spoke two or three languages, though rarely English or French. Often they had lived in areas that were Russian in one decade, Polish in the next and Austrian in the third. However, the one thing they had in common was their lingua franca—the Yiddish language. Yiddish is a development of thirteenth-century Rhineland German; it uses the Hebrew alphabet and combines words borrowed from a number

A Montreal market facing the harbour, 1904.
(National Archives of Canada C-003573)

of east European tongues. This new wave of immigrants was an unplanned, uncoordinated exodus. And they represented an endless profusion of philosophies. The Western Enlightenment had inched into the Jewish shtetls with its messages of secularism, science, history, and culture. Consequently, the immigrants reflected the immense chasm beginning to divide Jews. In the boats, bearded Hasids were outraged by the thinking of beardless youths who talked about Kant, Marx and Tolstoy. Religious Jews, bowed devoutly in prayer, were shocked when fellow brethren refused to join them or challenged them to discuss socialism and communism, the new religions for many. This new, second Jewish community represented a rich mosaic of personalities. Many held strong opinions. Factions joined the Zionists with the hope that ancient Israel would be reborn. Others turned to charismatic religious leaders. Still others saw their greatest hope for the future in chasing the American Dream.

J.S. Woodsworth, in his 1909 study of Canadian immigrants, wrote the newly-arrived Jews prioritized the acquisition of a "knowledge of English", adding: "It is almost pathetic to see old men, after their day's work, coming to night school to read from children's primers; and this is not merely that they may do business, for at once they plunge into all kinds of intellectual activities... Our librarians tell us that the young Jewish people patronize the public libraries more than any other class. They establish literary societies, social and dramatic clubs and political associations. They glory in their literary traditions."

MAKING A LIVING

The struggle to make a living began the day the immigrant stepped off the boat. Many of the newcomers were skilled workers, artisans, tradesmen, teachers and rabbis. They were tanners, carpenters, tinsmiths, bakers, butchers and milkmen. Labour union leader H. Hershman recalled, in 1928:

Levinsky's store, Montreal, c. 1910. (Jewish Public Library Archives)

"The Jewish craftsmen who came from Europe then were true artists in their work." For those who had been tailors in the old country, there were low-paying jobs in squalid quarters. In Montreal, Hershman said, the CPR became "a truly Jewish shop." The foreman used hand signals to tell the Jews what to do.

And about half of them, many with few skills who spoke neither English nor French, found work in the burgeoning garment manufacturing industry for a dollar or two a week. The light garment industry was scattered in ramshackle buildings in the area between St. Denis Street to the east and University to the west. Men would sit bent over a foot-driven sewing machine for eleven to fifteen hours a day. They dared not stop, even for lunch, as the work was seasonal. Conditions were worse for women and children workers, as families, including boys and girls as young as eight, were lugging unfinished garments into their tenement flats to be sewn for pennies a piece.

Others made their living as shop-keepers or peddlers. Companies provided them with merchandise on credit, and they circulated among the small villages and isolated farms of rural Quebec. They paid for food and lodging with small items from their stock, for example, a handkerchief or a pair of stockings. Wholesalers J.A. Ogilvy and Sons were keen on supplying the needs of Jewish peddlers. At the end of the nineteenth century, they printed a Hebrew religious calendar—the first ever in Canada—for their Jewish customers.

Some peddlers, after a few years, were able to afford a horse and wagon—a giant step up because they could see many more customers and carry much more merchandise. The horses often were old nags, but they were treated with great kindness and concern by the owners. After all, the horse was the motive power of their business. During the bitter Montreal winters, horse and owner would be colourfully arrayed in a combination of old blankets and used coats to keep out the cold. The horse was also the family pet, the only one they could afford. For younger children it was a supreme delight to be lifted onto the back of a bony old nag while father or grandfather led the patient animal for a block or two. It was even more exciting than seeing Tom Mix, the cowboy actor, in the movies at the nickleodeon.

The merchant worked from an open wagon in the warmer weather, selling what his customers wanted, but mostly fruit and vegetables, and chickens, and from an open sled in the winter when he peddled fish and chickens. He would take horse and wagon long before dawn to a farmer's market for supplies. And the oldest boy graduated to the seat beside his father the moment he was old enough to help out. The merchant often picked up merchandise to order for hard-pressed mothers, many of whom in those days had very large families. Ten or more children were quite common.

BE A MENSCH

The acceptance and utilization of Yiddish in general conversation apparently reflects a decline in anti-Semitism. Yiddish is a full-blown language, drawn mostly from German (72%), Hebrew (18%) and the Slavic tongues (16%). It has also borrowed words from Latin, French, Italian and English and it continues to absorb and adapt itself to change. There are manuscripts in Old Yiddish dating back to approximately 1200. And a Hebrew-Yiddish dictionary was published in 1534. The first English dictionary appeared only in 1721.

There is more to Yiddish than mere vocabulary. One good example is the word "*nu.*" Its meaning is changed by the way you say it. Nu?—how are you doing? Nu—accompanied by a hunch of the shoulders—what else could I do? Nu?—where's the money you owe me? And on and on. Another multi-use expression is "*hoo-ha.*" It may be taken to mean virtually anything, negative or positive. Did he make a lot of money?—Hoo-ha! You call him a businessman? Hoo-ha.

Fortunately, on the other hand, definite meanings exist for many words and, surprisingly enough, some are used by people who wouldn't know *kreplach* from *gefilte fish.*

Take "*mensch*", for example. It means someone who is a decent person, living up to their responsibilities in society. On the other hand, "*gonef*" means a thief. "*Tukus*"means a person's bottom as does "*tush.*" When you say "*l'chayim*" you're making a toast to someone's health. "*Mitzvah*" is a good deed and 613 different ones are listed in Jewish holy books. "*Chutzpa*", meaning nervy, aggressive, is in wide use. A "*kibbitzer*" is someone making a nuisance of himself. "*Nebish*" describes a person who is something of a nerd.

Oddly enough, the word "bread" from the Yiddish "*broyt*" means money! The word "deli" is an abbreviation for delicatessen and has roots in German, French and Latin. The final five letters "*essen*" means "eat" in Yiddish. Yet "eat your heart out" comes from the Yiddish expression "*Es dir oys s'harts*", meaning to be envious. "*Nosh*" means a snack.

Some other useful words and their meanings:

Shmeer—to bribe, or tip with unnecessary generosity.
Shamus—is taken to mean detective.
Shmoos—refers to a relaxed conversation.
Tsatske, from the Slavic—refers to anything ornate or someone who is over-dressed.
Tsores, from the Hebrew word Tsarah, means you have problems.
Yente is a woman who gossips overmuch.
Patsheke means to fuss with things.
Nudnik, from the Russian nudna, refers to a pest.
Messhugge means to be crazy.
Mazel is to have luck hence, *Mazel Tov*—congratulations and good luck.

Some other useful words include "*Gelt*" meaning money. When you have a "*pekel*", technically, you have a package but it suggests you have a pile of money.

Bobkes suggests you have been underpaid for something.
You have "*sachel*" if you have good judgement.
"*Kvetch*" means to grumble.
A "*Klutz*" is a clod.
The phrase "I need it like a hole in the head" comes from the Yiddish "*loch in kop.*"

Finally, take offense if someone says you're "*Zhlub*"; they're suggesting you're clumsy and bad-mannered. So be sure to be a *Mensch.*

Some made their rounds buying whatever they could sell for a profit. One trick of the trade was to bring along a son who would respond to cries from second-or third-floor tenants. The boy would run up the stairs and, with experience, know precisely how much or how little to offer for an item. Boys of eight or nine had their wits sharpened by bargaining for old clothes, pots and pans, or dishes, which their father or grandfather could sell for a modest profit. With time, an energetic and hard-working man with a horse and wagon could save enough to capitalize a small corner store.

The biggest adjustment to life in Montreal was required of religious scholars. In the Old Country, they had spent their entire lives studying holy writings, debating their meaning with colleagues, and others had maintained them. In Europe, a father-in-law was honoured to have a scholar in the family. On occasion, the wife worked while the husband pored over religious tracts.

The exodus from Eastern Europe changed all that. The scholarly ways of a quiet backwater shtetl were replaced by the demanding realities of the modern age. In Canada, they struggled to make a living. The lucky ones found work in Jewish schools. Other scholars, to earn a living, were forced to work in the needle trade, separated from their precious Torahs. Most had to accept whatever employment they could find in order to survive. On The Main, the opportunities for religious scholars were limited. A number were able to form small congregations, gathering in apartments or halls until—after many years—there was money for a synagogue. Even then, the small congregations often could not afford a full-time rabbi. A few were able to get by teaching children Hebrew for their bar mitzvahs. Others who had the training were able to perform circumcisions, or become ritual slaughterers to ensure meat was kosher. Most found themselves unable to make the transition from the near-medieval circumstances of their past life to the overwhelming differences of the New World. They were vanquished by modernity.

ROOM AND BOARD

Finding a place to live often meant compromise. Tiny flats frequently were shared by two families. And three or four people slept in one room. Hot water was available, in the winter, for one bath a week. During the summer, when the coal or wood stove did not heat water, the family used public baths. Families, despite the crowding, would take in boarders to help pay the rent. There was a seemingly endless stream of young unmarried men arriving who needed room and board.

BUILDING THEIR OWN WORLD

Despite working 60-80 hours a week, the newcomers laboured all day and created their own cultural and social world. They flocked to book stores and attended night school, created libraries, and amateur theatre troops, and assembled for heated discussions of world affairs. The immigrants organized centres for worship in apartments and halls. They set up schools where their children could learn about their history and their traditions. A travel agency was formed to help bring family and friends from the Old Country. And a "Debt of Honour Association" provided interest-free loans to Jew and non-Jew alike.

LANDSMANSHAFT

One of the most effective self-help organizations was the landsmanshaft, gathering together men and later women, to arrange for everything from health services to burials.

The Russian Polish Hebrew Sick Benefit Association, in its 1907 constitution, declared "no officer is to be elected unless he is able to read and write Jewish (Yiddish). The President, secretaries and treasurer must also be able to read and write English."

FOUNDING THE HERZL DISPENSARY

To provide medical services, the Community began to open dispensaries and clinics. In 1907, a group of Jewish doctors—in cooperation with the Ladies Auxiliary of the King Edward Benefit Association—created the Herzl Dispensary. Initially, it was accommodated in a small building at 832 St. Dominique Street. When the Dispensary outgrew this limited facility, it was moved to 632 St. Urbain Street, where an average of 1,000 patients a month was treated by a staff of twenty Jewish physicians.

The Herzl Dispensary's second home, acquired in 1914, at 632 St. Urbain Street; headquarters in 1917 for Federation.

Costs kept rising, rapidly, as immigration soared—nearly 39,000 migrants, many of them penniless, poured into the city in the years 1911-1913.

The Community, somehow, found the resources to care for the newcomers.

THE "Y" IS FORMED

Many immigrants saw a need for new services. In 1909, the Young Men's Hebrew Association was formed. The first meetings were held in a small room at the Baron de Hirsch Institute on Sanguinet

Street. The founders were mostly tradesmen and craftspeople—shirtmakers, boot-makers, carpenters, etc. The rent was $7.50 a month; the membership fee in 1909 was 25 cents weekly.

However, in a few years, the "Y" was in deep financial trouble. There was $15 in the bank, but the rent now was $25 a month, and the organization needed furniture and equipment. The ten young board members donated $2.50 each to help. The rent was paid; there was $9 for a down-payment on furniture and there was even $1 left in the bank. By 1912, the "Y" was on sounder footing; a membership drive had brought in 1,260 people—making the Montreal "Y" second in size only to the famous 92nd Street "Y" in New York.

GREETING REFUGEES

More than 300 Jewish immigrants on arrival in Halifax from the S.S. "Asia", 1924.
(Canadian Jewish Congress National Archives)

The Community was not unanimous in welcoming the new wave of refugees. Maxwell Goldstein, K.C.—who was to become the first President of the Jewish Federation in 1917—was critical of some immigrants. In a 1909 interview with the *London Jewish Chronicle*, Mr. Goldstein declared: "The cause of many of our troubles is the vast influx of foreign Jews into the Dominion. They form ghettos among themselves and create a great deal of prejudice. Certain of the French press are very antipathetic to the Jews. ....the difficulty with us is how to cooperate with these people" And, he added: "They must not be ignored."

THE HEBREW FREE LOAN
In 1911, a 48-year-old Polish immigrant, Zigmond Fineberg, founded the Hebrew Free Loan Association. It is impossible to

determine how many lives were changed by help from the Association. Loans of five dollars to $200 were made in the early years. Fineberg's charter for the group read that its task was to "loan money to those in need instead of giving alms." The Association granted loans to applicants "regardless of race or creed." Assistance was provided for everything from seed money for a new corner store or small factory, to underwriting a wedding ceremony or a bar mitzvah. The Association reported, after its first 13 years, that losses were one-tenth of one per cent.

JEWS: A COMMENDABLE RACE

"In close connection with the synagogue a very efficient social organization has grown; and by that is meant not the kind which will enable people to gamble and drink late into the night in comfortable little nooks, but the kind that will, if necessary, take huge human masses from the slums and uplift them. The synagogues themselves through their religious and lay officers do most of the work. When they do not lead, they help. The Hebrew Sick Benefit Association numbers 1,000 members; the Hebrew Ladies Relief Society 400; the Hebrew Ladies Aid Society 500; the Hebrew Young Women's Orphan Association 300; the Young Men's Hebrew Association 600; the Independent Sick Benefit Association 600; the Sons of Benjamin 400.

"The Baron de Hirsch Institute maintains night and day schools for the education of the immigrant, both in English and his native idiom, assists the destitute, protects the weak. Liberally endowed as it is, it gets active support from seven hundred local members. There is a Hebrew Sanitorium at Ste. Agathe, north of Montreal. There is a Hebrew Home for the Aged, and there is a Hebrew Association for the protection of orphans. The Montreal Jew is a self-supporting citizen and justly proud of it....A race that has no beggars, no drunkards, no prostitutes, no hoodlums, certainly has much to commend it."

Oliver Asselin "The Jews in Montreal" in The Canadian Century, September 16, 1911

THE GREAT FERMENT

The Jewish ghetto throbbed to a Yiddish beat. People worked, studied and romanced each other in this most expressive language. As time went by, the newcomers learned English and French but often they fell back on certain Yiddish words to convey the subtlety of the point they were trying to make.

The Jews brought with them yet another language—Hebrew, the "holy language." Hebrew was the language of the synagogue; Yiddish was the language of the streets.

Longtime educator and Zionist leader Zave Ettinger recalls how the Chinese laundryman in his area serviced the almost exclusively Jewish clientele in perfect Yiddish. The tradesman collected bundles in a wicker hamper on wheels and verified each item in flawless Yiddish!

Despite wretched poverty and poor health, many Jewish immigrants felt, for the first time in their lives, like human beings. In Montreal, they were free of fear. Best of all, the Jews found they were free to read what they wanted, to say or write anything they wanted.

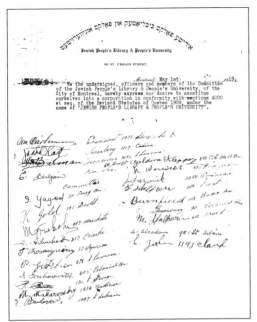

The Charter of the Jewish Public Library (from the Library's Archives)

MONTREAL'S FIRST JEWISH BOOK STORE

In 1903, M. Hershman founded the Jewish Library and Reading Room, described in its provincial charter as a University of the People—at 68 St. Lawrence Boulevard, in Zionist facilities. He took the train to New York with $20 to acquire stock. In 1914, the Library expanded into larger facilities at 669 St. Urbain Street. (A deposit of 50 cents per book was required; a book could be borrowed for one week and the fine for failing to return a volume on time was half-a-cent a day.) Through its books and lecture programs, the Library brought Yiddish-speaking literary figures to lecture in its crowded facilities. Montreal spawned a bevy of important Yiddish writers and soared to prominence in the Yiddish world. The city had a Yiddish newspaper, the *Keneder Adler*, and a Yiddish Theatre.

Jewish immigrants wrote frequently to those left behind in Europe. When no response came after years, they said prayers for the departed. However, where possible, they pinched pennies to gather enough money to bring over others.

Writing of this era, Israel Medres stated:

"The Jewish immigrant generally arrived here ahead of his wife and children.

"They had remained in the 'home' country while the father rented a room and, after securing employment, saved for the day when he could be reunited with his family. Room and board averaged three dollars a week and incidentals another dollar. Usually two or three dollars were sent home every

Amateur Yiddish Theatre actors after performing "Ruth" at the Monument Nationale Theatre in June 1914. (Canadian Jewish Congress National Archives) The first group to promote Yiddish Theatre was formed, by immigrants, in 1898 with the assistance of a Boston actor, L. Mitnick, who is regarded as the father of Yiddish theatre in Montreal. Mitnick and his associates brought the greatest Yiddish actors of the day—all appearing at the Monument National Theatre. The theatrical pioneer died in 1913, and his son carried on for a time, but the days of the great international Yiddish performers in Montreal was over.

week to the family, and the balance went as payment on the steamship ticket that would bring over the family."

HOLD THE BACK PAGE!
JEWISH NEWSPAPERS IN MONTREAL

When a breaking story would hit the wire, a reporter in the newsroom of the Yiddish daily, the *Keneder Adler*, would call out jokingly, "hold the back page!" instead of the usual "hold the front page." Yiddish and Hebrew are written from right to left, and the back page of a Yiddish paper is the front page of a regular publication.

The typesetting facilities of Keneder Adler, the important Yiddish Newspaper. (Allan Raymond Collection, Jewish Public Library Archives)

Hirsch Wolofsky was born in a little town in Poland and came to Montreal with his wife in 1900. He found a job as a cutter in a factory, but the work blistered his hands, and he quit after only a few days. Then he opened a small corner store, but it burned down. In 1907, Wolofsky started a Yiddish newspaper, called *"The Jewish Eagle,"* or *Keneder Adler* in Yiddish. Other newspapers came and went but the *Keneder Adler* soldiered on for seven decades, declining only as Yiddish declined in Montreal. In its golden age, the newspaper was the great political, literary and cultural voice of Canadian Jewry.

The first Jewish paper was published in English. The *"Jewish Times"* was founded by a number of community leaders, in 1897. Co-founders included Samuel W. Jacobs, a lawyer and MP, and Lyon Cohen, an important community leader. The *Times'* editor was an Irishman, Carroll Ryan, who remained at the paper's helm until his death in 1910. The paper's name was changed to *Canadian Jewish Times* in 1909. In 1915 it merged with the *Canadian Jewish Chronicle* of Montreal.

The *Times* became the voice of the Uptowners, the established wealthier Jews of Montreal. The brash *Keneder Adler*, on the other hand, reflected the views of the less affluent Yiddish-speaking immigrants, the Downtowners. The *Times* expressed concern about Jewish poverty and workplace exploitation but abhorred editorially the vigorous, left-leaning editorials of the Wolofsky family. Inheriting the editor's chair from his father, Max Wolofsky maintained the *Keneder Adler* as a daily until mid-century, when the declining use of Yiddish forced the paper to became a weekly.

In a bid to boost circulation, the *Keneder Adler* became a bilingual Yiddish-English paper. However, after more than 70 years, the paper was shut down, a fate shared by similar publications in Boston, Philadelphia, and Chicago.

In 1960, *Canadian Jewish News* was launched in Toronto by Meyer J. Nurenberger. In the 1970s, first the Toronto and then the Montreal Federations took over the *News* as a non-profit venture. The *News* continued to exercise full editorial independence. Currently it is the largest and most important Jewish publication in Canada.

The front page of first edition of the Keneder Adler Yiddish newspaper. Aug. 30, 1907.
(Canadian Jewish Congress National Archives)

TEACHING HATE

On March 10, 1910, a Quebec notary and journalist, Jacques E. Plamondon, speaking to a Catholic youth group, stated that the Talmud teaches that Christians should be put to death, that a Jew who has slain a Christian is not morally a murderer, that Jews may commit adultery with impunity where non-Jewish women are involved, and that Jews murder Christian children to get blood for ritual purposes. After the lecture, members of the audience smashed windows in a neighbouring synagogue and attacked a number of Jews in Quebec City streets.

The lecture was lengthened and published as a pamphlet in which Plamondon described Jews as "enemies of the Christian faith."

Two Jewish merchants in Quebec City, Benjamin Ortenberg, and Louis Lazarovitch, sued for damages. They contended that they had lost business because of the pamphlet. They hired Member of Parliament Samuel W. Jacobs to appear for them before the Quebec Superior Court. Jacobs told the court:

"It is to show that these charges are abominable falsehoods that we are before the Court, and we ask the Court to examine our books, and our teachings, examine these charges, examine these dispositions, and say after listening to the evidence whether the charges made by this man are true or whether they are malicious and slanderous libels for the publication of which the defendants ought to be held amendable to the law."

Rabbi Herman Abramowitz of Montreal's Shaar Hashomayim Synagogue, in giving evidence, declared that "similar charges had caused disaster to the Jews in the past, and they have been denied by the Popes of the past." The Rabbi testified that the so-called quotations were false and he offered evidence from the Catholic Encyclopedia. The Judge dismissed the case and noted that Plamondon had incriminated the Jewish race in general but did not attack the plaintiffs in particular. However, Jacobs appealed and Plamondon was found guilty in December 1914. Five years later, the *Canadian Jewish Chronicle* reported that Plamondon had been jailed for dishonest business practices.

Harry Hershman's store on The Main, 1906. From the Montreal Jewish Standard.
(Canadian Jewish Congress National Archives)

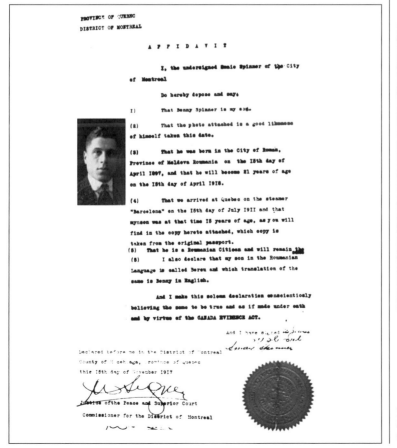

"A curious and interesting sight it is to watch the Jewish toilers every evening after six, going in one long stream to the Hershman store to buy the Yiddish newspapers. For the average workingman Jew is an omniverous reader, and, like his Gentile cousin, he must have his daily paper.

"Whenever the Jewish bulletins announce anything important, groups of Hebrews congregate together in and outside the Jewish newspaper stores, and have very heated arguments pro and con."
Canadian Century 1911.

The 1918 affidavit to permit Benny Spinner to emigrate to Canada.

CHAPTER TWELVE

THE MAIN
Building Blocks of Progress

To a middle-class stranger, it's true, one street would have seemed as squalid as the next. On each corner a cigar store, a grocery and a fruit man. Outside staircases everywhere. Winding ones, wooden ones, rusty and risky ones. Here a prized plot of grass splendidly barbered, there a spitefully weedy patch. And endless repetition of precious peeling balconies and waste lots making the occasional gap here and there. But, as the boys knew, each street between St. Dominique and Park Avenue represented subtle differences in income. No two cold-water flats were alike.

Mordecai Richler
from The Apprenticeship of Duddy Kravitz

The heart of the Jewish community, from late in the nineteenth century through to the Second World War, lay in the few blocks beginning at Craig Street (now St. Antoine) and running north to

TIMELINE 1911-1914
1911. The Montreal Hebrew Free Loan Society is incorporated.
1912. Po'ale Zion and the Socialist Territorialist parties organize the Peretz Schools.
1912. The Mount Sinai Sanitarium is created for the care of tuberculosis victims.
1912. Abraham Blumenthal elected alderman in Montreal.
1913. 20,000 Jewish immigrants arrive in Montreal; the Jewish population soars to 60,000.
1913. The Peretz School is founded.
1914. The First World War breaks out.
1914. The Jewish Public Library is founded as a library and "people's University."
1914. Jewish People's Schools are opened in Montreal (and Toronto).
1914. The Canadian Jewish Chronicle commences publication in Montreal.
1914. The Hebrew Maternity Hospital is opened.
1914. Louis Rubenstein is elected alderman.

Mount Royal Avenue. It sprawled about six blocks on either side of the island's north/south dividing line—the legendary St. Lawrence Main or Boulevard. This intensely Jewish neighbourhood was a bustling square mile of vibrant Jewish life for more than 50 years. A ghetto-by-choice, this self-contained ethnic enclave became widely known as "The Main". It was literally a road to opportunity and an incubator for greatness. Poor Jews landed as Europeans and, as they prospered and moved north, they emerged from this transition zone a mile later as Canadians, and as Montrealers. The children of The Main carried forward into the mainstream their parents' dream for a better life. They became the poets and painters, the professionals and professors, the authors and judges.

THE IMMIGRANT'S MONTREAL

The Jewish community began virtually on the waterfront. For most newly arrived Jews, their lives centered on the "lower Main," the southern-most portion of St. Lawrence Boulevard. A Jewish Quarter or ghetto developed in downtown Montreal as Jewish immigrants from Russia and Romania, Galicia, Estonia, Lithuania, Poland and Germany flooded into the city and gravitated toward the synagogues and homes established by earlier settlers. At first their numbers were comparatively small—only 2,500 in 1891. Then an explosive growth began, more than doubling through immigration in the next ten years. By 1911, the city's Jewish population had soared to 29,000.

Newcomers from eastern Europe could hear the reassuring sound of Yiddish almost from the moment they stepped down from the boat onto the bustling dockside, littered with cargo and the rope-tied baggage of poor immigrants. Most of them were met by family or friends, and failing that, there was someone from the established Jewish community. Confusion was great as adults and children circled anxiously looking for a familiar face. "Aunt Dora!" "Cousin Abe!" Shouting and tears were commonplace. The look of relief after a long and arduous journey was evident on hundreds of faces.

For many, there was the long walk up St. Lawrence, unless their friends or relatives had done well enough to afford a horse and wagon. The boulevard was lined with shops bearing signs in many languages, but most often in Yiddish. Familiar Jewish foods dominated the colourful scene. Barrels of herring and pickles were plunked down on the sidewalk. Haunches of meat dangled from hooks in butchers' windows bearing prominent "kosher" signs. Traffic thickened as the newcomers plodded north. There were noisy proprietors of pushcarts loudly extolling the quality and low prices of their merchandise: The best pots and pans. Clothing and shoes only slightly used. Bagels on a string. And books, mountains of books in a dozen languages, piled high in a peddler's cart. Everything that might have value was for sale. At their boarding house or tenement flat, if they were lucky, there would be a bed, to be shared with two or three others. If not, there was always the floor for that first night of exhausted sleep.

The corner of St. Lawrence Main Street and St. Catherine Street, c. 1910 (Notman Photographic Archives MP-0000.816.6 McCord Museum)

The day began at dawn with the clopping of horses' hooves on the streets. The milkman's horse knew the route so well he meandered through the streets, stopping at all the right places. The newcomers awakened to the clink of milk bottles in a metal carrier. Then came the iceman, making his deliveries. This was an oasis of plenty for those who had fled the terrors of Eastern Europe. All around them Jews bargained, argued, laughed, and worked with no interference from threatening Cossacks or brutal police. This indeed was the Golden Land.

AREA OF FIRST SETTLEMENT (C. 1901-C.1920)

Until the outbreak of World War I, Jewish immigrants filled the neighbourhood south of Ontario Street in the avenues flanking St. Lawrence Boulevard. They settled in areas where people from their region of the Old Country had found cheap accommodation. Many of the first arrivals lived in grinding poverty in high-density tenements where they shared tiny cold-water flats. In 1901, more than half of the Jewish population of Montreal lived in the area south of Pine Avenue and east of Park Avenue. However, new arrivals and the success of earlier migrants pushed the community north, block by block, until by 1921, they had reached St. Louis Square.

AREA OF SECOND SETTLEMENT (C. 1921-C.1940)

By 1931, the community had worked its way north to Mount Royal, and Greek and Portuguese immigrants began to move into tenements vacated by the Jews. From approximately 1921 to 1941, more than 86 percent of the community lived north of Pine

St. Urbain Street and Greenberg's corner store, c. 1920—for a time the heart of the Montreal Jewish Community. (Montreal City Archives)

Canadian Jewish Review, Sept. 3, 1926

and east of Park. Jews formed 55 per cent of the total population of St. Louis Ward. New community structures were built—a library, schools, synagogues, and the Davis Y.M.H.A. As the population moved, their institutions followed. There were 40 synagogues in the region. By 1940, six of Montreal's fifty synagogues were located on St. Urbain Street alone. At this time, St. Urbain Street was almost 100 per cent Jewish. The area became known locally as the St. Urbain Ghetto. According to author Mordecai Richler, "It was an all but self-contained world made up of five streets: Clark, St. Urbain, Waverley, Esplanade and Jeanne Mance, bounded by the Main on one side, and Park Avenue on the other." Richler immortalized the St. Urbain Street Jewish ghetto with his award-winning novel, The Apprenticeship of Duddy Kravitz. In 1974, the book was made into a movie, which was filmed in the district. A remarkable number of Canadians of national and international repute spent their childhoods within these city blocks. In addition to Richler, one of Canada's best-known writers, notables from the area include Nobel Prize winning author Saul Bellow, conductor and composer Alexander Brott, and artists Moe Reinblatt and Stanley Lewis.

Hyman's Cigar Store, 1920. (Jewish Public Library Archives)

"(The Main) was a great place to grow up. For a poet nothing could have been better. Nothing. Raw, vulgar, dynamic and dramatic: their smells and sounds and fights. It was altogether a rich and wonderful life. Sometimes I'm sorry for my children who lived in the suburbs and never had anything like this."

Poet Irving Layton in an 1970s interview with photographer Edward Hillel.

BARON BYNG HIGH

An important development in the history of the Jewish community came in 1921 when a high school was built on St. Urbain Street. It was named for a distinguished British soldier, Byng of Vimy. Lord Byng, who later became Governor General of Canada, opened the school himself in 1922.

The school enrolled about one thousand students and more than 90 per cent of them were Jewish. Many of them became outstanding figures. They included poets Irving Layton and A.M. Klein, novelist Mordecai Richler; David Lewis, a Rhodes scholar who became head of the New Democratic Party; Herbert Marx, one-time Justice Minister of Quebec and now a Justice of the Quebec Superior Court; physician and medical researcher Dr. Phil Gold; Fred Rose, the only communist member of Parliament; actor William Shatner (Star Trek's Captain Kirk); City Councillor Sid Stevens who created the Sun Youth organization; sociologist Lionel Tiger and politician Harry Blank.

Teachers at the school were under the iron direction of the principal, Dr. Astbury, who was a stickler for obedience and performance. In addition, some exceptional teachers, undoubtedly responding in good measure to the students' eagerness to learn, influenced countless young people to take up careers in art, the social sciences, politics, medicine, and law.

The outbreak of World War II marked the end of the Depression and the end of an era. Everyone either joined the armed forces or went to work in factories busy meeting the demand of the conflict.

After the war, returning veterans flocked to the universities and chose to live in the suburbs. By 1980, the high school was closed due to a declining enrolment, and was turned over to community agencies. The most successful of these is Sun Youth, directed by Sid Stevens, a graduate of Baron Byng.

TENEMENTS AND TORAH

For someone Jewish and new to the city, the St. Urbain ghetto was a turbulent but comforting place. There were familiar sights and sounds everywhere. The entire Boulevard was lined with shops selling traditional Jewish foods, clothing new and used, footwear and books. There were cafés and restaurants. At Horn's café, coffee was five cents, and on cold days, friends would sit for hours discussing world affairs, religion, and poli-

Mendel's Grocery Store, 1930 (The Allan Raymond Collection, Jewish Public Library Archives)

tics. The immigrants had lived through revolution, and no one was without a strong opinion. Synagogues and prayer halls flourished, and catered to the many variations in the Jewish faith, but mostly Orthodox. Passersby could hear youngsters chanting Hebrew in Jewish afternoon schools, tucked away in small homes. More than 40 synagogues, mostly Orthodox, were scattered throughout the ghetto; most of them were accommodated in rented quarters. The district had several mikvahs, public baths for ritual bathing. A number of clinics, often with Yiddish-only signs, provided medical care. In almost every shop, Yiddish newspapers were on display. Competition was keen as many converted their front parlours into tiny stores or rented a pushcart for 25¢. While husbands worked outside the home, wives took care of children, cleaned the house, ran the tiny family store, and accommodated boarders to help make ends meet.

In a memoir, author Mordecai Richler described the diversity of the ghettto:

Street Scene, 1935. (Lithography by Ernst Newman—from the art collection of Atara and Murray Marmor

"Within one block you could have disfiguring blackheads removed, talk with a miracle-working Rabbi, shoot a game of snooker, bet on a horse, consult a matchmaker, read newspapers in six different languages, furnish your bedroom for 20 dollars down, send a food parcel to a relative in Warsaw, and drop in on a herbalist with a sure cure for the most embarrassing of all ailments."

THE THIRD SOLITUDE

The Jews on the Main were positioned geographically between the anglophones residing mostly to the west, and the francophones dominating the eastern portion of the city. For decades, the Jews were the only considerable community other than the French and English.

Historian Ben Kayfetz, writing in 1959, suggested that the divided population helped Montreal Jewry develop their community:

"Montreal's French Catholic-English Protestant polarity may be the key to its Jewish development. It has given the impetus perhaps to a day school system that encompasses fully half of all Jewish children who get any Jewish education, to large institutions like a Jewish Public Library, a Jewish General Hospital and a Young Men's Hebrew Association."

The Bagg Street Synagogue. The last of some 40 synagogues on the St. Lawrence Main, it was converted from a duplex in 1921 and still has a small congregation. (The Ontario Jewish Archives Shuls Collection)

THE TEMPLE OF SOLOMON?

In 1921, a brown-brick duplex at the corner of Bagg and Clark streets, in the heart of the Jewish ghetto, was converted into a place of worship. The synagogue was named *Beth Shlomo*, meaning The Temple of Solomon. While the title evokes the magnificent original in Jerusalem, the Montreal version served a poor congregation and never had enough support to hire a full-time rabbi. The synagogue, which can accommodate 200 men and 100 women, was furnished with items donated by Shaar Hashomayim. When the Shaar, a rich congregation by comparison, moved from the corner of McGill College and Cathcart streets to its present Westmount location on Côte St-Antoine, members of Beth Shlomo moved the heavy wooden pews themselves, wrestling the long benches, and the ark, onto horse-drawn carts.

Commonly known as the Bagg Street Synagogue, it is the last remaining of the 40 or so synagogues dotting The Main in the period 1900-1950. Today a handful of parishioners gather on Saturday mornings to keep the 80-year-old congregation alive. On the Sabbath and High Holidays between 40 and 60 people attend. A small group interested in maintaining the synagogue call themselves Living Stones. Their goal is to convert the crumbling brick facility into a Museum of Jewish History. To raise money for building repairs and a possible museum, Living Stones has been striving to locate and contact the children and grandchildren of people who lived in the area during its heyday. According to architect Joshua Wolfe, "Whether or not we ourselves are religious, these buildings are important because they are heirlooms of our grandparents."

Poet Irving Layton, who lived in the area from his birth in 1915 until 1950, wrote of the Jewish district:

"It was a turbulent neighbourhood, full of Jews, French Canadians, Slavs, Italians. Along the Main it was all Jewish stores.

"Names like Cohen, Lidenberg, Margolis, Lindover and Goldberg lined the streets.

"It was the memorable combination of the starkness of daily reality, the meanness of drab, poverty-stricken streets, the pinched narrow lives that people led on those streets, and the religious piety that was so foreign to all this."

To the English and French, it seemed a strange world dominated by people dressed in dark clothing and speaking an odd guttural tongue. However, the more curious began to frequent this colourful neighbourhood, tasting the unusual foods and negotiating enthusiastically with push-cart operators for bargains. While there were tensions at times, the groups generally lived their separate lives with little association.

THIRD AREA OF SETTLEMENT (1940S-C. 1960)
"On Saturday afternoons the well-to-do Jews walked up and down Decarie Boulevard, which was their street. A street of sumptuous supermarkets and banks built of granite, an aquarium in the lobby of the Snowdon Theatre, a synagogue with a soundproof auditorium and a rabbi as modern and quick as the Miss Snowdon Restaurant, neon drugstores for all your needs and delicatessens rich in chrome plating. Buick convertibles and Cadillacs parked on

both sides; a street without a past. Almost all these Jews, who had prospered, craved for many lights. Wishing away their past and the dark." (Mordecai Richler from "Son of a Smaller Hero")

Murray's grocery, at 176-178 Dorchester West, in the 1940's; owned by the Kuchinsky family. (Allan Raymond Collection, Jewish Public Library Archives)

The flow of population to the north and then to the west began about 1914. It accelerated in the 30s, 40s and 50s, into lower Outremont, while the wealthiest Jews purchased homes in Westmount. By 1951, with Jewish veterans buying homes in suburban metropolitan Montreal, virtually every Jewish school and synagogue had followed the movement and had left the Main for Snowdon, Notre Dame de Grace, Côte des Neiges, Ville St. Laurent and Town of Mount Royal. In a later phase they moved into Hampstead and then, in large numbers, into Côte St. Luc, and into the west island suburb of Dollard des Ormeaux. According to the 1991 census, there were only 300 Jews living in the Old Jewish Quarter.

"Out of the ghetto streets where a Jewboy

Dreamed pavement into pleasant Bibleland,

Out of the Yiddish slums where childhood met

The friendly beard, the loutish Sabbath-goy,

Or followed, proud, the Torah-escorting band,

Out of the jargoning city I regret,

Rise memories, like sparrows rising from

The gutter-scattered oats,

Like sadness sweet of synagogal hum,

Like Hebrew violins

Sobbing delight upon their eastern notes."

A.M. Klein, from "Gloss Aleph: autobiographical"
1951

A SNIPPET FROM THE PAST

When Prince Charles was born in 1948, Irving the Barber on Clarke Street telexed Buckingham Palace that he would be honoured to cut the Prince's hair, without charge, any time His Royal Highness happened to be in Montreal. A formal reply acknowledging the offer came from the Palace. On magnificent crested stationery, a Palace spokesperson expressed appreciation for the offer. Irving the Barber immediately handmade a sign for his window reading "By appointment Barber to the Royal Family."

This is one of the favourite stories told by Stanley Asher, the professor who, for years, has conducted tours of the Old Jewish Quarter—the Montreal of Irving Layton, of Mordecai Richler, of Leonard Cohen.

Asher himself lived in the Main district, attending Baron Byng High School in the 1940s. "I had a very protective Jewish mother," he says. "When it was decided I would go to Baron Byng, we moved next door to the school so I wouldn't have to cross the road."

Professor Asher blends his academic career (at John Abbott College since 1971, teaching radio production, cinema history, Holocaust, and Montreal popular culture), with media involvement including radio, television, newspapers and film. Asher and Israeli filmmaker Dov Okouneff have recorded the oral histories of more than 100 early Jewish residents of Montreal.

THE LIFE OF A STREET

1672. A comprehensive street plan for Montreal includes a St. Lambert Street, a short road named in honour of Lambert Closse, second-in-command to Montreal founder Sieur de Maisonneuve.

1730. St. Lambert Street is extended to the new parish of St. Laurent; beyond the city walls, it is labelled Chemin de St. Laurent.

1777. The first Jewish synagogue is located at the corner of St. Lambert and Notre Dame streets.

1792. Montreal is divided into two districts with Rue St. Laurent as the dividing line between east and west. The thoroughfare is now called St. Lawrence Street.

1830s. The district of St. Laurent is labeled Faubourg Saint-Laurent, in French, and St. Lawrence suburb, in English; its principal street is called St. Laurent du Main or St. Lawrence Main, known familiarly as "the Main."

1870. A tidal wave of immigrants from Europe, including thousands of Jews, pours into Montreal and is funneled into cheap housing along the Main.

1905. St. Lambert Street, St. Lambert Hill and St. Lawrence Street are given the name: Boulevard Saint-Laurent or St. Lawrence Boulevard.

1920. Prohibition begins in the United States, and many Americans move to Montreal as a wide-open city. Many night clubs and bars, some with Jewish owners or partners, flourish along The Main. In the late 1950's, a young lawyer, Jean Drapeau, leads the fight to "clean up the Main."

JEWISH SPORTS PERSONALITIES

A number of Jews have been outstanding in various sports, including football, hockey and figure skating.

TOUCHDOWN!

Playing on the 1874 McGill University Football team, Henry Joseph (1855-1951) single-handedly changed the rules of the game in both Canada and the United States when he picked up the ball and ran with it.

Until then, the English version of football permitted only kicking the ball, as they do in Europe. By introducing the idea of carrying the ball, Joseph helped create North American style football.

THE HART TROPHY

The oldest and most prestigious award in professional hockey, the Hart Trophy, is named in honour of Cecil M. Hart (1883-1940), a direct descendent of Aaron Hart, Canada's first legal Jewish settler.

Cecil Hart organized, managed, and played for the Star Hockey Team 1900-1922. His team won the league championship in the 1914-1915 and 1916-1917 seasons. Hart then organized the first international amateur hockey series between Canada and the United States.

He entered professional hockey in 1921 and managed the Montreal Canadiens. The team played in the National Hockey League championship playoffs for six straight seasons. The Canadiens, under his direction, won the Stanley Cup in 1929-1930 and 1930-1931.

Dr. David A. Hart, Cecil's father, donated the Hart Trophy to the League in 1923. It is awarded annually to the most valuable player in the N.H.L.

LOUIS RUBENSTEIN (1862-1913)

World figure skating champion Louis Rubenstein.
(Jewish Public Library Archives)

In the northwest corner of Fletcher's Field (officially re-named Parc Jeanne Mance in 1964) is the Louis Rubenstein Fountain, honouring the memory of one of Canada's greatest athletes. Rubenstein was a Montreal council member, a world champion fancy skater, and president of several organizations including the Montreal Amateur Athletic Association, the Y.M.H.A., and the Royal Life Saving Society.

Rubenstein, son of Polish immigrants, was the Canadian figure skating champion from 1882 to 1889, American champion in 1888, 1889 and 1991, and North American champion in 1885. In 1890, friends collected $400 to sponsor his participation in the world figure skating championship in St. Petersburg, Russia, where he would compete against athletes from Austria, Finland, Norway, and Sweden, and from the cities of Moscow, Stockholm, and St. Petersburg.

En route to Russia, he stopped off in Berlin to practice at the Berlin Winter Gardens. He was not permitted to use the facility because he was Jewish. Later, in St. Petersburg, the police followed him around and told him to leave the city within 24 hours. Parts of Europe were rife with anti-Semitism at this time. Luckily, the Canadian Governor General Lord Stanley, one of Rubenstein's greatest fans, had given the skater a letter of introduction. The athlete took the letter to the British ambassador

(Canada had no consular representative in Russia then), who intervened with the authorities in St. Petersburg.

During competition, the judges were undoubtedly prejudiced against the Jewish athlete, but Rubenstein's performance won the day. The Czar Alexander 3rd made the presentation, probably with great reluctance; he is responsible for the persecution and murder of thousands of Russian Jews.

As the first internationally recognized figure skating champion, Louis Rubenstein's journey home was a triumph. This time, during a stopover in Berlin, he was received by the Kaiser. In addition, he was welcomed to London by the Prince of Wales (the future King Edward VII).

Louis repeatedly outperformed his brother Abraham on the ice, but another brother, Moses, was Canadian figure-skating champion in 1892 and 1897. Their sister Rachel won titles in both Canada and the United States.

Louis Rubenstein entered politics in 1914. He was elected Alderman by acclamation and held office until his death, 17 years later.

A bemedalled world "fancy" skating champion, Louis Rubenstein of Montreal, c. 1895. The term figure skating had not yet been conceived. (Jewish Public Library Archives)

RUBENSTEIN, RUBENSTEIN!!

FRIDAY EVENING, MARCH 14TH. 1884,

—AT THE—

MIRAMICHI SKATING & CURLING RINK, NEWCASTLE,

MR. LOUIS RUBENSTEIN,

THE Champion **FANCY SKATER** OF America!!

The Directors of the Rink have much pleasure in announcing that Mr. RUBENSTEIN has consented to remain over at Newcastle on his return to Montreal, and give an exhibition of his magnificent Fancy Skating.

RACES! WILL BE HELD AS FOLLOWS:—

5 Mile Race, free for all. 1 Mile Race, boys of 15 and under.

A first prize of a handsome Silver Cup will be awarded to the winner of the 5 mile race, with second and third cash prizes of $3 and $2. Cash prizes of $3 and $2 will be given the winners of the one mile race. There must be five entries in each competition.

THE RINK BRASS BAND WILL BE IN ATTENDANCE

The Event of ♯ Season!

Admission 25 cents, Children 15 cents, Entries to Races, 25 cents.

☞ TICKETS AT THE DRUG STORES.

CHAS. SARGEANT, President.   JOHN FERGUSON, Sec'y Treas.

Thousands attended his funeral, and among his eulogizers was Mayor Camillien Houde, who told the mourners "The City has lost a great man." The Montreal Gazette, in its coverage of the funeral, declared: "No greater tribute could be paid to any public-spirited man than that accorded to the late Ald. Louis Rubenstein when thousands of friends and acquaintances filled the residence, 3567 St. Urban Street, to capacity and overflowed to the sidewalks, roadway and adjoining premises in an endeavor to pay their last respects to one of the foremost Jewish citizens of this metropolis."

The small fountain is the only public monument to a Jew in the City of Montreal.

~~

FROM YPRES TO CANADA'S HUNDRED DAYS: JEWS IN THE GREAT WAR

An estimated 4,700 Jews donned Canadian uniforms to fight in the First World War (1914-1918). At least 100 were killed during the four-year conflict; and 84 were decorated for bravery. These figures are minimums. Many Jews enlisted in the Armed Forces without identifying themselves by religion.

Canadian Jews fought in every major engagement, from the first choking German gas attacks at Ypres, Belgium, through the Somme, the storming of Vimy Ridge, the bloody confrontation at Passchendaele, Flanders, and finally, in the dramatic Canadian breakthrough at Amiens in 1918. With fixed bayonets, the Jews participated in the historic advance known as Canada's 100 days.

Five Montreal Jewish officers on leave in Brighton, England, in 1918, to observe Yom Kippur. Black row: (l to r) Lieut. Nathan B. Cohen, Lieutenant Herbert A. Vineberg.
Front row: (l to r) Capt. Joseph Leavitt, Capt. Leo Livingstone, Capt. Horace R. Cohen.

RECRUTING THE SONS OF ISRAEL

The war pitted Britain and its Empire (including Canada by default), France, Imperial Russia, Belgium, Japan and Serbia, against Austria-Hungary, Germany and Turkey. The United States entered the war in 1918.

The Canadian government made a special plea to Montreal Jews to enlist voluntarily. Sir Sam Hughes, Canadian Minister of Militia, asked Captain Isidore Freedman to raise a Jewish battalion for service overseas. Colourful posters were printed, in English and Yiddish, declaring "Britain expects every son of Israel to do his duty." Captain Freedman agreed to raise a "Jewish Reinforcement Draft Company." After training, the unit proceeded overseas in 1917, and did not serve as a company. The soldiers were dispersed, as reinforcements, to various battalions. Captain Freedman was assisted by five Jewish Lieutenants—Alex Solomons, Herbert Vineberg, C. Lesser, Albert Freedman and Sol Rubin. Jews were in uniform in every one of the participating armies.

THE ZION MULE CORPS

The war had special significance for Jews. The involvement of the Ottoman Empire meant that the province of Palestine risked becoming a possible battleground. When Britain formed the Zion Mule Corps—dedicated to liberating the area from Turkish control—with mostly Jewish volunteers from Palestine, a number of

Montrealers enlisted. This was the first Jewish military fighting unit in the land of Israel since the Bar Kokhba rebellion in the year 132 (Common Era or A.D.). There were 562 members of the Zion Mule Corps who took part in the bloody but unsuccessful effort to capture Turkey's Gallipoli Peninsula. The Corp's casualties included six dead and 25 wounded. Three soldiers were decorated.

The Corps was disbanded in 1916, but re-born as a battalion of the Royal Fusiliers. They were posted to Palestine in June 1918 and were deployed in hills twenty miles north of Jerusalem, facing Turkish positions. An official account of combat in the area mentions that the battalion "at once assumed a vigorous offensive policy (that) thoroughly scared the Turks, so much so that they never once attempted to come anywhere near our front."

Late in the war, about 300 Canadians—more than half from Montreal—were members of the Jewish Legion, which completed training too late for participation in fighting, but became part of the occupation force in Palestine. A number of Canadians from both the Mule Corps and the Jewish Legion later settled in Palestine.

Capt. William Sebag-Montefiore, M.C.. He served in France and Palestine during World War One; he was awarded the Military Cross for bravery, and was twice mentioned in dispatches.

MYER T. MACCOHEN—A HERO IN A KILT

A large stained-glass window in the Anglican Church of St. Andrew and St. Paul on Sherbrooke Street pays tribute to a courageous Jewish officer from the First World War. The Black Watch window, as it is known, includes a Star of David, symbol of the Jewish people. It was installed in recognition of a lieutenant in the 42nd Highlanders, Montrealer Myer T. Cohen, winner of the Military Cross. He was decorated for his bravery and aggressiveness during October 1917 raids on enemy positions in Belgium. He captured six German soldiers.

The commander of the 7th Canadian Infantry Brigade, Brigadier A.C. MacDonell, wrote Cohen's battalion: "Well done, 42nd; well done, old Cohen. I herewith and hereby confer on him the brevet rank of 'Mac', to be used whenever and wherever he likes, but it must always be MacCohen in the kilt."

On November 3, 1917, Cohen led his men during the bloody battle of Passchendaele in Flanders, capturing the ruins of a strategic German position, called Graf House. (British casualties

A 1933 reunion of members of the Zion Cadet Corps. (Allan Raymond Collection; Jewish Public Library Archives)

in that battle numbered 400,000.) Cohen's unit, isolated by a German counter-attack, held their position bravely and stubbornly, but no reinforcements came to their assistance. All were killed.

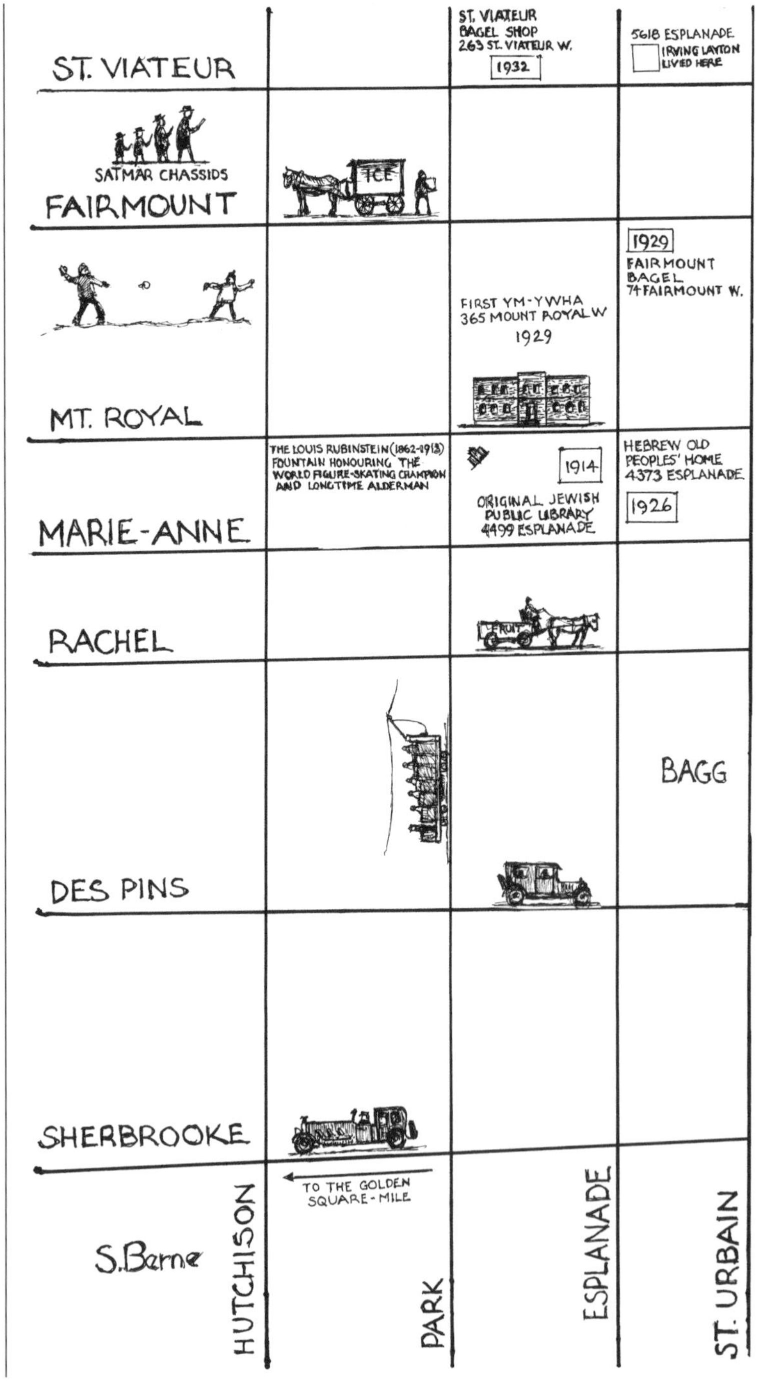

ST. VIATEUR

ST. VIATEUR BAGEL SHOP
263 ST. VIATEUR W.
1932

5618 ESPLANADE.
☐ IRVING LAYTON LIVED HERE

SATMAR CHASSIDS
FAIRMOUNT

ICE

1929
FAIRMOUNT BAGEL
74 FAIRMOUNT W.

FIRST YM-YWHA
365 MOUNT ROYAL W
1929

MT. ROYAL

THE LOUIS RUBINSTEIN (1862-1913) FOUNTAIN HONOURING THE WORLD FIGURE-SKATING CHAMPION AND LONGTIME ALDERMAN

1914

ORIGINAL JEWISH PUBLIC LIBRARY
4499 ESPLANADE

HEBREW OLD PEOPLES' HOME
4373 ESPLANADE
1926

MARIE-ANNE

RACHEL

FRUIT

BAGG

DES PINS

SHERBROOKE

TO THE GOLDEN SQUARE-MILE

S. Berne

HUTCHISON

PARK

ESPLANADE

ST. URBAIN

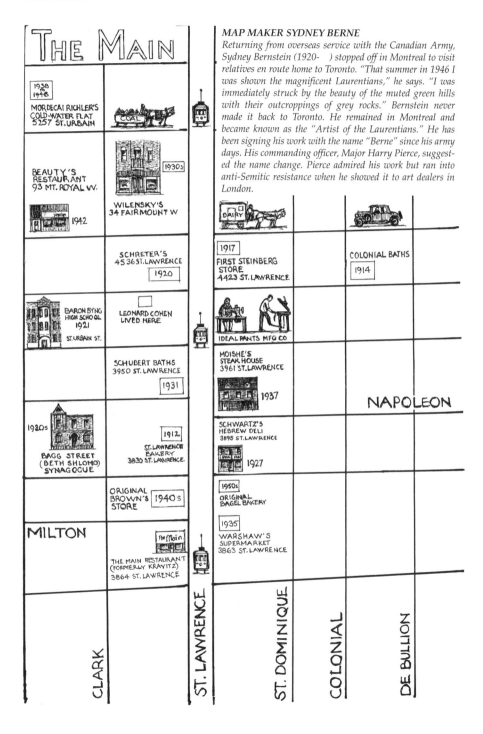

THE MAIN

1938 to 1948
MORDECAI RICHLER'S COLD-WATER FLAT 5257 ST. URBAIN

COAL

1930s

BEAUTY'S RESTAURANT 93 MT. ROYAL W.

WILENSKY'S 34 FAIRMOUNT W

1942

SCHRETER'S 45 36 ST. LAWRENCE

1920

BARON BYNG HIGH SCHOOL 1921 ST. URBAIN ST.

LEONARD COHEN LIVED HERE

SCHUBERT BATHS 3950 ST. LAWRENCE

1931

1920s

BAGG STREET (BETH SHLOMO) SYNAGOGUE

1912
ST. LAWRENCE BAKERY 3830 ST. LAWRENCE

ORIGINAL BROWN'S STORE

1940s

MILTON

The Main

THE MAIN RESTAURANT (FORMERLY KRAVITZ) 3864 ST. LAWRENCE

MAP MAKER SYDNEY BERNE

Returning from overseas service with the Canadian Army, Sydney Bernstein (1920-) stopped off in Montreal to visit relatives en route home to Toronto. "That summer in 1946 I was shown the magnificent Laurentians," he says. "I was immediately struck by the beauty of the muted green hills with their outcroppings of grey rocks." Bernstein never made it back to Toronto. He remained in Montreal and became known as the "Artist of the Laurentians." He has been signing his work with the name "Berne" since his army days. His commanding officer, Major Harry Pierce, suggested the name change. Pierce admired his work but ran into anti-Semitic resistance when he showed it to art dealers in London.

DAIRY

1917
FIRST STEINBERG STORE 4423 ST. LAWRENCE

COLONIAL BATHS

1914

IDEAL PANTS MFG CO

MOISHE'S STEAK HOUSE 3961 ST. LAWRENCE

1937

NAPOLEON

SCHWARTZ'S HEBREW DELI 3895 ST. LAWRENCE

1927

1950s
ORIGINAL BAGEL BAKERY

1935
WARSHAW'S SUPERMARKET 3863 ST. LAWRENCE

CLARK

ST. LAWRENCE

ST. DOMINIQUE

COLONIAL

DE BULLION

Poet A.M. Klein (r) with Congress' Munroe Abbey (l) and Saul Hayes. (Canadian Jewish Congress National Archives)

GRANDSONS OF THE PROPHETS

Abraham Moses Klein (1909-1972), one of Canada's greatest poets, was born in Ratno, Ukraine, and was a year old when he came to Canada, but he identified so strongly with Montreal that he claimed to have been born in the city. He attended Baron Byng High School where, in 1924, he helped form the Sholem Aleichem Club, named after the beloved Yiddish author. He later became interested in religion and studied for the rabbinate. In 1933, he graduated in law from the Université de Montreal, and was called to the Bar, two years before he married his childhood sweetheart Bessie Kozlov. During the Depression-era, Klein was compelled to find other ways of earning a living. In 1938, he became editor of the weekly *Canadian Jewish Chronicle* and he retained that position until 1955. Klein published four books of poetry, including: *Hath Not A Jew? Poems, The Hitleriad, and The Rocking Chair and Other Poems*, for which he was presented with the Governor General's Literary Award in 1948. Other awards include the Quebec Government Literary Prize, 1952; and the Lorne Pierce Medal in 1957 for "his outstanding contribution to Canadian literature". Writing about Klein's work, author Pierre Anctil declared "to fully appreciate Klein's work, the reader must be well versed in Judaic studies and in several languages, know how to appreciate all literary genres and be an expert on the subject of the immigration of the Ashkenazi Jews from eastern Europe—a formidable assignment indeed." As a speechwriter for Samuel Bronfman, Klein was one of the few people able to mitigate Bronfman's vicious temper. Klein returned to McGill 1945-48 as a special lecturer in poetry. He journeyed to Europe and North Africa, with financial assistance from Bronfman, to visit refugee camps in the wake of World War II and this experience inspired him to write his masterpiece and only published novel *The Second Scroll*. Critic Harvey Swados called the book "the most profoundly creative summation of the Jewish condition by a Jewish man of letters since the Eropean catastrophe." It was to be the poet's final publication. He became deeply depressed, and suicidal, while writing the book and stopped writing altogether during the final 18 years of his life. Critic Ludwig Lewisohn described him as the "first contributor of authentic Jewish poetry to the English language." Elaine Kalman Naves, in her "The Writers of Montreal" (1973) said Klein "was arguably the most important English-Canadian writer in the first half of this century, a genius with words whose profound knowledge of Judaica was twinned to a genuinely Canadian sensibility." When Klein died in 1972, Irving Layton wrote:

> "You were a medieval troubadour
> who somehow wandered into a lawyer's office
> and could not find your way back again."

"A poem is an Alka-Seltzer tablet," poet Irving Layton (1912-   ) wrote in his 1971 *Collected Poems of Irving Layton*. "Orthodoxies begin to fizz when one is dropped into their midst. Distrustful of abstractions, poetry is in love with the concrete and particular." Layton, whose real name was

Poet Irving Layton

Issie Lazarovitch, fell in love with poetry in high school when his teacher at Baron Byng, a Mr. Saunders, began to read poetry to the class. Irving Peter Layton was a year old when his parents arrived in Montreal from Romania. "My father was an ineffectual visionary; he saw God's footprints in a cloud and lived only for his books and meditations." He died when Layton was twelve years old, and Layton grew up in deep poverty. At times, there was not enough money to pay the electric bill. The family lived in a four-room shack with one room converted into his mother's grocery store, at 183 rue Sainte-Elizabeth. Layton and his three brothers worked as delivery boys. In his poem "The Yard", Layton wrote, "No one prospers outside my door..." Layton served in the Army during World War II and then attended McGill University. On graduation, he took a number of teaching positions and ultimately joined York University in Toronto as Professor of English. Poet Ralph Gustafson states that Layton is one of only two Canadian poets with what he termed "the Grand Style" with A.M. Klein as the other. In his poem "Irving", Gustafson wrote "This man, grandiloquent/Boastful.../Foolstruck,/in the glory of rage.../Like Joshua, commands/Contradictions." Author Hugh MacLennan labeled Layton as "the best poet... producing steadily within the (English) langage." In 1959, Layton received the Governor General's Award for his book of poetry *A Red Carpet for the Sun*. In his *Collected Poems*, 1965, he wrote: "To have written even one poem that speaks with rhythmic authority about matters that seem enduringly important is something to be immensely, reverently thankful for—and I am intoxicated enough to think that I have written more than one."

Canadian poets do not, with rare exception, earn a good living. Layton, in the preface to *The Laughing Rooster*, wrote:

> "In this country the poet has always had to fight for his survival. He lives in a middle class milieu whose values of money-getting, respectability and success are hostile to the kind of integrity and authenticity that is at the core of his endeavour...His concern is to change the world; at any rate, to bear witness that another besides the heartless, stupid and soul-destroying one men have created is possible."

In 1982, Italy and Korea nominated Layton for the Nobel Prize. Canada nominated Josef Skvorecky.

Louis Muhlstock (1903-) was seven years old when his parents brought him to Montreal from Poland. He began studying art at age 14, taking evening classes at the Monument Nationale. He continued to study at the Art Association of Montreal and *l'Ecole des Beaux Arts*, while he worked as a bookkeeper during the day. He was fortunate to study under one of Canada's foremost artists, William Brymner, and Muhlstock showed great promise as a young artist. In 1925 two portrait studies were accepted and hung at the Montreal Spring Exhibition. In 1928, at age 24, Muhlstock emptied his bank account of the $2,800 he had saved, and spent three years studying and working in Paris. Muhlstock was still astonished many years later that he had been able to get by on that

Louis Muhlstock

small sum and had enough to make trips to England and Belgium. Although he returned to Montreal in 1931, a year of economic depression, his career took off almost immediately. He sold drawings and earned enough to buy a house on Jeanne Mance Street, where he had his studio for more than 60 years. The Depression provided him with material, particularly subjects for drawings. He would visit Fletcher's Field where unemployed men gathered to wile away their time. Donald W. Buchanan, writing about Muhlstock, noted "here he did many drawings of men lying asleep on the grass or sitting staring morosely into space." His drawings, rich in social content, and later his nudes drew wide attention. He started painting in oil and these too found ready markets in Montreal and elsewhere. Paul Duval in the book "Four Decades" describes Muhlstock as "one of Canada's finest draughtsmen." The Museum of Fine Arts magazine *Collage* called him "one of Montreal's best loved artists." Muhlstock never married and retained his Left Bank Parisian bohemianism, jauntily turning up every day at his studio sporting a French beret.

J.I. Segal (1896-1954), known as Canada's foremost poet-in Yiddish—was 15 when he arrived in Montreal from Russia. His first name was Jakov-Otzchok, but he preferred using his initials. Initially he worked as a tailor in a men's pant factory but later obtained a job teaching in a secular Jewish day school. Finally, he became a journalist and editor for the Yiddish-language daily Keneder Adler. He began writing poetry in Hebrew and Russian but above all he delighted in writing in Yiddish. Segal was a secular Jew but was learned in the Torah, hassidic tradition, and folklore. Jack Thiessen in his "Yiddish in Canada" remarked that Canada had "talented artists" in all branches of Yiddish and Hebrew literature, but added "poetry deserves particular mention because of both its quality and quantity. The list of poets is headed by J.I. Segal." Although he only lived to 58, Segal spent the bulk of his life in Montreal, with the exception of the years 1923-28 in New York where he wrote many poems. In his "Late Autumn in Montreal", Segal wrote:

> "Our churchy city becomes even more pious
> on Sundays, the golden crosses shine and gleam
> while the big bells ring with loud
> hallelujahs and the little bells answer
> their low amens; the tidy peaceful streets
> lie dreaming in broad daylight murmuring
> endearments to me whom such a Yiddish Jew
> that even in my footsteps they must hear
> how the music of my Yiddish song sounds
> through the rhythm of my Hebrew prayer."

His name is honoured annually in Montreal with the awarding of the J.I. Segal Award, presented for the best book with Jewish content in fiction or poetry.

CHAPTER THIRTEEN

SHMATA BUSINESS
Sweatshops and The Rise
of the Jewish Labour Movement

She was only eight years old and small for her age, but she pumped the treadle on the sewing machine as well as her older sisters, aged 11 and 14. There were two rented Singer machines in the garret where they lived and worked. Her mother and sisters took turns stitching while her father spent his days, and evenings, making the rounds of the sub-contractors. Papa would be out at dawn and by mid-morning, with luck, he would return, triumphant, with bundles of cloth to be sewn.

The family, like hundreds in the city, worked from dawn until the moment when exhaustion dictated an end to labour. In this way, they earned five to seven dollars a week. A meagre sum. Nevertheless, they managed to get by.

*Corner of Pain and
  Anguish, there's a worn
  old house;
Tavern on the street floor,
  Bible room upstairs.
Scoundrels sit below, and
  all day long they souse.
On the floor above them,
  Jews sob out their
  prayers.*

*Higher, on the third floor,
  there's another room:
Not a single window wel-
  comes in the sun.
Seldom does it know the
  blessing of a broom.
Rottenness and filth are
  blended into one.*

*Toiling without letup in
  that sunless den:
Nimble-fingered and
  (so it seems) content,
Sit some thirty blighted
  women, blighted men,
With their spirits broken,
  and their bodies spent.*

*Morris Rosenfeld
(1862-1922)
The Sweatshop, translated
  from Yiddish*

The first years of the twentieth century saw the garment industry, known popularly as the *Shmata* or (rag) trade, expand enormously in Montreal. It was the first time Jews dominated a major industry from top to bottom, as employers and employees. The industry thrived coincident with the huge influx of Jews from Eastern Europe beginning with the 1880s, and it became one of the largest employers in the city. A small amount of capital was required to start up a business—even sewing machines could be purchased on credit—and many people were willing to work for the low wages current in the field. Competition was cutthroat. The system exploited men, women and children—almost all of them immigrants. Much of the work was done at home, on a piecework basis, or in "sweatshops"—crowded lofts and flats where workers worked long hours for low pay in unhealthy con-

An early sewing machine, activated by a foot pedal. Invention of the machine in 1864 made possible the mass production of stylish clothing for men and women at a low price. (original print)

A family carrying piece goods home to finish them. Often the entire family, including children as young as eight, worked for a pittance, to sew the outfits—earning less than a dollar a day. (Original Print)

ditions. Workers often put in an 80-hour week. The terrible working conditions in the needle trade led to the formation of a Jewish labour movement, and the Jewish radicals, in turn, had a profound influence on Canadian workplace standards.

The garment industry in its early days in Montreal was so small it did not rate mention in the Canadian census until after 1860. The first Jewish firm to manufacture clothing in the city was Moss Brothers, which set up production facilities ten years before the sewing machine was invented. The brothers brought with them from England £60,000—a substantial amount of capital for that time. They employed 800 men and women and exported 90% of their production, two-thirds of it to Australia.

Introduction of the sewing machine in 1864 permitted mass production and revolutionized the manufacture of clothing, making possible lower-priced ready-made fashion. Suddenly, shop girls could afford to dress well. At the turn of the century, women's outfits were available for $7; men's suits came off the rack at $5 to $20. The introduction of inexpensive clothing and a greater selection of styles was welcomed by everyone except dressmakers and tailors who suddenly found their businesses undermined.

As a substantial ready-to-wear woman's clothing industry began to flourish in Montreal, working conditions began to deteriorate. In 1897, the *Montreal Herald* reported in its Feb. 3 edition on the growth of the crowded, unsanitary sweatshops:

> "The operators and the victims of this system are mostly Hebrews, the number of whom is continually increasing. It is estimated by men who have made special enquiries that there are now over a thousand of them in the square bounded by Craig, Sanguinet, St. Catherine and Bleury Streets. Nearly all of them live in old, dark tenements. The overcrowding is general, there being cases where families have only one room each in order to save rent."

In 1911, *Canadian Century*, in an article on Montreal Jewry, reported:

> "The great majority of the Russian Jews are in the clothing trade as cutters, tailors, finishers and so forth. A good many work at home or in sweat shops under wretched physical conditions."

> "As long as the consumer insists on having an all-wool, ready-made, fit-you-as-a-glove suit of clothes for $9.99, someone will have to turn it out."

David Solomon, in a memoir on the history of the industry, wrote: "The impact of East European Jews on the garment

By 1910, the largest sub-contrac-
tor of Jewish firms and hence
the largest indirect employer of
Jews in Montreal and Toronto
was the T. Eaton Company.
With its enormous buying
power, the company dictated
the future of many Jewish companies.

*From the catalogue of the T. Eaton
Company for the year 1905-1906.*

industry was tremendous." Tiny manufacturing facilities sprang
up; some based on only one or two sewing machines. "In most
cases, the boss had worked in another sweat shop long enough to
save $50 or less, to set him up in business. All he needed was a
few sewing machines on credit." In time, workers bought their
own machines and worked from home. Solomon wrote:

"They and their families worked from sun-up to late at night
and lived in filth and misery all year round."

In the next two decades, the Shmata trade continued to flourish
and became an important sector of the Quebec economy. By 1890-
1891, the Canadian census indicated that the garment industry
employed 5,500 men and women; and provided jobs for more
than one-third of the manufacturing work force. A new group of
important manufacturers appeared, including Abraham
Gittelson, Jacob Waldman, Alan Hart, Joseph Dubrofsky, and the
Sommer brothers—Abraham and Charles. Some manufacturers
expanded into real estate development, constructing some of
Montreal's earliest skyscrapers. They erected buildings 10 to 15

Israel Medres, in a memoir, recalls industry conditions in the 1920s:
"A wage-earner received about ten or twelve dollars a week. The tailor or cloakmaker earned more, but he was each year faced with the 'slack season', when the employees worked part-time or not at all..."
When there were few orders, cloakmakers seeking work would trudge from factory to factory, with sewing machines belted to their shoulders.

storeys high to accommodate the burgeoning clothing business. Many of these buildings still accommodate manufacturing concerns.

By 1900, the manufacture of clothing was the second-largest industry in Quebec. The plants began to draw French-Canadian workers to the city, exposing them to efforts to organize unions. The Catholic Church became alarmed by the movement to the city and tried to discourage their constituents from taking urban jobs, or—if they did—to spurn the Jewish-organized unions and join francophone syndicates.

STARVATION WAGES

One of the first surveys of the "sweating" process was written by Jules Helbronner as an appendix to the "Report of the Royal Commission on the Relations between Labour and Capital" (1889). Helbronner referred to "starvation wages" and charged that many "evil practices" existed in the industry, including fining workers, reducing wages arbitrarily, and confiscation of workers' wages. In his conclusion, he wrote:

> "Working by the piece, although in principle one of the most equitable and just methods, has yet in certain industries been instrumental in lowering wages, or at least of obliging the workmen to supply a greater amount of work for the same amount of pay."

MACKENZIE KING INVESTIGATES

William Lyon Mackenzie King, the future prime minister, wrote a series of articles in 1897 on sweatshops for Toronto's *Mail and Empire* (a predecessor to *The Globe and Mail*). The series triggered his lifelong interest in labour issues. In one of his articles, he described how "appalled" he was by what he saw in the sweatshops. He visited a woman and her two daughters who did piecework in their homes. He wrote that the older girl, aged 16, worked 75 hours a week for two dollars. She had been working since she was six years old. Her younger sister was nine and had her own sewing machine. Although the three of them worked as many hours as their strength would permit, they were still—King wrote—"destitute."

In a report on Montreal conditions published in the *Herald* in 1898, King declared "sweating is the most odious form of labour to extract the most from a worker for the smallest wage under unhealthy working conditions." King said women are paid two or three dollars weekly for sixty hours of "drudgery" at a time when carpenters were earning three dollars a day.

M. Siematicki, in a paper entitled "Communism in One Constituency" wrote, "the very nature of the clothing industry lent itself to an intense exploitation of labour. As an industry which requires a limited degree of capital investment, the needle trades were characterized by a large number of relatively small firms waging intense competition."

The system was complex and led to abuse on different levels. Major contractors signed contracts with top retail outlets, and they in turn sub-contracted work to a variety of small shops. Each level was pressured to do work at the lowest possible price, and workers at the bottom of the production pyramid were forced to work for starvation wages.

EFFORT TO ORGANIZE UNIONS FAIL

Between 1900 and 1914, the unions organized 40,000 garment workers and encouraged them to participate in 158 strikes. However, many of these efforts failed to achieve concessions for workers or gain recognition of the union as a bargaining agent. The walkout launched in 1900 by the United Garment Workers of America (UGWA) against the Mark Workman factory is a case in point. The Montreal Trades and Labour Council, in 1901, decried the "scandalous conditions" at the Workman plant, which manufactured military uniforms for the Canadian and British governments. The union claimed that Workman illegally hired Romanian Jewish immigrants, at very low pay, and fired higher-paid Canadian workers. The UGWA claimed wages were as low as $5 a week for a six-day, 72-hour work week. When Mark Workman, who was also president of a congregation, arrived at the inauguration ceremony of a new synagogue, he found angry strikers had occupied all the seats in the sanctuary. Workman was compelled to deliver his prepared remarks to an openly hostile audience. Nevertheless, the strike was not successful. Out of a work force of 300, only 35 took part in the walkout.

SEEKING THE 45-HOUR WORK WEEK

Other strikes early in the century were more successful but marked by clashes between management and labour. As was happening in the garment industries of Toronto and New York, Jewish-led unions were often in confrontation with Jewish-owned companies. As the UGWA gained momentum with help from the American trade union movement, membership grew substantially in numbers. Four major strikes were called against the garment industry in the autumn of 1907. The UGWA wanted

The 1931 census noted that 16.49%—one worker in eight—of all Montreal Jews gainfully employed, worked in the garment industry. In 1932, there were 462 women's wear manufacturers in Canada—most of them in Montreal and Toronto—and most of them owned by Jews. Their production for that year was $45-million, making the industry the eleventh largest in the country. The garment industry remained one of the most important employers of Jews in Montreal, even as the city was gradually overwhelmed by the Great Depression.

a reduction in the work week to 45 hours. The norms in the industry, at the time, were 55 hours for men and 52 for women.

While some smaller firms caved in, the larger manufacturers locked out employees. Four major concerns threatened to move out of Montreal, and, in some cases, they hired goons to beat up strikers.

An employer named A.J. Hart—a Jew—called for "foreign agitators to be deported".

JEW VS. JEW IN 1912

Union efforts to organize the industry climaxed in 1912 when the union called a strike against all the member firms of the Montreal Clothing Manufacturers' Association. Membership included all the major men's clothing manufacturers in the city. Factory-owners at this time included some of the most prominent leaders of the Jewish community, such as Solomon Levinson, Harris Kellert, Noah Friedman, Harris Vineberg, Jacob Elkin, and Samuel Hart. They were working sincerely and sympathetically to alleviate poverty amongst their fellow Jews, but among those they assisted were some of their own underpaid, overworked employees.

Lyon Cohen, himself an immigrant in Montreal in the 1860's, owned the Freedman Company—one of the city's largest men's clothing manufacturers. He was one of the historic leaders of the Jewish community and later president of the Federation (1923-1924). Cohen was founder of the *Jewish Times* newspaper, president of the Baron de Hirsch Institute, chairman of a committee for Jewish students' rights in education, and a volunteer who personally greeted immigrants as they stepped off the docks.

Nevertheless, he denounced those who would unionize his factory and described them as "irresponsible demagogues" who sought to "dictate the terms upon which we will deal with those we employ."

The strategy for the 1912 strike owed much to the encouragement of Hananiah Meir Caiserman, an immigrant from Romania only two years earlier, who had been working in the industry and was determined to see working conditions and wages improve.

In a period of two years, from 1911 to 1913, Caiserman worked with three Jewish labour leaders—Louis Zuker, Victor Baranofsky, and Israel Cheifetz— to build a strong union organization. The 1912 strikers were supported by the Labour Zionists, a left-wing Jewish workers' movement, founded in Lithuania in 1905. The Labour Zionists taxed their own members to support the strike.

The workers were also supported and encouraged by Montreal lawyer Peter Bercovitch, and Reuben Brainin, editor of the *Yiddish Keneder Adler*.

The *Jewish Times*, edited by Marcus Sperber, expressed regret editorially that "most of the participants (in the confrontation) are Jews."

The strike ended in a compromise. The workweek was gradually reduced from 55 to 49 hours, and wages for piecework were increased to compensate the workers financially for the reduced workweek.

WAR BRINGS LABOUR PEACE

The menswear industry entered a period of relative peace after the 1912 strike as the outbreak of the First World War provided the industry with large orders and companies made concessions in terms of wages and working conditions to ensure uninterrupted production.

The United Garment Workers continued to recruit and they set up offices in Coronation Hall, at the lower end of St. Lawrence Boulevard. About 5,000 tailors employed at 20 major factories were signed up.

A NEW UNION APPEARS

However, the union movement itself split, with the Amalgamated Clothing Workers of America (ACWA) moving in to sign up workers. The ACWA called its first strike in 1916 against John W. Peck and Company Ltd., and it was successful. The 400 workers received a substantial pay boost, and the union was recognized as the employees' bargaining agent. In reaction, the manufacturers banded together. When another walkout occurred in 1916, strikebreakers were brought in. Union and management were at loggerheads. Efforts to mediate the dispute failed, and a general strike shut down the entire industry. The city agonized over a work stoppage affecting 4,500 employees in one of Montreal's major industries. The strike, the longest in the clothing industry, ended in 1917 with a memorandum of agreement signed by Michael Hirsch for the Manufacturers' Association, and Peter Bercovitch, acting for the union. They established a committee to study the situation; and two months later, it recommended establishment of a 46-hour week, an increase in wages, time-and-a-half for overtime, and most importantly, recognition of the union.

According to Statistics Canada 1996 census, there were 47,141 employees in 1,113 companies in the clothing industries in Quebec. Sales for the year totalled $4.3-billion. The manufacture of clothing was the eighth largest industry in the province.

CHAPTER FOURTEEN

BRISKETS AND BAGELS
The Jewish Originals that put Montreal on the Map

The year was 1908. Fanny Kravitz wiped her hands repeatedly on her apron as she bustled around her tiny cafe in the garment district. On the other side of the counter, a dozen women from the factories, with only half an hour for lunch, were calling out their orders for fruit and biscuits.

"They want sandwiches," an exhausted Mrs. Kravitz later told her husband Ben. "Why don't I try smoking some briskets?" Kravitz suggested. Ben Kravitz, remembering the technique his grandfather and mother had used in Lithuania, gathered the salt, garlic and spices and hand-rubbed them into the beef. Then he hung the cured brisket over a wood fire and smoked it for several days. The price for a "smoked meat" sandwich was five cents, but it was some time before customers accepted the new item. Before long, Montreal had a much-imitated delicacy, and, later, a new restaurant called Ben's.

One of the most pervasive aspects of the Jewish presence in Montreal is food. Two specialties—smoked meat and bagels—have given Montreal Jewry a national and even international reputation for excellence. Jewish immigrants from Eastern Europe brought their culinary traditions to the alchemy of The Main. Sesame and poppy seed bagels hot from a wood-fired oven won accolades and aficionados. As Montrealers of all persuasions were drawn to the plethora of delicatessens flourishing along much of St. Lawrence Boulevard, Montreal "smoked meat" became legendary. For many non-Jewish Montrealers, visiting a deli provided their first memorable experience of Jewish culture. Of the dozens of delicatessens that serviced The Main during its heyday, only a handful have survived the passing years, increased competition and changes in taste. The delicatessens moved, following on the heels of the Jewish population—first north into the St. Urbain Street area, and then into the Snowdon district and beyond.

The most time-tested Jewish eateries are Ben's Delicatessen—dating from 1908; the Montreal Hebrew Delicatessen—known as "Schwartz's, founded in 1927, Wilensky's Light Lunch, in business since 1932, and, more recently, "Beauty's", established in 1942 at 93 Mount Royal West. Many of these restaurants became Montreal landmark institutions, for example, names like Dunn's, Reuben's and Chenoy's. The city has also seen the development of a large food service industry, serving the needs of kosher families. Levitt's, founded on the Main in 1931, is a long-standing manufacturer of specialized kosher Jewish meat products, such as briskets, salami and hot dogs.

In the Snowdon district, the Snowdon Deli, established by the three Morantz brothers, survives after nearly 50 years, and the Brown Derby continues to soldier on in the Van Horne Shopping Centre, with its "old-fashioned" smoked meat and homestyle Jewish cooking. Perhaps the only thing more pervasive than the hype over Montreal Original Smoked Meat is the on-going debate, "who makes the best smoked meat?"

"Was it Etinson's or Rogatko's, Chenoy's Brooklyn Delicatessen or the Hebrew National? It was a question that was passionately debated on St. Lawrence Boulevard, the artery better known as the Main. On a warm summer evening in 1939, if you were to walk north on the Main from Prince Arthur, your nostrils would be assailed by the aroma of hot, spicy smoked meat wafting out of no fewer than seven delicatessens in less than a mile. Each had its own secret recipe, its own combination of pickling spices to encrust the noble brisket of beef. And as the clients of Putter's or Shagass's bit into their ten-cent sandwiches (rye bread, lots of mustard), they argued about quality and authenticity, just as they argued about just who it was that first brought smoked meat to Montreal from Romania, around the turn of the century, whether it was Old Man Kravitz or Old Man Wiseman." *(William Weintraub in "City Unique", 1996)*

BEN'S

Ken Johnson, writing in *Toronto Magazine*, said of Ben Kravitz's smoked meat sandwiches:

> "Between two slices of round rye bread baked especially to Ben's specification, the dark red smoked meat, slice upon slice almost half an inch thick, protrudes from the sandwich and its tantalizing aroma is akin in quality to its taste which some people say is akin to nothing less than ambrosia in a kosher form."

Canadian Jewish Chronicle, Nov. 6, 1931

Benjamin Kravitz later relocated his "Ben's Restaurant" downtown to De Maisonneuve West, where the walls are lined with the autographed portraits of celebrities from the delicatessen's earlier, more celebrated, days.

Charles Bronfman tells of his delight when his grandfather would visit from Winnipeg. "Gramps" would take Charles, his older brother Edgar, and his cousins Peter and Edward, for a sleigh ride on Mount Royal, concluding with a heavy lunch at Ben's delicatessen where Gramps would enjoy his conversation with Ben Kravitz in Yiddish. Former Prime Minister Pierre Elliot Trudeau enjoyed taking his sons to the restaurant.

THE HEBREW DELICATESSEN

Schwartz's Hebrew Delicatessen—named after the original owners, Maurice and Reuben Schwartz—is widely regarded as the top purveyor of smoked meat, but there are many delis and restaurants serving delicious smoked meat. In 1927, Schwartz's began serving smoked meat sandwiches and steaks. The diner is a landmark on the Main, and a waiting line is common. Schwartz's marinates and smokes its own briskets, using the Romanian technique. Montreal expatriates living in Toronto arrange for the delivery of Schwartz's smoked meat briskets when they gather periodically in the Queen City.

The legendary Schwartz's Deli on St. Lawrence Boulevard. Photo by Alan Kaufman. (Canadian Jewish Congress National Archives)

Papineau Street Butchers (The Allan Raymond Collection, Jewish Public Library Archives)

THE SECRET FORMULA?

Barry Lazar, writing in the *Montreal Gazette* (May 13, 2000) declared:

"Montreal's best known smoked meat emporium, Schwartz's, claims to smoke (its meat) for 10 to 14 days. But the length of smoking doesn't mean that it is better. Quebec Smoked Meat, which sells an excellent product used by many delis in Montreal, smokes for about 70 hours."

Better delicatessens (the word means "delicacies" in German) smoke or pickle their own meat. In Montreal, Schwartz's claims to be the only deli to smoke its own meat, but other delis most certainly would dispute that claim. Each shop, or delicatessen, has its own formula for achieving the taste and texture it desires. But all use garlic, herbs, and spices. A brisket of beef is cured in a mixture of salt with spices, garlic and pepper, then smoked, and finally steamed.

For some reason, smoked meat (pastrami is another name, used outside of Montreal) has been widely accepted in Montreal whereas, in the United States and in much of Canada, the preference is for corned beef.

Salt, pickled or corned beef goes by a variety of regional names. In Yiddish, preserved beef is called pickelfleisch; the same item is called salt beef in London, and pickled beef elsewhere in England. The delicacy became corned beef in America, because it is preserved with corns or kernel-sized grains of dry salt. Pastrami, or smoked meat, is likely of Romanian origin. Before refrigeration, meat was pickled or smoked to preserve it.

WILENSKY'S

Wilensky's, located in the north end of the old Jewish district on Clark and Fairmount streets, prepares the "Wilensky Special", fried salami and bologna slices, slathered with mustard, on a pressed kaiser roll. Wilensky's charges five cents EXTRA if you want the Special without mustard. When Moe Wilensky was busy behind the counter, his special increased in price to 12 cents. Today, his grandson Bernard supervises the cafe, with the sandwich priced at $2.25. Moe Wilensky came to Montreal from Russia at the turn of the century. His grandson says the founder made a success of his café through "long, hard work. He put in 60-70-80 hours a week to make $20 a month."

Wilensky's has gone through a number of phases on the long, hard road to success. It began as a barbershop, evolved into a cigar store and then became a combined café and smoke shop, with a barber working in the back. It is still a small cafe, with only a dozen stools at the lunch counter, which has changed very little in nearly seven decades. Wilensky's was used as a set for the filming of Mordecai Richler's "The Apprenticeship of Duddy Kravitz."

In Richler's books, Wilensky's was called Moe's Cigar Store.

BEAUTY'S

In 1942, Hymie Sckolnick opened Beauty's and waited on tables himself. The restaurant, located at 93 Mount Royal West, remains extremely popular, and often has long lineups.

Little has changed in the restaurant's decor from the early 40s. For those who lived on the Main a generation ago, a visit to Beauty's is a step back in time. Beauty's is known for Jewish specialties, such as toasted bagels, cream cheese with lox (smoked salmon), and cheese blintzes.

MOISHE'S

Moishe's Steak House is named after the founder Moishe Lighter, who was 14, and on his own, when he came to Canada from Bessarabia. He first worked as a busboy in a restaurant called the "Roumanian Paradise". In 1938, aged 25, he used his savings to establish his own restaurant. Moishe's has an international reputation for its steaks—based on the beef (imported from the U.S.), the aging process and cooking techniques Lighter and his chefs developed.

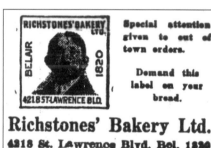

The Canadian Jewish Chronicle, Montreal, May 11, 1934

THE BAGEL: THE JEWISH HALO

The Montreal bagel is unique. Toronto and New York have their bagels, but they have a different texture and taste. One big reason for the difference is the fact that only Montreal still permits bakers to use wood-fired ovens. In other cities, they use gas-fired equipment.

Hyman Seligman is reputed to have started Montreal's first bagel bakery.

His Montreal Bagel Bakery was started around 1900. Using horse and wagon, Seligman delivered the Russian way—tied by the dozen with string. When Myer Lewkowitz, a survivor of several concentration camps, arrived in Montreal in 1950, he went to work for Seligman. When he had saved enough capital, he went into business with Jack Shlafman. They sold bagels from a pushcart, setting up their oven in a building entered from a lane immediately south of Schwartz's. When their partnership dissolved, they both set up competing ovens. This resulted in some temporary confusion. Both shops bore the name Fairmount Bagel Bakery, although Lewkowitz's was located on St. Viateur. The confusion ended when Shlafman died. Shlafman's son and grandson eventually reopened the Fairmount Bagel Bakery in the late 1980s. In his old age, Seligman—the doyen of the bagel bakers—regularly trudged, despite his 80-odd years, to St. Viateur street to buy his bagels there.

Emma and Myer Lewkowitz in their St. Viateur bagel bakery

Lewkowitz's bagels have an international reputation. The bakery received a call one evening, saying "Prince Charles would like to order 20 dozen bagels." The owner responded: "It's Saturday night, we're busy, so stop fooling around." An hour later, a fleet of limousines pulled up and a British naval officer marched into the store. I'm here," he announced grandly, "for Prince Charles' bagels." The clerk's reaction was brusque: "You'll have to wait like everybody else." It was, after all, a very busy night. The officer had to wait an hour while the limousines remained parked outside. Prince Charles, heir to the throne, was in Montreal Port aboard a naval warship, waiting patiently for Montreal bagels.

FROM THE YIDDISH "BEYGEL"

According to legend, the bagel was originated in 1683, in Vienna, when a Jewish baker wanted to thank the King of Poland for protecting his countrymen from Turkish invaders. The special hard roll he made was in the shape of a riding stirrup—Bugel in German—thus commemorating for all time the monarch's favourite pastime.

The bagel, from the Yiddish word "beygel", was the regular bread of Jews in eastern Europe, so it is not surprising that Jewish bakers brought them to America when they emigrated.

The shape of the bagel had great significance for Jews. They felt that it symbolized the eternal cycle of life and was believed to bring good luck. In the Old Country, bagels were frequently served at circumcisions, when a woman was in labour and during shivas (the seven-day period of mourning)—often with a hard-boiled egg. (The egg, again, symbolized eternity). The combination also, to the superstitious, warded off the evil eye.

Most bagel bakers today are not Jewish, but they function in the time-honoured way of the early bakers. The baker, with remarkable dexterity, quickly makes rings of risen dough, which are dipped into honey water for about five minutes. The bagel is the only bread product boiled before it is baked. An experienced baker can twist up to 1,000 bagels in an hour. White sesame seeds or black poppy seeds are added and rows of them are placed on a long wooden plank (a "shibba" in Yiddish) to be pushed into a wood-fired oven.

The famous Montreal cookbook, "A Treasure for my Daughter", published in 1950 by the Ethel Epstein Ein Chapter of Hadassah, states:

> "The first meal eaten by mourners on their return from the cemetery is hard boiled eggs and beigel. The roundness of the eggs signify the wheel of fortune, and the changes from happiness to unhappiness and back to happiness to which man is subject."

Don Bell, in his "Saturday Night at the Bagel Factory—winner of the Leacok award in 1972—wrote:

> "Hot, fresh bagels tumbling out of the oven like Jewish halos—the fragrance of life."

Restaurants competed briskly during the Depression years. In 1933, Manny Spinner, later Executive Director of the Jewish Cultural Association of Montreal, worked at Shaps, the soda fountain next door to the Mount Royal YMHA. Salmon sandwiches were 10 cents. Coffee was a nickel. An entire lunch, including soup, a main dish, dessert and coffee, was 49 cents. Spinner started working at the restaurant when he was 12, as a glass washer, for $3 a week. His fellow worker was Ben Weider, who later made his fortune in the fitness industry. Smoked meat sandwiches were 5 cents at Chenoy's, and two for 15 cents at Rogatkos. At the bakeries, rolls were 15 cents a dozen.

The Canadian Jewish Times, 1931

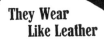

CHAPTER FIFTEEN

THE ISSUE IS EDUCATION
Fighting for Rights in a Christian Province

It was a red-letter day for the Pinsler family. Their son Jacob had won a scholarship to attend high school. It was 1901 and there were fees for attending high school—fees beyond the family's ability to pay. Unfortunately, the celebration ended with a formal letter from the Protestant School Board stating that Jacob Pinsler, honours student, was ineligible for the scholarship because his father was a tenant and not a property owner and therefore did not pay taxes to the School Board. Word got around. The neighbours were outraged. Who cares if the Pinslers rent, they said. They just don't want us in their schools.

The Pinsler scholarship case touched off a storm of controversy among Jews and Gentiles alike, and aroused the Jewish community to renew its demand for long-denied equal rights in the Quebec education system. The crisis triggered a 30-year campaign aimed at breaking the stranglehold of the Quebec School Act, the legislation denying Jewish children the legal right to attend school. It also sharply divided the community on whether Jewish students should go to Christian schools.

Pinsler was refused his scholarship at a time when the Jewish population was growing rapidly due to immigration and a high birth rate. Of 40 scholarship winners in Protestant schools that year, 10 were Jews. The Board was concerned that their schools would be overrun by Jewish students, with poor immigrant parents paying little, or nothing, in school taxes. However, more than money was involved; church leaders worried schools' Christian influence would be undermined by the presence of a large number of Jewish students. Many Christians were also opposed to having their children share schools with Jews. While the issue divided the Jewish community and the Protestants, too, the Catholics were quite clear: they did not want Jews in their schools. Jewish children had no option other than to attend Protestant schools where they were accommodated reluctantly.

In 1902, Montreal lawyer S.W. Jacobs took the Pinsler case to a Quebec City court, and lost. The court ruled that children of Jewish parents who were not rate-paying proprietors could not claim the right to attend Protestant schools or benefit from any scholarship program. Jewish children were attending school on sufferance—without any rights whatsoever. Jewish children were given Protestant religious instruction in schools where they were not permitted to observe Jewish holidays.

A LESSON IN RIGHTS

Until recent times, Jews had no actual legal rights to an education in Quebec. The 1841 Quebec School Act guaranteed education rights only to Roman Catholics and Protestants. In effect, Quebec was a Christian province. The British North America Act of 1867 was even more alarming to Jews. It constitutionally guaranteed the rights of Catholics and Protestants, and made no mention of Jews—their numbers insufficient to be deemed important. S.W. Jacobs turned to the Supreme Court of Canada to determine the legal rights of Jewish children to an education. The court verified the limitations.

The Montreal High School Class of 1922 (taken in 1919). Lavy Becker is in the bottom left of the photo; Louis Muhlstock is in the back row, 5th from the left; Max Wolofsky is in the back row, right.
(Canadian Jewish Congress National Archives, Montreal).

The Provincial Legislature, alarmed by all of this, in 1903 passed legislation, stating:

"Persons professing the Jewish religion shall for school purposes, be treated in the same manner as Protestants, and shall be subject to the same obligations and shall enjoy the same rights and privileges as the latter."

Furthermore, the Legislature declared:

"No pupil of the Jewish religion can be compelled to read or study any religious or devotional books or to take part in any religious exercises or devotions to which the father, mother, tutor or person having the care or maintenance of such pupil shall object."

THE SITUATION IS ACKNOWLEDGED UNFAIR

The Protestant School Board had won the Pinsler case, but it also acknowledged that justice had not been served. In 1903, a policy paper was issued by the board, and included the following guidelines:

— Jews would pay their school taxes to the Protestant "panel".

— Jewish children would not be compelled to take Christian religious instruction.

— It was conceded, that in terms of an education, "Jews shall be considered as Protestants with the same obligations, rights and privileges."

The Grade 7 class of Mount Royal School, early 1920's. The student population of this Protestant school was almost entirely Jewish during the 1920s and 1930s.
(Allan Raymond Collection, Jewish Public Library Archives)

Confirmation Class at Temple Emmanu-El, 1928. The Rabbi (back, centre) is Harry Joshua Stern.
(Allan Raymond Collection; Jewish Public Library Archives)

However, Jews still did not have the right to sit on school boards; it was a case of taxation without representation. Furthermore, the commitment to avoid exposing Jewish students to Christian teaching was frequently violated. Many students were forced to join in Christian prayers. One woman told the author that, in the 1950s, she attended a school where "more than ninety per cent" of the pupils were Jewish, but teachers still gave Christian religious instruction. In addition, parents could not keep their children home on Jewish holidays.

GROWING JEWISH ENROLLMENT

Jews, meanwhile, were flocking to schools, eager to absorb all the education they could afford. By 1914, 43.5% of the children in Protestant schools were Jewish. Nevertheless, the new arrangement functioned reasonably well until the 1920s, when the number of school children from Jewish families in the Protestant system rose to 12,000 out of a total enrollment of 32,000. At the high school level, there were more Jewish students than Protestant! Jewish parents were passionately committed to higher education, and were prepared to make sacrifices to that end.

A United Talmud Torah Class, 1934.
(Allan Raymond Collection, Jewish Public Library Archives)

Maxwell Goldstein (past president of the Federation) estimated in 1924 that Jews made up 90-100% of the enrollment in 12 to 15 large downtown Protestant schools. A leading spokesperson for the Protestant Board, Reverend Canon Elson I. Rexford, estimated that, in 1924, 13,594 Jewish children were attending Protestant schools. He figured the cost of teaching Jewish children at $837,240, whereas proceeds from school taxes on Jewish-owned property yielded, by his estimates, only $368,794. A *Canadian Jewish Chronicle* editorial countered that "labeling of Jewish ratepayers seems to have been based on some mysterious plan. Many a Jewish ratepayer has been set down either as a Protestant or Catholic." The *Chronicle* claimed that all Jews listed as Smith or Miller were registered as Protestant, while Pascal was categorized as Catholic. In other words, the Jewish contribution was greatly under-estimated.

MAKING CLASSES ALL-JEWISH AND SCHOOLS ALL-JEWISH

For many years, the policy of the Protestant School Board was to establish all-Jewish classes in some schools and where possible, as in the case of Baron Byng High School, make the entire school Jewish. However, there were no Jewish teachers in the high schools. In fact, of the 1,000 teachers employed by the Protestant Board, only 70 of them were Jewish. Nonetheless, the Protestants in 1921 asked the Provincial Government to overturn the 1903 legislation and wipe out even those minimal guarantees. In response, the Jewish community demanded that the Board employ a reasonable number of Jewish teachers and asked, furthermore, that Jews be made eligible for election to the school board and commissions.

PREMIER TASCHEREAU AND THE PROVINCIAL ROYAL COMMISSION

Liberal Quebec Premier Louis-Alexandre Taschereau shaped his reaction in consultation with the two Jewish Liberal members of the Legislative Assembly, Peter Bercovitch and Joseph Cohen. Taschereau heartily disliked racial and religious prejudice, and he wanted to see a deal made by moderate Protestants and Jews. At the same time, he made it clear he would not allow extremist Protestants to undermine Jewish rights. The Premier stated: "Jewish children have the same rights as Catholics and Protestants to receive education in schools which would not wound their religious sentiments." During hearings of a Provincial Royal Commission, formed to study the situation, the representative for the Protestant Board, Colonel J.J. Creelman, declared "It was impossib(le) (to) teach to Protestant children Protestantism, in a Protestant way, with Jewish teachers and in the presence of Jewish children." The Anglican bishop of Montreal, John Farthing, was concerned about the effect on the quality of Protestant education by the presence of Jewish children. "We have," he stated, "a distinct civilization to maintain which is based upon the Christian teaching." Inevitably, the Royal Commission's recommendations for a compromise arrangement were not acceptable to the many factions.

ADVOCATES FOR SEPARATE SCHOOLS

One of the most outspoken and influential opponents of having Jewish students in Christian schools, on any terms, was Hananiah Meir Caiserman, executive secretary of Canadian Jewish Congress, who charged:

"The Protestant school system implanted in the hearts of the Jewish children a Christian spirit...the same Christian spirit has reached into many of our homes."

The Jewish Community Council also advocated separate Jewish schools. Executive secretary, William Nadler, stated "Only by sending our children to school where the teaching of Judaism will play a prominent role, can we give to this country, a good Jew and a good Canadian."

JEWS WIN CONCESSIONS

In the end, money made the difference. When a Jewish faction called for a "third panel" that is, a neutral governing body to collect school taxes from Jews and fund a separate Jewish school system, the Protestant Board feared loss of revenue and compromised. Again, the compromise did not satisfy any of the dissenting groups. Nevertheless, the Protestant School Board became, in effect, a secular public school system open to all. Enrollment grew in the system as more Jews, other immigrants, and some Catholics switched to Protestant schools.

Teachers in 1931 at the Jewish People's School Mittelshule (l to r) Rifka Teitlebaum, Shirley Cohen, Mollie Schlossberg, Aron Schneiderman, Lehrer Dunsky and Gertie Kreisman. (Canadian Jewish Congress National Archives, Montreal).

UPTOWNERS VERSUS DOWNTOWNERS

The Jewish community remained split on the question of where Jewish children should go to school. On one side was the Uptowners, a group co-led by Peter Bercovitch, the first Jew to sit in the Quebec Assembly; Maxwell Goldstein, first President of the Jewish Federation; Michael Hirsch, President of the Montefiore Club, and Rabbi Nathan Gordon of Temple Emanu-El. They were against segregating Jewish students, fearing it would ghettoize them; they wanted the children to integrate comfortably into Canadian society.

The Downtown faction's leaders included lawyer Louis Fitch, Shloime Wiseman, Principal of the Jewish Folk School, and Rabbi Hirsch Cohen. They wanted a separate school system to strengthen the students' cultural identity.

The Downtowners literally did not speak the same language as the more established Jews. Most were recent immigrants from Eastern Europe and their first language was Yiddish. And they were poor—often painfully poor. However, they were proud of their Jewishness and energized the community.

The split surfaced in the *Montreal Gazette* when Downtowner Dr. A. Maxwell Lightstone wrote about the opposition:

"I can't for the life of me understand on what authority they base their claims as representing the Jews of Montreal regarding the School question. They belong to the Montefiore Club, the Shaar Hashomayim Synagogue and Temple Emanu-El. They have no direct interest in the Jewish community that send their children to the Protestant schools. I think the Jews living in the centre of the city and the north end know better what they need than those who live in the west end or Westmount."

On the other hand, Legislative Assembly member Peter Bercovitch wrote in a letter to the *Gazette*:

"I am opposed to separate schools. I do not want separate schools in this province. But I come from a proud race, and if my Protestant friends, the Protestant population of this province, feel they no longer want to carry on with us, I will be the first to ask for our own schools."

JEWISH SEPARATE SCHOOLS ARE ESTABLISHED

Jewish schooling appeared in Montreal late in the nineteenth century. It consisted of a number of independent programs run by various individuals, synagogues, and institutions. The first official Jewish school was the Talmud Torah, founded in 1896. It was a religious school providing afternoon instruction in Hebrew and English. As Talmud Torahs grew in number, they developed the first Jewish school system, The United Talmud Torahs (1917). Two secular afternoon schools were established—the Peretz School in 1913 and the Jewish People's School in 1914. In 1928, Jewish People's School opened the first Jewish day school. It was a secular school teaching in Yiddish, Hebrew, and English. The weekly fee was ten cents, and when a family enrolled three children, the discounted charge was 25 cents. The first school was in two rooms in a house at 502 St. Urbain Street. As there was no budget for staff, teachers worked without pay. These pioneer educators were dedicated and desperately poor. Some of them sold eggs to make a living.

MAKING A COMMITMENT

In the 1970s, the Jewish Federation made a powerful commitment to Jewish Education, declaring that every child had a right to such an education, no matter the financial circumstances of its parents. Quebec's first Jewish cabinet Minister, Victor Goldbloom, participated in negotiations leading to government funding of separate Jewish schools. Quebec is the only province assisting Jewish day schools. The substantial funding is directed to general education costs and does not apply to the Jewish curriculum. The issue of separate schooling remains contentious.

THE HIGHEST PROPORTION OF CHILDREN IN JEWISH SCHOOLS

Essential to the strength of the Montreal Community is the fact that the city has the highest proportion of students in North America receiving a Jewish education. A Jewish Education Council (JEC) was created in 1975 as an experiment, to strengthen the separate school system. Two years later, the JEC became a permanent organization. In the 1999 Federation local services budget of $15,563,746, Education and Culture was allocated $4.3-million.

CHAPTER SIXTEEN

THE FEDERATION
Jewish resiliency during the Great Depression

It was a crisis meeting dubbed "Save the Federation." The union of 14 service agencies, in 1923, was only six years old, but found itself in financial difficulties. In the wake of the First World War, a severe economic depression gripped Montreal. Many businesses had failed and thousands were jobless. Mrs. Esther (Ogulnik) Elkin electrified the meeting when she called on Jewish women to forgo tradition and go to Synagogue for the High Holidays wearing "last year's hat." Declared Mrs. Elkin: "Take the money you would spend on a new hat, and give it to the Federation." The suggestion spread like wildfire through the community and donations increased to the point that the Federation could survive. At the synagogue that Rosh Hashonah, as the shofar (ram's horn) was sounded to welcome the New Year, virtually every woman proudly wore a new hat.

TIMELINE—1917-1934
1917. The Federation of Jewish Philanthropies is established.
1917. Mortimer B. Davis is knighted by King George V in recognition of his philanthropic activities.
1917. Five separate Talmud Torahs are merged to form United Talmud Torahs of Montreal.
1917. Samuel W. Jacobs is elected MP.
1917. Peter Bercovitch is elected member of the Quebec Legislature.
1918. The Council of Jewish Women is founded in Montreal.
1919. Founding meeting of Canadian Jewish Congress. Lyon Cohen is the first Chairman.
1919. The Young Women's Hebrew Association (Y.W.H.A.) is formed through the merger of the Young Women's Association and the Welcome Club of Ladies.
1920. Jewish Immigrant Aid Society (JIAS) is formed.
1920. Camp B'nai B'rith is formed.
1922. First high school class opened by Jewish People's school in Montreal.
1926. The Old People's Home is founded on Esplanade Avenue.
1927. The first Old Age Pension Act is passed.
1927. Joseph Cohen, K.C. elected member of the Quebec Provincial Legislature.
1928. First Jewish Day School class opened by Jewish People's Schools.
1929. The Great Depression begins.
1929. Mortimer Davis building of Y.M.H.A. erected.
1929. Founding of the Jewish Laurentian Fresh Air Camp.
1931. Quebec has 60,087 Jews; 94% state that their mother tongue is Yiddish.
1931. The new Mount Sinai Sanitarium is opened.
1934. Canadian Jewish Congress is reorganized.
1934. The Jewish General Hospital is declared officially open.

The special 1919 issue of The Canadian Jewish Chronicle greeting delegates to the founding meeting of Canadian Jewish Congress.
(Canadian Jewish Congress National Archives)

Maxwell Goldstein, K.C., founding President of the Montreal Federation in 1916.

The creation, in 1917, of the Federation of Jewish Philanthropies had set the Montreal Jewish Community on a new course—a start to modernization of community services, and development of a central body to plan and coordinate services. This effort was strengthened by the growing muscle of a united fund-raising effort.

In the years following establishment of the Federation, the Community experienced comparatively rapid change—with new agencies appearing, old agencies disappearing and still others merging. On the national scene, in 1919, the Canadian Jewish Congress was formed as the "parliament" of Canadian Jewry. A resolution passed at the opening meeting triggered formation of the Jewish Immigrant Aid Society with the cooperation of the Romanian, Ukrainian and Polish Verbands. JIAS developed into a powerful instrument for assisting immigrants, greeting them on arrival, assisting them in the first difficult months of adjustment and making authoritative submissions to various levels of governments on behalf of newcomers. By this time, the Jewish Community had grown to 46,000—an increase of 18,000 in just nine years!

However, the 1920s were different than the previous decade. War had left a volatile world economy and inflation was rampant. As conditions worsened, families tightened their belts. Despite the Depression and its devastation, the Jewish community continued to flourish and realized many important projects, such as hospitals, the "Y" and a senior's home. Women's efforts began to be recognized as their own division of Federation was formed. Woman began to assume increasingly important leadership roles. With a spirit of resiliency and cooperation, the community continued to create and to build its social network and cultural institutions despite hard times.

A FEDERATION IS FORMED

In 1916, the Federation of Jewish Philanthropies was incorporated in the Quebec Legislature. Canada had its first Jewish Federation. The Federation was founded to bring a sense of order into an increasingly complex scene, to combine and rationalize fund-raising efforts, to "co-ordinate the various charitable bodies,

(A) Mortimer B. Davis, honorary chairman; (B) Mark Workman, honorary chairman; (C) Garfield A. Berlinsky, executive director. 1, B. J. Hayes; 2, Sol. Z. Fels; 3, Dr. A. P. Ship; 4, I. Lande; 5, I. H. Kaplan; 6, P. Popliger; 7, N. L. Schloman; 8, Wm. Albert; 9, David Blumer; 10, Paul Ogulnik; 11, P. B. Glickman; 12, Fromson; 13, L. Lehrer; 14, M. J. Heillig; 15, I. L. Berman; 16, Max Goldberg; 17, Hiram Levy; 18, Edgar M. Berliner; 19, A. Kellnor; 20, Harry Sessenwein; 21, Dr. E. C. Levine; 22, H. M. Levinoff; 23, J. Elkin; 24, S. Vineberg; 25, T. Glickman; 26, A. Harry Wolfe; 27, H. S. Sourkes; 28, D. M. Chorlton; 29, J. N. Neuman; 30, Sam Holstein; 31, Lawrence Tannenbaum; 32, H. E. Herschorn; 33, Louis Lewis; 34, S. M. Ogulnik; 35, H. M. Levine; 36, A. J. Livinson; 37, A. Rudolph; 38, Douglas Mire; 39, P. Adelstein; 40, Louis Vineberg; 41, B. Rubin; 42, H. N. Friedman, 43, David Kirsch; 44, H. E. Davis; 45, Julius L. Gittleson; 46, A. D. Caltiel; 47, J. Duchow; 48, M. Rittenberg; 49, Louis Vinberg; 50, I. Bald; 51, J. Ginsberg; 52, Alan J. Hart; 53, J. L. Gittleson; 54, Y. Certcoff; 55, C. L. Sommer; 56, L. H. Jacobs; 57, Arthur Schalek; 58, M. Bernstein; 59, S. Moscovitch; 60, A. A. Markus; 61, M. Markus; 62, Mike Bernstein; 63, B. Wilanski; 64, Lionel Coviensky; 65, Abe Rill; 66, David Gordon; 67, C. Feigin; 68, Herman Singer.

Leadership of the 1917 Federation Campaign (Canadian Jewish Congress National Archives, Montreal)

with a view to obtaining the greatest efficiency with the least possible expense and labour." Essentially it was a response to the community's explosive but uncoordinated growth of organizations. Author John Irwin Cooper, in his 1969 History of Montreal, states "the success of the Federation was an object lesson to other groups which, like the Jews, experienced the loss of homogeneity and the disappearance of a well-defined area of settlement. The Federation idea originated in New York, when half-a-dozen benevolent societies were merged to form the "United Hebrew Charities". (There are now 800 Jewish federations in the United States and Canada.)

The initial campaign on behalf of the new Montreal Federation ran from Jan. 2-5, headquartered in the Montefiore Club, and raised—despite snowstorms every day—the impressive sum of $127,000—$56,000 more than the Federation's member agencies had raised, on their own, the year before.

In the published list of gifts for that first, 1917, campaign, is the contribution of one dollar given by "Master E. Barkoff." Twelve-year-old Edward Barkoff had given up lunches for an entire week to collect a dollar in nickels, dimes and one quarter. He became President of the Federation, 1959-1961.

THE TWELVE FOUNDING AGENCIES
The twelve founding agencies of Federation were The Baron de Hirsch Institute, Mount Sinai Sanitorium, Ladies Hebrew Benevolent Society, Herzl Dispensary and Hospital, the Montreal Hebrew Orphans' Home, the Montreal Hebrew Sheltering Home, the Ladies Jewish Endeavour Sewing Society, the Young Women's Hebrew Association, the Beth Israel Day Nursery and Infants' Home, Hebrew Ladies Aid Society and the Friendly League of Jewish Women. (By 2000, only two of these organizations continue to exist as independent agencies—the Baron de Hirsch Institute and Mount Sinai, now a specialized hospital. The others have either disappeared or been folded into other organizations.)

In the first Federation fund-raising effort, the Trades Divisions included Rags and Junk, Hat Manufacturers, Retail Clothing and Gentlemen's Furnishings, Manufacturers of Ladies Coats and Suits, Export, Wines and Liquors, Ladies' Ready-to-Wear, Clothing Manufacturers, Cigar Manufacturers, Uniform Manufacturers, Lawyers and Leather Coat Manufacturers.

Originally, the Federation was housed in the Herzl Dispensary on St. Urbain Street and 90% of the Jewish Community lived within a mile of that location.

CREATING HOSPITALS

In 1913, Mount Sinai Hospital was built, in the Laurentians, to provide free treatment to victims of tuberculosis—a common disease among new immigrants in those years. Founders included Sir Mortimer B. Davis, Jacob A. Jacobs, M.A. Vineberg, Ascher Pierce and the estate of S. Wolsey.

The Mount Sinai Sanitorium, in Ste. Agathe, Quebec, built in 1913.

The Jewish women of Montreal, in 1914, established a new medical facility, the Hebrew Maternity Hospital, with Dr. J.R. Goodall as Chairman of the Medical Board; physicians included Doctors Eidlow, Fishberg, Wieseman, Schachter and Tannenbaum. The idea for the hospital originated with Mrs. Toba Kaplan, affectionately known as the "Greene Rebitzin" or the "Greene Yidene." She was the person who envisioned and worked hard to make the maternity hospital a reality. It was intended to care for poor and expectant Jewish mothers and their newborn children.

Toba Kaplan, known as the "Greene Rebitzin", who strove to establish health services for the Montreal Jewish community.
(Canadian Jewish Congress National Archives)

And Mrs. Kaplan (the "greene" indicated she was a new-comer; Rebitzin denoted the wife of a Rabbi) was at the forefront of those seeking and collecting money for the planned institution.

She also lived up to the best Jewish tradition of "Matan be-seyter"—that is, giving to charity in secret. When Mrs. Allan "Lucy" Bronfman disclosed they intended to name a ward at the Jewish General Hospital in her honour, she declined and urged that Sir Herbert Samuel, a prominent British diplomat, who was Jewish, be honoured instead.

THE CONTRIBUTION MADE BY WOMEN

It is impossible to describe, accurately, the enormous contribution made by women to the development of the community. The women were most aware of human distress; they saw the difficult living circumstances of the more vulnerable segments of the community. They often suggested how services could be modified, or even originated. When an organization was formed, the men

Turning the first sod for the Jewish General Hospital. (Canadian Jewish Congress National Archives, Montreal).

assumed leadership positions (unless it was an organization— like the Hebrew Ladies Aid Society—identifying women as founders) because, at that time, women were not expected to be in the forefront of the community.

The development of medical facilities represents an excellent example. The women originated the Hebrew Maternity Hospital— responding to apparent need—and a Committee of the Hospital, in 1925, suggested that funds be raised for a "Jewish General Hospital."

The Jewish community was ready to make its biggest step forward in terms of the health of its constituents. A study, to determine whether the Jewish community needed a general hospital, estimated the shortage of hospital beds in Montreal at 2,000. Allan Bronfman and Michael Hirsch co-chaired the Campaign in 1929, seeking $800,000. Despite the onset of the Great Depression, the campaign raised double its goal, and the 205-bed hospital opened in 1930.

The hospital was nonsectarian and its services were available to all "irrespective of race, creed and religion". This was in sharp contrast with the employment discrimination Jewish doctors and nurses had encountered in many non-Jewish institutions.

While everyone who came to its doors was treated, the Jews looked on the Jewish General Hospital as their own personal institution. It was, and is, referred to as "The Jewish." Its first Executive Director, Dr. Samuel S. Cohen, was brought in from New York. He was patrolling the halls one day, ensuring that everything was going well, when he encountered a Jewish woman visiting her husband, outside the posted hours. When Dr. Cohen admonished her, she responded, with spirit, "Rules! Rules! If I wanted rules, I'd go to the Royal Victoria Hospital."

Israel's future Prime Minister Golda Meir (then Myerson) on a visit to Montreal in 1929 to meet with local Zionists. (Canadian Jewish Congress National Archives, Montreal)

HONOUR THY MOTHER AND FATHER

Services to the elderly were modified with the merger of two older agencies—the Montreal Hebrew Old People's and Sheltering Home and the B. and S. Steinhouse Home—to become a new Old People's Home on Esplanade Avenue. For the first time, the Provincial Government helped—donating $50,000 towards the cost. An important new development for older people, and their families, was the introduction, in 1927, of federal old age pensions. The initial payments amounted to $20 a month, a useful sum at that time; it was enough to enable some seniors to rejoin their families, at home.

WALL STREET WOES

In 1929, the New York stock market collapsed—devastating the western world's trading system. Canada, with its heavy dependence on foreign trade, was particularly hard hit. Jews in Montreal shared in the grief.

Corner stores closed...factories shut down...homes were lost when mortgage payments could not be met. Many Jews involved in small commercial enterprises, or in handicraft operations, quickly went under.

Wages were lowered for those fortunate enough to keep their jobs.

Small shops extended as much credit as they could and furniture and jewelry stores emphasized low weekly payments. Agents called on customers once a week for payments of 25 or 50 cents. People moved out of their flats in the middle of the night when they could not pay the rent; others were dispossessed and found themselves, homeless, on the street with their furniture strewn over the lawn and sidewalk.

In 1931, with the help of a Provincial government grant of $125,000, a new Mount Sinai Sanitorium was opened in the Laurentians. In 1918, in its earlier building, the Sanitorium housed 23 patients. Thirteen years later, it was attempting to care for 57 patients in the same space.

A WOMEN'S DIVISION IS FORMED

The Federation's Campaign was strengthened in 1931 when, with Saidye Bronfman as first Chair, a women's division was formed. This was the beginning of a new visibility for women of the community, and it began when they made their own gifts—in their own names—to philanthropies, rather than having their gifts lumped in with that of their husband or their family.

Women were an increasingly important part of the household economy. While most Jewish women stayed home, many of them found work to help their families in difficult economic times. More than half the employed women were store clerks and salespeople. Many women working in the manufacure of clothing took bundles home with them and would work their sewing machines, clean and cook, and take care of their children. They had little or no trade union protection.

A 1931 study showed one in four working Jews were "independent business people and managers." Another 30% were clerks and salespeople. Only 5% were professionals at that time.

COMMUNITY DOING RELATIVELY WELL

The Jewish community was doing relatively well even as the Great Depression shattered the economy. A 1931 Federal census monograph stated:

"The Hebrews are the outstanding commercial race in Canada, from the point of view of occupational distribution within their own ranks, with five times the proportion of gainfully occupied men and two and one-half times the proportion of women than the population as a whole being so engaged."

In 1931, a deep Depression year, more than 7,200 Jews had manufacturing jobs and of this number, nearly 5,500 were in the needle trades and another 582 in the closely related fur and leather industries. Manufacturing provided jobs for more than 83% of the Jewish working force at this difficult time. The work did not pay well, but did provide, barely, a living wage at a time when more than 30% of Quebecers were unemployed. As the Depression continued to stifle the economy, employers continued to lower wages, or reintroduce piecework. Time spent at the work bench escalated to as much as 60 hours a week.

Her father had been out of work now for two years. Every day in his shabby clothes, he went from building to building..."I'll do anything". He cleaned offices...ran messages...anything. They paid him ten cents...a quarter...half a dollar from a kind-hearted janitor.

By 1932, one-third of Montreal's residents were on relief; the dependence of jobless Jews was proportionally less than that of the broader community, but still crushing for the community. The burden of helping the poor grew rapidly and soon exceeded the capacity of community agencies to meet minimum needs. When a Jewish-owned store lost its tenant, it became a kosher soup

"The average Jewish merchant in Canada is a small retail storekeeper, working himself with the help of some other members of his family or at most one or two hired assistants. There are several reasons for this constant concentraton of Jews in the small, retail trade. Firstly, the immigrant community represented a distinct market for the sale of goods and services which members of that community could best satisfy. Moreover, the small, retail trade required relatively small amounts of capital and provided the owner with a measure of independence in his economic affairs. The most prevalent Jewish retail outlets in Montreal were general stores, groceries, meat markets, bakeries, furniture stores and clothing stores. Among these transplanted Shtetl people trust was therefore common in employment in stores as clerks or as principals."
Louis   Rosenberg, "The Jew in Canada", 1931

kitchen. Shabby men, faceless, stood in line quietly waiting for bread and soup.

During the Depression, one man recalls being sent once a week to Schwartz's Delicatessen to buy five cents of "scraps". The countermen provided the boy with enough bone shavings to feed the entire family. He thought, for years, that scraps referred to a particular cut of meat.

By 1933, 23% of the Canadian labour force was unemployed, compared to 3% in 1929.

EVERYONE AFFECTED

The Depression affected virtually everyone. With widespread layoffs in business and industry, demand dropped sharply. People had less money to spend and, therefore, bought less; it was a downward spiral that ran for years. A pound of meat selling for 22 cents in 1913 had cost 36 cents in the peak year of 1929 and declined to 20 cents in 1936. It is important to note that, for those who continued to work—and that was always 70% or more of the work-force—things often were better than in pre-Depression days. Prices declined and the buying power of their dollar increased.

Depression Soup kitchen in Montreal. In addition to the food centres, mostly for unemployed, homeless men, there were kosher kitchens set up by the Jewish Community to serve observant Jews and others. (Jewish Public Library Archives)

The Baron de Hirsch Institute, as breadlines lengthened, resumed the task of finding jobs for its clients. In 1931, about 1,346 applicants asked for help in finding work, and the Institute was successful in placing about half. It was even tougher in 1932, when 1,925 registered but only one-third found placement. The community was not ready, at this time, to venture into an agency exclusively devoted to job-finding and vocational training. This only occurred when thousands of servicemen were demobilized in 1945, and the Jewish Vocational Service was created.

CAMPAIGN '34

The Federation Campaign in 1934 talked bluntly about "Fear":

"The ghastly spectres conjured up by hunger...march with our poverty stricken people in their desperate, frenzied search for a few paltry pennies that will buy bread to keep body and soul together..."

The "Y" served as a meeting place for the poor and unemployed. Recreational and educational programs were designed to help young people overcome anxieties about their future. The "Y"

Searching the newspaper for job possibilities, in the Depression year 1933.
(Lithography by Ernst Newman—from the art collection of Atara and Murray Marmor.)

opened an evening High School—staffing it with volunteers from McGill University.

The Depression aroused widespread opposition to immigration, coincident with the rise to power of Adolf Hitler and the Nazis in Germany, and their open oppression of the Jewish population. About 4,000 Jewish immigrants a year had been allowed into Canada from 1923 until 1931, when Ottawa closed the country's doors to all but British and American migrants.

Every corner had its tiny confectionary store. "Our's was Sam's at Esplanade and St. Viateur." A treat was a "scrapbag".... a crumpled kraft bag filled with broken candy. They cost two cents. Ice cream cones were also two cents. Wilensky's was the place to go for comic books. They were two cents—unless the cover was missing. Then they went for a penny each.

Meanwhile, another major change in the community was the continuing increase in the number of working Jewish women. The proportion of Jewish women with jobs had been well below the Canadian average in 1921 but by 1931, in the depths of the Depression, their participation was the highest of any ethnic group at 22% of all women over age ten. In the face of unemployment or lower wages, families often required two jobs to get by.

At the same time, Jews were flocking to schools. Jewish attendance at public high schools was far above the national average. Jewish enrollment at universities climbed steadily, particularly in the faculties of medicine, law, dentistry, and pharmacy. In 1935-36, despite quotas (McGill University required Jewish students to have higher marks than non-Jews during pre-World War II years), more than 14% of Canadian medical students were Jewish, as were 17 per cent of students in dentistry.

Many of them would graduate in time to serve in the Second World War—and preparations for that confrontation stimulated the economy and ended the Great Depression.

HIRING THEIR OWN

The Depression, if anything, led to increased discrimination against Jews in terms of job opportunities. Nevertheless, because the community's responsibility had been to do everything possible for its own, the proportion of Jews working despite depressed conditions was higher than the national average. Denied equal opportunities, Jews were more likely to go into business for themselves, and the availability of interest-free assistance from the

Etching/drypoint of man gathering wood to make a fire.
(by Moses Reinblatt)

Hebrew Free Loan permitted many to launch enterprises during these hard times.

RESCUING JEWISH WAR ORPHANS

On November 24, 1919, more than 30,000 Montrealers participated in the largest demonstration in the history of Jewish Montreal to

The Montreal Daily Star.

'CANADA'S GREATEST NEWSPAPER'

TUESDAY, NOVEMBER 25, 1919.

PROTEST AND REPROACH.

IN solemn protest against massacres of Jews in Eastern Europe, many thousands of the Jewish people made pilgrimage through the streets of Montreal yesterday. The city has never witnessed a more touching spectacle than this mourning procession, which was but one several conducted in America.

Those who take merely a superficial interest in world affairs, now that the great war is may well be recalled by this mass protest realization that all is not well. It is reproach to civilization that the victory the democratic nations has not brought Jewish race its right to peace and from outrage. Never was there a more

JEWS HERE HELD MOURNING PARADE

Resolution Asks Help to End Massacres of Countrymen

Large banners with deep bands of black were carried by the Jews yesterday in their march to mourn the dead in Ukraine and to try and impress on the Canadian public of the atrocious state of affairs in Eastern Europe. "We mourn the murdered in Ukraine" was the wording of the first banner carried. It was written in white letters on a black background. The doleful strains of the band added a touch of pathos to the whole scene. Mothers with their babes in arms marched along with, in some cases, the aged and infirm. The small school children who generally during a procession march along with smiling faces and youthful antics preserved an attitude of extreme reverence during the entire route of parade. Another banner which bore the biblical "Thou shalt not kill"

LA PARADE DES ISRAELITES A MONTREAL

WE MOURN THE MURDERED IN UKRAINE

protest the murders of an estimated 100,000 Ukrainian and Russian Jews. *The Montreal Daily Star*, on Nov. 25, 1919, reported:

"In solemn protest against massacres of Jews in Eastern Europe, many thousands of the Jewish people made pilgrimage through the streets of Montreal yesterday. The city has never witnessed a more touching spectacle."

From 1919-1921, in the aftermath of the Russian Revolution, more than 1,200 pogroms took place in the Ukraine alone. Entire Jewish communities were destroyed, and 100,000 Jewish children were orphaned.

Many survivors of the pogroms ultimately found refuge in Montreal—often after wandering destitute for months in eastern Romania.

Ukrainian orphans destined for adoption in Montreal, 1919. (Canadian Jewish Congress Archives)

In 1920, the Jewish War Orphans Committee, dedicated to rescuing Jewish orphans and bringing them to Canada, was formed under the leadership of Mrs. Lillian Freiman, of Ottawa. (Mrs. Freiman had previously organized Canadian Hadassah in 1919, and was in 1934 the first Canadian Jewish woman named an Officer of the Order of the British Empire.) Mrs. Arthur Meighen, wife of the prime minister, agreed to be honorary president of the War Orphans Committee. The Canadian government granted permission for 200 to enter the country. Ultimately, 146 children were rescued and brought to Canada. Montrealers Hirsch Hershman and Dr. J. Levitt journeyed to Europe to escort the first group of orphans to Montreal.

As more orphans arrived in the city, Hershman made ad hoc arrangements for finding them homes. On Fridays, he would take an orphan by the hand and walk up and down Esplanade Street, through the heart of the Jewish community, looking for a suitable parent. In this remarkable way, Hershman obtained homes for more than 100 children. He even adopted a little girl and brought her home without first advising his wife! On one occasion, while trying to spot a suitable parent for an eight-year-old orphan named Yankel, who was nervously clutching his hand, Hershman spotted a man named Abe Cooperberg. "You won't regret it," Hershman assured the wary Cooperberg. Many years later, an elderly Hershman was referred to an eye specialist named Dr. Cooperberg. The doctor immediately recognized Hershman and examined him without charge. Hershman, telling friends about the incident, did not focus on the role he had played in saving Yankel Cooperberg's life. Instead, he chuckled over his good luck in saving $25.

CHAPTER SEVENTEEN

THE MERCHANT PRINCES
From Pushcart to Pecuniary Prominence

He first sold goods from a pushcart. Then Herman Reitman, an immigrant from Romania, opened a shop in 1909 to sell groceries. Later, with two partners, he handmade coats and suits at the back of a store on St. Lawrence Boulevard. In 1926, Reitman took the plunge—opening a woman's retail clothing store on Ste. Catherine Street. He was so successful that, four years later, he was operating a chain of five Reitman's stores—with four sons in management positions. When someone suggested opening a sixth branch, Herman asked: "But who would run it? I have no more sons."

The tremendous wave of immigration inundating Montreal around the turn of the century included some names destined to become household words for Jews and non-Jews alike. Among the poor families reaching the city during this period were Reitmans, Pascals, Steinbergs, and Cummings. Each of these families was to build commercial empires in Quebec, in Canada, and in some instances, internationally. They created brand recognition magic that crossed the boundaries of ethnicity. Steinberg's was the word for groceries, Pascal's for hardware, Reitman's for ladies' fashions. These families, painfully poor, emerged from the shtetls of Eastern Europe without capital or skills, but with a storehouse of resilience and determination. They found themselves in Montreal at a time of tremendous economic growth and opportunity. They had families with mouths to feed and nothing to lose. Second-generation Jews, such as Mortimer B. Davis, built empires on the foundations developed by their fathers and grandfathers.

THE REITMANS

The Reitmans' success was remarkable. They had only one money-losing year—1933, at the bottom of the Depression, when the company lost $500. From the quintet of Montreal stores, they spread across Quebec, then Canada. The company started out selling lingerie and hosiery, and later added dresses. One of Herman's grandsons, Cyril Reitman, says the company was successful because of a very simple formula: they offered women the best possible quality, for the lowest possible price. Reitman's built a reputation of scrupulous honesty with both customers and suppliers. By the year 2000, Reitman's was Canada's largest ladies' apparel specialty chain. The company, with Herman's great-grandson Jeremy Reitman as President, operated several major chains in addition to the namesake company and had a total of 588 stores; in the year ending January, 2000, it had sales of $477 million.

THE PASCALS

Two Community giants—Arthur Pascal (l), founder-President of the Jewish Community Foundation of Montreal, and Allan Bronfman, co-chairman of the Campaign to establish the Jewish General Hospital.

Jacob Pascal, an immigrant glazier, established Canada's largest hardware business. Jacob opened his first store, in 1903, in the St. Lawrence market. He worked hard—unlocking the door each morning at six, for the convenience of tradesmen who needed supplies for the day's work. The store remained open until 11 p.m. At peak, Pascal's operated sixteen hardware stores and two furniture outlets, and had 3,400 employees.

Three of Jacob's sons, Max, Arthur and Cecil and two sons-in-law, Martin Levine and Sydney Glazer, served as general chairmen of the Combined Jewish Appeal. It was an extraordinary family contribution. In addition, the family always made an exceptionally large annual gift to the community.

Arthur Pascal, a decorated captain in World War II, was a Jewish community leader with great loyalty to Quebec. After the pro-separatist Parti Québecois assumed power in the 1960s, Pascal said: "We came here with very little, and this country and this province have been good to us. When things looked hard, and people were leaving, I felt that, we, as an important Jewish family, had a special responsibility to stay."

The Pascal's hardware empire folded in the late 1980s due to a failure to keep pace with marketing techniques. Pascal's continued to have its clerks serve customers, decades after competitors introduced self-service, which reduced costs.

THE STEINBERGS

As her husband was a religious scholar who did not actively support the family, Hungarian-born Ida Steinberg started her own business with $200 in savings. In 1917, she opened the first grocery store, at 4419 St. Lawrence Boulevard. Ida was determined to "give customers a little more than they expect." Her sons and daughters worked in the store, or made deliveries after school. Sam Steinberg was 12 when the store was

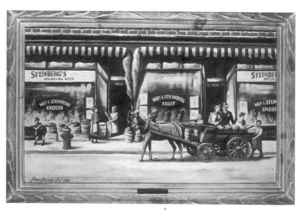

Painting of the original Steinberg's grocery store, 1917. (Canadian Jewish Congress National Archives)

opened, and by age 14, he knew he would spend his life in food retailing. The teenager expanded his mother's store by renting the premises next door. By the time he was 25, Sam Steinberg was president of a chain of eight grocery stores. In 1933, in the pit of the Depression, he opened a tenth store—the first featuring self-service. The revolutionary marketing technique was the result of poor planning. Sam Steinberg found that the new facility he had rented was too narrow to accommodate service counters. In desperation, he removed them, and let customers make their own selections. Until then, virtually all grocery stores were "full-service." A clerk would dart from shelf to shelf to gather the customer's order. Steinberg cut out delivery and made his operation cash and carry with prices as much as 20% lower than the competition. In 1937, he opened two innovative supermarkets, the first in Canada with separate coolers for meat, dairy products, and produce. He also pioneered the use of cellophane packaging. Steinberg originated the concept of aisles with arrows to indicate and facilitate traffic flow. Another Steinberg innovation that drew crowds was the introduction of parking lots.

American, as well as Canadian, grocers came to study his ingenious merchandising techniques. Sam always insisted on top quality. When company executives convinced him they had to carry eggs other than grade "A" large, Sam gave in—but insisted they "...charge lower-than-market prices for grade 'B'." The Steinberg empire ultimately comprised 224 supermarkets, as well as 32 Miracle Marts in Quebec and Ontario, and 200 restaurants across Canada. They had 26,000 employees and sales of $2.5 billion. Only Bell Canada had more employees than Steinberg's among private concerns in Quebec.

Sam Steinberg's daughter Mitzi Dobrin was the first Jewish woman appointed to the Board of Directors of the Royal Bank of Canada. Steinberg's were ahead of their time in accepting the French Fact. The company recruited francophone university graduates in the 1960s. In 1965, Steinberg's made French the working language in its Quebec operations—a dozen years before it became law. Arnold Steinberg, an influential business executive and nephew of Sam, recalls with delight getting up at 2 a.m. to accompany his father, Nathan Steinberg, on his regular morning jaunt to the Bonsecours Market, in Old Montreal, to purchase fresh fruits and vegetables for the stores. Nathan Steinberg did all his dealings in French. Premier René Levesque, shortly after his election to power in 1976, told Mitzi Steinberg Dobrin, at a reception, "You're one of the few anglophones who doesn't have a poisoned mind."

Sam Steinberg died in 1978, and the family decided to sell out after a highly publicized split developed among the three sisters and their husbands. Mitzi Steinberg Dobrin, wife of former company president Melvyn Dobrin, sued her sisters—Marilyn Cobrin and Evelyn Alexander—for control. To settle the dispute, the company was sold in 1989 for $1.8 billion, but the new operators had no experience in grocery retailing and the company folded. Despite the nostalgia of loyal customers, the name Steinberg—a name synonymous with grocery retailing for almost two generations—disappeared.

THE BROWNS

When Benjamin Brownstein opened a small department store in 1937, he found that French customers had trouble pronouncing his name—so he abbreviated it to Brown. Brown's Credit House on St. Lawrence Boulevard carried everything but hardware and food on four floors. In 1940, he began to specialize in shoes—opening a store on Ste. Catherine Street West. When fire destroyed the first shop in 1954, the family decided to change their merchandising policy and became a retailer of high quality fashion footwear. To stock their first new shop—opened in 1959 in the Rockland Shopping Centre in the Town of Mount Royal—the Brownsteins journeyed to Spain, Italy and France, purchasing for their new shop the finest European shoes. Rockland remains the flagship store and, with 7,700 square feet, is the largest of the 30 Brown's stores scattered across Canada from Quebec City west to Vancouver. Brown's also has installations in major stores of the Bay and Holt Renfrew, and operates four shoe shops in Chicago. Sales exceed $65 million annually. Two Brownstein brothers— Morty and Harold—have chaired the community's annual Combined Jewish Appeal. Morty Brownstein has led highly successful fund-raising efforts on behalf of the Jewish General Hospital.

THE CUMMINGS

The Cummings family arrived in Canada late in the nineteenth century. The family patriarch, David Cummings, did not have a good head for business. He opened a shoe shop in Saint John, N.B. It failed. He moved to New England at the same time as his neighbour, Louis B. Mayer (later of Metro-Goldwyn-Mayer Motion Pictures) and tried operating a Nickelodeon—an early movie picture theatre, where the charge was five cents. However, that also was not successful. Meantime, sons Nathan, born in 1896, and Maxwell, in 1898, became involved in various family enterprises in New England. At ages 12 and 14, respectively, they were forced to quit school and help support the family. In the early 1920s, the Cummings moved to Montreal, where their second shoe store did better (they called it, brazenly, Eaton's Shoes, borrowing the name of one of Canada's most important department stores at that time). The boys then made a fortuitous mistake in judgement. They decided to expand the business and rent a property. It proved to be too large for them, so they partitioned it and rented the smaller facility for more than they were paying for the entire building. The Cummings family thus entered the real estate business, which boomed in the housing shortage of the post-World War II period. When grandsons Jack and Bob returned from military service, the family built 1,000 homes, each sold for $100 down. The thousand units were snapped up in two hours! From housing, the family expanded into office buildings and shopping centres. In the 1970s, they sold much of their real estate to the Trizec Corporation. Today Maxwell Cummings and Sons is a corporate umbrella of merchant banking and real estate enterprises.

NATHAN CUMMINGS BAKES PIES AND BUILDS SUBMARINES

Meanwhile, Nathan Cummings, Maxwell's older brother, was after bigger game. He started his business career as a clerk in his father's shoe store but by age 21 was manufacturing his own footwear. He set up an importing firm, specializing in tea and coffee; he also bought and sold a small company manufacturing biscuits and candy.

In 1939, at the age of 43, Nathan Cummings decided he could do better in the United States. With a $5.2-million loan, he acquired a Baltimore, Maryland wholesale distributor of sugar, coffee and tea. When he retired in 1968, he had built one of America's largest multinational companies, with manufacturing plants in some 40 countries and distribution branches in more than 140 countries. The former shoe store clerk had constructed a corporation manufacturing everything from Sara Lee baked goods to Playtex undergarments. Furthermore, he was a major stakeholder in General Dynamics, manufacturing diverse products including supersonic aircraft and nuclear submarines! His Sara Lee Corporation employed 100,000 and had annual sales exceeding $11 billion. Nathan Cummings maintained a strong connection to Montreal and his family. He spoke to his brother Maxwell in Montreal on the telephone almost every day.

No family name is more visible in the Montreal Jewish community than that of the Cummings. The Jewish Community Campus, where many agencies are congregated, is called Cummings Square. It is located at the corner of Cote Ste. Catherine Road and Westbury in the Snowdon district. The Federation's imposing five-story headquarters is called Cummings House, and nearby is the Cummings Jewish Centre for Seniors. Moreover, the auditorium at the Montreal Museum of Fine Arts is named in honour of Maxwell Cummings, one of its most important patrons.

THE MORTIMER B. DAVIS STORY

Mortimer Barnett Davis, a leading industrialist and philanthropist, shared the title "Tobacco King of Canada" with Sir W.C MacDonald. He was the first and only Canadian Jew to be knighted.

Davis' father, Samuel, had introduced cigar manufacturing to Montreal in 1861.

After completing high school (a good education by the standards of that time), Mortimer Davis and his two brothers entered their father's tobacco business. Samuel Davis put his son to work as a travelling sales representative to learn the business from the ground up. After an apprenticeship of several years, Mortimer assumed greater and greater managerial responsibilities and helped make the family business grow swiftly.

In 1895, the American Tobacco Company was formed, and Mortimer Davis was named President. That same year, the father retired and died within a few months, aged 61. Mortimer Davis

Sir Mortimer B. Davis— knighted in 1917 by King George V, in recognition of his "munificent philanthropic work."

acquired another company and founded the Imperial Tobacco Company of Canada, which by the turn of the century was employing 3,000.

BUILDING THE TOBACCO BUSINESS

Davis was largely responsible for the establishment of a market for Canadian-grown tobacco. Of course, this was at a time when the harmful effects of smoking were not known. (The Jewish General Hospital, named in honour of Sir Mortimer in 1934, was one of the first health facilities in Montreal to forbid smoking on its premises.)

Davis worked on the development of a milder tobacco leaf, because the Canadian tobacco plant was bitter. He recruited two American brothers versed in the flue curing of Virginia leaf tobacco, which was suitable for cigarettes. Around the time of the First World War, cigars and pipes were declining in popularity and cigarettes were becoming the rage. Imperial Tobacco moved to the forefront of the industry.

SIR MORTIMER AND THE MOUNT ROYAL CLUB

In 1908, Sir Mortimer applied for membership in the most prestigious private club in Montreal, the Mount Royal. He was well aware that he risked being turned down despite his prominent position in the business world and his knighthood. Much to his surprise and pleasure, he was accepted. However, a lot had gone on behind the scenes before his application was approved. One of Davis' employees was a son of Lord Shaughnessy, and the young man went from member to member warning them that if the Jewish tobacco magnate were blackballed, he—a Shaughnessy—would resign and join the rival St. James Club. Because of this quiet backroom pressure, Davis' application was approved.

THE DAVIS FAMILY LEGACY

In Community affairs, Davis was an outstanding leader. In 1921, he served as General Chairman of the Federation's annual fundraising campaign, the community's most important position. The Y.M.H.A. programs expanded enormously in 1926 with the gift of $420,000 by Davis for construction of a modern community centre at 265 Mount Royal Avenue West. He died as the "Y" building, bearing his name, was nearing completion. When "Y" officials advised his executors that they had run out of money for the building, they donated a further $30,000 from the estate.

The Jewish General Hospital is named in his honour, and the Medical Research Institute memorializes his wife, Lady Henrietta Davis.

"...Tell a story about a Little Jewish Guy who was dying. Calls all the children over. He says 'Children, I'm dying. Are you all here' They say, "Yes, daddy, what do you want?' Old Jewish Guy says, 'Who the hell is watching the store?'"

—From Saturday Night at the Bagel Factory by Don Bell.

Advertisement from the Keneder Adler, 1931.

CHAPTER EIGHTEEN

FROM RAGS TO GREAT RICHES
The Bronfman Story

He was one of the richest men in Canada. But he frowned on waste. He became the most powerful leader Canadian Jewry has ever known, yet Samuel Bronfman could never forget his childhood poverty, and the humiliation of attending school in rags. One way it showed was his concern about wasting money on electricity. "Mr. Sam" was often the last to leave his castle-like Seagram offices on Peel Street. At the end of the day, he went from floor to floor, checking that the lights were turned off. As an honoured guest in Ireland, touring a distillery, Bronfman finished a guided tour of a Quonset hut filled with barrels of whiskey, turned to his host, and said: "Aren't you forgetting something? You forgot to turn out the lights."

Samuel Bronfman, who lived ten years more than the Biblical three-score and ten, left an indelible mark, during that long life, on Canada, on Montreal and particularly on the Jewish people. With the help of his family, he devoted much of his life to strengthening the Jewish Community in Montreal, in Canada and around the world. Bronfman was the longest-standing President of the Montreal Jewish Federation. He was also president of Canadian Jewish Congress, the voice of Canadian Jewry, during the momentous developmental years, as the community struggled with the Great Depression, the rise of Hitler and the horrible reality of the Holocaust, the arrival in Canada of thousands of survivors and the rebirth of Israel. To Montreal Jewry he was "the King of the Jews."

"Mr. Sam" was born at sea, on February 17, 1889, to immigrant parents from Bessarabia, Russia, en route to the Canadian West. The family arrived in Canada destitute, and failed in their first efforts at making a living. Ekiel Bronfman, his wife Mindel, and their eight children, were dirt poor for years. The elder Bronfman had owned a gristmill and tobacco plantation in the Old Country, but was driven out by pogroms. He first tried his hand working the land at a Jewish farm settlement in Wapella, Saskatchewan (a settlement built with financial assistance from Baron Maurice de Hirsch), but failed. Samuel was the third son, in the staunchly Jewish family, which included four sisters— Rose (or Rebecca), Jean, Bessie (or Bea), and Laura, and three brothers—Harry, Abe and Allan. The boys were angered when their classmates discovered that Bronfman, in Yiddish, meant whiskeyman, and jibed them about their name. The boys had the last laugh. After dabbling in the sale of liquor in small hotels they owned, the family moved to Montreal, set up a distillery and became the world's greatest spirits manufacturers.

Samuel Bronfman (l-r), Cote St. Luc Mayor Sam Moscovitch and Prime Minister Lester Bowles Pearson.

ENTERING THE WHISKEY BUSINESS

The venture into whiskey came almost by accident. Ekiel Bronfman, searching for some way to make a living for his large family, tried a number of ventures. One of them was horse-trading. During one transaction, Samuel, still a boy, watched horse-traders downing whiskey at a bar. "Instead of selling horses, we should be selling drinks," he told his father.

The elder Bronfman borrowed money and went into the hotel business, where he could sell spirits. They gradually drifted into the distilling of whiskey. In fact, Sam Bronfman's first independent business venture was in 1916, when he purchased a liquor store in Montreal.

A few years later, the Bronfman brothers built a distillery in Lasalle, and in 1924 established Distillers Corporation Limited, headquartered in Montreal. In 1928, Sam Bronfman acquired the troubled 71-year-old Joseph E. Seagram and Sons and merged the companies to form Distillers Corporation-Seagrams Limited.

OF BOOTLEGGERS AND PROHIBITION

During American prohibition, the Bronfmans sold their products to distributors who smuggled liquor into the United States where there was a huge underground market. Allegations were made that the family were bootleggers, but the Bronfmans followed the same business practices as other Canadian distillers. However, only the Bronfmans were pilloried in the press by anti-Semitic government officials. When Prohibition was repealed in 1932, the Bronfmans were ready with a huge stockpile and made millions. The Bronfman name became synonymous with great wealth.

Sam Bronfman created an entirely new category of alcoholic beverages, blended whiskey. "Distilling is a science," he would say. "Blending is an art." And, in 1930, he brought in a Scottish Jew named Calman Levine as master blender. In 1934, Levine created Seven Crowns. It became the best-selling whiskey in the United States within two months and the top seller in the world in less than ten years. Bronfman aggressively built profitable partnerships with some of the most important Scottish whiskey distillers. They made up unlikely teams—the Scottish liquor barons and the upstart Montrealer.

On an overseas trip, in 1932, a wine merchant introduced Bronfman to Joachim von Ribbentrop, later Foreign Minister of Nazi Germany. Ribbentrop, who had lived in Canada for about four years while he sold champagne across the country, had joined the Nazi party only a few weeks before. In later years, Sam reported that von Ribbentrop had said to him, "I can assure you that nothing will happen to the Jews when we take over. This is all politics. Everything will be fine. In fact, some wealthy Jews secretly supported us and we will remember that." After the war, Von Ribbentrop was tried at Nuremburg, and hanged in 1946.

LIFELONG ROMANCE

Saidye and Samuel Bronfman on their honeymoon, 1922. (Canadian Jewish Congress National Archives)

Sam Bronfman met Saidye Rosner in 1920, and they married in 1922. As a friend put it, "he was on his honeymoon from the day he was married to the day he died." The Bronfmans had four children, Edgar, Minda, Charles and Phyllis. They were partners in raising a family, and in working for the community.

Saidye Bronfman's efforts during World War II won her the rank of Officer of the Order of the British Empire. Sam was also intensely loyal to the British Empire. He grew up at a time when Canadians looked to the monarchy for inspiration and leadership. When Elizabeth, not yet Queen, and Prince Philip toured Canada, Bronfman created a new whiskey in their honour— "Crown Royal"—in a bottle shaped like a crown. Bronfman offered the Princess 10 cases of the whiskey. The offer was accepted.

LEADING THE WAY

For decades, Sam and Saidye Bronfman hosted the reception launching the annual Montreal Combined Jewish Appeal, raising funds for Jewish services locally, nationally, and internationally. They had a large reception room on the lower level of their Westmount mansion, perched on the flanks of Mount Royal. (At the top of the stairs leading to the lower level was a painting by the Russian-born painter Marc Chagall of a white vase, filled with flowers. Below the painting was the actual vase Chagall had used, and it was filled daily with fresh flowers, matching those in the oil.) Each fall, for nearly 40 years, heads of the most important families in the Jewish community gathered in their home to make a pledge for the coming year. Mr. Sam always led off, naming a sum, which set the benchmark for increases expected from everyone else. And, traditionally, the "leading families", as they were called, followed the leader. Mr. Sam called the large room in which these sessions were held "the sweatshop" because of the pressure he would put on guests to increase their contributions to the community.

PRESIDENT OF THE FEDERATION

Despite the burdens of running an enormous industry, he still found time for a tremendous communal participation. Sam Bronfman was President of the Montreal Jewish Federation for 17 years (the normal term of office is two years), from 1933-1950. He also served as President of Canadian Jewish Congress, from 1939 to 1962. He led the way in providing funds to Israel from its inception. The Bronfman family made the largest annual charitable gift donations in North America for many years.

DISTILLING THE LEGEND

Sam's temper was legendary. "Some of Sam's language would make a longshoreman very proud indeed," observed Saul Hayes, who worked with Bronfman for decades at Canadian Jewish Congress. Sam's nephew Gerald Bronfman once cautioned his uncle to watch his temper or he might get ulcers. "I don't get ulcers," Sam snapped back. "I give them." However, Sam mellowed with the passing of time. For his eightieth birthday—his last—hundreds of people gathered in the elegant reception hall of Congregation Shaar Hashomayim. Guests came from all over the world, and included Teddy Kollek, longtime mayor of Jerusalem. Later, in Mr. Sam's den in his red-brick mansion at 15 Belvedere, Westmount, the 80-year-old business tycoon, once feared for unpredictable outbursts of temper, talked gently with guests about gifts he was giving his grandchildren.

Sam Bronfman left many enduring gifts to his beloved Canada. One of them is the Seagram Collection of Canadian art—56 paintings of 26 Canadian cities by 23 members of the

Sam Bronfman's secretary worked with him for more than 40 years and one of her daily tasks was to pour a gin and mix for the boss. One Saturday at the office, Mr. Sam wanted his customary late morning drink, but did not have a key to his personal liquor cabinet. He strode down the corridor to the office of Vice-President Mike McCormick, who quickly concluded a meeting and sent a secretary out for mix—Schweppes' ginger beer requested by Bronfman. As they were sipping their drinks, McCormick—making conversation—mentioned that Schweppes made more money "out of the mix than we do out of the booze. The mix is 60 cents." Mr. Sam was astonished and, when he wanted a second drink, told the secretary, "Only one bottle this time. It costs 60 cents, you know."

prestigious Royal Canadian Academy. His own favorite was a painting of downtown Place d'Armes, by J.S. Hallem. However, when Pope Pius the Twelfth admired the painting, Mr. Sam presented it to His Holiness as a gift.

Munroe Abbey (1) presents the original Samuel Bronfman medal to Bronfman at his 80th birthday party.

OTHER BRONFMANS PLAY A ROLE

Samuel's brothers—Abe, Harry, and Allan—played outstanding roles in both commerce and community. The oldest brother, Abe (1882-1968), was involved in supporting the Federation, Combined Jewish Appeal, Mount Sinai Hospital, the Jewish General Hospital, Montreal General Hospital, the Verdun Protestant Hospital (now the Douglas Hospital), the YM-YWHA and Canadian Jewish Congress. In addition, he was active in international organizations aiding Jews in distress worldwide. Mildred Lande, daughter of Abe Bronfman and his wife, Sophie Rasminsky, became the first woman to serve as General Chairman of the Combined Jewish Appeal—the most challenging and difficult job in the community.

The second son, Harry (1886-1963), played a similar leadership role in Montreal Jewish and non-Jewish institutions. Harry was a strong supporter of Jewish education, and was a major contributor to the United Talmud Torahs, an important network of private schools. In addition, he and Samuel were involved in the activities of State of Israel Bonds from their inception in the 1950s. His memory is honoured through the naming of two community housing facilities for seniors, Harry Bronfman Square Number One, and Two.

The youngest of the four Bronfman brothers, Allan (1895-1980) is the only sibling born in Canada. He is also the only one with a university degree. After graduating from the University of Manitoba, he practised law for nine years in Manitoba before joining Seagram's. Allan, noted for his gentle disposition, is best known for his leadership of the successful campaign to fund the Jewish General Hospital. In addition, he was deeply involved with the Hebrew University in Israel, where a student residence at the Jerusalem University is named in his honour. Allen is the only person to have chaired two Combined Jewish Appeals—the very first one, in 1941, and the difficult 1968 campaign, immediately following the Six-Day War in Israel.

HIS DESK IS STILL DUSTED
Samuel Bronfman's office in the Seagram's building remains as it was. On the large mahogany desk is the annual report, rendered in gold, in which sales first topped the billion-dollar mark. At the bottom of the desk ornament are the words "Thanks a billion, Dad" signed by Mr. Sam's two sons, Charles and Edgar.

Three Montreal Expos baseball fans (r to l) Prime Minister Pearson, Sam Bronfman and Governor General Michener. (Canadian Jewish Congress National Archives)

Charles Rosner Bronfman paid the following tribute to his late father:

"In 1939, when (Sam Bronfman) was elected President of the Canadian Jewish Congress, he became head of a tiny, ragtag, fractious Community, just about to face the trials of the Jewish refugee crisis, the Second World War, and the Nazi Holocaust. This was the darkest moment in the history of modern Jewry, when the doors of immigration slammed shut at home and murder roamed freely abroad. In the agony that followed and during the subsequent birth of the State of Israel, it was Sam Bronfman who heard the cries of pain, who responded to the appeals for financial aid to the fledgling Jewish State. and who helped bring into being a remarkably successful network of Jewish public institutions in Canada. For some thirty years, as Canadian Jewry came of age, he was the foremost Jew in the country, putting his stamp on a community that has become one of the most successfully integrated pieces of the Canadian mosaic."

Well groomed, we stand on broadloomed floors
Inhaling deeply the smell of money
Well-adjusted children of the new era
Blankly awaiting the next pogrom.
David Lewis Stein
"First Flowering" 1956

PART THREE

PRAYERS AT SUNDOWN
Years of Turmoil

Quebec becomes a centre of vicious anti-Semitism and a cradle for Fascism, with open support by the Church and political hierarchy. Canada adopts the most discriminatory immigration regulations in the western world—a brutal policy of exclusion for imperiled Jews in Nazi Germany. In Montreal, Jews participate in organized gambling, the city's "second largest industry." The left is fractured in Montreal as Jews elect Canada's first and only Communist MP, and a moderate socialist heads a national Canadian political party. During World War II, 16,000 Jews—almost half from Montreal—join the Canadian Forces to battle European Fascists on land, in the air and on the high seas. In the wake of the war, Canada adopts liberal new policies and becomes the largest haven in North America for survivors.

CHAPTER NINETEEN

S.W. JACOBS, MP
A Dissenter in the Corridors of Power

Liberal Samuel Jacobs—the sole Jewish Member of Parliament in Ottawa—rose from his seat in the House of Commons to repeat his bitter opposition to his own government's increasingly restrictive immigration policy. Canada had closed its doors to Jews; a cabinet ruling had placed them on the bottom rung of desirable immigrants. Raising his voice above the din, Jacobs said:

"None of the founders of the early Christian Church could enter Canada under the present regulations," he told the House. "There are, in the case of Jesus of Nazareth—and I am saying it with all respect—four orders-in-council which would prohibit him from coming here. There would be first," he went on, "the order relating to the non-agriculturist class. Carpenters are not permitted to enter this country coming from that district. And then he would not have a proper passport; he would not be travelling by a continuous journey; and he would have no relatives in this country."

Montreal lawyer Samuel William Jacobs (1871-1938) was an outstanding figure in Canadian Jewish history, as a brilliant parliamentarian, an exemplary servant of the community and a true voice of liberalism. For 21 years, beginning with his 1917 election in the largely Jewish Cartier riding, he carried—often single-handedly—the burden of fighting for all Canadian Jewry, particularly with regard to Ottawa's policy of cutting back on Jewish immigration. On one occasion in the Commons, when it was stated that migrants were undermining the country, Jacobs (a son of Lithuanian immigrants who had risen to the level of King's Counsel) responded:

Montreal Member of Parliament S.W. Jacobs. Sir Wilfrid Laurier picked him out as one of the great white hopes of the Liberal Party, but he never left the back benches of the Commons. (Canadian Jewish Congress National Archives.)

"We know that under the Liberal administration (of former prime minister Sir Wilfred Laurier) from 1896 to 1911, we had a vast immigration and that the foundation of the prosperity of Canada was the immigration which came in that period."

However, the governments succeeding Laurier, headed by Conservative/Unionist Sir Robert Borden (1911-1920), and Liberal W.L. Mackenzie King (1921-26,1926-30,1935-48), had a less favourable attitude toward immigration. In the wake of the First World War, Canada experienced painful social and economic adjustments and responded by tightening its immigration policy. As industry converted to peacetime production, returning veterans and others found jobs hard to find. Unemployment soared to 15 per cent in 1921. Inflation and high interest rates discouraged investment. The volatile stock market tumbled in 1921-22, and crashed seven years later. Trade unions went on violent strikes and were vocal opponents of immigration. At the same time, disillusioned Canadians were concerned about widespread unrest in Europe—Revolution in Russia, the economic collapse of Germany, and the rise in strength of Bolshevism. In the aftermath of war, Jews in Europe, particularly Poland, faced growing anti-Semitism and extreme hardships and were anxious to emigrate. However, Canada's generous policies of the past were essentially discarded with the election of Mackenzie King in 1921.

CANADA CLOSES THE DOOR ON JEWISH IMMIGRATION

King, who had campaigned on a platform of greater immigration, introduced the first of a series of orders-in-council limiting immigration, almost exclusively, to people from "preferred countries"—that is, the British Isles and northern Europe. The tightening of Canadian immigration laws coincided with similar restrictive policies in the United States. Canada officially closed its doors to refugees and "less desirable" immigrants in 1923 with passage of Order-in-Council 183, which classified potential immigrants as "preferred", "non-preferred" and "special permit". Jews were placed on the lowest rung of the immigration ladder, with blacks and Asians. The restrictions also included new limits on reuniting families. The Montreal Yiddish newspaper *Keneder Adler* noted that the Germans, who had been "Canada's mortal enemies" a few years before, were now among "preferred immigrants." Every year, additional orders-in-council were passed, piling restriction on restriction—each narrowing the opportunity for distressed Jewish families to come to Canada.

BREAKING THE BARRIERS
Occasionally, Jews were admitted, but on a case-by-case basis. Numerous appeals were made directly to Jacobs' offices in Montreal, and some exceptions were negotiated. One example involved a young law student, H. Carl Goldenberg (later a Senator), whose family was admitted from Austria. In these individual cases, Jacobs did not waste his time meeting with government immigration officials who adhered strictly to the orders-in-council. Instead, he campaigned at the cabinet level, or pressured the prime minister, to have exceptions made.

JEWISH IMMIGRANT AID SOCIETY
Jacobs had joined Lyon Cohen, a prominent clothing manufacturer in Montreal, in leading the newly formed immigrant advocacy group, the *Jewish Immigration Aid Society*. JIAS grew to be an increasingly effective instrument in pressing the government for greater cooperation in allowing refuge for Jews, and the organization created programs to help migrants as they arrived in Canada. As bewildered Jewish migrants stepped onto the docks in Montreal, Quebec City, or Halifax, many were greeted by representatives of the agency. JIAS services included language lessons, financial assistance, and vocational guidance. They also helped newcomers find accommodation.

Sam Jacobs tried another tack in the face of stiff government resistance to relaxation of its tough immigration policies. He dipped into the Jewish tradition of **shtadlanut**; that is, he would make the rounds of offices in Ottawa accompanied by important members of the Jewish Community. While he was unsuccessful in modifying the government's policy, Jacobs' efforts over a span of ten years led to the admission of several thousand Jews into Canada. And he and his associates had to fight for every one.

About 4,000 Jewish immigrants a year were allowed into Canada from 1923 until 1931, when Ottawa closed the country's doors to all but British and American newcomers.

A FIRST GENERATION SUCCESS STORY
Jacobs was born in 1871 in Lancaster, Ontario, and moved to Montreal shortly thereafter with his family. He was called to the bar in 1906 after studying at McGill and Laval universities. In addition to his law practice, he was active in the Jewish community, serving as President of the Baron de Hirsch Institute 1912-1914.

Jacobs' influence on people is well demonstrated by a 1912 incident involving a run on the City and District Bank. Bank president Sir Thomas White wired the Receiver General's Office to release gold to restore depositors' confidence. However, the

CJC REBORN
Created with great enthusiasm in 1919, Canadian Jewish Congress, intended as the Parliament of the Jewish people of Canada, lay dormant for 15 years, except for the single-handed faithful efforts of H.M. Caiserman. Because of the increasingly urgent problem of endangered Jews in Europe, the organization had to be revitalized. The community needed a top leader. In 1934, they chose S.W. Jacobs to be president of the renewed institution.

THE WIT AND WISDOM OF S.W.
S.W. Jacobs was a charismatic public speaker with a sharp wit. The *Montreal Herald*, reporting on his campaign for fellow Liberal James A. Robb in Huntingdon, Quebec, noted:
"Speaking of Sir Joseph Flavelle and his profiteering in bacon, Mr. Jacobs made the meeting laugh with his declaration: 'Moses was a real prophet when he invited the children of Israel not to eat pork and bacon. He must have known that in 1917 Sir Joseph Flavelle would run the cost of bacon up to 60 cents a pound.'"
Later, after Robb had been named Federal Minister of Finance, Jacobs—during a friendly argument on taxation—remarked, "Yours is a very appropriate name for the cabinet post you have."

public was not convinced, particularly immigrants who worried they would lose their life savings. Thousands gathered menacingly one evening around a branch on St. Catherine Street East and the situation threatened to get out of hand. Senator Raoul Dandurand pleaded with the mob, urging them to disperse. However, the crowd refused to listen and ugly threats were uttered. The senator turned to Sam Jacobs for help. Jacobs spoke to the crowd in English, then French and finally in a mixture of Yiddish and German. He assured them their money was safe and that he personally would guarantee every penny. The crowd calmed down and drifted off, confident Jacobs was telling them the truth.

THE RISING STAR OF MONTREAL

In 1917, Jacobs accepted a Liberal party nomination and went into politics. On the campaign trail, Jacobs, who was fluent only in English and French, relied on enthusiastic supporters to extol his virtues in Yiddish. In fact, at Jewish political meetings, he was the only one who spoke English! His fluency in French made him popular with francophone voters. When he rose to speak at rallies in Montreal the audience chanted, *"Il a gagné ses épaulettes."* (He has won his spurs).

Former prime minister Sir Wilfred Laurier had singled out two men in his Liberal party as outstanding leadership prospects, Mackenzie King and Samuel W. Jacobs. (King became Canada's longest-serving prime minister, and Jacobs had a long career as an MP but was consistently denied a cabinet position.)

In 1917, the Union government was re-elected, but Liberal Jacobs trounced his two opponents, registering a majority of 5,342. His first public appearance as a member of Parliament was at a Zionist mass meeting to celebrate issuance of the Balfour Declaration by Britain calling for Palestine to be the "national home for the Jewish people." Jacobs, in his remarks, referred to the "remarkable coincidence" that British General Henry Hynman Allenby had captured Jerusalem on the first day of **Hannukah**, the day recalling the triumphant entry into Jerusalem of Judas Maccabeus in 164 B.C.E. after defeating Syrian occupiers.

Being a Jewish member of the Commons did not guarantee automatic support from the Montreal community. In his first election campaign, Jacobs came under fire from other Jews. But the Yiddish *Keneder Adler* defended him, stating: "The socialists charge that he has done nothing for the working class. In the last tailors' strike he was the first to send in one hundred dollars and worked day and night to settle the strike."

When Jacobs stood for re-election in 1921, the *Keneder Adler*, which had admonished him to be "faithful to the trust reposed in him", commented: "He is positively the right man in the right place; he has brought us honour and great service."

The *Toronto Globe and Mail* referred to him as "The Growing hope of Liberalism in Canada." As a protégé of Laurier, Jacobs believed that a Liberal government would be more receptive to Jewish concerns, such as immigration. He hoped the Conservative Unionists under Robert Borden would be defeated. In October 1921, he wrote a friend in Winnipeg:

> "Should this (Unionist) government be returned it is all up with Jewish immigration to Canada as I am satisfied that everyone in the department of immigration is strongly and bitterly opposed to our people. I am, however, confident that things will right themselves in a few weeks."

Jacobs was hoping that his party, the Liberals, would win the general election with its new leader, Mackenzie King. He had reason for optimism. He and King had met frequently in Ottawa and Montreal. Before the leadership convention, where Jacobs supported the candidacy of King, the latter had consulted him on policy. After a pleasant visit to Jacobs' home, King was so impressed by the Jacobs family that he confided to his diary that he should marry and have a family, too. King never married, nor did he honour promises he made to Jacobs on Jewish affairs.

The 1921 election returned the Liberals to power, and Jacobs was re-elected with a majority of 4,271 over four opponents. The Jewish MP was widely seen as potentially a senior personality in government. The *Montreal Star* picked Jacobs as a likely candidate for cabinet, calling him the 'rising star of Montreal' and stating:

> "The addition of the name of S.W. Jacobs, member-elect for Georges Etienne Cartier, to the list of possible ministers in Hon. Mackenzie King's cabinet has brought into the spotlight Quebec's distinction of being the cradle of Jewish political emancipation in the British Empire."

But when the prime minister's new cabinet was sworn in, it did not include Jacobs. He found himself a lonely, embittered figure on the government side of the house. Nonetheless, he diligently represented the interests of the entire Jewish community of Canada in a hostile Commons.

Jacobs guided and encouraged a number of lawyers who in time became titans in their field. They included Sen. Lazarus Phillips, Sen. H. Carl Goldenberg, Louis Fitch, Henry Weinstein, Marcus Sperber, Nathan Gordon, Maxwell Goldstein and Henry Weinfield.

Anger on the Main. Jews demonstrate in Montreal to protest the Arab atrocities at Hebron, Palestine, in 1929. (Jewish Public Library Archives)

Montreal in the '20s was the major Jewish community of Canada, with about half of all Jews in the Dominion. In 1921, the census listed 52,287 Jews. During the next decade, the population rose by 26.6%, almost entirely from a high birthrate.

In the next general election, in 1925, Mackenzie King's Liberals were soundly thrashed. The prime minister and eight members of his cabinet were defeated. But S. W. Jacobs was re-elected and remained a member of the Commons until his death in 1938.

The first Jewish MP of the twentieth century, Jacobs is best remembered as the man who debated seminal civil rights issues in Canada: the right of Jews to go to school, to work on Sunday, and to become Canadian citizens equal under the law. He was the eloquent voice that spoke for the Jewish people and for all disadvantaged individuals, in court and Commons. Although he worked within the system along the corridors of power for 21 years, he was denied his rightful place in cabinet. Nonetheless, he did manage to break through bureaucratic barriers and win admission to Canada and Montreal for thousands of Jewish individuals and families.

CHAPTER TWENTY

MAYHEM IN THE METROPOLIS
Gamblers, Gangsters and Gunslingers in the Dirty Thirties

Charlie Feigenbaum was looking forward to a weekend in the country as he parked his car in front of his sister-in-law's triplex on Esplanade Street one sunny August afternoon in 1934. He was planning to drive her, and his 18-year-old son, Jackie, to the family cottage at Val Morin. He and Jackie were loading parcels into the car when a man slipped out of a Hudson automobile parked across the road and sauntered leisurely toward him. As neighbours looked on in horror, the stranger pulled out a revolver and emptied six shots into Feigenbaum, who fell to the ground, fatally wounded. The killer calmly turned around, strode back to the vehicle, and stood on the running board of his getaway car as it sped away.

Welcome to Montreal in the Dirty '30s—the crime capital of North America. The city had been taken over by a variety of criminals, many of them Americans driven out of their own country by a police crackdown. With a reputation for anything goes, Montreal was a wide-open city, and it became a magnet for gangsters and gamblers. It was riddled with houses of prostitution, sleazy nightclubs, blind pigs, and gambling dens. Mayor Camillien Houde, city officials, and the police welcomed their new citizens and often cooperated with them—for a fee.

As Montreal became a haven for the lawless, many Montreal Jews became deeply involved, particularly with gambling. According to the Caron Inquiry report, Jewish crime lords included Harry Ship, Max Shapiro, and Harry Davis. Equally well known was the lone Jewish crime-fighter Ben Greenberg, who was for 36 years what the *Montreal Star* called "the scourge of law

The Montreal Star covers the demise of two members of Montreal's Jewish Mafia. CJC archives

breakers". The era of mayhem ended when numerous killings triggered a formal investigation and ultimately brought about the election of a crime-busting mayor, Jean Drapeau.

When the Kefauver investigation in the United States drove out organized gamblers, they moved to Montreal, where gambling was controlled by a local Jew named Harry Ship. He loved to gamble, and regularly made and lost fortunes. He rented facilities for bookies, set up dummy companies and installed telephone lines. For two years, Montreal was the bookmaking capital of North America. **For a time, it was claimed that gambling was the second largest industry in the city, second only to the manufacture of women's clothing.**

Harry Ship's gambling casino on Côte St. Luc Road was the most luxurious in town. Gamblers could nosh on filet mignon and champagne "on the house" without having to leave the roulette wheels or crap tables. Ship also had an extensive bookmaking operation in downtown Montreal, on two floors of an office building.

"LUCKY BEN" NAILS THE KIKI GANG

In the 1930s, the tough northern division of the Montreal Police force covered St. Lawrence Boulevard ('the bounding Main') and Chinatown, and was supervised by Divisional Detective Inspector Ben Greenberg, one of the few Jewish police officers in the city. He had applied and been accepted by the RCMP, but his mother opposed his leaving home to train in the West. Greenberg joined the Montreal police force in 1928. At that time, the force had about 800 men and was "99 per cent French", he recalled in a 1978 interview with the *Montreal Star*. A rookie cop earned $800 a year.

Ben Greenberg, one of Montreal's top policemen for 40 years from the mid-1920s.

The hefty Greenberg, who spoke six languages, received quick promotion. In three short years he was promoted from beat cop to sergeant to captain. In 1959, he was named detective inspector, the highest rank ever attained by a Jew. He was repeatedly cited for bravery and won a number of medals.

"I was very aggressive," Greenberg said, "not pushed around by the **goyim** (non-Jews) and had a reputation as a fighter. We had a lot of anti-Semitism in the force then. There were a couple of other Jewish constables but they quit and I was the only one who remained."

Probably Greenberg's most famous exploit was the time he nailed the notorious Kiki gang. The burly, 200-pound Jewish police officer had been tipped off that the gang, which had been terrorizing part of Montreal, had gone to ground in a house at the corner of Sanguinet and Dorchester streets. Greenberg led his uniformed squad in a raid on the house. While handcuffing rank-and-file members of the gang, they were told the "boss" was upstairs, asleep. The inspector bounded up the stairs two at a time and threw open the first door. Sure enough, there was the gang leader stretched out on a brass bed with his gun drawn, and pointed directly at Greenberg's head. "I thought I was a goner," the police officer said later. After a moment's hesitation, he leapt onto the thug. The gun went off. The bed collapsed under the impact. And the floor caved in. It was an interesting way to deliver his suspect to the officers waiting below. "In the confusion, I was able to grab him and get the handcuffs on," he said.

"As late as 1932 we had only one automobile for the entire detective force. It was a two-seater Ford. If we caught two suspects, we had to spread-eagle them over the hood to bring them in. Fortunately we were never very far from headquarters."

One of nine children of immigrant parents from Kiev, Greenberg was born in Russia in 1903 and brought by his family to Montreal when he was four. His father owned a grocery and liquor store and "had a big keg of de Kuyper gin on the floor of the store as well as barrels of molasses and coal oil. Gin sold for about ten cents a quart." Ben quit school early to work in the store and to take care of horses stabled behind the shop. Motivated by a childhood experience, Greenberg created in the 1950s the Montreal police bicycle squad, the first of its kind in North America. "When I was a little guy I had two bicycles stolen and never got them back. It was heartbreak. Bicycle thefts were mounting to big business in Montreal when I set up the squad. At first I worked alone but later had a staff of 10 with three trucks...we didn't ride bicycles, we found stolen ones." Greenberg was one of the detectives who travelled to Toronto to arrest a nursemaid who had kidnapped the infant son of a well-known Montreal Jewish family. Greenberg retired at age 61, the retirement age set by city by-law, having never missed a day of work. He wound up his working career as a private investigator with the Acme Detective Agency, and security officer for the Montreal Expos VIP lounge.

"Following the release (from wartime internment) of Mayor Houde and his return to power at City Hall after the war, many of the old houses (of prostitution) were back in business. The other rackets had never stopped flourishing. The click of the ivory dice in a game called barbotte could be heard across the city. On the street they called the Main—St. Lawrence Boulevard—Benny Cohen ran

a big barbotte game. If your weakness was the horses, Barney the bookie, operat-
ing under the cover of the Brotherhood Bridge Club, was one of hundreds in the
illegal gambling fraternity. In fact, Montreal became headquarters for illegal
bookmaking for the whole continent when authorities turned on the heat south
of the border. Illegal drinking establishments called blind pigs were everywhere.
The suspicion grew that illegal gambling, bootlegging, prostitution and nar-
cotics peddling flourished with the connivance of certain key police officers and
public officials."

Brian McKenna and Susan Purcell in "Drapeau", 1980.

THE FINK, THE OVERLORD AND THE GANGSTER
Before he was gunned down in broad daylight, Charlie
Feigenbaum had been a small-time hoodlum, smuggling silk
fabrics into Canada via the port of Montreal. When he made a
deal with a group of Montreal and New York narcotics smug-
glers, he was in over his head. His contact in the customs service
confessed to police; Feigenbaum went to jail. From his cell, he
learned that his old cronies, after promising to keep his rackets
going, instead were taking over. He decided to get even, and his
testimony sent another Jewish gangster, Harry Davis, to the pe-
nitentiary for seven years, plus ten strokes of the lash. Davis was
the reputed overlord of drug trafficking in Montreal, and was
involved in gambling and illegal betting. Feigenbaum's testimony had put the mob boss in jail for a long time.
    At the time of his murder, Feigenbaum was to have testified in
twenty days' time against Pincus Brecher, a gangster from New
York with interests in Montreal. In the meantime, freed from
prison because of his confession and implication of other crime
figures, he had gone back to his old ways. In fact, he was trying
to take over the illicit activities of the imprisoned Davis.
Feigenbaum, of course, did not get to be the kingpin, nor did he
testify. Nevertheless, Brecher was convicted of drug offences. On
the way to a Montreal prison infirmary, he committed suicide by
leaping from a gallery.

SETTLING OF ACCOUNTS
Harry Davis, having served his sentence, was released in 1945. A
year later, he was checking betting slips in his bookmaking parlour on Stanley Street when Jewish mobster Louis Bercovitch
walked in and fatally wounded Davis with three shots.
Bercovitch wanted revenge because Davis had prevented him from
opening a bookie joint. The killer then fled and surrendered him-

self to the managing editor of the *Montreal Herald*, Ted McCormick. When police came to the *Herald* building looking for their man, McCormick hid him in the women's washroom. The newspaper took down Bercovitch's 10-page confession and ran the story with the front-page headline: "Davis Slayer Surrenders to *Herald*", before turning him over to the authorities.

Five thousand people attended Davis' funeral, overflowing from the limited capacity of Paperman's funeral home on St. Urbain Street.

The Davis killing caused a huge public backlash, and led to a campaign to clean up Montreal. Assistant police director Pacifique (Pax) Plante wrote articles in 1949 and 1950 in *Le Devoir* that exposed the collaboration of police with organized crime. He revealed that key figures in Montreal's enormous gambling industry included Max Shapiro, Abie Noodleman and Benny Cohen. Plante arrested Harry Ship in 1946 but the gambler, released on bail, laughed it off. He confidently told reporters, "In two weeks, nobody will remember who that guy Plante was." He was wrong. Though Ship was found guilty of operating an illegal gambling establishment and sent to Bordeaux prison for six months, and Plante was fired for making public disclosures, the die was cast. Authorities could no longer look the other way.

THE CARON INQUIRY

A Judicial Inquiry was ordered with Judge François Caron as Chairman, and his two investigators were Plante and a young lawyer named Jean Drapeau. Ship acknowledged in his testimony at the Caron Inquiry that none of the bookmakers could have functioned without the cooperation of the police. The officer who headed the morality squad for nine months, Captain Arthur Taché, was asked how, on a salary of $3,000 a year, he could afford to buy a $3,000 car, a $3,000 diamond ring and other luxuries. Taché responded that he earned extra money doing housekeeping!

Disclosures of civic corruption in the Caron Report brought about the retirement from politics of Mayor Camillien Houde. The Inquiry had detailed how, under Houde's administration, corruption was blatant and the city was wide open for gamblers and prostitutes. Houde could not understand what all the fuss was about. "Montreal is wide open," he acknowledged, "but honest." A police narcotics raid turned up, by chance, a document listing the names of underworld figures who had contributed to a $100,000 slush fund, and detailed ruthless plans to defeat the crusading mayoralty candidate Jean Drapeau. The paper also included a false electoral list, which included the name of a 10-month-old child!

In 1954, Drapeau was elected mayor, despite bribery and brutality at the polls, and proceeded to clean up the city.

SPORT HERO OF THE ERA
Max (Maxie) Berger (1916-2000) fought his way to the top in the ring; he was one of the greatest pugilists in Canadian history. He started his boxing career with the Montreal YMHA, won a silver medal for Canada in the British Empire Games, captured the Canadian lightweight and welterweight titles and, as a professional, fought six world champions. Berger's first loss in nearly 100 professional bouts was to Sugar Ray Robinson, one of the greatest fighters of all time, in New York's Madison Square Garden in 1942.

THE NOTORIOUS UNTOUCHABLE WILLIE OBIE

An official inquiry in 1975 into the criminal activities of Quebec, American and Italian Mafia leaders, identified one Jew, William Obront. (The Inquiry called him W.O. Bront, and some stories have mistakenly labeled him as William O'Bront!) The Crime Commission alleged that between 1964 and 1975, Obront laundered $84-million from the Cotroni gang's loan-sharking operation.

Former police investigator Pax Plante called Obront and gang leader Vic Cotroni "the untouchables" because they were shielded by high political connections. Obront, known to his associates as "Willie Obie", was born in Montreal in 1924, and was under periodic police surveillance, beginning in the 1940s, for much of his adult life. He had an annual declared income of $38,000 but was known to bet as much as $50,000 on American football games. He was the nominal head of 38 companies, one of which appropriately enough, was a laundry. It was his job to take the millions the Mafia garnered through gambling, drug smuggling and other activities, conceal the origin of the funds, and invest them.

On one occasion, the police taped a conversation between Obront and a member of the Cotroni gang, Angelo Lanzo. The gangster called Willie Obie from a pay phone in the Sirloin Barn Restaurant, at 5050 Paré. Part of the tape ran like this:

Obront - *Going to see the Egg (Vic Cotroni) tonight?*
Lanzo - *Yeah. That's why I called you. He wants to see you.*
Obront - *You know, calling me on the phone, you know, it's like the worst possible thing, eh Angie. This phone is like 100% tapped.*
Lanzo - *So what?*

Police investigations launched in the '60s continued into the early '80s and Obront, feeling the hot breath of police on his neck, fled to Florida, where he was a partner in a mob hang-out, the Pagoda North restaurant. A year after he arrived in the U.S., Obront became a naturalized American citizen. The normal waiting period is five years.

When Obront learned that Canadian authorities were working to extradite him from his Florida lair, he fled to Puerto Rico, and then Costa Rica. Montreal authorities caught up with him in Central America and brought him back to face charges of fraud, forgery, and conspiracy to commit forgery and issuing false documents. The police also wanted to question him about the bombing of the home of a Steinberg's supermarket official, after the company stopped buying meat from one of Obront's companies.

Appearing before a Superior court in Montreal in 1976, Obront was sentenced to four years in jail for defrauding Obie's Meat Market and its creditors of $515,991, plus two years for contempt of court. While he was believed to have been involved in other illegal activities, he was not prosecuted beyond the improper declaration of bankruptcy for two butcher shops.

A year later, the Quebec Police Commission Inquiry into Organized Crime referred to Obront and Vincent Cotroni, charging that they used bank credit to finance a "whole range of illegal activities". The Inquiry also alleged that some bank managers "were bribed or followed the instructions of crime figures without question." Obront and Cotroni, the Police Commission stated, then used the "legitimate money...in the financing of illegitimate schemes such as loan-sharking, gambling and drug distribution."

TWO-GUN COHEN

One of the most colourful Jewish personalities to reside in Montreal was Morris Abraham "Two-Gun" Cohen, a retired general of the Chinese Nationalist Army and dual-pistol-packing gunslinger. His early years were not promising. He was born in a London slum and had to struggle to find enough to eat in his childhood. Cohen had been sent to the first Jewish reform school at age 10 for fighting and petty theft. In 1905, his Orthodox parents in London had banished him to Saskatchewan after, at age 18, he had been convicted of picking pockets. Wandering in the Canadian west, Cohen tried his hand at ranching, peddling and smuggling liquor. He became widely known throughout western

General Two-Gun Cohen, the Jewish senior officer in the Nationalist Chinese Army.

Canada as a crack shot and a gambler. When two cowboys unwisely called him a "dirty Jew," he pulled out a revolver and wounded them both. In his youth, Cohen was frequently in trouble with the law, and in and out of jail.

Around 1910, Cohen walked into a Saskatoon Chinese restaurant, which doubled as a gambling den, to find a gun-wielding thief holding up the proprietor. "I saw it was a hold-up, but I wasn't heeled—that is, armed—and I had to be careful," he said later in an interview. Cohen sidled carefully up to the bandit "until I was too near for him to use his rod and socked him on the jaw." He waited until the thief regained consciousness, and then he "gave him a kick in the pants—maybe two kicks—and told him to beat it." To Mah Sam, the elderly proprietor of the restaurant, and the local Chinese community, Cohen was a hero.

TWO-GUN FIGHTS FOR THE CHINESE

Cohen became genuinely interested in the Chinese, who suffered greatly from Canadian prejudice; he learned to speak Chinese and became a champion of Asian rights. The hefty Cohen enlisted in the Canadian Army in the First World War, and for a time, led a Chinese labour battalion in France. His unit laid railway tracks for the movement of troops, equipment, and supplies to the front. He survived several of the bloodiest battles of that costly conflict, including the slaughter at Passchendaele in 1917. The British suffered nearly 400,000 casualties in that one offensive.

At loose ends after the war, he packed a kit bag and sailed for Shanghai, where his contacts and reputation as a tough guy earned him the job of bodyguard to the head of the Chinese Nationalists, Dr. Sun Yat Sen. It was in China that Cohen earned his nickname because he always packed two pistols. The legendary Two-Gun is said to have saved the Chinese president on more than one occasion from assassins' bullets. When Sun died in 1925, his successor, Chiang Kai-Shek, promoted Two-Gun to the rank of General, and Cohen handled the training and arming of the 19th Route Army, one of the most effective Chinese units in resisting the invading Japanese during the years leading to World War II. (The Chinese called him "Mah-Con", shortening his name and using "Mah" to honour him.) When the wider conflict broke out in 1941, he was in Hong Kong, where he saved Madam Sun's life. However, the Japanese captured him, and he spent 21 months in an internment camp, where he lost 81 pounds. During that time, he was tortured and, in 1944, sentenced to death before a firing squad. Fortunately, the British negotiated his release and he was repatriated to Canada. He had lost almost half his weight, but soon regained it with a return to good living.

A MONTREAL CELEBRITY

On arrival in Montreal, he moved into the Windsor Hotel on Peel St. Shortly thereafter, the Jewish community held a welcome dinner for 500 at the posh Mount Royal Hotel. The event was organized by the YM-YWHA and chaired by Samuel Bronfman. Within months, Cohen, 57, had courted and married a 38-year-old divorcee named Ida Judith Clark, who ran an upscale dress shop near the Ritz-Carlton hotel. As Cohen was lionized in Montreal, he and his wife were invited everywhere. He was the guest of honour and speaker at many elegant functions. However, Two-Gun was a restless individual, and prospects for a gunslinger in Montreal were not promising. Within a year, he travelled to Britain, the United States, Western Canada, and China to seek a role for himself. In China, the Chinese paid his hotel bills, but otherwise Two-Gun's high life drained his wife's financial resources. He was a flamboyant character who spent money like water. To impress his family in Manchester he would send them gifts, including briskets of Montreal smoked meat. When the marriage collapsed after less than a year, Two-Gun moved back into the Windsor Hotel.

In 1945, when 50 nations of the world gathered in San Francisco to formally establish the United Nations Organization, Samuel Bronfman, as President of Canadian Jewish Congress, invited Two-Gun to attend. The Congress delegation wanted the retired General to use his influence on the Chinese leader, Chiang Kai-Shek, to support a campaign through the UN to bring about the rebirth of Israel. He was able to convince China to support Jewish efforts to recreate Israel. As one of the few people welcomed in both Peking and Taipei, Cohen was concerned about the split in the Chinese nation—Communist against Nationalist. He explained his life-long support for the Chinese by stating that they were the only people who had never persecuted the Jews.

Cohen returned to England in 1950 and died in Manchester in 1970.

CHAPTER TWENTY-ONE

FASCISM AT HOME
An Ugly Time in La Belle Province

In every community there is a class of people profoundly dangerous to the rest. I don't mean the criminals. For them we have punitive sanctions. I mean the leaders.
Montreal-born Nobel Prize winner Saul Bellow, from his novel "Herzog", 1964

Joseph Cohen, a Liberal member from the Montreal riding of St. Lawrence, was addressing the Quebec Legislative Assembly when the recently elected Union Nationale Premier, Maurice Duplessis, stood up and rudely interrupted the opposition MLA. "Members need not listen to the only Jew in the room," declared Duplessis. "No," Cohen responded immediately. "There are TWO of us," he retorted, pointing to the crucifix over the speaker's chair. An eyewitness to the exchange, Jean Martineau, said he "never knew Duplessis to suffer such a put-down before or after."

It was 1936. Not a good year for Quebec Jewry. Joseph Cohen, regarded as "one of the finest criminal lawyers in the Dominion of Canada", was a King's Counsel, and held a position of eminence in law and society, yet he, like most Jews, witnessed an alarming growth of anti-Jewish prejudice and discrimination in the province. That year, the Liberals under L. Alexandre Taschereau, an open-minded tolerant premier who condemned anti-Semitism as anti-national and anti-Quebec, had gone down to defeat, and Duplessis and his ultra-nationalistic party had taken office. The new premier boasted he had dictatorial powers, *"L'Union Nationale, c'est moi"*. On another occasion, he asserted, "The bishops eat out of my hand". The premier openly suggested he was not interested in democratic procedures when he

Several times a week French-Canadian toughs from the east-end congregated outside the YMHA building at Park Avenue and Mount Royal and thumped Jewish youth—until the Jewish youngsters decided they would retaliate. The next time the bullies came, the Jewish boys had equipped themselves with baseball bats. The hoodlums never returned.

stated, "Do you wish to know what public opinion is? It is the opinion of those who are against us." The rise to power of three Fascist dictators in Europe—Adolf Hitler in Germany, Benito Mussolini in Italy and Francisco Franco in Spain—was paralleled by the formation of a number of Fascist groups across Canada, but the extremists were strongest in Quebec. Fascism, a socio-political ideology of the extreme right that relies on pseudo-religious attitudes and the use of force to obtain and retain power, manifested itself in the province in expressions of anti-Semitism and nationalism. The philosophical underpinnings of extremism in Quebec came notably from the work of Adrien Arcand and Abbé Lionel Groulx, with approval from the official Catholic press.

The 1936 election of Premier Duplessis and his Union Nationale touched off a wave of attacks on Jews. In the Legislative Assembly, Duplessis repeatedly denounced Communists—and he lumped Jews in that category. He charged Jewish MLA Peter Bercovitch with being the Communists' "echo in the legislature". The premier's vitriol encouraged sporadic street violence. For example, in 1936, Université de Montréal students terrorized Jews on the Main while pretending they were hunting Communists. These incursions were repeated on numerous occasions without fear of police interference.

Duplessis was to remain in power in Quebec until 1959, with the exception of five years in opposition (1939-1944).

A FUHRER IN QUEBEC

When selecting his first cabinet, Duplessis chose Adrien Arcand as labour minister. Arcand was the well-known head of a Fascist party and a vocal anti-Semite, who in 1933 had written in his newspaper *Le Patriote*:

"Now more than ever we have to fight against the Jews. We just have to look at the state of affairs in our province to see to what extent the Jews have managed to infect not just our economic life, but our very laws, with their subversive ideas and their despicable methods."

"We don't attack Jews," he declared. "We simply defend our country against their conspiracy."

Arcand began spreading his poisonous views in 1929, after being fired from *La Presse* for trying to organize a union. In August of that year, he established a satirical weekly *Le Goglu* (the bobolink) that launched repeated attacks on the Liberal government of Premier Taschereau. Arcand's partnership with a printer named

Joseph Menard made possible the publication of several papers, including *Le Miroir* and *Le Chameau*. Their editorial policies were uniform. Aside from being staunchly nationalistic, they were all fiercely against capitalism and the presence of Jews in Quebec. Montreal Mayor Camillien Houde paid a subsidy to Arcand's publications but later denounced the Fascist leader's anti-Semitism.

With the support of Menard, Arcand organized a political movement called the *Ordre patriotique des Goglus*, a group created along the lines of the Italian Fascist Party. (At the time, Mussolini was greatly admired in Quebec in part because he was supported by the papacy.) Arcand made grandiose claims of having signed up 50,000 members within a year. The party platform included a range of positions, such as the need to purify society, and to engage in what Arcand termed " the cleansing of politics." The party actively supported the campaign *Achat Chez Nous*, or "shop from your own".

When a bill to create a separate Jewish school commission was introduced in the assembly in 1930, Monsignor Georges Gauthier, Auxiliary Bishop of Montreal, hired Arcand to organize opposition to the measure. Arcand's strategy was to blame Jews for all the ills of the world, borrowing from the extreme right in Europe, and particularly the words of Adolf Hitler. The journalist charged that Jews sought to dominate the world and to destroy "Christian civilization."

ARCAND AND THE NAZI

By 1932, Arcand was in touch with international Fascist organizations that he called "enlightened patriots". He was in direct communication with Nazis in Germany through Nazi agent Kurt Ludecke. In his book, "I knew Hitler", Ludecke recalled a fund-raising tour of America: "(We) drove to Montreal to keep our appointment with Adrien Arcand, the fiery leader of the *'Ordre Patriotique des Goglus'*". Ludecke found the Order "violently anti-Jewish in the main...with three publications, all very demagogue and clever". He presented Arcand with an autographed picture of Hitler, which Arcand proudly displayed at headquarters. According to Ludecke, "We understood each other perfectly and agreed to cooperate in every way."

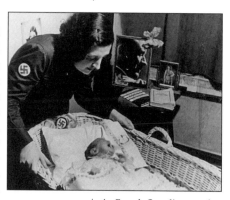

A French-Canadian mother, wearing a Swastika armband, with her baby in a bassinet decorated with the Nazi emblem. (Canadian Jewish Congress National Archives)

In 1930 and 1935, Arcand campaigned for the federal Conservatives and was paid by that party for his services. For example, in 1930, Conservative leader R.B. Bennett offered the Goglus $25,000 if they helped him win more than 12 Quebec seats in the general election of that year. Bennett won 24 seats in Quebec. Arcand and Menard received a large sum from the Tories; estimates range from $18,000 to $27,000—substantial sums for the times. Despite such financial backing, Arcand's papers were in trouble. Facing lawsuits from Jews and non-Jews, and without adequate advertising revenue, the Arcand publications folded in March 1933.

Despite never recruiting more than 7,000 supporters from among the 4 million French-Canadians, Arcand remained undaunted. In 1934, Arcand replaced his *"Ordre patriotique des Goglus"* with the "Parti national social chretien" (National Social Christian Party), a carbon copy of Hitler's Nazi Party. He adopted the swastika, symbol of the Nazis, for his own party and dressed his followers in blue shirts, imitating the German black shirts. The Party announced its intention of ultimately seizing power in Ottawa.

Throughout the mid-to-late '30s, Arcand orchestrated periodic recruitment marches in the downtown core. On one occasion, the parade could have taken place in Munich, Germany, but it was Dorchester Street. Men dressed in swastika-decorated uniforms goose-stepped down the wide thoroughfare, cheered on by mothers holding babies swaddled in blankets bearing the Nazi emblem.

YOUNG QUÉBÉCOIS TAKE UP THE REFRAIN

Arcand's group was not the only Fascist organization in Canada. In 1933, young Quebec intellectuals formed *Le Jeune Canada*, and published an anti-Semitic pamphlet *Politiciens et Juifs* (Politicians and Jews). One of the authors of the pamphlet was André Laurendeau, who alleged "Jews aspire to dominate the world."

Laurendeau later acknowledged he was mistaken, and went on to serve as Chairman of the Royal Commission on Bilingualism and Biculturalism.

(In 1952, Laurendeau wrote in *Le Devoir*: "After the assassination of six million Jews under Hitler's reign, one must have a too delicate stomach to swallow these fanatical denunciations without heaving. Such anti-Semitism is so stupid that it turned us into philosemites.")

PHILOSOPHICAL UNDERPINNINGS OF EXTREMISM IN QUEBEC

Anti-Semitism began to appear in early twentieth-century Quebec with the publication in 1913 of a small book of anti-Semitic cartoons entitled *Montréal Juif: Dessins Gais*. The cartoons vilified and stereotyped Jews, charging that Jews were cheating French-Canadians and plotting to seize control of the province.

In 1922, the young Catholic priest Lionel Groulx published a novel (under a pseudonym) called *L'Appel de la Race*. The novel, which was widely read, declared that there was no room in Quebec for any "foreigner", including Jews. Abbé Groulx declared:

> "The Jews bring us popular corruption through the cinema and fashion. The Jews have passed from the adoration of the true God to the adoration of Satan."

A move to boycott Jewish stores arose in Quebec in the early 1920s and received enthusiastic support from Nationalists and priests. In early 1924, the newspaper *La Croix* (the Cross) called on Québécois "to get rid of them by elimination or annihilation." This publication included in its pages excerpts from "The Protocols of the Elders of Zion," a forged document said to have been authored by the Czar's secret police. The Protocols (still in circulation) claim Jews plan to conquer the world. The document first surfaced in 1905 and was proven a forgery in 1921.

The Great Depression (1929-39) created widespread unemployment, particularly in Quebec, where the number of jobless rose to one-third of the work force. (The social benefits of the future—unemployment insurance, family allowance and medicare—did not exist then.) Jews were vulnerable targets as scapegoats. The English were a larger minority in the province but held too much power and prestige to be easily attacked. According to sociologist E.C. Hughes, who studied the textile town of Drummondville, Quebec, of the 1930s: "The symbolic Jew receives the more bitter of the attacks which the French-Canadians would like to make upon the English or perhaps even upon some of their own leaders and institutions. Many of the accusations made against the Jew would be justified if made against the English...It is the English who have introduced the new form of economic enterprise which threaten the French-Canadian way of living and working."

Economic activities in the city were drawing thousands from rural parishes across the province. Church officials deplored and publicly denounced the trend, but could do little to prevent it.

In 1930s...

...There were 57,997 Jews in Montreal, and about 2,000 scattered throughout Quebec.

...The *Montreal Gazette* had a Jewish editor, Abel Vineberg.

...A debate raged whether women should have the right to practise law in the province.

Tenement, 1936 (Etching and drypoint by Frederick B. Taylor—from the art collection of Atara and Murray Marmor)

OFFICIAL CATHOLIC PRESS ANTI-SEMITIC

The campaign against the Jews was strengthened through the official Catholic press. *L'Action Catholique*, which published anti-Semitic articles and influenced many clerics, declared:

> "The Jew is perfidious because he adores the blasphemous Talmud, because he has plotted for centuries against Christian states, because he has founded the Socialist movement, because the B'nai B'rith is associated with Freemasonry, and because Jewish bankers have financed the Russian Revolution."

(The Talmud is a compilation, by scholars, of ancient Jewish law and tradition, and is considered a guide to moral living. The very core of the Talmud is the **Mitzvah**—the doing of good deeds.)

One of the extreme writers of the era was Abbé E.V. Lavergne, who declared in 1922, "Jews, as a race, are our enemies. Their goal is to destroy Christianity, but in order to achieve this goal, it was necessary to shed floods of blood."

"QUEBEC, A PARADISE FOR MINORITIES"

In 1932, the only two Jewish MLAs—both Montreal lawyers—Joseph Cohen and Peter Bercovitch, introduced a group libel bill in the Legislature. The bill, a measure intended to prevent libel based on race, religion or nationality, was aimed at anti-Semitic papers, namely those of Arcand. However, press reaction was hostile. *L'Action Catholique*, in condemning the proposed legislation, commented:

> "The Province of Quebec, a paradise for minorities, does not merit the affront of a law which would give her the appearance of being more of a persecutor than her sister provinces." The bill was shunted aside and never came up for a vote.

GROULX: THE PHILOSOPHER OF THE FASCIST MOVEMENT IN QUEBEC

Of great significance to the history of Jews is the activity of avowed Fascist Abbé Lionel-Adolphe Groulx, who in recent times has been called the spiritual leader of modern Quebec. Though Groulx expressed his fascism mostly in a campaign of fervent nationalism, many of his comments are blatantly anti-Semitic.

Shortly after Hitler became Chancellor in 1933 and assumed control of Germany, Abbé Groulx wrote: "Jewish internationalism (is) one of the most dangerous forces of moral and

When Alderman Max Seigler of Montreal was nominated for deputy mayor, *Le Club Ouvrier Maisonneuve* led a campaign against his nomination, declaring "it is a shame to see that our French Canadian aldermen could not find anything else but a Jew as deputy mayor...(and) that we must humble ourselves before the Jews."

social decay on the planet." In that same year, Pope Pius XI signed a concordat with Hitler, an agreement that helped make Nazism more acceptable to French-Canadian Catholics. Some clerics, such as Father Georges-Henri Levesque, the founder of the School of Social Sciences at Laval University, went against the tide and campaigned for more liberal ideas in Quebec.

In 1933, Abbé Groulx began publishing his own newspaper, *L'Action Nationale*, charging that all Jews were pro-Communist, that they had created a monopoly over business and the professions and should be limited to an even smaller quota of students in the university. In editorials, Groulx expressed admiration for various dictatorial governments—particularly those of Benito Mussolini in Italy and Francisco Franco in Spain. The Abbé had a vision of a "racially pure" Quebec, mirroring the propaganda of Hitler's Germany and the "Aryan" ideal of a white, blue-eyed master race. (Aryan is actually the Indo-European family of languages, and has nothing to do with race.) In Quebec, the Abbé had tremendous influence. He had taught thousands of students since he began lecturing at the Université de Montréal in 1915. In addition, the newspaper of the intelligentsia, *Le Devoir*, provided him with space for his theories and opinions.

NATIONALISM NOT ANTI-SEMITISM
Commenting on the *Achat Chez Nous* campaign in 1933, Abbé Groulx clarified his position:

> "Anti-Semitism not only is not a Christian solution, it is a negative and silly solution. To solve the Jewish problem it would be sufficient for French-Canadians to recover their common sense. There is no need for extraordinary legislative machinery, no need for violence of any kind. We would not even give our people this order 'do not buy from the Jews!' We would simply tell French-Canadian customers 'Do as everyone else does, do as every ethnic group does, 'Buy at Home'."

The campaign endured for about 10 years, winding down in the mid-1930s, but not before the St. Denis branch of the St. Jean Baptiste Society weighed in with a campaign to 'Save the corner store'. A widely circulated flyer read:

> "Just so long as we neglect our merchants, our corner grocer, to give our money to foreigners, our race will play a secondary role in commerce and our patriotism will be reduced to empty words which do no good to anybody if not to those who have interest in keeping us down."

In 1935-1936, Canadian Jewish Congress called on the Canadian government to withdraw its athletes from the 1936 Berlin summer Olympic Games. The Trades and Labour Congress of Canada supported the Jewish organization's call for a boycott of the Games and of German goods. The Labour Congress pressed Ottawa "to break off diplomatic relations with the Hitler government until such time as this government ceases their persecution of the organized working class of Germany, and to express abhorrence for the regime which has overthrown civil and religious freedom." The Canadian government did not respond.

The Achat Chez Nous campaign did not do well; most Jewish merchants spoke French and got along well with their customers.

A WARNING ABOUT FASCISM IN CANADA

Fascist activities in Quebec, particularly Arcand's Nazi Party, alarmed many in Canada. In its April 15, 1938 edition, *Maclean's* magazine warned "there is a Fascist movement in this country and it is growing." The magazine charged that Arcand was "potentially dangerous" and called his anti-Semitism "fanaticism." According to *Maclean's*, Arcand has "a savage scorn of Judaism and everything connected with it."

Canadian Jewish Congress echoed the magazine's words of warning: "Fascist and Nazi organizations in Canada are plotting to obtain political control of this province (Quebec) and to destroy the Jewish people." A Congress bulletin circulated in Quebec and the Maritime provinces stated that "the rising tide of anti-Semitism throughout the world is having its repercussions in Quebec, (where) the National Social Christian Party, led by Adrian Arcand, already boasts of having 15,000 members...Scurrilous and malicious propaganda continues to pour out and poison the minds of innocent people." In 1938, Arcand claimed he had 80,000 members in his party, but disenchanted party members put the figure at 1,800.

The Fascist movement in Quebec died quickly in 1939 when Canada went to war against Germany and Italy. Arcand and his deputy, Dr. Noel Decarie, were interned in 1940 under the War Measures Act for "disloyalty and subversion of the democratic process." The RCMP, making the arrest, seized documents indicating that Arcand's party had, at that time, 7,803 members across Canada. Of these, 98 per cent were in Quebec. Arcand remained in custody until the war ended.

Arcand was regarded as dangerous even after the war. In October 1952, the Paris magazine "Droit de Vivre" said of the Fascist leader:

"Arcand is the most dangerous Canadian anti-Semite for he is truly eloquent. He knows his people; he can present sophistry with consummate art and put forward the worst lie so sincerely and so seductively that his listeners, in the main ignorant and illiterate, accept the lie as religious truth."

In 1965, Arcand renewed his call for the formation of a Fascist party which would be "federalist, Corporatist, monarchist and pro-western." Furthermore, he wrote a book, *"A bas la haine"*

(Down with Hate) in which he claimed that Hitler never persecuted the Jews.

Arcand died in Montreal on August 2, 1967, his views
unchanged. Abbé Groulx died in that same year—the 100th
anniversary of Confederation. They and their associates had led
Quebec dangerously close to becoming a Fascist state. Despite
open support for Fascists in Europe, and blatant anti-Semitism,
Groulx remains a revered figure in Quebec.

DR. DELISLE MAKES HER CHARGES

The French-Canadian historian Dr. Esther Delisle was ostracized
by her fellow francophones when she published, in 1992 a book
based on her Ph.D. research called "The Traitor and the Jew". The
book includes harsh comments on Abbé Groulx and his "myths"
about the "purity" of the French Catholic "race". In a second
book, "Lies and False Memories", published in 1999, Delisle
charges that a secret branch of the "Iron Guard" existed in
Quebec and its membership included "many" Quebec
Nationalists. Membership in this extreme right-wing organization, she alleged, included Abbé Groulx.

She also wrote that the American Consul in Quebec City
advised President Franklin Roosevelt about the danger that
Quebec might become a Fascist state.

In 1937, the Duplessis government moved closer to a dictatorship with the passage of the "Padlock Law," giving provincial police almost unlimited power. The Law had been preceded by passage of a series of measures curtailing freedom of speech and press in the province. Theoretically, the Padlock Law was aimed at Communists and authorized the state to padlock any facility suspected of being used "to propagate Communism or Bolshevism." However, the law was used to suppress public expression and permit censorship of publications and movies.

ORDRE DE JACQUES CARTIER

On June 22, 1944, a Senator from Quebec, Télésphore-Damien Bouchard, triggered a great deal of outrage when he stated during his maiden speech in the Upper House that a secret society existed in the province with the goal of creating an independent Fascist state along the lines of the dictatorial regimes of Spain and Portugal. Senator Bouchard charged that the Ordre de Jacques Cartier society was anti-English and anti-Semitic, and that it enjoyed church support. The existence of the quasi-Fascist society had been mentioned previously in an article in the newspaper *Le Jour*. The paper called it the "Ku Klux Klan of French Quebec." Bouchard told a shocked Senate that the movement had 18,000 members and included "some of the most prominent and powerful people in Quebec." According to Bourchard, membership included leaders of Catholic trade unions, top officials of the nationalistic St. Jean Baptiste Society, school commissioners, and politicians. Furthermore, he stated that the kind of state the organization wanted would "bring us back to the social and economic status of the Middle Ages." He charged that members of the society had been instrumental in the 1936 election victory of Maurice Duplessis, which gave Quebec "the poorest and most abusive government in the history of the province."

Senator Bouchard's remarks came during a Senate debate on a proposal for adopting a national textbook of Canadian history. He charged that "false history" was being taught in Quebec schools, and that such books were tools of "subversive propaganda in the hands of those who are aiming to disrupt Confederation and overthrow our form of democratic government."

The reaction to the charges was widespread condemnation by politicians and church people and Bouchard paid the price for speaking up. He was fired from his position as President of Hydro-Quebec. The reaction of newspapers to this punishment was interesting. The French newspapers approved of the dismissal; the English papers denounced it as an interference with freedom of speech. Richard Jones, in an article on the Ordre de Jacques Cartier in the Canadian Encyclopedia, remarks that its "actual influence remains debatable" and he added the group was "officially disbanded" in 1965.

The diplomat asked the President to intervene. Delisle also declares that sympathy for fascism did not end with World War II. Her book claims that as many as 200 Nazi collaborators from France found shelter in Quebec—assisted by francophone Nationalists including priests, politicians, and academics.

EASTER TIME IN MONTREAL

In a multi-volume study on anti-Semitism, historian David Rome suggested that "the concept of violence was eschewed in Canada by all concerned, even by the preachers of race hatred, contradictory as this may seem. Unlike European parallels, there was little violence upon person or upon property here." Rome suggested "to a large part this restraint had Christian religious roots; justice, love and moderation were meaningful terms even in the milieu of the Fascists." Not everyone would agree with this assessment.

Poet Irving Layton, who lived in the downtown Jewish district from his birth in 1913 until 1950, told an interviewer:

> "The strongest memory I have is of clashes. Around Easter, during the death and resurrection of Jesus Christ, something seemed to happen to the gentiles. They took it as a cue to come and beat up on the Jews.

> "So, without fail, every Easter, they would descend on the embattled Jews with bottles and bricks, and we'd be waiting for them on the roofs, like an army, with sticks and stones, with anything.

> "There would be pitched battles and a number of serious injuries."

For Jews who witnessed the ugly face of anti-Semitism in Quebec, or who experienced any of the sporadic violence, the experience was not soon forgotten.

JOHN BUCHAN, ZIONIST/NO ANTI-SEMITE HE

Author and Governor General of Canada John Buchan (1875-1940) is best known for his popular adventure stories, some of which (The Thirty-Nine steps, 1915, Greenmantle, 1916 and The Three Hostages, 1924) contain anti-Semitic references. However, Buchan was not an anti-Semite, but instead was a fervent pro-Zionist. In having characters make anti-Jewish remarks, Buchan was only mirroring popular speech. The writer, who became Baron Tweedsmuir, served as Governor General of Canada from 1934-1940. In Britain and in Canada, he was outspoken in his support for the idea of a Jewish State in Palestine. Buchan was both a friend and admirer of the great Jewish scientist, Dr. Chaim

Weizmann, who became the first President of Israel.   As Chairman of the Palestine Committee, Buchan referred to "the centuries of cruelty and wrong which have stained the record of nearly every Gentile people." In 1930, Buchan wrote an article in the *Graphic* entitled "Ourselves and the Jews" in which he described the Balfour Declaration and Britain's support of a Jewish Homeland in Palestine as a "categorical promise."

In 1936, John Buchan visited Montreal and told a Zionist meeting "no social or political or intellectual barriers" were erected against the Jewish people. Referring to Benjamin Disraeli, he noted "we have made a Jew our Prime Minister."

Even the Nazis knew where Buchan stood. In a "hit list" prepared in anticipation of a successful siege of England, the Germans labeled him a pro-Jewish Briton.

> *"I fought the street*
> *with my flesh and bone*
> *for every breath I took.*
> *The mockery and the abuse*
> *the ugly hand*
> *that fell on my shoulders*
> *when I had to ransom my existence somehow*
> *and answer to the day before the next day came.*
> *I went down under my enemies' attacks*
> *and the acts of fate*
> *into depths*
> *where songs were sunken ships*
> *and the bones of unborn generations slept."*
> > *Montreal poet J.I. Segal*
> > *from "In The Book of Beauty."*
> > *Translated from the Yiddish*

CHAPTER TWENTY-TWO

A BAS LES JUIFS
No Dogs or Hebrews Allowed

Sam Rabinovitch was full of enthusiasm when he reported to Notre-Dame Hospital for his first day as chief intern. He had graduated at the head of his class from the Université de Montreal's Medical School in 1934 and had been immediately offered a position at the Roman Catholic hospital. When he reported for duty, he was dismayed to learn that the other 34 student doctors—all French-Canadian—had staged a walk-out at midnight the night before because they refused to work with a Hebrew. The afternoon editions reported that interns in four other French hospitals (St. Jean de Dieu, Ste. Justine, Hotel Dieu, and Hôpital de la Miséricorde) had joined the walkout in sympathy. Some priests had even joined the picket lines. With almost the entire staff of interns having deserted their post, Rabinovitch was called to 50 different places in the hospital and needed the help of nurses to maintain basic services. The medical board of the faculty of medicine, which had voted to honour their contract with Rabinovitch, issued an ultimatum to the strikers. However, after the strikers— about 75 medicos—refused to care for patients or answer ambulance calls for 90 hours, Sam Rabinovitch felt he had no choice. He resigned, saying "I feel my decision will meet with the approval of the entire Jewish community because the care of the sick has always been of first importance with the Jewish people."

Discrimination against Jews, or anti-Semitism, was rampant in Canada, and at its most intense in Quebec throughout the 1930s. While not solely a by-product of the Great Depression (1929-39), deteriorating economic conditions helped spread the contagion. Historian Pierre Berton described the era in less than glowing terms: **"Canada was a racist country. The vast majority of Canadians, from the Prime Minister down, were at least pas-**

sively anti-Semitic. Everybody knew what the warning sign 'restricted' meant at golf clubs and tourist resorts. It bothered few that banks, insurance companies, department stores, financial firms, and a variety of other institutions, from Procter and Gamble to Maclean Hunter, barred Jews from employment. Jewish doctors couldn't get hospital affiliations. Law firms rarely hired Jews. The universities and professional schools refused to hire Jewish faculty and devised quotas for Jewish students."

DISCRIMINATION IN MEDICINE

Outside of Jewish-run medical clinics, Jewish doctors faced extensive prejudice. To find an appropriate position, doctors often had to practise in the United States. Anti-Semitism was widespread in the United States as well as Canada, but larger concentrations of Jews in American cities provided greater opportunities for doctors in hospital facilities owned and operated by co-religionists. Sheila McLeod Arnopoulos and Dominique Clift, writing about this period in their book "The English Fact in Quebec", declared:

"Until World War Two, Anglo-Protestant Hospitals such as the Royal Victoria and the Montreal General admitted only limited numbers of Jewish interns and rarely offered them top appointments. It was in response to these policies that the Jewish community raised funds to open the Jewish General Hospital."

Interestingly, the newly opened Jewish General Hospital—created specifically for the Montreal Jewish community—did not offer Rabinovitch a post.

The *Gazette*, commenting on the Rabinovitch dispute, wrote in an editorial on June 20, 1934:

"The striking interns of the Notre-Dame Hospital and four other French Canadian hospitals have returned to their posts, but the strike was not won by them; it was won by Mr. Sam Rabinovitch, who was willing to sacrifice his position in order that the hospitals might maintain the efficiency of their services and that their patients might have all the care and the attention available under normal conditions. Dr. Rabinovitch did what no one of the other interns did; he placed the standards of his profession, the moral responsibility of the physician, above every personal or racial consideration."

Indeed, Rabinovitch sacrificed his own position to prevent further disruption of service at the hospital. In his letter of resignation, Rabinovitch wrote: "In view of the distressing, serious and dangerous condition to which the patients of the Notre-Dame and other hospitals have been exposed because of the refusal of a number of their interns to take orders from their superiors, I feel it is my duty as a Physician to tender my resignation as intern to your hospital."

The Montreal doctor received support from Jewish doctors in the United States. Dr. Benjamin Jablons, Physicians Division, American Jewish Congress, sent him a telegram stating: "Greatly admire your stand and appreciate your attitude. If we can be of any help please communicate with me."

Rabinovitch did not have to wait long for another position. Less than 43 days after he resigned, he was taken on staff at the Mount Sinai Hospital in Baltimore. Six years later, he returned to Montreal as a specialist in internal medicine. While he went on to have an outstanding career in the United States and Canada, the disgraceful events of that June weekend had a profound effect on him.

ANTI-SEMITISM FRONT AND CENTRE IN QUEBEC SOCIETY

The discouraging experience of Sam Rabinovitch was just one of many blatant examples of discrimination faced by Jews in all levels of society and commerce. In 1931, the prominent demographer Louis Rosenberg noted in his immense study "Canada's Jews" that Jews, in their occupations, were "confined" to the entertainment industries, the clothing industry, retail trade, and professions that were "self-employing" because anti-Semitism denied them wider opportunities.

Jews seeking relaxation in the Laurentian mountains north of Montreal encountered signs splashed across the road in bold white paint with the message: A Bas Les Juifs (Down with the Jews). It was trendy for Jewish families in the '20s and '30s to rent a car for 50 cents (including gas) to spend a summer weekend getaway outside the city. Anti-Semitic organizations, such as Adrien Arcand's Nazi Party, targeted these areas for particularly insidious campaigns.

A handbill circulated in one town read:
> "NOTICE
> Jews are not wanted
> Here in Ste-Agathe
> Scram while the going is good."

An anti-Semitic sign in the laurentians, north of Montreal. (Canadian Jewish Congress National Archives, Montreal).

GROWING ANTI-SEMITISM

In 1937, Canadian Jewish Congress, which had been revived in 1934 in part due to the rise of anti-Semitism, reported:

Montréal, 15 juin 1933.

Sir George Perley,
Premier ministre intérimaire du Canada,
Ottawa.

Monsieur le ministre,

Sur recommandation de la Société St-Jean Baptiste, Section Immaculée-Conception de Montréal, nous vous prions instamment de refuser l'entrée au Canada aux juifs d'Allemagne, que leurs coreligionnaires veulent faire venir parmi nous.

En vous faisant remarquer, monsieur le ministre, les difficultés que chacun de nous avons à surmonter par ces temps de crise et de chômage aigus, où une telle immigration serait injustifiable au point de vue social et moral. Ce qui augmenterait davantage le fardeau de l'Etat.

Espérant votre bienveillante attention à nos remarques, nous demeurons,

Vos très respectueux serviteurs.

Président.

Secrétaire,
Société St-Jean Baptiste,
Montréal.

FB/.

Anti-Jewish letter by the St-Jean Baptiste Society. (Montreal Holocaust Centre Archives)

"During the past few years, we have witnessed an amazing growth of anti-Semitism.

"The minor and more spectacular evidence of this programme against the Jews have been the many instances in which Jews have been barred from hotels, beaches, golf courses and parks."
The report continued:

"The most pernicious results of this movement have been the startling increase in the number of individuals and companies who refuse to rent living quarters to Jews; the spreading policy of not employing Jews; the boycott of all Jewish firms; the sporadic attempts by various organizations to involve Jews in disturbances and in violence."

DISCRIMINATION IN EDUCATION

Montreal Jews ran into open prejudice in the field of higher education. In the 1930s, the author of discrimination at McGill University was R.A. MacKay, Dean of Arts. "The simple obvious truth is that the Jewish people are of no use to us in this country," he declared. He was able to limit Jewish enrolment in his faculty to 20 per cent and required Jews to have a 75% average in high school whereas Gentiles would be admitted with 60% or better. Other McGill faculties fell in line and, by 1939 the percentage of Jews in the university declined to 12 per cent in arts and medicine, and 15 per cent in law.

A Canadian Jewish Congress dispay of Canadian anti-Semitic publications. (Canadian Jewish Congress National Archives, Montreal)

McGill Medical School limited Jews to 10 per cent of its total enrolment until the 1960s. At the same time, the Université de Montréal had no quota for Jews. Historian Irving Abella wrote in the Canadian Encyclopedia about the effects of exclusivism:

> "There were scarcely any Jewish teachers and—most notably—no professors. Jewish nurses, engineers and architects had to hide their identity to find jobs in their fields."

DISCRIMINATION IN LAW

In 1948, Jewish members of the Quebec Bar Association were horrified to learn that the Annual Convention of the Association was to be held at the Mont Tremblant Lodge, in the Laurentians, which had a policy of "no Jews and dogs." When the Jewish lawyers protested, they were told it was too late to change the venue. The incident so outraged hundreds of Jewish lawyers that, after a series of meetings, they decided to boycott the Convention, and they created the *Lord Reading Law Society* to "lobby for fair representation of Jews on the Bar and the Bench."

The Society's first victory was the Bar Association's amendment to its constitution to ensure Jewish representation on the Bar of Montreal. (There had been only two Jewish members prior to this—Maxwell Goldstein, K.C., in 1922, and Peter Bercovitch, K.C. in 1930.)

The first Montreal Jewish lawyer to break through the web of anti-Semitism in legal circles was Samuel Jacobs, MP for Cartier. He had been admitted to the Bar in the late 1890's. (The first Jew admitted to the practice of law, in Lower Canada, was Aaron Ezekiel Hart.) Later a new generation of outstanding legal personalities emerged, including Benjamin Robinson, Joseph Shapiro, Philip Meyerovitch, and Harry Batshaw. They did pioneer work in the then new field of tax law. Cohen is regarded as "The Father of Criminal Law" and his career as a lawyer, politician, and teacher endured into the 1960s. Cohen and Philip Vineberg lectured in corporate law and their lectures were described as "spell-binding."

NO JEWISH JUDGES

In 1931, there were 350 Jewish lawyers in Canada, but not a single Jewish magistrate or judge in the entire country. This vacuum stemmed from two factors—anti-Semitism, on the one hand, and the tradition of balancing appointments of English and French-speaking candidates. In 1950, Harry Batshaw was the first Jew appointed a Justice of the Superior Court of Quebec. Batshaw was sworn in on the Old Testament, causing considerable consternation.

"Anti-Semitism was open and acceptable until at least the 1950s," Daniel Francis wrote in his 1997 book "National Dreams; Myth, Memory and Canadian History". "Jews were denied jobs and professional appointments, excluded from clubs and public facilities, subjected to hiring quotas, and refused admittance to the country, even when their lives were imperiled by the Nazi regime in Europe. All of these restrictions, and many others," wrote Francis, "were implemented on behalf of the Anglo-French majority in an effort to ensure that it retained economic, social and cultural preeminence."

While the disgraceful events surrounding Sam Rabinovitch's appointment to a French hospital made international headlines, most cases of discrimination went unreported and undocumented. Jews, after all, had lives to live. Families to feed. Goals to achieve. Anti-Semitism became an irritation at best, another obstacle to circumvent, another challenge to surmount on the road to their future.

"Fifty years ago the Jew was a stock character with a hooked nose in Canadian vaudeville, who got hit on the derby with a length of salami. Today, he is respected, often esteemed, sometimes the voice of our conscience...Jews have made contributions out of all proportion to their numbers in Canadian business and trade, art, literature, music, entertainment, medicine, law, science, research and university life."

Phyllis Lee Peterson, in Maclean's (1959), on the 200th anniversary of Jewish settlement in Canada.

CHAPTER TWENTY-THREE

"NONE IS TOO MANY"
How Canada Denied Sanctuary
to Endangered European Jews

There were five of them, nervously shifting about the waiting room of the office of Mackenzie King, the Prime Minister of Canada. The members of the Canadian Jewish Congress delegation—Parliamentarians Samuel Jacobs, A.A. Heaps, Samuel Spector, and Jewish Congress—President Samuel Bronfman and Executive Director Saul Hayes wanted to stress the urgency of allowing European Jews to immigrate to Canada. It was November 1938. Adolf Hitler had been in power five years. The terrible shadow of Nazi tyranny and terror had fallen across the German Jewish community of 300,000. In those pre-War days, the Germans would let Jews go—if they could find a country to take them. However, Ottawa repeatedly rejected their pleas. Later , in Cabinet, the Prime Minister, shaken by the Jewish delegation's presentation, suggested that Canada relax its strict regulations on Jewish refugees. However, King's Quebec Lieutenant, Justice Minister Ernest Lapointe, looked glum, and the subject was dropped.

Appeals to the government did move the Prime Minister. He confided to his diary: "The sorrows, which the Jews have to bear at this time, are almost beyond comprehension." In addition, he added: "Something will have to be done by our country." Mackenzie King acknowledged that it would be "difficult politically" but he would fight, in Cabinet, for the admission of some Jewish refugees, because it was "right and just, and Christian." By the time he met with the Jewish delegation, he had been convinced that he had to stick to his government's restrictive immigration policy. The government was under great pressure, particularly from unions, to curb immigration due to poor economic conditions. However, even when the world economy began to recover in 1936, Canada's doors remained closed. Mackenzie King said he sympathized with the plight of the Jews, but had to "consider the constituencies and the views of those supporting the government."

According to the distinguished historian Irving Abella, **"Canada had by far the worst record of any Western country in providing sanctuary to the Jews of Europe in the mid 1930s and 1940s."** Longtime Prime Minister of Canada, Mackenzie King firmly believed that the bicultural nature of Canada—English and French—should be protected. At an international conference, he declared:

"We must seek to keep Canada free from unrest and too great an intermixture of foreign strains of blood."

King, who welcomed immigration from the British Isles, was in power during the critical war years, 1939 to 1945, a period during which Canada only reluctantly accepted a handful of Jews who had escaped the Nazis. Tens of thousands of immigrants, many with large amounts of capital and others with exceptional abilities, were turned away. Jews could only enter through special orders-in-council. Barriers were erected to Jewish immigration in the form of demands for documentation impossible for refugees from embattled Europe to obtain. The numbers allowed in, when tens of thousands needed a refuge, tell their own tragic story: 1935—880 Jews allowed in; 1936—619; 1937—584 and 1938-39, on the eve of World War II, 890.

POLITICAL INACTION IN OTTAWA

Much of the blame for the Canadian position is dumped on F.C. Blair, Deputy Minister of Immigration, who, when asked how many Jews should Canada accept, cruelly remarked: "None is too many." The moral bankruptcy is shared by two prime ministers, R.B. Bennett and Mackenzie King, Justice Minister Ernest Lapointe and two Immigration ministers—W.A. Gordon and Thomas Crerar—and Canada's High Commissioner in London, Vincent Massey.

Lapointe was extremely influential. He dominated the Liberal Party in Quebec, and electoral support from that province was vital to Mackenzie King's re-election. Quebec members of the cabinet opposed the prime minister's attempts to liberalize immigration policy, and the cabinet decided the provinces should determine how many Jewish refugees to admit. Quebec was already critical of Ottawa for the number of immigrants coming into its depression-racked jurisdiction.

However, public opinion was not totally against the Jewish people. The French-language daily "La Patrie" published a "Letter from Ottawa", stating:

"In this country, we welcome with open arms all those who wish to become good citizens, all those who obey our laws and support our institutions.

"The Jewish colony is growing in scope and importance. It now numbers thousands of citizens such as any country would be proud to admit."

DARKNESS DESCENDS ON EUROPE

When the second letter to his sister in Austria came back marked Address Unknown, he knew instinctively that she had become a victim of the Nazis. However, he couldn't mourn her in the traditional manner; it would mean taking off eight days to sit shiva. He worked for the city parks department and if he took time off, he might be fired. So, in lieu of normal mourning, for eight days he worked with loose gravel in his boots as a painful reminder of his loss.

Few in Germany and fewer elsewhere believed that Adolf Hitler would carry out his threats, clearly enunciated in his book "Mein Kampf", to exterminate the Jews. Even the half-million Jews in Germany, when Hitler came to power in 1933, doubted that he would or could do exactly what he wrote and said. However, Hitler quickly disabused them of any notion that he was only talking. He oppressed the Jews, publicly humiliated them, stole their possessions, and barred them from almost all positions of significance in German society. In 1933, as his rule as Chancellor began, he ordered the dismissal of 1,700 Jewish scholars from teaching positions. An international organization was established in Switzerland to find positions for them. About 650 academics were able to emigrate in 1933 and 1934.

The League of Nations reported that, out of 366 engaged in research, only two were able to continue their work in Canada. In addition, only four others from among 248 academics were accepted for permanent positions in Canadian universities. Quebec universities did not accept a single person out of hundreds of highly qualified Jewish scientists and academics.

CANADA CLOSES ITS DOORS DURING THE JEWISH REFUGEE CRISIS

In the pre-War years, the Nazis did not prevent Jews from leaving. They wanted them to go. The problem was who would accept them?   Few visas were available for Jews agonizingly ready to leave an increasingly oppressive Germany. In addition, many Jews could not believe their country would turn against them; many considered themselves more German than Jewish. In the years 1934-37, 65,000 left the country. Of these, one in four journeyed to Palestine, while most of the others remained in Europe—not knowing that, in 1940, the Nazis would over-run Western Europe and they, once more, would be in their clutches. Most of them settled in France. Therefore, by the time tens of thousands of German Jews realized their danger, there was no refuge for them. Even in Palestine, the British shut down Jewish immigration after Arab protest riots in 1936.

In that same year, the Nazis introduced the vicious anti-Jewish Nuremburg Laws. In 1938, the campaign against the Jews rose to a terrible tempo. On November 9, the savage pogrom called **Kristallnacht** (Crystal Night) occurred; Germans attacked Jews in their homes, in their businesses, in their synagogues. They seized a multitude of Jewish men, women and children—beating some and shooting others. The streets were littered with broken glass. The event in "civilized Germany" shocked and panicked the world Jewish community. The crisis had begun.

Before long, Nazi military aggression left a million stateless Jews wandering the continent desperate for sanctuary.   However, Canada did not welcome them. Only a trickle of Jews was permitted to enter Canada—about 3,000 in the critical period 1935-1939. During the twelve years of the Hitler regime, the United States accepted more than 200,000 Jewish refugees. About 125,000 made it to Palestine. And Britain, under threat of invasion, accepted 70,000.

Canada's reputation, among European Jews, was so bad that the facility in the Auschwitz concentration camp, where victims' possessions were stored, was called "Canada"—a place of great wealth, but with access denied.

Shortly before World War II broke out, one of the three Jewish members of Parliament, A.A. Heaps, told a Canadian Jewish Congress conference:

> "The attitude of the Canadian government towards the immigration of Jewish refugees is inhuman and almost brutal...No country in the world has done so little for the Jewish victims of persecution in Europe."

SEEKING JUSTICE IN VAIN

In 1938, the League of Nations Association formed the *Canadian National Committee on Refugees and Political Persecution*, and the country's first woman senator, Cairine Wilson, became its chair. The Committee joined in the campaign to relax Canada's tight restrictions on Jewish immigration. During the year, 35 mass meetings were held across the country, calling on Federal authorities to modify its policy. Each of the gatherings heard from prominent non-Jews who angrily and emotionally denounced the government's rigid stand. Protest letters were sent by 66 organizations and individuals. Opposition to letting in Jewish refugees was expressed in 19 letters, nine of which came from Quebec. At a public rally in Montreal, supporting increased Jewish Immigration many non-Jews turned out, including Protestant clergy and the highly regarded Senator Raoul Dandurand.

Some individuals were outstanding in lobbying government to circumvent the restrictive refugee policy. Herman Gottleib, a post-First War refugee, succeeded in rescuing at least 17 people, mostly members of his own family. (He also built from scratch the Dependable Slipper Company, which in the late 1930s employed more than 1,500 people. Gottlieb started his shoe business using his bed as a workbench.)

THE EVIAN CONFERENCE

The United States took the lead in seeking help for victims of religious, racial and political persecution in Nazi Germany. In 1938, the U.S. State Department financed the formation of the "Evian Committee". This was an international conference, held at the Hotel Royale in Evian, Switzerland, intended to determine how problems arising from Hitler's anti-Jewish measures could be solved. However, there was no moral leadership. Country after country went on record as being unable or unwilling to help. One of the most negative participants in the talks was Frederic Charles Blair, Canadian Commissioner of Immigration. He told the conference that, in his view, the Jews were responsible for their own suffering. Only three countries went on record as being willing to accept Jewish refugees. They were the Netherlands, Denmark and the Dominican Republic. In addition, Australia told the conference it would admit 15,000 German refugees over the period 1939-1941. In the same year as the conference, the German Jewish journal *Der Morgen* bluntly told its readers, "You will be in terror all day and all night, and you won't be safe, so that you will say in the morning: if it were only evening, and in the evening: if it were only morning."

MACKENZIE KING: "THERE WILL BE NO WAR."

In 1937, Prime Minister Mackenzie King journeyed to London for two major Empire events—the Imperial Conference and the

Coronation of King George VI. From London, he flew to Berlin where—on June 29—he met Adolf Hitler. The Allied leaders in World War II, Winston Churchill, Joseph Stalin and Franklin Delano Roosevelt, never met Hitler, but Mackenzie King did—and he felt that the dictator was a fine and honest man!

When the Canadian Prime Minister arrived in Germany, the Nazis set out to impress him. They took him on a whirlwind tour of Hitler Youth camps.

They showed him aspects of German prosperity (stemming from rearmament in violation of the Post-World War I Treaty of Versailles).

King had coffee with the head of the German Air Force, Hermann Goering.

Finally, the Canadian leader was ushered into the presence of Adolf Hitler—who was dressed in white tie and tails for the occasion.

Mackenzie King was impressed and later commented:
"My sizing up of the man as I sat and talked with him was that he is really one who truly loves his fellow-men and his country.... His eyes impressed me most of all. There was a liquid quality about them which indicate keen perception and profound sympathy."
Hitler presented the Canadian PM with an autographed photo. Mackenzie King wrote in his diary, "Looking back over the German visit, I can honestly say that it was as enjoyable, informative and inspiring as any visit I have had anywhere...I have come away from Germany tremendously relieved. I believe that there will not be war."

The outbreak of war on September 1, 1939 broke off contacts between the Canadian leader and Hitler.

The "St. Louis", the vessel involved in the "Voyage of the Damned." (The Eiran Harris Collection, Canadian Jewish Congress National Archives)

WAS MACKENZIE KING AN ANTI-SEMITE?
Prime Minister King's diaries indicate that the Canadian politician admired many Jews and was often sympathetic to their plight. However, he was a consummate politician; he did not lead, he tried to placate fickle public opinion. In the final analysis, his policies were drafted simply to win votes.

A classic example is his handling of the unfortunate events surrounding the "St. Louis" refugee issue.

In 1939, the liner St. Louis, with 1,936 passengers aboard including 930 Jews, departed Hamburg, Germany, for Cuba. The refugees had been permitted to leave Germany but only after they had been stripped of all their possessions; their homes and businesses had been confiscated.

Their one hope was Cuba; they all had official Cuban landing certificates. However, when they reached Havana only 28 passengers were allowed to leave the vessel. The passengers were unaware of the fact that their certificates, which had been bought for $235 each, had been invalidated by Cuban President Frederico Laredo Bru in a dispute over which corrupt official should be paid off.

The ship turned north and the passengers sent a telegram to President Franklin D. Roosevelt appealing for help. There was no reply other than the appearance of an escort of U.S. Coast Guard cutters sent to ensure that no passenger swam ashore.

In Canada, a committee headed by Professor George Wrong of the University of Toronto pressed Prime Minister King to allow the exiles to land in Canada. At the time, the prime minister was in Washington accompanying the Royal family on a visit to the United States. Mackenzie King directed the plea from the St. Louis passengers to his Quebec lieutenant Ernest Lapointe. King knew many Quebecers were opposed to immigration in general and against Jewish migrants in particular. (A year before, Quebec's nationalistic St. Jean Baptiste Society had presented the Federal government with a petition with 127,000 signatures calling on Ottawa to turn away all refugees and "especially Jews." In Montreal, the influential Le Devoir asked its readers: "Why allow in Jewish refugees? The Jewish shopkeeper on St. Lawrence Boulevard does nothing to increase our natural resources.") It was a foregone conclusion that Ottawa would turn down the appeal.

The St. Louis continued its voyage back to Europe, but its anti-Nazi Captain Gustav Shroder steamed as slowly as he could. The refugees appeared to be en route to almost certain death. However, at the last moment, the frantic efforts of an international Jewish relief agency, the Joint Distribution Committee, paid off. With the JDC posting a bond, the Netherlands accepted 194 of the passengers; Belgium and France took in 250 each, and Britain accepted the rest.

Of the 621 who took refuge in continental European countries, all but four are said to have perished the following year during the German Blitzkrieg.

"DANGEROUS ALIENS" ARE SHIPPED TO CANADA

Canada unwittingly became a refuge for thousands of Jews when—with the outbreak of war—the British had no time to

THE ATTITUDE OF MIKE PEARSON

During the pre-war years, Lester B. "Mike" Pearson, the future Canadian prime minister, was a member of the diplomatic corps in London, and he showed his sympathy and concern for the harassed Jews of Germany during a BBC broadcast. When a broadcaster suggested that Jews caused their own problems by not mixing, Mike Pearson responded: "Even if that were true, who's responsible for this tendency? It wasn't so many centuries ago...when Jews were forbidden to be anything but Jews, no matter how long they'd lived in a country; they were herded together into separate communities, they were kept there as a separate people." About ten years later, L.B. Pearson was External Affairs Minister for Canada and, at the United Nations, helped ensure a positive vote for the establishment of Israel, through the partitioning of Palestine.

investigate the background of refugees from Germany and Italy. They were all classified as "enemy aliens" and shipped to Canada and Australia. In fact, the vast majority of these people were anti-Nazis and anti-Fascists who had escaped to the United Kingdom, and most of them were Jews. Canada agreed to accept 7,000 such "aliens", and Britain shipped 4,500 civilian internees and made up the remainder of the quota with 2,500 prisoners of war. Many of them ended up in a large detention camp at Farnham, Quebec. One of the "dangerous aliens" shipped to Quebec was Gideon Rosenbluth, now Professor Emeritus, Department of Economics, University of British Columbia. Professor Rosenbluth wrote, in the secular Jewish publication "Outlook":

> "My family was among the first German refugees to arrive in England in 1933. My father had been a member of a delegation sent to England by Jewish organizations in Berlin to alert British Jews, politicians, and media to the escalating persecution of German Jews."

Despite his family's impeccable anti-Nazi credentials, Rosenbluth was shipped through submarine-infested waters to Canada. One shipload of detainees was sunk by a German submarine and most perished.

The campaign to free the anti-Nazis to work or to study was led by an outstanding humanitarian, Alex Patterson, a prominent Montreal lawyer. Rosenbluth wrote that Patterson convinced the Canadian military and civil authorities to recognize the distinction between Nazis and anti-Nazis, and to make some effort to treat the anti-Nazis decently. Rosenbluth said, "(Patterson) did a job which nowadays would require a large committee with a platoon of assistants. He had help from Jewish and Quaker Committees."

Other people involved in the successful effort to free the detainees were Samuel Bronfman, as President of CJC, and Saul Hayes, Executive Vice-President of Congress. They visited the camp near Sherbrooke several times to interview inmates and determine how they could help them.

One man who impressed them particularly was Henry Oelberg. They were able to negotiate his release to study and work. Oelberg in time became Director of Finance of the Federation.

His story began in Germany, where his Austrian-born father was a major importer and exporter. When the Germans seized Austria, Oelberg urged his son to leave. Henry Oelberg nervously boarded a train for Holland, and sat with an Australian who

Lavy Becker with a shipment of Jewish books recovered from the Nazis. (circa 1949) (Canadian Jewish Congress National Archives, Montreal)

spoke no German. When Nazi officials asked for their documents, Oelberg translated for the Australian.

The border officials were distracted and only glanced at Henry's passport. Oelberg made it to Britain but, with the outbreak of war, he was rounded up and shipped to Canada where, as a potential immigrant, he would never have been admitted.

By the autumn of 1943, the camps in Canada and Australia were closed. Of the internees, more than 1,500 returned to Britain while others settled in Canada and the United States. In 1945, Canada formally invited the internees to become citizens and 972 accepted the invitation.

In its issue of May 15, 2000, *Maclean's Magazine*, reporting on the internees, noted that "more than 70 became university professors, including two Nobel Prize winners and collectively they received more honourary degrees than anyone has cared to count. Of the nearly 1,000 who chose to remain in Canada, dozens have contributed to Canada's cultural life as authors, musicians and scientists, and at least nine have been named members or officers of the Order of Canada."

Canada's refugee policy did not change until the war ended, and stories and pictures of the Holocaust modified public opinion. However, a post-War open-door policy did not reflect any change in the thinking of Canada's longest-serving prime minister. As late as 1947, Mackenzie King declared, "Immigration must not distort the present character of the Canadian population." In a debate in the House of Commons on May 1, 1947, Mackenzie King stated:

> "With regard to the selection of immigrants, much has been said about discrimination. I wish to make it quite clear that Canada is perfectly within her rights in selecting the persons whom we regard as desirable future citizens. It is not a 'fundamental human right' of any alien to enter Canada. It is a privilege."

493 Sherbrooke West—home for Federation 1950 through 1972 when Cummings House was built on Cote St. Catherine Road.
(Canadian Jewish Congress National Archives, Montreal).

In 1946, Canadians were asked in a survey "if Canada allows more immigrants, are there any of these nationalities which you would like to keep out?" The highest negative response was to Japanese at 60 per cent. Jews came second at 49 per cent.

Members of the Sir Mortimer B. Davis Building Committee of the Y.M.-Y.W.H.A., 1944-1951. Many of these men dedicated much of their adult lives to building and supporting the "Y". (Allan Raymond Collection, Jewish Public Library Archives)

CHAPTER TWENTY-FOUR

GOING TO WAR
16,880 Jews Enlist in Canada's Armed Forces

In the face of considerable anti-aircraft fire, Pilot Sidney Shulemson carefully aimed his twin-engined Beaufighter attack aircraft at the warship below him in the Bay of Biscay. Through his gun-sight, he could see the swastika flag flapping on the ship's mast. Carefully, he squeezed the red button on his control column and his four 20-mm Oerlikon cannon began spitting shells. He watched the path of the tracer rounds as the projectiles slammed into the German ship. He and his observer saw the vessel burst into flames, and watched as sailors leapt into the water from their sinking craft. The two young airmen cheered wildly before gunning their engines and heading back to home base. It was the second Nazi warship they had sunk, off the French coast, that day.

TIMELINE—1939-46

1939-1945. World War II; 17,000 Canadian Jews—nearly half of them from Montreal—serve in the Canadian Armed Forces.

1941. The Combined Jewish Appeal is formed by Federation, Jewish General Hospital, and the United Jewish Refugee and War Relief Agencies.

1942. The Jewish Hospital of Hope is created to care for the chronically ill.

1942. Nahum Goldman reports on the Nazi "Final Solution" to a Canadian Jewish Congress Plenary.

1944. Jewish Vocational Service becomes operational.

1944. The B'nai Brith Hillel Foundation is established to serve thousands of war veterans flocking to universities in the post-war era.

1946. Squadron Leader Gerald Bronfman of Montreal is awarded the Legion of Merit by the United States for "outstanding service" with the Canadian Joint Staff in Washington.

During WWII (1939-1945), more than one million Canadian men and women served in the Armed Forces and more than 42,000 died. Canadian Jewish Congress, chronicler of the war effort of Canadian Jews, notes "with pride" that 9.6% of the Canadian Jewish population served in the three armed forces— 10% higher than the national average. *"The Jewish community as such has subscribed generously, away out of proportion, not because they consider it a 'Jewish' war, but because they understand the clear cut policy of decency versus brute force much better than people who take their freedom too much for granted."*

RCMP Report, December 1940

Recruiting in World War II in Yiddish, English and French. (Canadian Jewish Congress National Archives).

The Jews of Montreal have a long and often distinguished record of fighting on behalf of Canada. In World War II, more than one-fifth of Jewish males enlisted in the Canadian Armed Forces. At least 16,880 Canadian Jews, including 279 women, are confirmed to have served—10,440 in the Army; 5,870 in the Air Force and 570 in the Navy. These are minimum figures. Unquestionably, more Jews served but were not identified as such. During the five-and-a-half-year conflict, 421 Jewish servicemen died, including 104 from Quebec. (One Jewish woman, Rose Goodman, from New Glasgow, N.S., was fatally injured in an accident in Canada.) Military decorations were awarded to 1,971 Jews. The most decorated Canadian Jew was Montrealer Sydney Simon Shulemson, who received both the Distinguished Service Order and the Distinguished Flying Cross.

Shulemson, a graduate of Baron Byng High School and McGill University, served for 18 action-filled months with the 404th Squadron of the Royal Air Force Coastal Command. He flew an attack aircraft doubling as fighter and bomber armed with four cannon and rockets. In one sortie, he inflicted what was described in dispatches as "heavy damage" on three enemy destroyers. On another occasion, he sank "heavily-defended enemy vessels." Single-handedly, he did great damage to the German naval forces patrolling the Atlantic coast of occupied Europe. Known as an aggressive daredevil flyer, Shulemson's bold tactics encouraged others in the squadron to follow his lead in striking at the enemy. The citation for his D.S.O. read: "He is a skillful, courageous and determined leader, whose example has inspired all. " The citation details what happened to Shulemson after he destroyed part of the German convoy in the Bay of Biscay: "As course was set for home one member of the formation was attacked by a fighter and sustained damage. Flying Officer Shulemson immediately turned and joined the fight. Some 18 minutes later the enemy aircraft was forced to terminate the engagement and Flying Officer Shulemson flew on to base and landed safely in spite of a burst tire on one of the landing wheels."

Cartoon on Flt. Lieut. Sydney Shulemson, D.S.O., D.F.C., published by Canadian Jewish Congress.

Another Montreal pilot, Wing Commander Harry Shapiro, was awarded two distinguished Flying Crosses for his "cheerful courage, determination and devotion to duty."

Squadron Leader Sydney Shulemson, DSO, DFC, with the Bristol Beaufighter fighter-bomber he used to destroy several German vessels during World War II. (Canadian Jewish Congress National Archives)

Wing Commander Harry Shapiro, DFC and Bar.

1.5-MILLION JEWS IN UNIFORM

Jews throughout the world were determined to see the Axis powers—Nazi Germany, Fascist Italy and Imperial Japan—defeated, in a war that inflicted more casualties on civilians than on men and women in uniform. An estimated 55-million people died in the conflict. Of that immense total, approximately six million were Jews, mostly in Eastern Europe, annihilated by the Nazis in what has come to be known as the **Shoah**, or Holocaust.

An estimated one-and-a-half million Jews served with the Allied Forces. The United States and the Soviet Union counted half-a-million each in their armed services. In Palestine, 50,000 Jews enlisted. There were 50,000 British Jews in England's armed services.

NAZI CAMPAIGN COMES TO LIGHT

By late 1942, reports were reaching Canada of the mass murder of Jews by the Germans, but few—including many Jews—believed the horror stories. Squadron Leader Monty Berger of Montreal, an intelligence officer with an RCAF Spitfire fighter wing, recalled in an interview:

> "Not unlike other Jews in Canada, I had heard of cousins and relatives who had disappeared, or were killed in the nightmarish world that descended on Europe's Jewish population in the late 1930s. My identity as a Jew ran deep. I felt fully the sense of frustration seeing Hitler and the Nazis go unchecked."

A JEWISH BRIGADE GROUP (1944-46)

An international volunteer contingent of fighting Jews was formed midway through the war and commanded by a Canadian

Jew, Brigadier Ernest Frank Benjamin. *The Jewish Brigade* included in its ranks a number of Canadian Jews, 40 of whom were Montrealers. The Brigade unit formed part of the legendary British eighth army, and had a strength of 5,000 men. It fought the Germans savagely on three fronts—Egypt, Northern Italy, and Northwest Europe— during the years 1944-45. In Italy, they went up against some of the crack units of the *Wehrmacht* (Germany army) and inflicted heavy casualties. After fighting on the River Senio front, the Brigade was moved to the Italo-Austrian-Yugoslav border where it made its first contact with Jewish survivors and members of the Jewish underground.

A veteran of the unit told a Montreal synagogue audience about an emotional encounter between members of the Brigade and Jews in a Displaced Persons Camp in Germany. A Brigade messenger on a motorcycle was preceding the convoy of military vehicles when he stopped near a fenced-off camp for Holocaust survivors. They were amazed to see the Star of David on his uniform armband. "You're a Jewish soldier?" they asked incredulously. "Tomorrow morning," the messenger told them, "5,000 Jewish soldiers will be coming down this road." The stunned survivors stayed up all night, leaning against the fence. They did not want to miss the Jewish soldiers. When the convoy reached the encampment, the soldiers tumbled out of their vehicles, crying. They embraced the survivors and gave them all the rations and cigarettes they had.

The Brigade returned to Palestine in 1946 and was disbanded. In the end, 44 had been killed in action or died of wounds. There were 21 members of the Brigade who were decorated and 78 were mentioned in dispatches for particularly courageous efforts.

ON THE HOME FRONT

Jewish organizations, particularly Canadian Jewish Congress, worked hard to promote the war effort. Headquartered in Montreal, Canadian Jewish Congress, with the highly patriotic Samuel Bronfman at the helm, spearheaded most of the home-front initiatives. They organized Jewish veterans of the First World War to staff recruitment depots across the country. Posters appeared in Montreal in English, French, and Yiddish.

Jewish servicemen enjoying themselves at one of Canadian Jewish Congress' clubs for men and women in uniform. (Canadian Jewish Congress National Archives, Montreal)

In 1940, Congress set up a *National War Efforts Committee* "to stimulate and guide the contribution to the national war effort by Canadians of the Jewish faith." The Committee marshalled many

Jewish organizations across the land to support endeavours such as the War Savings Campaign, War Service Campaign, Victory Loan Drives, and other undertakings in support of the government. Thousands enlisted in the Civilian Protection Corps.

Canadian Jewish Congress set up recreation facilities for servicemen "regardless of race or creed" across the country. The centres were intended to provide off-duty servicemen from bases in the region with places to relax and socialize. Volunteers, mostly women, provided snacks and home cooking. And more than one wartime romance blossomed.

Many of the servicemen were overseas for three or more years, and links with home were important. The community was encouraged to write letters, knit scarves or sweaters, and send small gifts.

While there was a handful of Jewish women who served in women's divisions of the Armed Forces, most Jewish women made their mark on the home front. The contribution of women to the war effort should not be underestimated. Many had to shoulder the burden of raising families alone with sharply reduced incomes. Others worked long hours in war-related industries. In addition, the community counted on them to be on the front lines of local and overseas relief efforts. They collected and packaged huge quantities of clothing and non-perishables as part of an international effort to aid refugees from war-torn Europe.

> **THE LEACOCK HISTORY OF CANADA**
> In 1942, the war was not going well for the allies, and Samuel Bronfman, a passionate Canadian, was concerned about the country's morale. He commissioned McGill University Professor Stephen Leacock to write a history of Canada. Leacock asked if he could be provided with a comfortable place to work, and Allan Bronfman accommodated him in a magnificent panelled den in his home. The book, which glorifies the British Empire and Canada's place within it, was widely read and circulated. Allan Bronfman later donated the room, panels and all, to McGill University where it became the Leacock Room of the Rare Books Collection—honouring one of Canada's most famous writers.

IN MEMORIAM
Quebec Jewish servicemen killed or presumed dead in World War II

Aaron, Elmer Oscar	Chizy, Harold	Galt, John Elliot
Abelson, Charles Robert	Cohen, Hyman	Garber, Sydney
Abrams, Hyman David	Cohen, Samuel	Gaskin, Donald
Adelman, Archie	Cosoff, Joseph	Gaskin, Jack Hyman
Albert, Saul	Dlusy, Nat	Gelman, David
Backler, Herman	Elias, Issie	Gertel, Joseph
Baittle, Horace David	Epstein, Irving	Gilbert, George Lyon
Baum, Hyman	Epstein, Max Mendel	Glassberg, Jack
Beigleman, David	Erlick, Muni	Glickman, Bertram W.
Bell, Issie	Feldman, Arnold Lepine	Godfrey, Joseph G.
Berger, Nathan Louis	Fine, Joseph	Goldberg, Harry
Brown, Moe	Flexer, Alex Ellis	Goldberg, Louis
Charton, Moses	Fried, Carl M.	Goldin, Louis

Goldstein, Peter
Goldwater, Mark
Goresky, William
Gorodetsky, Reuben
Greenberg, Percy
Greenblatt, Moses
Haberman, Joseph
Hockenstein, Benjamin
Holden, George
Horn, Joseph B.
Hurwitz, Samuel Moses, DCM, MM*
Ittkin, Abe
Jacobs, Aaron Avrom
Jacobs, Michael Stein
Jacobson, Joseph Albert
Kirsch, Abraham
Kirsch, A. Lionel
Klein, Hyman
Knobovitch, Harry, DFC*
Kugelmass, Jack
Lassner, Arthur Joseph
Levine, Samuel Meyer
Levitt, Samuel I.
Lewis, Manuel Zack
Livis, Mortimer
Lupinsky, Jack
Marcus, John Joseph
Mayoff, Issie
Michaels, John Lewis MM*
Morris, Lionel J.
Munk, Milan

Nagley, Arthur Harold
Nelson, Wlliam Henry, DFC*
Newman, Sydney
Nutik, Louis
Ofner, Sidney
Oiring, Morris Nathan
Padveen, Issie
Pappelbaum, Sydney Sol
Park, Samuel
Pascal, Fred
Pervin, Tim Israel
Portuguese, Joseph
Rabiner, Joseph
Regenstrief, Mortimer
Rezven, Hyman
Reznick, Harold
Rochlin, Ab e
Rosenthal, Wlliam G.
Russman, David
Sager, Harry
Samuels, Bernard Edwin
Saxe, Samuel Leo
Schachter, Moses
Schwartz, Frank
Schwartz, Gerald I.
Schwartz, Moses
Schwartz, William
Seigler, Robert
Shapiro, Martin
Shatzky, Michael
Shulman, Joseph
Shvemar, Max

Silver, H.
Simon, Edward David
Singer, Jack Harry
Slabotsky, David
Spector, Samuel
Stein, Isidore
Stein, Wilfred
Steinberg, Abraham
Sterlin, Mitchell
Stromberg, Bennie
Sturm, Issie
Tafler, Sydney A.
Teitlebaum, Nathan
Titleman, Daniel
Tritt, Jack
Usher, Moses Lewis
Van Geun, Furneau M.
Weiss, Herbert Stanley
Weshler, Frank
Winkler, Louis
Yellin, Benny
Yellin, Philip
Zareiken, Joe
Zareiken, Samuel

* Explanation of Decorations:
DCM—Distinguished Conduct Medal
DFC—Distinguished Flying Cross
MM—Military Medal

When our efforts loose the bonds of evil,
When we feed the hungry, clothe the naked,
Strive for peace, for righteousness and justice—
Yea, 'tis then that we have become immortal,
Deathless, timeless, living on in others.

From *Yizkor*, the Jewish memorial service

THE WEIDER BROTHERS

It was an oft-repeated tale in the neighbourhood. The story of how two local boys made good. Joe and Ben Weider were gangly teen-agers who discovered to their dismay that they were simply not big enough or strong enough for wrestling and boxing. Things changed when Joe came across a second-hand magazine called *Strength,* showing pictures of powerful men who had trained hard to develop a magnificent physique. Says Joe: "This was when I was 13-years-old and weighed 115 pounds. I was fascinated." Joe was working as an errand boy for $2 dollars a week, half of which went to his parents. Nonetheless, he bought a pair of barbells for $7, paying for them at 50 cents a week. Young Weider began weightlifting at a time when "experts" frowned on the idea. He began selling weight-lifting equipment and then writing about his personal bodybuilding experiences.

Ben (left) and Joe Weider flank actor/strongman Arnold Schwartzenegger as they receive the "Lifetime Achievement Award of the Governor's Council on Physical Fitness and Sport (1995), in California.

Three years later, Joe Weider alarmed his mother by announcing he planned to publish bodybuilding magazines. It was not a promising time to start something new. It was the 1930s, and people were more concerned about where to find their next meal rather than building up their muscles. Mrs. Weider urged her husband to find Joe a job. Mr. Weider, who pressed pants for a living, thought the boys should be given some leeway.

The brothers, now dedicated to bodybuilding, both found their performances getting better in the ring—Joe in wrestling and Ben in boxing. So many people asked Joe and Ben how they had become so strong and fit that they started a mimeographed magazine in 1940 called *Your Physique.* At first, the Weiders worked out of their parents' living room. They ordered barbells—on credit—from a foundry in La Prairie. By the mid-40s, monthly circulation of *Your Physique* had grown to more than 40,000. In 1946, after serving in the army during World War II, Ben became active in the business.

WORKING WITH AN AUSTRIAN ACTOR

The Weiders' biggest break came in the 1960s when they hired, as the symbol of their physical development program, a muscular Austrian named Arnold Schwarzenegger. That proved to be a promotional masterstroke for a growing empire of products— weight-lifting equipment and a steadily growing family of publications. Schwarzenegger won numerous bodybuilding championships and became a major film star. The Weiders began marketing nutrition products at almost the precise moment the public became receptive to the idea of sports nutrition and dietary supplements. And their nutritional supplement business grew apace.

The Weider array of publications was launched with *Muscle and Fitness* and now includes *Flex, Shape, Jump, Natural Health, Men's Fitness,* and *Fit Pregnancy*. Shape is the most widely read women's fitness magazine in the world, with monthly newsstand sales of a million copies. Their specialty magazines have 25 million readers worldwide. In addition, Weider bodybuilding equipment is sold in more than 100 countries. Joe Weider lives and works out of California, while Ben, who became an authority on Napoleon and has a major collection of Napoleonic memorabilia, runs his wing of the Weider Brothers empire from Montreal.

SHOAH

IN MEMORY OF 6,000,000
STORIES UNTOLD

THE COMMUNIST AND THE SOCIALIST
Rose versus Lewis in a politically divided community

Two Jewish politicians faced off in the predominantly Jewish fed-eral riding of Cartier in Montreal. David Lewis was a Rhodes scholar and dynamic secretary of the moderately Socialist CCF (Co-operative Commonwealth Federation) Party, while his main opponent, an electrician named Fred Rose, carried the banner—the red banner—of the Labour-Progressive Party, a thinly dis-guised cover for his Communist affiliation. Rose won the by-elec-tion with a substantial margin of 2,476 votes. The election result, on August 9, 1943, gave Canada its first and only Communist Member of Parliament.

The Russian Revolution caused great ferment across the globe; it was as if a large stone had been thrown into the placid pool of world politics. Many Canadians, disillusioned with the vagaries of the unpredictable free enterprise system, looked to other eco-nomic and social philosophies, and new political parties, for answers. In Montreal, radical thinking imported from Russia brought about a clash between those who favored the extreme left—the Communists—and those inclined to back a more moderate Social democratic philosophy—the Socialists. The climax was an electoral confrontation between two Montreal Jews, David Lewis and Fred Rose. The former was to become the only Jew to head a national political party in Canada and the latter, the first Communist in the House of Commons, holds the dubious distinction of being the only Montreal Jew tried and found guilty of spying for the Union of Soviet Socialist Republics.

THE COMMUNIST PARTY IN CANADA

Soviet Russia's first leader, Vladimir Ilyich Lenin, had drawn widespread interest and support when he presented the Communist credo: "From each according to his ability, to each according to his needs." The Marxists talked about the brotherhood of man—a magnetic proposition to Russia's huge population of serfs, and even more attractive to the long-oppressed Jews of Europe. Longing for a land where they would be treated with respect, and granted equal rights and opportunities, many Jews believed Lenin's propaganda.

In 1921, 22 fervent young Communists met secretly with an agent from Moscow in a farmhouse near Guelph, Ontario to organize the Canadian Communist Party. Many who joined had fled Russia after the failed 1905 Revolution and believed that the success of the 1917 Revolution was a call to liberate humankind. Membership in the Canadian party also drew heavily on immigrants from Eastern Europe who had suffered persecution, poverty, and pogroms. While the Communist Party never had a large following in Canada, there were many sympathetic to the theories of the party. These sympathizers were known as Parlour Pinks. Communism was almost non-existent in Quebec, other than in the industrial areas of Montreal, where it regularly drew a few thousand votes. In 1937, the Committee on Gentile-Jewish Relations published "Facts and Fancies About Jews" and stated that of an estimated 15,000 Communists in Canada, only 450 were Jewish.

During the 1940s, Jews formed as much as 70 per cent of the Communist Party's strength in Quebec. They dominated the membership for a number of reasons. Other ethnic groups were generally not interested; French-Canadians for religious reasons rejected "godless communism", and the English were doing well economically and had little incentive for radicalism.

In 1931, the Communist Party, which proposed the violent overthrow of existing governments, was outlawed in Canada. Party leaders were arrested and jailed under Section 98 of the Criminal Code. Aliens (landed immigrants) who were suspected of Communist activity were arrested and often deported. Later it became known that the Royal Canadian Mounted Police (RCMP) had planted an undercover agent or "mole" in the party from its inception.

THE FIRST CANADIAN COMMUNIST MP

Fred Rose was born Fred Rosenberg in Lublin, Poland, in 1907. He moved with his parents to Montreal and shortly after joined

"In January 1938, an Anglo-Canadian journalist estimated that there were 20 Fascists for every Communist in Quebec. Anti-communism was as safe a platform as motherhood, both of which were strongly promoted by the Catholic Church."— Lita-Rose Betcherman in "The Swastika and the Maple Leaf" (1975).

the Young Communist League in 1924. During the Depression years, he organized unions of unemployed and unskilled workers. The RCMP monitored his activities and he was arrested twice—in 1929 and 1931. He was charged with sedition under Section 98 of the Criminal Code and served a year in Bordeaux Jail.

In 1930, he went to Russia for what has been described as a "course of instruction." On his return, he went into politics, running for office unsuccessfully in provincial and federal Montreal ridings. In 1942, Rose was arrested again. He was charged with "subversive activities" as a member of the Communist Party of Canada. He confessed and promised to cease working for the party. He was released after a few weeks. Internment, however, did not discourage Rose's political ambitions. By this time, the Communist Party decided to change its name. The Labour-Progressive Party, a Communist front organization, was established in 1943. (It remained in existence until 1959 when it reverted to its original name.) Under the new banner of the Labour-Progressive Party, Rose (known to French-Canadian voters as *Le Petit Fred*) was finally elected to the Commons in the 1943 by-election. The Communist candidate did well in his Montreal constituency for a number of reasons:

Fred Rose (left), former Member of Parliament, entering court with his lawyer, Joseph Cohen, to face charges of conspiring to pass sensitive information to the Soviet Union, 1946. (photo by Andy Graetz, National Archives of Canada, negative PA 115249)

■ The Communists had an efficient party organization in the Cartier riding, which encompassed the northern part of the Main, around St. Louis Square.

■ Many voters were showing their hatred of Fascism and their anger at French Quebec's widespread anti-Semitism.

■ The Soviet Communists were now Allies of the West, and had just won the Battle of Stalingrad.

■ The Communists managed to obtain some union support.

UNMASKED AS A SPY

Rose was re-elected in 1945; however, his political career was cut short when he was arrested for spying. Soviet embassy cipher clerk Igor Gouzenko had defected in Ottawa and provided the RCMP with confidential documents implicating Rose and others in a Soviet spy ring in Canada. It was the night of September 5, when 25-year-old Gouzenko stuffed 109 confidential documents under his shirt, and walked from the Russian Embassy to the offices of the *Ottawa Journal*. At first, reporters did not believe his story of a Soviet espionage ring in Canada, nor did the RCMP, until four Russian embassy people were caught breaking into Gouzenko's apartment. (The Russians paid the landlord $5 for damage to the door.)

The Gouzenko documents revealed that Fred Rose was a senior liaison agent responsible for forwarding information to the Soviets regarding Canada's explosives program. When the RCMP arrested Rose in his Ottawa apartment, he blurted out: "Honest to God, I'm innocent." Rose claimed he did nothing wrong because, at the time, the Soviets were Allies in the war. He was tried in the spring of 1946 and sentenced to six years in prison for "communicating official secrets to a foreign power." Evidence showed he had recruited spies for the Soviets and organized espionage on their behalf. The Jewish community of Montreal, many of whom lived in the Cartier riding and had voted for Rose, were stunned. Harry Binder, chief organizer for the Communist Party in Quebec (1946-55), declared: "Who would believe that Fred Rose would be stupid enough to get into that position?" When Rose was released from prison in 1951, he returned to Montreal for a few months but was shunned by virtually everyone. In 1952, he returned to his native Poland and accepted a government job in Warsaw. He died there in 1983.

A naïve positive view of communism persisted until the 1950s when the murderous policies of Dictator Joseph Stalin were exposed by successor Nikita Krushchev. Millions of people had been starved to death or executed in a mad push for dictatorial powers. The victims included 24 prominent Jewish writers, and other Jewish leaders identified by Stalin as "enemies of the people". Jewish support for the Canadian Communist Party disappeared after World War II in protest against the Kremlin's silence on the Holocaust.

THE RHODES TO POWER

David Lewis was born in Russia in the same year as Rose, 1907. As a child, he experienced the bloody turbulence of the German invasion of World War I, and then the Russian Revolution. When his family moved to Montreal in 1921, Lewis found himself at age 12 unable to speak or read English. At school, he was relegated to a classroom for six-year-olds. He begged his father to let him quit school and go to work. However, Morris Lewis was adamant. His son must be educated! Frustrated and angry, David Lewis trotted to a nearby bookstore and bought the thickest English-language book he could find. It was Charles Dickens's "The Old Curiosity Shop". By the end of the year, he could speak perfect Dickensian English. With command of the language, he was able to excel in school. In six years, he completed elementary and high school. During holidays, Lewis would work in his Uncle Eli's clothing factory alongside his father and Uncle Max. Upon graduation from

David Lewis (r.), who became leader of the New Democratic Party (NDP), at a 1947 Cooperative Commonwealth Federation (CCF) meeting with (l. to r.) Party leader M.J. Caldwell, D.C. MacDonald and Lorne Ingle. The NDP evolved from the CCF. (National Archives of Canada photograph negative PA 130730)

McGill University, **Lewis became one of the first Canadian Jews awarded the prestigious Rhodes Scholarship to study at Oxford.** He also was the first Canadian elected President of the Oxford Union.

David Lewis demonstrated his forthrightness in an interview he had when under consideration for the Rhodes Scholarship. The Chairman of the Selection Committee, Sir Edward Beatty, President of the Canadian Pacific Railway (CPR), asked Lewis "What would be your first act if you became prime minister of Canada?" "Nationalize the CPR, sir," responded Lewis.

FIRST JEWISH NATIONAL PARTY LEADER

During his three years of study in England, Lewis met members of the British Labour party and was inspired by their Socialist policies. His father, Morris Lewis, had been a Socialist leader (and anti-Communist) in their hometown, Swislocz, Poland, and greatly influenced Lewis' interest in politics.

Back in Canada, Lewis began to practise law in Ottawa. In 1936, he became national secretary of the CCF. He ran for election to Parliament in four elections in the 1940s and was defeated on each occasion. However, after helping to found the CCF's successor, the New Democratic Party (NDP)—which had the support of the Canadian Labour Congress—Lewis ran in six elections in the Toronto riding of York South—winning four times. In 1971, **Lewis—regarded as one of the most devastating debaters in the Commons—was chosen leader of the NDP, and became the first Jew to lead a national political party.** His greatest electoral success as party leader came in 1972 when he held the balance of power during the Liberal minority government of 1972-1974.

His most quotable utterance during his political career was his condemnation of companies seeking government funding as "corporate welfare bums." After his defeat in the 1974 federal election, he stepped down as leader and ended his career teaching at Carleton University in Ottawa. He died in Ottawa in 1981.

Stephen Lewis, David Lewis' son, was also prominent in Canadian politics. Born in Ottawa in 1937, Stephen became active in the Ontario NDP Party. He represented Scarborough West in the Ontario legislature from 1963-78, assuming leadership of the party in 1970. In 1975, the NDP became the Official Opposition. However, the party had a setback in the '77 election and he resigned. He became Canada's ambassador to the United Nations in 1984.

JEWISH POLITICAL ACTIVIST ORGANIZATIONS

The Jewish emphasis on social justice inclines most voters, religious or secular, towards small "l" liberal thinking. A majority of Jews support the (mostly moderate but sometimes extreme) left. This tradition began among early twentieth-century immigrants to Montreal, who believed that ameliorating the deplorable conditions in which they and others had lived in Eastern Europe called for extreme measures.

Waiting for results of the 1950 provincial election opposite the offices of the Keneder Alder (Canadian Eagle).
(Canadian Jewish Congress National Archives, Montreal).

In Montreal, Yiddish-speaking immigrants formed a variety of left-wing self-help organizations. These included the *United Jewish People's Order*, a Communist and anti-Zionist (until 1948) group, the Workmen's Circle and the Labour Zionists.

The *Workmen's Circle* (Arbeiter Ring in Yiddish) was established in 1900 to provide its members with fraternal services including mutual aid, health, and death benefits.   This group of Yiddishists supported labour and Socialist movements throughout the world. Some of their members were anarchists.

Founded in 1903, the *Labour Zionists* (Po'ale Zion) fought for the rebirth of Israel and for the rights of labour in the new state. They organized sick benefits, and encouraged education through Jewish folk schools (including two in Montreal). The Labour Zionists were split between the left and the right—the left (linke) were Marxists who promoted the use of Yiddish, and the right (rechte), known as the Farband, promoted the use of both Yiddish and Hebrew.

All of these organizations, with the exception of United Jewish People's Order, were still active in the year 2000. In the last century, they have been extremely active politically and socially, striving for the betterment of all humankind while concentrating on fuller lives for the local Jewish community.

Baron Byng High School's Class of 1948; enrollment in the school was 99% Jewish. Class President was Mordecai Richler and Dr. Sholom Friedman was secretary.

THE FORMIDABLE LÉA ROBACK

Dynamic. Courageous. Remarkable. Understatements to describe Léa Roback, the passionate Communist and social activist who fought successfully for the rights of workers—especially women in Montreal's garment industry. Léa Roback (1903-2000) was a survivor too—a survivor of pitched battles in an unstable Germany before Hitler took power and a survivor of the difficult and often violent organization of labour unions. **One of her greatest achievements was bringing 4,000 women, working in what she called the "cockroach shops" of ladies' clothing manufacturers, into the new International Ladies Garment Workers Union (IGLWU).** By this achievement, she made the IGLWU a force in the industry. Fluent in Yiddish, English and French, Roback won the trust of the mostly Jewish and French-Canadian employees who until then had worked for marginal wages under appalling conditions. In 1937, she led a massive strike, winning unprecedented concessions.

Léa Roback, the Jewish activist and Communist who helped organize the International Ladies Garment Workers union, 1940s. (Jewish Public Library Archives)

Roback became a Communist after a chance meeting with Dr. Norman Bethune, the Canadian doctor who served in the Spanish Civil War (1936-39) and later became a hero to the Communist Chinese. Before launching her trade union activities, Roback campaigned for Fred Rose, a candidate for Parliament for the Labour-Progressive Party, a thinly disguised Communist organization. In addition, she opened Montreal's first Marxist bookshop, on Bleury Street. It became a centre where like-minded people gathered to discuss how to spread their Marxist philosophies. Interestingly, the young Communist also worked for a time as program director of the *Young Women's Hebrew Association*, where her patron was Saidye (Mrs. Sam) Bronfman.

Léa Roback was born in Montreal in 1903, but grew up in Beauport, near Quebec City, where the family operated a general store. She was the second of nine children, and the big family was crammed into a house so small that every room served as a bedroom with two children to a bed. Her Polish-born parents spoke Yiddish at home. And they impressed on their children values of tolerance, hard work, and education. Despite her own poverty, her mother stressed the importance of helping others who were less fortunate.

Roback was 14 when her family moved back to Montreal. At 16, she began working in various factories, where she learned firsthand about the huge gap in living standards between English-speaking factory owners (many of whom were Jewish) and the mostly French and Jewish workers. She became angry at what she saw and that experience coloured her entire life.

Her life took a detour when, by chance, she was hired to sell tickets at Her Majesty's Theatre. An actor suggested that Roback apply to attend the University of Grenoble in France. "I did and I was accepted. I borrowed $90 for a one-way boat passage and spent two wonderful years there, supporting myself teaching English to students and professionals," she said in an interview.

In 1928, her older brother Leo, studying medicine in Berlin, invited her to visit. She enrolled at the University of Berlin, took courses in sociology, and added German to her language skills. She studied in the German capital during the critical period 1928-1932 when the country reeled from depression and runaway inflation. The country was close to revolution, with extremists vying for control—the Communists on the left and the Nazis, led by the charismatic Adolf Hitler, on the right. "Everyone was either far left or joining the Nazis. I joined the left, met Communists, and read Karl Marx," she said. "Every day in 1929 was a day of battles. I saw the Nazis, helped by the Berlin police, attack us, my friends beaten. I was shaken." As the depression worsened, the Nazis became even more aggressive. "It got so bad I couldn't even pass out leaflets without being beaten by them."

Léa Roback returned to Montreal in 1932 and her political inclinations and contacts drew her into the trade union movement. On one occasion, when a Jewish manager had turned away a black applicant without good reason, she stormed into the man's office and blasted him in Yiddish. The mortified manager hired the black woman and later conceded she was one of his best employees.

During the war years, Roback worked at RCA. She became an organizer for the United Electrical Workers and business agent for 3,000 plant employees. In addition, she found time to campaign for better working conditions for disadvantaged people in poor Montreal districts. "That was an exciting period, exciting and full of experiences. I worked with people in the St. Henri community on housing, jobs and better conditions."

However, Roback lost her union jobs, one by one, as she developed a reputation for being uncompromising and too radical. While she made a living as a salesclerk, she continued to campaign for poor people. "In my time, I lived through some terrible and also some wonderful years and I am grateful I was able to experience that period. And I still have faith that humanity will survive to live in a better world."

On her 90th birthday, friends established the Léa Roback Foundation "to promote education for personal and collective fulfillment and emancipation, as well as promoting universal access to education for all." In 2000, she was awarded the *Ordre du Québec*.

CHAPTER TWENTY-SEVEN

OUT OF THE FIRE
Holocaust Survivors Build A New Life in Montreal

The child answered:
My father is dead, my mother is dead,
and my home is a place where miracles happen,
and I am going to it.
Then the child departed
and left the fear with me.

And then I realized that I hadn't heard a child's weeping,
that I was weeping,
that I was the one waiting for a miracle.

> Melech Ravitch
> Montreal poet

"There is a Jewish child, in a European DP camp, who is waiting for you to let him begin to live. He is leaving behind him a nightmare of death and ashes...Today, no longer anonymous, no longer separated from your succour by an ocean, he stands at your very doorstep, needing a home, a family, the love and guidance of a father and mother."

> *From a letter to Montreal Jews by Canadian Jewish Congress seeking homes for more than 1,000 war orphans.*

TIMELINE—1947-1952

1947. 1,100 youngsters from concentration camps and hiding places are welcomed to Montreal under a War Orphans Program negotiated by Canadian Jewish Congress.

1947. Dr. Reuben Rabinovitch of Montreal is awarded the Medal of Freedom with silver palm by the United States for "disregarding his personal safety, (when he) rendered medical aid to Allied airmen whose planes had been shot down over enemy-occupied territory."

1947-52. 11,064 Jews are admitted to Canada with 40% settling in Montreal. An order-in-council admits 2,138 tailors and 500 furriers—60% of them Jewish.

The end of World War II brought with it the horrifying disclosures of brutality to Jews, and others. The Allied armies with their tanks and half-tracks rolled into and liberated the concentration camps, and the world saw the handiwork of the Nazis—and condemned it. The planned genocide of 6,000,000 Jews was one of the greatest crimes in history. After 2,000 years, the entire continent of Europe, with the exception of France and Britain, ceased to have a significant Jewish presence. The United Nations, which succeeded the League of Nations, promulgated sweeping declarations on human rights. In a complete reversal of its immigration policy, the Canadian government, committed to the UN, opened its doors to survivors of the Holocaust. **Canada became the first non-European country to approve emergency measures to expedite the admission of refugees from the Displaced Persons (DP) camps.** Through the humanitarian efforts of Canadian Jewish Congress (CJC), 1,100 orphaned Jewish children were brought to Canada, and 525 were adopted by Montrealers. And countless families and friends were reunited. As thousands of refugees poured into post-War Canada, Montreal became home to 35,000 survivors, more than any other city in North America.

"All human beings are born free and equal in dignity and rights. They are endowed with reason and conscience and should act towards one another in a spirit of brotherhood."
Universal Declaration of Human Rights, 1948

CANADIAN POLICY CHANGES

During the 12 years of the "thousand-year Reich", Canada had reluctantly accepted fewer than 5,000 Jewish refugees. This small number brought in millions of dollars of new capital, and in one year, industrialists who had fled Hitler's Germany created 31 new industrial plants in Montreal alone. The reversal in Canada's racist immigration policy was more than a gesture of good will. It was the practical reaction of Liberal politicians, troubled by the rising strength of the left, in the form of the mildly socialist CCF party and growth in support for communism. Furthermore, Canada's economy was expanding and labour was needed to keep it rolling. Prime Minister Mackenzie King, in the final years of his long stewardship of Canadian affairs, remained the consummate politician, devising policies and programs designed to draw votes. Canada required skilled workers and European Jews, known for their apprenticeship tradition in various crafts and trades, were finally welcome.

The Cabinet's Order-in-Council #2180 admitted 2,138 tailors and 500 furriers. These migrants helped build the modern clothing manufacturing industry in Montreal, as well as the fur industry in Montreal, Toronto and elsewhere in Canada.

Representatives of relief agencies visited the camps, and cleared the way for 3,000 refugees, including 150 Jewish women, to come to Canada as "domestics". About 260 "dressmaker" families came from Sweden, where they had found sanctuary during the war. They also came from the DP camps—facilities set up to shelter survivors after they were liberated from Nazi concentration camps. Many more Jews were admitted under the "Skilled Workers' Project", including chemists, industrial mechanics, cutters and nurses' aides.

LEAVING THE TENTS

Shoah survivors, often skeletal and diseased, had been sheltered in makeshift camps located near the notorious Holocaust facilities. Some had lived in tents for as long as two years. People had married in the camps; they had had children. CJC negotiated with the Federal government a special arrangement for the admission of 1,100 Jewish orphans. A few months later, embarrassed Congress officials were back in Ottawa to arrange emigration for parents of some of the "orphans". Fathers and mothers, lost in the turmoil of five years of war, had surfaced from hiding places, where Good Samaritans had concealed them. One Jewish couple in Poland had hidden in a well for four years and was cared for by a Catholic neighbour. After making it to Montreal, they sent their protector a gift every year, and visited her when circumstances permitted. *Righteous Gentiles* are honoured in Jerusalem by a tree-planting ceremony in a special grove on the pathway leading to the Yad Vashem Museum.

CHILDREN OF THE SHOAH

Many of the orphans had witnessed the brutal death of their parents, and had been terrorized themselves. They only lived if they were useful to the Nazis as slave labour. However, some had managed to escape into the woods and survive by joining partisans fighting the Germans. The children emerged after the cease-fire, hungry to find surviving family members. Often, there were none.

Representing Congress, Hananiah Meir Caiserman journeyed to Poland in 1946 to document the condition of Polish Jews and to help Canadians locate, if possible, surviving members of their families. Caiserman reported, "I was not prepared to understand the real meaning of finding 65,000 Jews from 3¼ million who lived there

H.M. Caiserman, a key personality in the work of Canadian Jewish Congress in its first 30 years. (Canadian Jewish Congress National Archives)

In Jerusalem, adjacent to the Yad Vashem Holocaust Museum there is a special child memorial, designed by Israeli-born Montreal architect Moshe Safdie. Visitors hear a continuous reading of all the known names of the million young victims of the Shoah.

before the war." The Congress representative, visiting a children's shelter in Warsaw, had a moving conversation with nine-year-old Yechiel Leben. "My father and mother were both burned alive," said the boy. "I only have my little brother, David, one year old." He knew of an uncle named Leben living somewhere in Canada or the United States. "Find him for me," the boy cried. Caiserman wrote in his report, "I cried with him."

In the devastated town of Bialystok, Caiserman met with a group of survivors, and later wrote in his report:

"The 25 people who had supper with us each had a number burned on their arm while in the concentration camps. Each has a story of horror and slow death both physical and moral. I was especially moved by the fate of children who escaped annihilation and wandered about the forests and fields of Poland, often dying friendless and without finding the peace of a grave."

The Congress representative was deeply moved by what he saw and experienced. "All is desolation and dust." Nonetheless, the CJC agency began the heartrending task of finding adoptive parents for the displaced children of war. In Montreal, there was no shortage of applicants. However, most of them were hoping for a five-year-old poster girl, and were crushed when they learned that almost no little ones had survived the ordeal. Among the victims of the Shoah had been approximately one million Jewish children. Dr. Paul Freedman, an American psychiatrist who after the war spent a great deal of time with survivors, estimates that of the 100,000 Jews who survived the camps, only 4,000 were young children, mostly teenagers capable of hard labour.

Montreal-bound. 17-year-old war orphan Gisela Lazar (left) is one of 1,100 youngsters brought to Canada to start new lives. With her in this 1947 photograph taken in Paris is Lotte Levinson, an official of the Joint Distribution Committee (JDC), a Jewish organization active in assisting Jews in distress worldwide. Arrangements for bringing the children to Canada were made by Canadian Jewish Congress. (Canadian Jewish Congress National Archives)

Of the 1,100 children who came to Canada, most were teenagers. There was only one child of five—the youngest of the patriated orphans; two six-year-olds; three seven-year-olds; nine eight-year-olds; and eight nine-year-olds. The six oldest were 18. Though 24 could not identify their country of origin, the orphans were discovered to be from 15 different countries.

Joseph Rothbart, an orphan who later became executive director of Mount Sinai Hospital in Montreal said, "You had to find the strength to save yourself."

Another orphan wrote about the experience of coming to Canada:

"We were very much impressed with the difference between Europe and Canada. In Europe, we seldom saw a smiling face, we saw more often a tearful face; in Canada, wherever

we go, we are greeted with a smile. It is interesting that I
found it hard to become accustomed to smile once more."
Devastated by his experiences in Poland, Caiserman needed
upon his return to Canada a hiatus of several days in Halifax to
recover his emotional equilibrium. He also carried with him 1500
letters from survivors to Canadian relatives and friends. Nor did
he ask of others what he would not do himself. Among those
adopting orphans was Caiserman himself.

His daughter, Ghitta Caiserman-Roth, tells of the great day
when an orphan adolescent who had survived Auschwitz arrived
by train. Caiserman's wife, Sarah, the only member of the family
who could drive, met Necha and drove her to the Caisermans'
cottage at St. Donat where Ghitta excitedly awaited her new sister. "We talked for three days", Ghitta recalled, "and Necha
changed her name to Nella." Despite the trauma of the concentration camp, Nella Caiserman married and raised a family in
Montreal. Her three children settled in Israel.

A war orphan donating a Torah to Canadian Jewish Congress, repre-sented by Benjamin Robinson. The Torah cover was hand-made in a Displaced Persons Camp in Europe. (Canadian Jewish Congress National Archives, Montreal)

Longtime JIAS worker Joe Kage (left) in 1947 with a group of young immigrants.

CANADA A MAJOR SANCTUARY

Representatives of Congress were not
the only ones seeking to rescue displaced Jews. Delegations from the
Jewish communities of Australia, South
Africa and Palestine were also working
to find homes in their countries for displaced children. In the end, Canada
became one of five major sanctuaries for
European Jewry—taking in 123,000,
while the other main countries of reset-
tlement were the United States (329,000);
Australia (182,000); Israel (132,000), and
Britain (86,000).

Extraordinary tales of courage and chutzpah during this era have become known. When Austria's
champion soccer player was arrested by the Nazis
and taken to the infamous Dachau concentration
camp, his wife, a former Miss Vienna, dressed
as a nun, marched into the prison wih false
papers, and told the authorities, "this man is not
Jewish." It was 1940, and she and her husband
walked out of the camp—and away from

Jewish refugees arriving in Canada in 1946. (Canadian Jewish Congress National Archives.)

certain death. They eventually made it to New York, where their son Jim Torczyner was born in 1945. Torczyner became a notable professor of social work at McGill University, and created Project Genesis, a social service agency protecting the rights of vulnerable people, with storefront operations in Montreal, Israel and Jordan.

MAKING DO IN A NEW LAND

As in the past, members of the Jewish community often did not warmly welcome newcomers. The more integrated population of earlier settlers has regarded each wave of immigration with some distaste. The population of the Montreal Jewish community, which for a generation had hovered around 60,000, increased by one-third in the few years after the war, to reach 80,000 in 1951. Many established Jews were disturbed by the sudden influx, and embarrassed to acknowledge as "their own" newcomers with strange dress and accents, with lifestyles from a "foreign place" or another time.

Three orphans in Paris in 1947—packed and ready to leave for Montreal. (Canadian Jewish Congress National Archives).

> *They were obviously mother and daughter, aged perhaps 60 and 30. They paused, nervously, at the top of the stairs. Below, a Golden Age Association group was meeting. But after barely escaping alive from Poland, how would they be received in their shabby European clothes? They had their answer when they reached the foot of the stairs. There was a babble of Yiddish and Polish and they were warmly welcomed into the arms of a score of people who had had similar experiences.*

STRENGTHENING THE COMMUNITY

The survivors revived or created 35 organizations in Montreal with more than 4,000 members. Today, Canada is home to 27,000 survivors, and of these, 8,430 live in Montreal. A large proportion 30 per cent of Montreal's Jewish elderly—are survivors. By the 1991 census, more than 6,500 were 63 or older.

Many survivors, often toughened by their horrendous experiences, learned to adjust to their new living circumstances and did well in Montreal. A McGill University study declares that survivors "played a pivotal role in the institutional and cultural development of Montreal's Jewish Community." The Report continues: "Despite portrayals of Holocaust survivors as victims with an overwhelming number of physical and psychological 'traumas' and 'symptomatology', survivors have shown a great resiliency and love of community and family as they rebuilt their lives in Canada."

The hours of humiliation,
hours of grandeur
hours of pain;
They are not necessary,
For there stands an ancient covenant
Between myself and the silence—-
And there is a road to buried dreams
From a place beyond words.

Leah Goldberg (1911-1970)
"Of Myself"
Translated from Hebrew

Harvey Golden (1904-1990) served the Montreal Jewish Community in a communal leadership role for five decades. He was born in Russia and moved with his family to Winnipeg where he studied at the University of Manitoba. In the late 1920s after graduating from Harvard, he was named Executive Director of the new Davis YMHA on Mount Royal Avenue in Montreal. Golden played a particularly important role in integrating immigrant youth into Canadian society. After World War II, he pushed for construction of a new "Y" in the Snowdon district following the shift of the community westward. Golden was important as a philosopher of the community and a patient personal guide to hundreds of young men and women at critical stages in their lives.

Saul Hayes (1906-80) was a lawyer who first became involved in community work in 1940 as executive director of the United Jewish Relief Agencies of Canada. Two years later he assumed the professional leadership of Canadian Jewish Congress at a time of crisis for World Jewry. Hayes and Samuel Bronfman teamed up to do what they could for endangered Jews in Europe, strengthen Canada's war effort, rescue survivors and press for a United Nations vote to set the stage for the rebirth of Israel. Hayes became the Ambassador of Canadian Jewry to the nation's various government bodies, but most importantly to Federal authorities.

Hayes' successor was **Alan Rose** (1921-95), a Scottish-born Jew who, as a tank commander in World War II, was one of the first military men to reach the Bergen-Belsen concentration camp. Years after the war, a survivor recalled Rose and that his tank was marked by a drawing of a chicken. As executive-director of

---

REMEMBERING THE HOLOCAUST
In 1999, Liberal member of the Quebec National Assembly Lawrence Bergman, with Parti Québécois member André Boulerice, introduced a private members' bill seeking proclamation of an annual Holocaust Memorial Day in the province. The measure passed without a dissenting vote. Quebec became the third province in Canada—after Ontario and Prince Edward Island—to commemorate the tra-gedy in this way.
Manuel Schachter, Q.C., Chair of the Canadian Jewish Congress-Quebec Task Force on Yom Hashoah, commented: "It is our hope at Congress that Yom Hashoah (Holocaust Memorial Day) will be a signal to Quebecers to never allow the propagators of hate, racism and violence to stand unchallenged."
Yom Hashoah is marked worldwide.

Canadian Jewish Congress Executive Vice-President Alan Rose. The story of his achievements can not yet be fully told for security reasons.

Congress, Rose travelled extensively in an effort to aid oppressed Jews. Much of what he accomplished remains confidential but one of his known accomplishments was arranging visas allowing 700 Jews to leave Iraq for Canada. He was also involved in rescue efforts in Syria and Egypt, and was often successful under diplomatic conditions that denied access to Americans and others. In the campaign to free Soviet Jews, Rose spoke for the International Jewish community at Helsinki, Finland, where he pressed the Russians to allow Jews the right to emigrate. "It was Alan Rose who was largely responsible for the Canadian government's posture," activist Wendy Eisen wrote in her book "The Struggle to Free Soviet Jews."

In 1981, Rose was awarded the United States Presidential Citation of Honour as a Concentration Camp Liberator. In 1987, the government of Czechoslovakia awarded him the Terezin Anti-Fascist Fighters Decoration. When he died, Montreal priest Father John Walsh commented "whenever and wherever peoples of the world suffered human indignity, Alan brought people to respond."

"I was born on Prince Arthur Street in 1905," stated **Lavy N. Becker** a Montrealer who enjoyed three careers—as a social worker, a rabbi, and an executive. "My father came to Montreal in 1903 to work as a cantor." He trained as a rabbi and social worker, graduating from the Theological Seminary of America in New York in 1930. During World War II, he went overseas and helped survivors of the Holocaust to reach Palestine before partition. He established Montreal's only Reconstructionist synagogue in 1960 and served as its spiritual leader, unpaid, for 17 years. Latterly, he entered the family business, Rubinstein Brothers, because "I had to make a living for my family." Becker and his son, Hillel, are the only father and son to be honoured with Canadian Jewry's highest honour, the Bronfman medal.

Dr. Alton Goldbloom (1890-1968) pioneered modern pediatrics in Quebec and eastern Canada. He played a prominent role in the development of the Montreal Children's Hospital and the Department of Pediatrics at McGill. The Alton Goldbloom Drive in Laval honours the pediatrician.

The Jerusalem of Canada and the Vilna of the New World
a vicarious city in the heart of French Canada,
with its Churches, its river and its mountain
and its popular languages which keep us from forgetting
the loss of the other country.
David Roskies
Canadian Jewish Congress' "Viewpoints"
March, 1990

PART FOUR

THE NEW JERUSALEM
Years of Transition and Triumph

Montreal Jews celebrate the rebirth of Israel, enlist to fight in the War of Independence and set a worldwide pace in financial support. An influx of French-speaking North African, Hungarian, and Soviet Jews enriches the Montreal Jewish mosaic. As Jews move steadily up the ladder of prosperity, they begin a migration north and west. The population of the Old Jewish Quarter dwindles as residents move to new suburbs, creating new neighbourhoods. It is a golden age for the Jews as they forge to high levels in business, industry, the professions, and the arts. Jews move into the Federal and Quebec cabinets, and on to the benches of the highest courts of the nation. The election of a government intent on separating the province from Canada alarms the community and triggers an exodus of Jews, and others. Despite worrisome demographic changes, the Community enlarges its federation building, a symbol of determination to stay and thrive in Montreal.

CHAPTER TWENTY-EIGHT

ISRAEL IS REBORN
Montrealers Help Realize the Age-old Dream

In Israel, in order to be a realist you must believe in miracles.

David Ben-Gurion,
first Prime Minister of Israel

Jews in Montreal, tense and apprehensive, crowded around their living room radios to listen to the live broadcast from the United Nations Assembly. Would Palestine be partitioned into a Jewish State and a Palestinian entity? Jews in Montreal, across Canada, and around the world had lobbied for years to end the British Mandate, and to create a homeland for the Jewish people. Jews from Montreal were in New York as observers for the crucial vote. As each country was called, a representative stood and stated Yes or No; Oui ou Non. The date was November 29, 1947, and when the rollcall was complete, the vote was 33-13 in favour, with ten abstentions, including Britain. In a rare display of agreement, the two superpowers, the United States and the Soviet Union, had supported partition. Across the Jewish world, there was great rejoicing. However, the Arabs rejected partition and went to war.

After an absence of nearly 2,000 years, Israel returned to the pages of history. The United Nations vote that permitted the reestablishment of a Jewish homeland touched off a wild celebra-

---

TIMELINE—1947-1949

1947. United Nations vote to partition Palestine.
1948. The Israeli War of Independence begins.
1949. The first Jewish lecturer is appointed to a Canadian Catholic University; Rabbi Chaim Denburg teachers Medieval Jewish Philosophy at Université de Montréal.

Jews celebrate the rebirth of Israel at a rally in the Montreal Forum, 1948.
(Gazette Photograph, National Archives of Canada, negative PA 116478)

tion in the St. Urbain Street area. Author Mordecai Richler described the scene in these words:

"People charged out onto the street to embrace. Men and women who hadn't been to a synagogue since last Yom Kippur surprised themselves, turning up to offer prayers of gratitude and then toss back glasses of schnapps with slices of schmaltz herring. Horns were honked. Photographs of Chaim Weizmann or Ben Gurion, torn from back issues of *Life* or *Look* were pasted

up in bay windows. Blue-and-white Star of David flags flapped in the wind on some balconies. Many wept as they sang 'Hatikvah,' the Zionist anthem."

At meetings, they congratulated each other that after 100 generations theirs was the one blessed to witness the re-creation of **Eretz Israel**, the State of Israel. After all, once a year, in their High Holiday prayers, they chanted in Hebrew "If I forget thee, O Jerusalem, let my right hand forget her cunning. Let my tongue cleave to the roof of my mouth, if I remember thee not, if I set not Jerusalem above my chiefest joy." In the synagogues, elated rabbis recalled the words of God in Genesis: "I will make of you a great nation." Montreal Jews responded with outstanding generosity to every appeal on behalf of the new Jewish State, whether it was to help finance the integration of tens of thousands of immigrants or provide food for an embattled people. In per capita terms, Montreal Jewish support for Israel was the largest in the world throughout the critical first decades of statehood. In addition, many Montrealers made notable contributions in support of the War of Independence.

"A COUNTRY WORTH LIVING FOR IS A COUNTRY WORTH DYING FOR"—a popular saying among Jews who had been interned by the British.

AN INTERNATIONAL FIGHTING FORCE

Only half the size of Nova Scotia, tiny Israel was wedged between the Mediterranean Sea and nine invading Arab armies, including Palestinian volunteers, the Armed Forces of Egypt, Jordan, Syria, Lebanon, Iraq, Saudi Arabia, Morocco, and the Sudan. Jews around the globe were anxious to help. Gaunt survivors of the concentration camps, who during the British Mandate had been denied the right to land in Israel and who had spent years in British internment camps, such as on the island of Cyprus, were finally free. With enthusiasm and elation, they boarded rusty outdated freighters to cross the Mediterranean—destination Israel. On arrival, the men were recruited into Israel's fledgling defence forces, and some were handed weapons dating from the First World War. With not more than an hour of training, many were sent directly to battle and perished within days of their arrival.

The Arab countries each had trained and well-equipped armies and air forces. Israel had only its poorly armed underground force, the Haganah. And, no air force. A secret meeting was held in New York of representatives of Jewish communities in many countries. Sydney Shulemson, the much-decorated World War II

The all-Canadian 52nd Battalion of the Givati Brigade, participants in Israel's 1948 War of Independence. In the picture are: (front row - left to right) Allan Brown, Moe Dankevy, Gerry Gross, Art Lashinsky, Irving Kaplansky, Murray Cappel, (first name not known) Loeb. (Mid-row seated) Sam Cohen. (back row) Albert Spiegel, Joe Abramson, Murray Ginsberg, Abe Danovitch, Sid Halperin, Ben Ocupnick, Jack Berger. (Bus driver; name not known), Joe Gerstl and the Israeli commander, Yosef Horowitz. (Reclining) Avrom Siegel.

pilot, was asked to represent Canada. The discussion in New York was urgent. How could trained and experienced fighting men be recruited, and where would arms, and especially aircraft, be obtained?

Back in Montreal, Shulemson—working with Canadian Jewish Congress, his Masonic Lodge and the Jewish Air Cadet Squadron—invited Jewish veterans of World War II to a briefing at the Spanish and Portuguese Synagogue. About 400 veterans attended the session, and 30 of them signed up that evening to fight for Israel. Across the country, similar meetings were held and, ultimately, 450 Canadians joined an international fighting force of 3,400 volunteers.

Jews had fought in many armies, but under other flags. Finally, with a homeland, many Montreal Jews were eager to fight for Israel. As Golda Meir put it, "The Arabs can absorb many defeats and attack us again, but we cannot afford to lose even once." As its first army in 20 centuries, the Israeli army lacked a definitive recruitment policy and turned to the Bible for guidance. According to Deuteronomy 20:7, "Is there anyone here who is engaged to be married? If so, he is to go home. Otherwise, if he is killed in battle, someone else will marry the woman he is engaged to." In addition, those who had just built a house or planted a vineyard were considered ineligible to serve.

CANADA'S #1 FIGHTER PILOT VOLUNTEERS

Further meetings were held in New York, and at one of them, Shulemson pressed for establishment of an Israeli Air Force. Back home, he consulted former airmen who suggested that the greatest Canadian ace of World War II, George Frederick "Buzz" Beurling, would be interested in flying for Israel. Beurling had destroyed 32 enemy aircraft, 28 of them in four months while defending the island of Malta in 1942 (before being dismissed from the Air Force for being too free-spirited and unruly). Why would this outstanding flyer (and a non-Jew) want to risk his life for Israel? Shulemson had no money to offer, and rumour had it the Egyptians were offering Beurling $5,000 a month to fly for them. Shulemson, busy acquiring arms and equipment for Israel and arranging for volunteers to fly to the Middle East, decided he had nothing to lose. He invited Beurling to lunch, explained what he wanted and added, bluntly, all Israel could offer him was three meals a day and "a chocolate bar for dessert." "Fine",

responded the Verdun native, "when do I leave?" The recruitment of Beurling was kept as secret as possible, but a complica-
tion arose when the pilot wanted his girlfriend to come with him.
Beurling was flown to New York, then Rome, where the Israelis
had a clandestine air base. It is still not known who broke
security on the deal. Could it have been an inopportune remark
by an innocent girlfriend? In any event, Beurling and another
veteran of Malta, Leonard Cohen (not the poet), had been
assigned the task of ferrying a Canadian-built Noorduyn
Norseman to Israel. On a training flight, the aircraft crashed,
killing both flyers. "It would have been easy to sabotage the
aircraft," said Shulemson, who had the difficult task of informing the Beurling family of the loss of their son. The
Canadian ace was buried, as his family wished, in Jerusalem's
cemetery for its fallen warriors. Beurling was a member of
Plymouth Brethren—a fundamentalist Protestant sect that
believes the Jews are God's Chosen People. This explains why
Buzz Beurling turned down an enormous fee from the Arabs to
fly for Israel without pay.

PROVIDING ARMS AND EQUIPMENT
The first two vessels to transport so-called "illegal" immigrants to
Israel, before statehood was formally declared, were converted
Canadian Navy corvettes. The 'Beauharnois' was renamed the
'Josiah Wedgewood' and the 'Norsyd' became the 'Hagana'.
However, as the volunteer crews were clearing Montreal harbour,
the harbour-master recalled them. "You can't sail an armed warship out of a Canadian port," the official declared, pointing at the
4.3-inch diameter guns mounted on the foredeck of the vessels.
Obediently, the Jewish crew sailed back to the jetty. Using a
crane, they lowered the weapons into the holds of their ships.
Then, with the deck guns as cargo, they set sail for Haifa with the
harbour-master's approval. In the Israeli port, it was a matter of
minutes to raise the guns and reposition them on the prow of
each warship.

Canadian Jewry cooperated when they could in the war effort.
On one occasion, when the Israeli Forces needed communications
equipment, their military procurement office in New York called
Shulemson. He checked around and found that a Toronto Jew
had recently purchased an entire warehouse full of war surplus
items. Among them were 125 radio sets Israel could use for its
military vehicles. Shulemson called Toronto and asked the price.
"Just pick them up" was the response.

HAGANAH IN CANADA

An Israeli pilot who had illegally purchased a B-17 bomber through a dummy New England company was en route to the Middle East when his engines began to malfunction. He made an emergency landing at the Shearwater Canadian Naval Air Station, near Dartmouth, Nova Scotia. "What now?" he asked himself as a rather portly gentleman in a business suit approached him at the airport. "Have a cigarette," said the man. "And keep the package." Inside the flap was written, "follow me." The pilot's unlikely contact was long-time Montreal resident Sam Jacobson, the Canadian representative of Haganah, the underground army that later became the Israeli Defence Force. Jacobson kept the pilot in touch with Israel, via New York. The Haganah suggested the pilot abandon the plane and crew. He was too valuable to lose, they said. But the pilot was reluctant to give up the aircraft with its concealed cargo of much-needed weapons. Ground crew at the air base secretly helped him refuel his plane, and sympathetic RCMP let him know when three U.S. fighter planes, sent to escort him back to the States, were unserviceable. The pilot and his crew abandoned their luggage in a Dartmouth motel, and flew away at night without lights and without their engine cowlings, which were left on the tarmac to fool their intended escort. They flew to the Azores, where the bomber was seized. The pilot, "Swifty" Shindler, spent two years in jail in the United States for violating a ban on acquiring and exporting weapons to Israel. On release, he went back to Israel and helped establish one of the country's largest industries, manufacturing and servicing aircraft.

ZIONISM TRIUMPHANT

The Jewish armed forces, with limited armament but tremendous courage and intelligence, defeated the nine invading Arab armies. During fierce battles, they seized more territory than was allocated to them in the United Nations partition plan. However, Old Jerusalem fell to Jordanian troops, trained, armed and led by British officers, and was to remain a divided city for nearly twenty more years. **Montrealer Dov Joseph (1893-1968) became a hero in the story of world Zionism by becoming the first Jewish governor of Jerusalem since Pontius Pilate.** Bernard Joseph was only 17 when he formed *Young Judea,* a youth branch of the Zionist organization, in Montreal in 1910. Then, two years later, he did what the movement called on Jews to do—he made **Aliyah**

Dov Joseph (right), the Montreal Jew who became military governor of Jerusalem, photographed at a Washington Conference with Canadian Jewish Congress National Executive Vice-President Saul Hayes (left) and Britain's Lord Jenner.
(Canadian Jewish Congress National Archives)

(emigrated) to what was then Palestine, changed his name to Dov Joseph, and joined the Jewish Legion in the British-inspired effort to end Turkish rule. During World War II, Joseph raised Jewish units for the British Army. When the United Nations partitioned Palestine in 1948, Dov Joseph became military governor of Jerusalem and a commander in the bloody battle to control the city. In his book "The Faithful City: The Siege of Jerusalem", published in 1960, Joseph wrote: "The last governor of Jerusalem we had known as a people was Pontius Pilate. For the first time in over two thousand years, Jerusalem once again had a Jewish governor." In later years, Joseph was an Israeli cabinet minister, and worked for the Jewish Agency, the body representing the interests of World Jewry in the Holy Land.

FINANCIAL SUPPORT FOR THE JEWISH HOMELAND

International studies of giving patterns confirm that Montreal Jews were the most generous in their support of Israel, in financial terms. **The per capita gift of Montreal Jewry to Israeli fund-raising campaigns was the highest in the world—exceeding even those of the great American Jewish communities.** Montreal was the only major community in North America to give a higher priority to Israel's concerns than its own local needs in dividing up the proceeds of its annual Combined Jewish Appeal.

In 1953, the State of Israel Bond organization was created in Canada under the joint leadership of Samuel Bronfman and Edward E. Gelber. Money invested in Bonds, purchased by non-Jews as well as Jews, was used to build Israel's infrastructure—roads, airports, seaports. Many banks and other financial institutions invested in the Bonds, which never failed to meet their obligations. In the first 13 years of operation, $664-million worth of Bonds were sold in Canada. Leaders in this effort included Sam and Allan Bronfman, Charles R. Bronfman, Rubin Zimmerman (who later moved to Israel), Thomas Otto Hecht, Melvyn Dobrin and Norman Spector. Bonds remained an attractive investment for Canadians. In 1999, sales topped $100-million for the second time.

Cash gifts to Israel were used largely to absorb the flood of immigrants that overwhelmed the Jewish State in its first decades. The money was also used to rescue Jews in peril around the globe. However, gifts from Jews worldwide never exceeded five per cent of the Israeli budget.

The Canadian Jewish Legion, and members of the Association of Former Concentration Camp Inmates, march in Montreal, 1961. (Canadian Jewish Congress National Archives, Montreal)

> We shall live forever and forever.
> We shall wander from land to land,
> From nation to nation,
> Sometimes driven, sometimes tormented;
> We shall suffer sharp blows and many deep-hurting wounds
> However, this place will be with us
> And this warmth
> In addition, this rejoicing...
> For this is the great, the many-faceted "Shalom".
>
> Ellen Grindel (1913-)
"Shabbat"

Canadian Champion Jewish basketball players—the Snowdon Blues in 1957. Manager Joey Richman holds the trophy. Photo by Ted Harrison.
(Canadian Jewish Congress National Archives)

In 1843, the *B'nai Brith* (Hebrew for People of the Covenant) fraternal order was founded in New York by a dozen idealistic young men to involve American Jewry "in the work of promoting their highest interests and those of humanity." The first Montreal lodge was formed in 1881 and disbanded in 1903. In 1913, Mount Royal Lodge, then the 729th Lodge worldwide, was chartered in Montreal with 32 members, and later became one of the largest in the system. The order was important in Montreal in many ways, but particularly in its support for Camp B'nai Brith and the Hillel Foundation, serving university students. In later years, these agencies were funded through allocations from the Combined Jewish Appeal and their own campaign efforts.

In 1964, Canadian lodges were united into their own District (#22), and counted more than 100 lodges in nine provinces; the exception was British Columbia, where the formal association is to the American Pacific District 4. District 22 organized the first French-speaking lodges in North America, to accommodate Jews from North Africa. It also welcomed and assisted Vietnamese Boat People.

The B'nai Brith's longtime Anti-Defamation League evolved into the *League for Human Rights*, which counters racism and anti-Semitism, and distributes an annual audit of anti-Semitic incidents. The Media Human Rights Award is presented annually to journalists who have contributed to the "advancement of human rights and to the exposure of bigotry and anti-Semitism."

CHAPTER TWENTY-NINE

LES SÉPHARADES
The Other Children of Abraham
in the Ashkenazi domain

He was a handsome young man, but no girl would dance with him when he went to YM-YWHA socials. Jean-Claude Lasry had a problem fitting in because he was a Moroccan Jew, and most English-speaking Jews had never before encountered a French-speaking Jew. This was 1957, and hundreds of thousands of French-speaking Sephardi Jews were fleeing North African and Middle Eastern countries where their ancestors had lived for centuries. Thousands were drawn to Montreal, the world's second largest French-speaking city, where they could realize the American Dream—in French. Many Ashkenazim were reluctant to accept the newcomers so different in language, customs, and mentality. In desperation, Lasry had a T-shirt made, reading "I am Jewish too."

TIMELINE—1950-1966

1950. Gov. Gen. Viscount Alexander opens the new headquarters for Jewish communal services at 493 Sherbrooke W.

1950. The *National Council of Jewish Women* launches a pilot program for the elderly that evolves into the *Golden Age Association*.

1951. Federation of Jewish Philanthropies is renamed the *Federation of Jewish Community Services*.

1951. The Ezra Ladies' Group receives a charter to operate a convalescent home. It was the beginning of the *Jewish Rehabilitation Hospital*.

1952. The Jewish population of Montreal is 85,000.

1956. More than 4,500 Jews fleeing the Hungarian Revolution immigrate to Canada, and 1,500 of them choose Montreal as their new home.

1957. Moroccan Jews begin arriving in Montreal, settling in the Outremont area where they establish the first francophone synagogue, *Congregation Mogen David* on Darlington St.

1957. Lester B. Pearson is awarded the Nobel Prize for his diplomatic efforts to solve the Suez crisis.

HISTORY
Sephardim are Jews descended from those expelled from Spain and Portugal in the fifteenth century. Forced out of the Iberian Peninsula, they journeyed across the globe, searching for freedom to be Jewish. Some Jews found havens in North Africa, and along the Mediterranean shore, especially in Turkey. Others fled to Western Europe—to the Netherlands, England, and France. They spoke, in addition to the language of the country where they resided, a fifteenth-century romance language called Ladino. In synagogue, they follow the Sephardic rite of Judaism, an order of worship that differs from the Ashkenazi rite in variations of pronunciation and cadence in sung prayers.

Most of the Jews in Montreal before the mid-twentieth century were Ashkenazim (of Central and Eastern European descent). They named their first synagogue (1768) the Spanish and Portuguese only to maintain close ties with existing synagogues in London and New York. With a mixed congregation, the synagogue maintains the Sephardic rite to this day.

In the 1950s, French-speaking Jews from North Africa, finding it increasingly uncomfortable and even dangerous to live in bitterly anti-Israel countries, began to leave. The number of Sephardic Jews in Montreal had grown only slowly in the period 1910 to 1945, coming from such countries as Lebanon, Syria and Egypt. Iraqi Jews began arriving in Montreal in the 1950s but quickly integrated themselves without fanfare into the English-speaking (anglophone) community. However, between 1957 and 1965, a flood of French-speaking (or francophone) Sephardic immigrants arrived in the province. More than 3,000 Moroccans emigrated to Canada and three-quarters of them settled in Montreal. The records show that the newcomers, during this eight-year period, also included 222 Iranians and 57 Algerians. Montreal now had two different Jewish communities—the older Ashkenazi community, and the newly arrived *Sépharades*. The francophones of Quebec welcomed the Sephardim—recognizing that **this was the largest infusion of immigrants with the French language and culture to reach Quebec since before the Conquest in 1759**. However, the newcomers' integration into the Ashkenazi-dominated Jewish society was far more complicated. The tensions and ambivalence between the two branches of the Jewish world mirrored the friction between anglophones and francophones in Quebec society. French and English Jews began a process of learning to live together productively, drawing strength from a shared Judaism.

1957. Moroccan Jews begin to move to Montreal in substantial numbers. Between 1957-1966, 3,000 come to Canada and 75% settle in Montreal.

1959. Plans are made for a new hospital and home for the aged, and a capital fund raises $2.8 million which, coupled with federal-provincial grants of $1.1 million, creates the *Maimonides Hospital and Home for the Aged*.

1960. The Canadian Bill of Rights is approved by Parliament.

1962. The Federal Government introduces new immigration regulations "to eliminate all discrimination based on colour, race or creed."

1963. Women's Division is reorganized as Women's Federation of Combined Jewish Appeal.

1965. Federation is renamed *Allied Jewish Community Services*, reflecting a new stage of development, and an emphasis on providing social services.

1966. The *Francophone Sépharade Association* is founded.

PIONEER SEPHARADS

Jean-Claude Lasry, a well-regarded psychologist and teacher at the Université de Montréal, was a pioneer Moroccan immigrant. His family was the third Moroccan family to settle in Montreal. "My father, brother and I arrived first (in January 1957), followed quickly by my mother, to whom we had written. Some friends were curious about our experience, including a very well known family in Morocco, the Malkas, who joined us soon afterward and have done very well in real estate. That's sort of how Sephardic immigration has taken place, through families and friends." (Footnote: The teenage boy who could not get an Ashkenazi girl to dance with him eventually married a French Jew, and raised a family in Montreal. In his research career, he took a special interest in the well-being of his people and in the evolving relationship between the two Jewish communities, and he did comprehensive studies on the living conditions of Sephardim. One of his foremost accomplishments was his successful campaign to have a French-language Jewish school, *École Maimonide*, established in Montreal.)

1960—and the Haim Abenhaim family from Morocco is welcomed to Montreal. (Canadian Jewish Congress National Archives, Montreal)

DESTINATION MONTREAL

From the mid-1960s, the numbers of French-speaking Jewish migrants increased sharply when about 10,000 immigrants, mostly from Morocco, arrived in the city over a period of twenty years. Jacques Langlais and David Rome wrote in *Jews and French Quebecers* (1991), that "by choosing Quebec as a refuge, Jews have signaled their confidence in the laws and institutions of the land and the openness of its people. Five thousand years of history have taught them to recognize a hospitable environment". The co-authors suggested that the sources of Jewish immigration "constitute a barometer of the social climate prevailing in different parts of the world". Indeed, emigration intensified after the 1967 Six-Day War between Israel and her Arab neighbours. Almost the entire Jewish populations of Algeria (130,000), Morocco (250,000), and Tunisia (150,000), were driven out by Arab hostility.

~~~

"As a land of many races Canada has benefited from the contribution of its various ethnic groups. Those of the Jewish faith have particularly enriched our business, academic and cultural life. In so doing they have placed Canada in their debt. Perhaps their most notable achievement, however, has been that they have helped to promote a spirit of tolerance and an opposition to discrimination in all its forms." T.C. Douglas, leader of the NDP (1961-71) in a letter, 1962.

Costumed Sephardic children celebrate the holiday of Purim.

"When we left Morocco," recalls Joseph Levy, an anthropologist from the *Université du Québec à Montréal (UQAM)*, "in the sixties, we had three possible destinations: Israel, France or Canada—particularly Quebec which presented the advantage of the American dream...in French...We were quite surprised, when we arrived in Quebec, to find that English was the language of work."

WELCOMED INTO FRENCH SOCIETY

The North Africans came to Quebec because they knew that French was widely used here, and they hoped to prosper like Americans but still retain their French language and culture. They were unaware of the Quebec Nationalists' push for independence from Canada, a movement with which they have little sympathy. Nevertheless, many French Jews found it easier to relate to francophone Canadians than anglophones. In Quebec, the Sephardim moved freely into industry and academia. An early settler from Morocco, Dr. Joseph Levy was readily accepted into French academic circles. "At UQAM where I've been teaching for twenty years," stated the anthropologist in the late '80s, "I have experienced no problem because I am Jewish or perceived as an immigrant."

ANGLO AND FRANCO JEW

While the French Jews blended seamlessly into French Quebec, it was not as easy when it came to relationships with the Jewish community. The English-speaking Jewish community had laid out the welcome mat for their francophone co-religionists, but there were strings attached. The Ashkenazim already had an outstanding and comprehensive service network, and they expected the Sephardim to fit into the existing communal structure. Over generations, the Ashkenazim had become accustomed to making substantial financial gifts to the community—a tradition the Sephardim did not share. The francophone Jews had their own idea of how they wanted to organize themselves and they developed their own array of community institutions. However, they have also steadily, and increasingly, become lay and professional communal functionaries in the wider Jewish community.

COMMUNAUTÉ SÉPHARADE DU QUÉBEC

The newcomers began, almost immediately, to organize their own service institutions and build a parallel community.   The North African Jewish
Association was founded in 1959. In 1962, Sephardic
delegates, for the first time, participated in national
meetings of Canadian Jewish Congress.   The
Francophone Sépharade Association was formed in
1966 and, by 1978, the Sephardic community was
ready for a major move: *the Communauté Sépharade
du Québec*, created two years earlier, became a

*Members of Le Bel Age Sépharade
model traditional ceremonial dress-
es from Morocco during the
Sephardic cultural festival of the
Centre Communautaire Juif,
Montreal 1991. (Photo courtesy of
the Centre Communautaire Juif.)*

constituent member organization of the Jewish Federation. That
meant that Sephardim had representatives sitting on the Allied
Jewish Community Services' powerful board of trustees. This
was a big step in integrating Sephardim into the mainstream
Jewish community.   However, the ambivalent relationship
between Ashkenazi and Sephardim at cultural and social activities was a source of concern for many community leaders, and
prompted many programs of rapprochement. In 1972, Jean-
Claude Lasry undertook a survey covering "more than 2,500
households, representing approximately 10,000 to 13,000 persons,
probably the whole universe of North African Jews at the time."

   Dr. Lasry found that 46 per cent of Sephardim surveyed perceived French Canadians as the "best colleagues", and 41 per cent
felt that they were the "best bosses." One surprising finding was
the fact that 23 per cent said they disliked Ashkenazim. On closer analysis, it turned out that the North Africans perceived
"Ashkenazim" as immigrant Jews, still speaking with a noticeable accent, while "Canadian Jews" were, in their thinking,
native-born Canadians who spoke English without an accent.
Canadian Jews were appreciated as "friends" by only 23 per cent,
while 68 per cent preferred other North African Jews.
Interestingly, 75 per cent preferred their children to have
Canadian Jews as friends, suggesting the importance Sephardim
placed on development of a Jewish identity. However, Sephardic
immigrants who wished to integrate fully into the **Jewish** milieu
were forced to participate in a Jewish culture dominated by the
Ashkenazi majority and faced difficulties preserving a meaningful Sephardic identity. In 1987, Haim Hazan, writing in the peri-
odical La Voix Sépharade, summed up the Sephardic community's concerns for its linguistic and cultural survival:

   "We are a small vulnerable community because we are isolated and because, in a continent of six million anglophone

The policy of Multi-cul-turalism adopted by the Federal government in 1971 was a critically important development for Canadian Jews. It meant, essentially, that Canada was no longer simply a bicultural Christian country domi-nated by French-speak-ing Roman Catholics and English-speaking Protestants. As a decla-ration of tolerance and diversity, the policy out-dated restrictive immi-gration policies—a long-standing thorn in the side of the Jewish Community. The revi-sed view of immigrants and their role in a multi-cultural society had been outlined in 1946 by Professor Watson Thomson, addressing the Senate Committee on Immigration:
"British political wisdom, Jewish cosmopolitanism and realism, French lucid-ity of mind and expres-sion, German emotional depth and capacity for work, Slavonic spontane-ity and verve—all these are there in the riches of our Canadian life, and each set of qualities can be learned and assimilated by all."

Jews, we 25,000 francophones want to remain Sephardic in a totally Ashkenazi milieu...The status quo can only lead to suffocation and in time to our disappearance as a distinct community."

THE MOSAIC

While Sephardic Jews come from a variety of backgrounds, Moroccans form the largest segment of the population, and were estimated in 1994 to number 18,000. The majority speak French but some hundreds speak Spanish. There are 1,500 Jews from the Iberian countries—Spain and Portugal. The Egyptian Jews num-ber 1,000 and they came to Montreal in two groups—the first shortly after the First World War, and the second during the period 1940-1960. Dollard des Ormeaux is home for almost all the 800 Syrian Jews living in Greater Montreal. Some 50 Lebanese Jews fled that country during the bitter 10-year civil war in 1975. There are very small communities of Jews from Iraq and Iran.

FROM THE CASBAH TO COTE DES NEIGES

The Sephardim have maintained close ties with what remains of their ancestral Jewish community in Morocco. There had been a particularly close bond between Montreal Sephardic leaders and the late King Hassan, who had done his best to protect his Jewish residents from wide-spread Moroccan hostility during upheavals related to the re-birth of Israel. The King on more than one occasion tra-velled incognito to Canada to attend Sephardic celebrations. In Quebec, the Sephardim retained many of their local customs. For example, at least one local Moroccan leader—ranked as a Prince in

The Torah Scrolls of the Spa-nish and Portugese Synago-gue...a congregation founded in 1688—the first in Canada. (Ontario Jewish Archives Shuls Collection)

the North African Kingdom—had a throne room in his Hampstead home and, on occasion, was called upon to mediate or arbitrate disputes among members of the community. Despite the animosity that prompted them to leave their homeland, Montreal Jews frequently visit Morocco, and do business there.

FACILITATING RAPPROCHEMENT

According to the Federation CJA study *Sépharade 2000: Challenges and Perspectives for the Sephardic Community of Montreal* (Shahar), significant diversity remained between the English and French-speaking Jewish communities 40 years after settlement. As the Sephardim are younger and have higher birthrates, **Sephardic Jews are expected to form the majority of the community within the next generation**. Approximately one Sephardi in four is under the age of 15. However, research indicates that the face of Sephardic culture is changing. "It seems that the children of Sephardim are increasingly becoming more anglophone."

Only 11.3 per cent of Sephardim are aged, while the figure for Ashkenazim is 26.3 per cent. Both have low intermarriage rates but the Sephardim, in their early years of settlement, intermarried widely with non-Jews. According to the 1991 census, between 1940 and 1959, about 20 per cent of Sephardic immigrants—one in five—married non-Jews. However, the rate dramatically decreased, by 1991, to 6.8 per cent (8.0 per cent for the Jewish community in general). Among those migrants who arrived after 1980, only 2.3 per cent marry out of Judaism.

There is a high level of religious observance among Sephardim. There are at least 42 synagogues serving the community, of which Petah Tikvah, the Spanish & Portuguese, and Hekhal Shalom were the most popular. The Federation survey also reported that "in terms of specific rituals: 63% of respondents keep kosher at home; 47.7% keep kosher outside the home; 80% always buy kosher meat; 47.4% strictly observe Shabbat; and 75.9% always observe Shabbat dinner."

The arrival of Sephardic Jews has meant new taste treats for all Montrealers. Sephardic dishes, smacking of their Mediterranean origin, range from shish kebabs to sesame-sprinkled pastries and are wildly popular. A wide range of cafés and bakeries featuring the specialties of Middle Eastern and North African Jews dot Montreal. One of the most popular items of North African cuisine is the "cigar," a paper-thin rolled crust stuffed with spiced liver and beef.

Quand je te lis Voix Sépharade
Mon coeur bat la chamade.
J'ai mal à mes racines
Celles que le temps doucement déracine.

Pourtant je t'écris Voix Sépharade
Preuve qu'en toi j'existe malgré la dérobade.
De mes tripes tu es la substance
Celle qui guide ma plume comme un pas de danse.

ALDO, A SEPHARAD SUCCESS

In the late '60s, Moroccan-born Aldo Bensadoun was living in New York when he made a weekend trip to Montreal and fell in love with the city. He later transferred from New York University to McGill. When Bensadoun went to France to honour his military service obligation, the French assigned him to teach economics at an academy in central France. Back in Montreal in 1972, Bensadoun started manufacturing and selling stylish footwear under the Aldo name. He later expanded the business and created six retail chains, including Pegabo, Simard, Transit, Calderone and Feet First. The 600 stores, in Canada, the U.S., and Israel, reported sales in 1999 of $450 million.

The 1991 census showed 21,049 Sephardim and 77,131 Ashkenazim living in Greater Montreal.

Quand je te parle Voix Sépharade
Je fais partie de la parade
Et avec elle d'un brin d'éternité
Du Sacré que tu lègues à la postérité.

Éliane Acoca, 1999
Hymne à la voix sépharade

PROUD OF ARAB HERITAGE

Iraqi-born author Naim Kattan (photo by John Evans)

Novelist, essayist, author and critic, Naim Kattan is a cultural icon of the Montreal Sephardic community. He was born in the fabled city of Baghdad, and wrote his first story, in Arabic, at age 14. He moved to Montreal in 1954 after attending the Sorbonne in Paris. "To live in Canada, to write in French, is for me the pursuit of an undertaking that did not end in my ancestors, the Jews of Babylon." Kattan is comfortable in his multilingual world. "I am Arabic-speaking," he declares. "I was a writer in Arabic; I come from that civilization. And I still belong to it. I write about it. But, also, I belong to one of the oldest Jewish communities in the world, maybe the oldest, and I feel that also very strongly."

His first job in Canada was with Canadian Jewish Congress, where he launched *Bulletin Cercle Juif*, a publication targeted to the French-Canadian community, with the goal of heightening understanding between the two communities. In 1967, after 13 years in the editor's chair, he joined the Canada Council as Director of its Writing and Publishing Section. He remained in that post for 23 years, guiding and assisting other authors. He also found time to do a great deal of important writing on his own.

In 1992, he joined Université du Québec à Montréal as writer-in-residence and, in 1994, as a Professor. Kattan is a member of the *Royal Society of Canada, Société des Cent Associés* and *Académie des Lettres du Québec*. He is also an Officer of the Order of Canada and a member of the Order of Arts and Letters of France.

CHAPTER THIRTY

ISRAEL IN PERIL
Montreal Jews and the Other Side of the Shekel

Federation President Gordon Brown and Samuel Bronfman were flying to Quebec City on business. With deep concern, they discussed the crisis in the Middle East. It was May 1967 and Arab countries, armed to the teeth by the Soviets, were threatening to drive the Jews of Israel into the sea. How could Israel survive? She was surrounded by enemies. Sam Bronfman made up his mind. "We will have a national meeting next week, in Montreal," he announced. Allan Bronfman went on the telephone, calling Canada's most important Jewish leaders. Within 48 hours, virtually every prominent Jewish family in Canada sent a representative to Montreal for the meeting in the prestigious Montefiore Club. Sam Bronfman did not mince words; he never did. After the situation was authoritatively summarized, Sam stood up and announced "our family is going to triple its gift to the campaign." Almost every leader present followed suit. Some even exceeded the guideline.

The Jewish State of Israel had been in modern existence for only 19 years and the young country was heavily burdened by war, terrorism, and an incredible number of immigrants, many in dire straits. In the first three years of Independence, the Jewish population had doubled from 650,000 to 1.3 million. It had nearly doubled again, to 2.5 million, by 1967, when Egyptian President Abdel Gamel Nasser announced his army would "drive the Jews into the sea." Nasser demanded that the United Nations Peacekeeping Forces be removed from their positions between Egyptian and Israeli forces in the Sinai desert. Remarkably enough, the UN complied. Then, in an act of war, the Egyptians blockaded the Gulf of Akaba, cutting Israel off from sea routes to Asia and Africa. The Arab League countries, including the main armies of Syria, Jordan, and Iraq, joined in with threats to destroy Israel. On May 30, 1967, Radio Cairo stated:

> "There are now two courses open to Israel—either of which is drenched in her own blood; either she will die of strangulation under the Arab military and economic siege, or else she will perish under the fire of the Arab forces encompassing her on the north, the south and the east."

The dream was about to become a nightmare. Israel was in peril and in desperate need of help. Jews around the globe recognized the urgency of strengthening Israel at this critical moment. The landmark meeting at the Montefiore Club not only raised several million dollars, it galvanized the Montreal community to help mobilize the Diaspora and to provide leadership to the whole Jewish world. In general, the response from Montreal Jews—historically in the forefront of support for Zionism—was spontaneous, unanimous, and exceptional.

A TIDAL WAVE OF MORAL AND FINANCIAL SUPPORT

Without an official campaign or marketing effort, gifts—large and small—poured in to Federation headquarters, located since 1950 at 493 Sherbrooke West. Non-Jews as well as Jews brought in contributions. Gifts ranged from the contents of a child's piggy bank to the deed to a home. Children gave their lunch money. So many coins came in that more than a dozen young accountants volunteered to count the contents of large canvas bags stored in the Combined Jewish Appeal's walk-in safe. Montreal's contribution exceeded $5 million and all but what was necessary to maintain essential services in Montreal was sent to the Jewish Agency, the Parliament of the Jewish people in Israel.

Israeli war hero Moshe Dayan (with eye patch) on a visit to the Montreal Jewish Community. General Dayan is flanked (l to r) by former Combined Jewish Appeal General Chairman Thomas Otto Hecht, the author and Gordon Brown, onetime President of Federation.

THE TERRIBLE SWIFT SWORD

On June 5, 1967 Israel struck first with a lightning offensive against the Egyptians. In six days, the Israelis swept away the Arab Armies, seizing the Gaza Strip and Sinai desert from Egypt; Old Jerusalem and the West Bank of the Jordan River from Jordan; and the Golan Heights from Syria. Tiny Israel, instead of being destroyed, suddenly became a military titan in the Middle East. All the peace talks since the Six-Day War have focussed on pressing Israel to return territory conquered in the defensive battles of '67.

The stunning 1967 victory tremendously affected Jews everywhere, including, of course, Montreal. A sense of relief that the
state had survived was followed by euphoria. Jews now had a
different opinion of Israel, and of themselves. They were proud of
Israel's incredible victory, and they carried that pride around
with them from that moment on. Jews around the world who
had been less than enthusiastic about Israel realized how important it was to them personally, and they intensified their commitment. The Diaspora had undergone a trauma of conscience and
identity during the summer crisis. According to *Israel and World
Jewry*: "Each year of Israel's independence and consolidating
strength had blurred the memory of refugees adrift on the seas
like Flying Dutchmen; of Jewish intermediaries hats in hand,
waiting in foreign consulates for the revision of a visa quota; even
of the *numerus clausus* that once had excluded Jewish students
from good universities and professional schools. The memory
had all but faded—until May 1967." The shared experience of a
threat to Israel's existence coupled with the relief of military victory welded the Diaspora Jews and the Israelis into one people.

FROM DAN TO BEERSHEBA

Relieved Jews, including many from Montreal, poured into Israel.
One of the first groups to arrive was a *Combined Jewish Appeal
Study Mission* led by Federation President Gordon Brown and
including some of the community's top leaders. In an intense ten-
day visit, they journeyed literally from Dan to Beersheba—from
the wreckage-strewn Golan Heights, where they were shot at by
snipers, to the Suez Canal, where looking down from an aircraft,
they could follow the retreat of Egyptian soldiers by discarded
boots in the sand. The Mission studied the human needs of the
Jewish State in the wake of the Six-Day War, and their report,
After the Storm, described the damage suffered by Israelis and recommended how Montreal Jewry might assist. Details of the difficulties encouraged many people, including a number of professionals, to voluntarily visit the Jewish State for long periods to
provide medical and other services.

ISRAELI LEADERS VISIT MONTREAL

After the war, the reaction of Jewish communities overseas, such
as Montreal, shared front-page space in Israeli newspapers with
reports on UN negotiations and Arab developments. The heightened importance of Montreal in the Jewish world was underscored by the fact that virtually every important Israeli leader

Charles Bronfman (l) with Abba Eban, Israel's longtime Foreign Minister, during a 1979 visit to Montreal.

On January 31, 1961, the old Mansion on Stanley Street, home to the Hillel Foundation, was a crowded scene as a world-famous historian and an Israeli diplomat/scholar debated. Professor Arnold Toynbee, who in lectures and print had stated that the Jews were a "fossil" people, was up against one of Jewry's most articulate representatives, Yaacov David Herzog, the Israeli Ambassador to Canada. The consensus was that Toynbee was roundly defeated as Ambassador Herzog declared: "We are the only people today in the Middle East speaking the same language, practising the same religious faith, living in the same category of aspiration and spiritual continuity as our forefathers thousands of years ago." Toynbee's view was that "the Jews are living on as a peculiar people long after the Phoenicians and Philistines lost their identity." The debate was broadcast live over CJAD radio and a recording was made and circulated widely.

visited the city repeatedly. David Ben Gurion, the first Prime Minister, came a number of times. The great generals and heroes of the Six-Day War, Moshe Dayan, Yitzhak Rabin and Uzi Narkiss, also visited. Shimon Peres, Menachem Begin, and Golda Meir were among the prime ministers who made the journey.

During the unrest in Montreal in the 1970s, when terrorists were active with bombs and kidnapping, plans for a Golda Meir dinner were changed from Montreal to Toronto. Security was particularly tight during the numerous visits of Moshe Dayan, Israel's defence minister during the Six-Day War, who was regarded as Arab terrorists' number-one target. General Dayan would often stay at the Queen Elizabeth Hotel in a corner suite so members of the Israeli secret service and RCMP could occupy the adjacent rooms.

The Israelis brought symbolic gifts of appreciation to community leaders. For example, Yigal Yadin, the world-renowned archaeologist responsible for the dig at Massada—a mountain fortress from pre-Roman times in the Negev Desert—gave Maxwell Cummings an enormous vase discovered in the ruins of the fortress.

YOM KIPPUR WAR

Israel from its inception has been in conflict with its neighbours. In addition to five wars, the Jewish State has been continuously harassed by terrorists.

On the state's holiest day, Yom Kippur, the threat of destruction was renewed in 1973 when Egypt and Syria attacked from the south and north respectively. Young conscripts—many not old enough to shave—patrolled the Israeli defence lines. While most Israelis were in synagogue, the sirens wailed, calling the soldiers to arms. In a hastily organized offensive, the Israeli Defence Forces attempted a counterattack on October 8, which failed. The Jewish world waited with apprehension. Recovering their strength and maintaining morale, the Israelis eventually pushed the Egyptians back across the Suez canal, and stopped within 100 kilometres of Cairo to avoid street fighting in a metropolitan area. In the north, they pushed the Syrian army to less than 50 kilometres from the Syrian capital, Damascus.

During the imposed cease-fire, Montreal Jewish leaders once more journeyed to Israel to report on conditions and identify where help was most needed. The General Chairman of the 1973 Combined Jewish Appeal, Thomas Otto Hecht, went so far as to visit the Israeli entrenchments along the Suez Canal, where Egyptian gunners continued sporadic shellfire at Israeli positions. In military jeeps, Hecht's party careened on an erratic course to avoid being hit by snipers as they visited soldiers in their fortifications.

> Between 1946 and 1973, there were 23,636 Israeli immigrants to Canada. Most settled in Toronto. Bob Luck of the Jewish Immigration Aid Services estimated in 1999 that the Israeli community in Montreal numbered between 3,000 and 3,500.

ISRAELI IMMIGRATION TO CANADA

Small numbers of Israelis began to move to Canada almost from the moment the Jewish State was created. Not everybody could cope with the repeated wars and the economic disruptions linked to the conflicts. During the 1946-1950 period, 435 Israelis came to Canada. Their numbers swelled to 6,842 between 1951 and 1957. Immigration from Israel peaked in the period between the 1956 Suez War and the Yom Kippur War in 1973.

The young soldier pretended he was dead after an Egyptian attack on the Holy Day of Yom Kippur. He and other members of his unit had been playing soccer on the banks of the Suez Canal when the Arab assault took place. When he could move around, he found the bodies of all his companions littering their playing field. He was the only survivor. His family sent him to stay with a cousin in Montreal. He found a job as a shipper and stayed six months until, it was felt, he could return home.

BUILDING ON THE FERTILE CRESCENT

Canadian business leaders have made their mark in Israel by developing commercial and industrial projects. In the mid-1950s, Charles R. Bronfman collaborated with American executives to set up Israel's first chain of modern supermarkets, Supersol.

Later, Bronfman and Montrealer Jonathan Kolber (son of Sandra and Senator Leo Kolber) purchased five Israeli companies and became the largest foreign investors in Israel. They provided the Jewish State with its largest high-tech corporation, ECI Telecom, and branched out into pharmaceuticals. The Bronfman-Kolber partnership created Koor, Israel's largest conglomerate, with 25,000 employees.

Montreal real estate developer and architect David Azrieli conceived and built Israel's first enclosed shopping mall—the Canion Ayalon in Ramat Gan, in 1985. As Israelis flocked to the new facility, Azrieli built two similar centres in Beersheba and

Montreal developer David Azrieli with his huge development in Tel Aviv—the largest structure of its kind in the Middle East.

Jerusalem. In 2000, the Azrieli Center in Tel Aviv—the largest project in Israel and, indeed, in the entire Middle East—was under construction. The 340,000-sq. metre Azrieli Center includes three high-rise towers (one with 50 floors), a shopping mall, recreation areas and public spaces. David Azrieli is a Polish-born survivor of the Holocaust whose postwar route to Canada involved a trek across war-torn Europe, and service with the Israeli Defence Forces in the 1948 War of Independence. He moved to Canada in 1954 and began designing and building homes, apartments, and malls. In 1985, Azrieli returned to Israel. When his credentials were questioned, he enrolled in Carleton University and, at age 73, earned a Master's Degree in Architecture in 1997. The School of Architecture at Tel Aviv University, Israel's largest institution of higher learning, bears his name.

Women's Division Study Mission from Montreal to Israel in the early 1970s on behalf of the Combined Jewish Appeal.

MISSIONS TO ISRAEL

In the aftermath of the 1967 War, and the reunification of Jerusalem, tens of thousands of Montreal Jews flocked to Israel as tourists on packaged tours or as part of "Study Missions" organized by the Combined Jewish Appeal, or Israeli-based organizations.

A 1997 study conducted by Federation's Charles Shahar and Randal F. Schnoor of McGill University found that three-quarters of respondents have visited Israel at least once. The study concluded, "(that this) is by far the highest rate of any North American community." The rate for Toronto, 63%, is also very high, but for the entire United States it is only 26 per cent.

The high percentage of travellers to Israel included young people. Another Shahar study showed that more than half of those surveyed—56.8 per cent—had travelled to the Jewish State after graduation from high school, and almost half of Jewish high school students had visited Israel as part of their educational program. Jewish high schools incorporate a visit to Israel in their study plan. And for the more religious schools, students spend an entire term in Israel—studying and travelling.

MARCH TO JERUSALEM

Montreal Jews have always had an unusually deep attachment to Israel. The Shahar-Schnoor study showed 67.4 per cent of respondents agreed "strongly" with the statement "caring about Israel is a very important part of being a Jew." The spirited **March to**

Jerusalem, initiated to help mark the 25th anniversary of Israel, draws 20,000-25,000 participants a year, or about one-quarter of the city's Jewish population—a figure that does not include thousands of supportive bystanders, many of them non-Jews. Nuns, priests, and foreign students walk alongside young and old waving blue-and-white Israeli flags. Volunteers march a 25-kilometre route through western Montreal in order to raise money for cultural and recreational projects in the

March to Jerusalem '94

Jewish State. The route includes the challenging climb up the slopes of Mount Royal, re-named Massada for the day. The Montreal March, first organized by Manny Spinner and his Jewish Cultural Association, is one of the largest in North America. The success of the March prompted other communities—including Jerusalem—to request help organizing a similar event in their city, and Spinner advised a number of other groups, including Chinese, Arab and Shi'ite Muslim organizations. In addition, the Montreal organizers of the March prepared a handbook that was circulated to many world Jewish communities.

MARCH OF THE LIVING

In the mid-80s, Montrealers began participating in the **March of the Living**, an annual event sensitizing young people to their heritage and history. The program involves an escorted visit to Holocaust sites in Eastern Europe, followed by a tour of Israel. It is a deeply emotional experience for the young people and their adult escorts, as they tour the concentration camps and then experience a thriving Israel.

In 1999, Charles Bronfman teamed up with American philanthropist Michael Steinhardt to create **Birthright Israel**, a program to send young Diaspora Jews on 10-day visits to Israel. About 6,000 students took advantage of the offer during the winter of 1999-2000, half of them by arrangements made through Hillel, the Jewish campus organization. In Montreal, 750 students applied to go, and 200 were accepted in that first year. Many others were on a waiting list for future visits. In the spring of 2000, Birthright Israel was extended for five years, to 2004. Funding of the immense project is shared among 14 philanthropists, local Jewish federations, and the State of Israel.

Before taking part in the program, many of the young Jews reported having little interest in Israel, or Judaism. Many later said that the reality of Israel—a vibrant and dynamic democracy—had moved them to change their attitudes.

FEW MAKE ALIYAH

Despite interest in and widespread support for the Jewish home-land, few Canadians actually "make **Aliyah**", the term for mov-ing to Israel. In 1999, for example, only 184 Canadians emigrated to Israel, and that figure included people retiring to the Jewish State, businesspeople, and a dozen fervent Zionists from Cote St. Luc who moved to the West Bank town of Ariel. The number of émigrés in 1998 was comparatively small, at 256. In 1999, immi-gration from other countries to Israel ranged from 31,000 from Russia and 23,118 from the Ukraine to 1,328 from the United States, 322 from England, 227 from South Africa and 84 from Australia. While Israel is the most prosperous and advanced country in the Middle East, the western world still has many advantages in terms of creature comforts! Nonetheless, the very existence of a Jewish State is vitally important to Jews in the dias-pora. Not only is the nation a sanctuary for Jews in distress around the world, it remains for the Diaspora, after 2,000 years in Exile, a powerful and enduring symbol of security and source of great pride.

A formal occasion in the 1960's (l to r) Samuel Bronfman, Samuel Moscovitz (longtime mayor of Côte St. Luc) and Prime Minister Lester B. Pearson, (Allan Raymond Collection; Jewish Public Library Archives)

THANK YOU, PRIME MINISTER

Canada has had and continues to play an important role in Middle Eastern politics. In 1947, Prime Minister **Lester B. Pearson**, then Minister of External Affairs, was one of the authors of the Partition Resolution submitted for UN con-sideration and played a pivotal role in negotiations leading to the crucial vote. After the 1956 War, when Israel was pressed to pull back from its territorial gains in the Sinai Desert, Pearson proposed the idea of UN peacekeeping forces. He was awarded the Nobel Peace Prize in 1957 for his role in solving the Suez Crisis. In receiving his award, he declared: "The grim fact is that we prepare for war like precocious giants and for peace like retarded pygmies." Pearson, who was prime minister from 1963-1968, did not visit the Middle East until his retirement from politics.

No prime minister was more outspoken in support of Israel than **Brian Mulroney**, Prime Minister from 1984-1993. During a 1993 Washington press conference with U.S. President Bill Clinton, Mulroney told reporters: "I am always concerned when people start to lecture Israel on the manner in which it has to look after its own internal security because, for very important historical reasons, Israel of course is better qualified than most to make determination about its own well-being." Later that same year, at a Canada-Israel Committee Parliamentary dinner in Ottawa, he declared: "You may rest assured that I will always remain a firm and faithful friend of Israel."

Former Canadian Prime Minister (1984-1993) Brian Mulroney (centre), with mem-bers of the Cummings Family when Tel Aviv University conferred an Honorary Degree on him in 1994. Members of the family in the picture are Maxwell, seated, Jack (left) and Stephen.

Jean Chrétien was the first Canadian prime minister to visit Israel while in office. His tour in 2000 included the memorial to the Holocaust, Yad Vashem, where he apologized for Canada's failure to help rescue threatened European Jews. "Errors were made in the past," he stated, "but as you know, Canada is the most open nation today for refugees all over the world." In the Yad Vashem guest book, Chrétien wrote:

"As Prime Minister of Canada I pledge to you that Canada will take a leading role to ensure that such atrocities never happen again."

October 1973: Mass demonstration in support of Soviet Jewry, seen from overhead perspective, Doctor Penfield Avenue. Rallies around the time of Simchat Torah were for many years a hallmark of the Soviet Jewry movement across Canada.
(Canadian Jewish Congress National Archives)

In the mid-seventies, tight Soviet emigration controls were relaxed, and Russian Jews poured out in their tens of thousands. Most went to Israel or the United States, but the Russian Jewish community in Montreal is authoritatively estimated—by Jewish Immigrant Aid Services—at more than 8,000.

Nathan "The Matchmaker" Scott

NATHAN THE MATCHMAKER

The tradition of using a matchmaker to bring young men and women together persists in modern times in many societies, but the concept faded away in the New World among Jews—until Nathan the Matchmaker set up shop in Montreal. In Europe, the matchmaker in the *Shtetl* was almost always a widow who got by on small fees she collected for her services. But onetime businessman Nathan Scott saw a need for this kind of service in 21st century Montreal.

Scott departs from tradition, however, in his *modus operandi*. His technique is to be constantly aware of the potential compatibility of people he meets. He has 80 to 100 clients in his "registry", mostly women in their 30s and 40s. "Women are more interested in marriage than men," he says. "It's easier for a guy to call a girl; it's harder for a girl to phone a guy."

Scott manages to match up about a dozen couples a month. He is aggressive in his style. If, for example, he spots a suitable male for one of his clients, he will approach him and propose a meeting.

He charges clients $250, and for that he will arrange to put the prospect in touch with "three to five potential mates." He won't cash his client's cheque until they've been in contact with potential partners. And he will refund the fee in full if the prospect is not happy with his services.

Scott emphasizes he is not running a dating agency. "I only help people who are serious about getting married."

CHAPTER THIRTY-ONE

BUILDING A GREAT CITY
Montreal Jewry sparkles at home and on the World Scene

Montrealer Sheila Kussner did her best to be cheerful as she went from bed to bed in the military hospital near Tel Aviv. In the ward were many young men, barely old enough to shave, who had been maimed and mutilated in the Yom Kippur War. Kussner, a Strathcona High beauty queen who became a respected Jewish community leader, had taken a crash course in Hebrew and hurried to the Jewish State to comfort the wounded. Although Kussner distributed gifts and talked as encouragingly as she could with her limited vocabulary, one of the soldiers—who had lost his right arm—snapped, "How can you know how we feel?" Kussner, who had lost a leg to cancer when she was 14, quietly reached down and unscrewed her artificial leg—holding it up for the wounded men to see.

TIMELINE—1967-1975

1967. The Jewish Community opens Pavilion of Judaism at Expo '67, the World's Fair in Montreal.

1967. The Saidye Bronfman Centre for the Arts opens.

1969. The unused nurses' residence of the Jewish Hospital of Hope is renovated to become the Jewish Nursing Home.

1969. Ecole Maimonide, the first French-language Jewish school in Canada, is established.

1971. Samuel Bronfman House at the corner of Cote Des Neiges and Docteur Penfield is inaugurated as the new National headquarters of Canadian Jewish Congress.

1971. The Jewish Community Foundation is created by the Allied Jewish Community Services, Jewish General Hospital and other agencies.

1971. A policy of Multiculturalism is adopted by the Federal Government.

1972. Cummings House, funded with the help of a substantial gift from the Cummings Family, is opened at 5151 Cote St. Catherine Road.

The Pavilion of Judaism at Expo '67 in Montreal. The picture includes the President of the Foundation for Judaism, Sam Steinberg, 4th from the right; Architect Max Roth, who designed the exhibits in the Pavilion, and Rabbi Wilfred Shuchat, longtime spiritual leader of Congregation Shaar Hashomayim.
(Canadian Jewish Congress National Archives, Montreal)

The period from Expo '67 until the Montreal Olympic Games in 1976 saw the Montreal Jewish community flourish and expand despite a slump in the Canadian economy, and a recession in Quebec aggravated by political ferment. In 1967, Canada celebrated its centennial year and the tremendous growth and opportunity of the previous decade; from 1957-67, the Canadian Gross Domestic Product had doubled from 35 billion to 70 billion. Expo '67, Canada's first world's fair, was a showcase of the strength of Canadian multiculturalism and diversity. As evidence of its new prominence, the community organized the world's Judaica pavilion, celebrating 50 centuries of Jewish history. Sam Steinberg headed the committee that raised $400,000 and created an important Jewish presence on the fairgrounds. The community, like the city, had reached a pinnacle. Montreal had become a world-class cosmopolitan city, and Jews had been among the most important contributors.

The Jewish community, which for the most part had begun in the poverty of the St. Lawrence Boulevard "Main", was *on the move* literally and figuratively. The population was growing, peaking in 1971 at 114,000. Jews graduated from downtown tenements to apartments, duplexes, and then finer homes in Westmount, Outremont, Cote des Neiges, Hampstead, Ville St. Laurent, and Laval. The migration north and west to the suburbs meant the creation of new neighbourhoods; Jews built the cities of Cote St. Luc and Dollard des Ormeaux. The island was open to them and they built synagogues, schools, and shopping centres.

1972. Baron de Hirsch Institute is divided to provide government-funded programming as Jewish Family Services.

1972. A federally funded study that shocks the Community reveals one Jewish family in six lives at or below the poverty line.

1972. Caldwell Residences agency is formed to develop dignified housing for elderly with low incomes.

1972. Fondation B'nai Brith de Montréal is established to serve francophone university students.

1973. The March to Jerusalem is created by the Jewish Cultural Association to help mark the 25th Anniversary of a reborn Israel.

1974. The Herzl Health Centre merges with the Jewish General Hospital and becomes the Herzl Family Practice Centre.

1975. The Jewish Education Council is formed to coordinate the activities of Jewish schools.

MOVING IN TUNE WITH A CHANGING SOCIETY

Jews who had graduated from peddler's packs to family stores, Jews who operated corner candy stores, delicatessens, bakeries, grocery stores, corner newspaper stands—sometimes working 12 to 18 hours a day, seven days a week, began moving up the ladder of prosperity. Their sons and daughters formed the highest component proportionately in high schools and studied at universities in impressive numbers—although quotas shunted them into certain disciplines. Second-generation Jews chose the professions—medicine, the law, accountancy—or science and advanced business degrees. As they graduated, changes in society, and the economy, provided great opportunities. Industry was becoming increasingly complex, with science and technology opening the door to new products. In *Viewpoints*, Joseph Baumholz described the radical change in the Montreal Jewish community:

Saidye Bronfman triumphantly cuts the ribbon inaugurating the Centre for the Arts bearing her name—a birthday gift from her children in 1967. (Canadian Jewish Congress National Archives)

> "The economic boundaries for Jewish shopkeepers exploded with the development of Jewish chains such as Steinberg's, Reitman's, and Pascal's. Junk dealers became equipment and structural steel suppliers, while clothing manufacturers became construction real estate companies."

Jews took their advanced degrees into the marketplace—and they were wide open to change. Having been excluded from leadership in existing industries, they focussed on what was new. In the boardrooms of major corporations, many of their own making, they undertook enormous real estate developments, created new industries, expanded older ones, and remained on the cutting edge of a diversifying Quebec economy. Moreover, they entered government as the civil service grew. One Jewish lawyer negotiated the major trading agreements with the United States—the Auto Pact and the Free Trade Agreement—setting the Canadian economy on its course for decades to come. A Jewish economist became Governor of the Bank of Canada. Another Jewish lawyer, born in the heart of The Main, became Chief Justice of the Quebec Provincial Court. In every area of Jewish endeavour, there was success and vitality. The reputation of Montreal as a world centre for the Jewish Diaspora was well established, and local community leaders confidently became major players on the World Jewish stage. A number of outstanding personalities emerged on the city scene—pre-eminent thinkers, artists and industrialists, scientists, medical researchers, town planners, lawyers, activists—revolutionizing the city and dazzling the world.

Sheila Kussner, founder of Hope and Cope at the Jewish General Hospital.
(Drummond-Jacquot Photo)

Sheila Kussner (1931-) emerged from her devastating experience with cancer determined to help others. Her efforts led in 1981 to the formation of *Hope and Cope*, a volunteer organization meeting the needs of cancer patients and their families, a concept that started at the Jewish General Hospital but has been adopted in many hospitals in Canada and the United States. Kussner raised millions for Cancer Research at the Jewish General and for McGill University, which awarded her an honorary degree. One of the world's greatest research facilities, the Sloan-Kettering Cancer Centre in New York honoured her with its Robert Fisher Fellowship Award.
In 1977 she became the first woman to receive the President of the State of Israel Award, the highest recognition bestowed by the

THE BATSHAW ERA

In 1968, **Manuel G. Batshaw** (1916-) became executive director of Federation, then known as *Allied Jewish Community Services (AJCS)*, and the 12-year period in which he held this post was a time of unparalleled growth and is described as the "Batshaw Era." Fresh from,

CUMMINGS HOUSE-FEDERATION'S NEW HOME FROM 1972. This modern four-storey structure became the central address for the Montreal Jewish Community. (Photo from Federation/CJA)

senior positions within the American Jewish Community, the McGill-trained social worker readily accepted an invitation to be professional leader of the community. It became a period of intense growth for the central community body with Batshaw working in tandem with seven presidents—Gordon Brown, Boris G. Levine, Monty Berger, Charles R. Bronfman, Joe Ain, Hillel Becker and Irving J. Halperin. Over 12 fruitful years, AJCS modernized itself and followed the move of population by building a new headquarters in the Snowdon district—finally, a central address for the community.

Responding to demographic change, AJCS moved, in 1972, from the weatherbeaten stone building it had occupied since 1950 on Sherbrooke Street at Aylmer to **Cummings House** located on Cote St. Catherine Road, at Westbury Avenue, across the road from the Snowdon YM-YWHA and its similarly, black-glass-clad Saidye Bronfman Centre. In 1972,

Manuel G. Batshaw, (l) Honorary Executive Vice-President of Federation/CJA, receives the Order of Quebec from Premier Jacques Parizeau.

Caldwell Residences was formed to develop dignified housing for elderly people with low incomes. The agency eventually built four apartment facilities in line with its mandate. In the next few years, a **Golden Age Centre** was constructed next door to Cummings House and three low-rental housing projects for seniors—**Harry Bronfman Square One** and **Two**, and **Pollack House**—were erected to the east.

When a newspaper reporter asked the intake social worker for Harry Bronfman Square One, Ruth Fisher, how the older people would move their fragile collectibles, Fisher laughed and responded: "Almost all of these people are either survivors of the Holocaust, or refugees from the Hungarian Revolution. Most of them have never had so much as a room of their own. When they close the door on their modest apartment in the Square, it will be the first time in their lives they had the luxury of space of their own."

The building program was all on land bought for the Jewish General Hospital in 1930, at depression-level prices, and sold— lot by lot—to AJCS at one dollar per purchase. The movement to the west continued with the erection of the Jewish Nursing Home and the Jewish Hospital of Hope, moved from their original homes in east-end Montreal, and thereby creating a Jewish medical complex, adjacent to the Jewish General Hospital. When Batshaw became distressed over conditions for youth in detention centres, he investigated personally and later chaired a Provincial Commission. The Batshaw Report led to significant changes in the way services were provided to children in Quebec and the new network of youth-serving agencies was named in his honour.

MOVING UP; MOVING OUT

The Jewish population continued its trek westward, with the most spectacular movement into what had been the tiny, picturesque, French Canadian village of Cote St. Luc. In 1931, there were no Jews in the community. Ten years later, 13 pioneers had built homes there, and according to the 1951 census, there were 34 Jews living in the village. Then the dam burst. By 1961, 8,307 Jews were Cote St. Luc citizens. The Jewish population continued to increase rapidly: to 17,460 in '71; and 20,495 in '81. By the 1991 census, the municipality with the greatest concentration of Jewish residents was **Cote St. Luc**, with 21,160. Jewish schools and synagogues were built to accommodate the new arrivals. Cavendish Mall shopping centre was built (in 1973) across the road from the City Hall and Public Library, generally held to be the finest municipal public library in Greater Montreal.

As younger couples found the western portion of the island— far from downtown—attractive, older Jewish districts declined in popularity. Outremont was a good example. The city welcomed thousands of Jews in the 1940s and '50s (so many, in fact, that a

Combined Jewish Appeal. In 1983, she received the State of Israel Bonds Eleanor Roosevelt Humanitarian Award in acknowledgement of her across-the-board fund-raising efforts for the community. In 1982, she negotiated a $200,000 endowment from Gerald and Marjorie Bronfman to launch Hope and Cope.

future Prime Minister, Pierre Elliot Trudeau, learned street Yiddish playing with neighbourhood children) peaking at 11,566 in 1951. By 1991, the city had a Jewish population of only 3,765 and that included hundreds of Hassidim (a sect of ultra-Orthodox Jews). In the trend toward the suburbs, developers erected bungalows and cottages on large lots and Jewish couples chose Dollard des Ormeaux, in particular, as an ideal place to raise a family. The D.D.O. Jewish component soared from 16 in 1961, to 9,150 in 1991. Schools and synagogues sprang up to serve these new constituencies.

OUT OF THE GHETTO

Although World War II hastened the movement out of The Main ghetto to suburbia, the shift in population had begun much earlier, as the Depression waned. In 1931, in the depths of the economic tragedy, the Jewish population of the Old Jewish Quarter and the Laurier district totaled 28,667. By 1941, when World War II was underway, it had declined to 25,767. In 1951, after the war, only 18,658 were listed as resident in the area. The decline then became precipitous—dropping to 1,985 in 1961, 705 in 1971, and a mere 335 in 1981 and, finally, 300 in 1991, according to the most recent census.

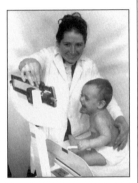

The expansion of community services didn't go over well with everybody.
(Jewish Public Library Archives)

Snowdon and **Cote des Neiges/Wilderton**, known as the areas of third settlement, became the new area of choice for immigrants, but the rise and fall of population reflects the rapid progress made by newcomers who often arrived with very little. By 1970, the geographical centre of the Jewish community was the junction of Decarie Boulevard and Van Horne. More than half the Jewish population was living west of Decarie at that time.

	Snowdon	C.D.N./Wilderton
1931	3,281	316
1941	4,726	3,572
1951	15,435	4,241
1961	27,650	12,067
1971	24,260	7,165
1981	17,545	2,520
1991	12,855	855

As Jews moved into new suburbs, some population shifts, such as in **Hampstead**, were dramatic. The statistics for **Town of Mount Royal**, where residents initially resisted Jewish newcomers, and where municipal documents in the 1930s clearly prohibited the sale of property to Jews, are telling:

	TMR	Hampstead
1931	1	0
1941	12	52
1951	298	538
1961	2,617	1,560
1971	4,305	4,805
1981	3,720	5,590
1991	4,010	5,490

Westmount, the most exclusive district in Montreal, has seen a slow but steady increase in the number of Jews resident there:

1931	1,764
1941	1,578
1951	1,675
1961	2,322
1971	2,855
1981	3,735
1991	4,405

According to 1991 Census, the Jewish population of St. Laurent was 8,790.

TOPS IN MUNICIPAL POLITICS

During Mayor Jean Drapeau's long reign, his only Jewish City Councillor was Alderman Max Seigler. In the post-Drapeau era, a number of Jewish politicians appeared and were influential. **Samuel Moscovitch, a lawyer, was elected Mayor of Cote St. Luc in 1963, the first chief magistrate of a Montreal area municipality.** Bernard Lang, an engineer, succeeded him in the mid-1970s. In 1974, Hampstead elected Irving Adessky, a lawyer, as Mayor. Numerous city councilors made their mark. They included Michael Fainstat, Abe Limonchik, Marvin Rotrand, Sam Boskey, and Hassid politician, Saulie Zajdel. Two grassroots activists have made a particular contribution to city life. After four years on Montreal City Council, **Arnold Bennett** became involved in community work and specialized in landlord-tenant relations. **Sid Stevens** (council member 1978-82) was only 12 years old when he started Sun Youth in donated space at the back of a shoe store. Stevens was drawn into community service when he repeatedly saw people left homeless by fires on St. Urbain Street in the 1950s. Sun Youth became one of the largest facilities for providing food, clothing, and other services to the downtown poor, and fire victims.

CRISIS IN QUEBEC

The political struggle over Quebec's place in Confederation began to bubble to the surface. The Front de Libération du Québec, separatist extremists, waged a terrorist campaign of bank robberies and bombings, creating tremendous political uncertainty and fear. In the October Crisis of 1970, the FLQ had kidnapped two people—James R. Cross, the British trade commissioner in Montreal, and Quebec labour and immigration minister Pierre Laporte, who was later murdered. The federal government invoked the controversial War Measures Act (Oct. 16), which suspended civil liberties across the country, and led to the arrest of 465 people. When Cross was freed on December 3, after being held 60 days, British officials brought him to the Jewish General Hospital. While soldiers and police swirled around the hospital, Cross was whisked through the hospital's delivery entrance, and rushed to a private room for examination and tests. Several hospital officials—Executive Director Dr. William Slatkoff, President Dr. André Aisenstadt, and assistant Director Fred Goldstein, visited Cross to welcome him. They brought with them a bottle of 12-year-old whiskey and four glasses. Raising his glass, Cross said, "Cheers." Slatkoff, responding, suggested an additional, Jewish toast: "l'chaim"—Hebrew for "to life."

SECOND-GENERATION BRONFMANS

Following the death of his father, Sam Bronfman in 1971, **Charles Bronfman,** (1931-) assumed the mantle of leadership in the Montreal Jewish community. The venue was changed from the Mansion on the mountain slopes in Westmount to tony Forden Avenue, as Charles and his wife Andrea continued the family tradition of hosting the launch of the annual Combined Jewish Appeal, beginning in 1972 and continuing for a quarter of a century. At the end of summer, before the Jewish High Holidays, representatives of about 100 of Montreal's leading Jewish families gathered to pledge support for the community for the following year.

The ritual remained unchanged from the days of Sam Bronfman, including the tactful footnote on the invitation, "Minimum gift of .... required." The minimum gift changed periodically to reflect the problems facing the community locally, nationally and internationally. The evening began with a cocktail reception (serving only Seagram's products) on the huge balcony overlooking the swimming pool and tennis courts. Then the family representatives would gather in the enormous living room where more than 100 could be seated. The General Chairman of the Campaign would open the meeting by describing the problems Jews in distress were facing in Montreal, across the nation and elsewhere in the world. Then the Chairman would announce his gift, including an increase from the previous year reflecting the community's greater responsibilities. Charles Bronfman would follow announcing his family's gift—the largest annual gift made in North America to a charity—and one by one representatives of the prominent families would rise as their name was called to announce their pledge. The Allan Bronfman family...the Pascals...the Steinbergs, and so on. In approximately 45 minutes, the routine would be complete. An accountant in the nearby sunroom (a shrine to the Montreal Expos established in 1968 by Charles Bronfman with memorabilia including a baseball for each year of his ownership autographed by all members of the team) would rip the strip of paper off his calculator, and hand it to the General Chairman for an immediate announcement. One time, $10 million was raised in 45 minutes. In those years, the community could boast that 99% of the pledges were honoured. Rarely did financial problems force a contributor to cut his or her gift. The high rate of collection started to slip in the 80s with the recession.

Charles Bronfman continued to support many other projects in Montreal, across Canada and internationally. His name attached to a fund-raising effort was magic. Organizing committees knew their event would be a success if Bronfman would participate as Chairman of a dinner or Honorary Chairman of an event. His endorsement stamped the campaign as being worthwhile.

So many charities, Jewish and otherwise, made submissions to the Bronfman offices that a former Executive Vice-President of Federation, Manuel G. Batshaw, was taken on as an advisor primarily on "Jewish affairs." For 18 years, until Bronfman left Montreal, Batshaw would evaluate a proposal and if it won approval, Bronfman would make a gift of 10 per cent over and above what the organization raised. Batshaw, commenting on

Bronfman's philanthropy, declared, "His generosity wasn't just in doling out money. The money had to have meaning."

EMPHASIZING CANADIAN AND JEWISH HERITAGE

The Bronfman family has always been passionately committed to Canada, and in 1986 Charles Bronfman crystalized his interests through the creation of the $100 million CRB (standing for Charles Rosner Bronfman) Foundation. It is intended to promote "the enhancement of Canadianism" and the "unity of the Jewish people whose soul is in Jerusalem." The Foundation produces Heritage Minutes, dramatizations of Canadian historical vignettes shown on television and in movie theatres. In addition, the Foundation organizes Heritage Fairs across Canada, maintains a website (www.Heritageproject.ca) on Canadian history, and develops learning resources for teachers and students. Bronfman's interest in promoting Canadian heritage was stirred in 1981 when he was inducted as a Companion (the highest level) of the Order of Canada. "While listening to the citations of the distinguished people receiving this same honour," he commented, "I thought it was such a shame that, except for those in the room, few Canadians would ever know how many superb citizens they have."

In 1997, Batshaw retired from his advisory role and the following year, the Charles Bronfmans sold their home to spend more time in residences in the United States and Israel. They maintained an apartment in Montreal, and visit the city frequently to monitor their interests and attend important community functions. Charles Bronfman's son Stephen (1964-) remained a resident of Montreal and became increasingly involved in community affairs. His sister, Ellen (1969-) moved to Europe.

Bronfman's sister **Phyllis Lambert** (1927-) an architect, founded Heritage Montreal in 1975 in an effort to save historically important buildings in the city. In addition, she created and directs the Canadian Centre for Architecture, one of the greatest architectural museums in the world. It incorporates Lambert's own personal collection of architectural prints valued at $20 million. The Museum is housed in a new building attached to and protecting the historic Shaughnessy Mansion in downtown Montreal. Architect Michael Fish acknowledges "She has been THE key figure on the Montreal conservation scene. Without her, little would have happened here."

Phyllis Lambert, founder of the Canadian Centre for Architecture in Montreal.

The oldest son of Sam and Saidye Bronfman, **Edgar Miles** (1929-), succeeded his father as head of Seagram's Distillers in New York until 1994, when he accepted the Presidency of *World Jewish Congress*. Edgar Bronfman successfully focussed on recovering from Swiss banks hundreds of millions of dollars in deposits made by Jews before World War II, for survivors and their descendents.

Sam Bronfman's second daughter **Minda** (1925-1976) married a titled French banker, became the Baroness Alain de Gunzberg, and through the marriage became related to the legendary European Jewish family, the Rothschilds. (When Sam Bronfman moved to kiss the bride at her wedding, Minda jokingly demurred. "Father, don't you know you should bow to a baroness?")

Edgar M. Bronfman, elder son of Sam Bronfman

FOR SONS ONLY! NEPHEWS NEED NOT APPLY

The contest for succession to the family business had periodically flared, but Sam Bronfman was determined that his sons would succeed him. Therefore, he had to oust from the company the ambitious offspring of his brothers, Allan and Harry. When Allan's sons, **Edward** (1927-), and **Peter** (1929-1996) were pushed out of the company, they received a golden handshake of $25 million, which they parlayed into Edper Enterprises, the largest corporate conglomerate in Canada. In 2000, Edward resided in Toronto but remained involved in Montreal Jewish affairs.

Edward Bronfman

Another ousted nephew was **Gerald Bronfman** (1911-1986), Harry Bronfman's son. Gerald designed the classic purple and gold cloth bag for Seagram's Crown Royal. A Company executive was so impressed that he suggested during a company meeting in New York that Gerald should be the next company president. A furious "Mr. Sam" quickly arranged for his nephew's departure with generous compensation. Gerald went into the milk business and was reputed to be worth $200 million at his death. He had been a Squadron Leader in the Royal Canadian Air Force in World War II and received the U.S. Legion of Merit. He and his wife **Marjorie Meta Schechter** (1917-), an American-born social worker, were prominent patrons of the arts and leaders of the Montreal Jewish community. In 1999, the Jewish Community Foundation chose Marjorie Bronfman as its "Person of the Year" for her community work.

A daughter of Abe Bronfman, Sam's brother, rose to top positions in the Montreal community. **Mildred "Millie" (Mrs. Bernard) Lande** (1914-) was the first and only woman to undertake the General Chairmanship of the Combined Jewish Appeal, the toughest assignment in the community. She also served as President of the *Jewish Community Foundation*, which chose her as their "Person of the Year" in 2000, and as the first woman President of the Shaar Hashomayim Congregation.

BREAKING DOWN THE BARRIERS

In the 1960s, Jews were no longer confined to their own small businesses and professional associations, and they began to slowly ascend to top positions in the social and economic institutions of the ruling Anglo-Protestant community. In 1965, John Porter published his groundbreaking The Vertical Mosaic. In it, he suggested that Canadian Jews, in the same manner of American Jews, had been driven into marginal and high-risk businesses because of the "exclusiveness at the social periphery of business. For example, the Jews who were in the economic elite did not belong to the same clubs as did the charter group members of the elite. They were not members of the important trade associations, and their philanthropic activities rarely overlapped with those of other members of the elite." Porter reported that in 1965 only two Jews were serving on the Boards of chartered banks. As cultural pluralism in the English community, created by the arrival of Italians, Greeks, blacks and other ethnic minorities identifying with the English, forced an end to exclusivism, barriers began to fall, and Jews were poised to participate fully in all aspects of society. Decades of anti-Semitism were relegated to history, as the doors of Canadian society opened and Jews began to rise to great prominence.

IN ECONOMICS

Montreal native **Sol Simon Reisman** (1919-) negotiated the Auto Pact of 1965, and the 1988 Canada-US Free Trade Deal, two landmark agreements that ensured the strength of the Canadian economy in the 21st century. In 1974, he received Canada's Outstanding Public Service Award. He also negotiated an important Aboriginal Land Claim agreement with Natives of the western Arctic, the Inuvialuet.

Montreal-born **Louis Rasminsky** (1908-1998) became governor of the Bank of Canada (1961-73), and established the rules covering relations between government and banks. He is credited with playing a major role in the creation of the International Monetary system. In 1968, he was named to the highest rank in the Order of Canada—Companion.

IN LAW

The first breakthrough was **Harry Batshaw's** appointment as a Justice of the Superior Court of Quebec in 1950, and 10 years later, **Michael Franklin** became the first Jewish Senior Crown Prosecutor. In 1967, when Canada marked the 100th anniversary of passage of the British North America Act, almost one lawyer in five (391 out of 1,960) registered with the Bar of Montreal was Jewish. In that year, Canada had 19 Jewish judges and five of them were in Quebec. Lawyer Yoine Goldstein, pressing for more Jewish appointments to the Bench, wrote Justice Minister Otto Lang in 1973:

"Since the anglophone membership of the Montreal bar is half-Jewish, it would be appropriate, given all the circumstances and the eminent positions which some of the Jewish members occupy before the Bar, that a Jewish appointment to the Court of Appeal be considered." That same year, **Fred Kaufman** became the first Jew appointed a Justice of the Court of Appeal of Quebec.

Alan B. Gold (1917-), son of a door-to-door salesman in the Eastern Townships, received his first judicial appointment in 1961, to the Provincial Court. Four years later, he became associate Chief Judge and in 1970 Chief Judge of the Provincial Court of Quebec. Finally, in 1983, he became Chief Justice of the Quebec Provincial Court. Gold was born on St. Dominique Street in the heart of The Main, where his father prospered as an important figure in the Montreal clothing industry. As the family climbed the ladder of success, they moved to Jeanne Mance Street. Unable to enter McGill because of the quota, he went to the Université de Montréal, where he was treated like royalty and made friends for life, among them Jean-Jacques Bertrand and Jean Drapeau. The Lord Reading Society held a sell-out "Evening of Gold" to honour his appointment as Chief Justice. When Irving J. Halperin called for reservations, he was told that the downstairs dining room was full and he would have to sit upstairs. However, room was found for Grace and **Irving Halperin** when it was learned he had just been appointed a Judge of the Superior Court.

Hon. Alan B. Gold, former Chief Justice of the Quebec Superior Court (photo by Laszlo, Montreal)

IN THE SENATE

Carl Goldenberg (1907-1983), named to the Senate in 1971, was one of Canada's most outstanding mediators, called upon for assignments as far away as the West Indies. He was Special Counsel to the Prime Minister on the Constitution, 1968-71. Born in Montreal in 1907, the son of a merchant, Goldenberg graduated with honours from McGill. He decided to study

Undoubtedly, Montreal's most controversial Jewish citizen was Dr. **Henry Morgentaler**—the point man in the fight to make abortions legal and more accessible. He was a survivor of both the Auschwitz and Dachau concentration camps; both his parents and a sister were murdered by the Nazis.

Morgentaler came to Canada in 1950 and by 1969 was a national personality because of his advocacy of legalizing abortions. As he put it, "I am not pro-abortion any more than I am pro-appendectomy." Parliament had made abortion a crime in 1869. Mortgentaler, making no secret of the fact that he was performing abortions, repeatedly faced the courts, but juries found him not guilty of any crime.

In 1988, the Supreme Court of Canada ruled that the anti-abortion law was illegal.

Doctors in Canada who performed the operation had been attacked (three had been wounded) and the police urged Mortgentaler to wear some form of body armour. He refused; "I won't give in to terrorism."

government at first hand. In Ottawa, he encountered by chance Prime Minister Mackenzie King walking home from his office. The young lawyer brashly introduced himself to the Prime Minister. King invited him to walk down Rideau Street with him while the excited Goldenberg rattled on about how he felt the country could be run better. On a whim, the government leader invited Goldenberg to have dinner with him in Rideau House. "We've just received a shipment of lobsters from New Brunswick," King said grandly. "I don't eat lobsters," Goldenberg said. "They're not kosher." The Prime Minister was taken aback but responded, "We'll find something else for you." The two became friends for life. One of Goldenberg's most dramatic achievements was settling the 1943 Montreal Tramways Co. strike in less than 24 hours, a coup considering it was wartime and essential industries were being seriously affected.

Lazarus Phillips (1895-1991), one of Canada's greatest senators, only served in 1968-70 before being forced into mandatory retirement from the Upper Chamber at 75 years of age. In that short time, he developed a formidable reputation. "I can say of Senator Phillips," Hon. Paul Martin (Sr.) declared, "who stands in the tradition of that great member for Cartier, the late Sam Jacobs, and in whose shadow he has always walked, that at the present time there is no greater parliamentarian than Senator Phillips." Phillips was a major figure in the Liberal party, an important adviser to the Bronfman interests, and founder of the Canadian Tax Foundation.

IN ARCHITECTURE

Moshe Safdie (1938-) came to great prominence at Expo '67, the Montreal World's Fair, with his innovative Habitat '67, an unusual concept of assembling apartment buildings from precast concrete cubes. Safdie's graduate thesis at McGill interested planners for the world's fair with its emphasis on a more humane style of building. He called for a more imaginative use of space, less massive structures and room for individual outdoor gardens. Acknowledged as one of the world's greatest architects, he made his home in Montreal although his work took him all over the globe. Lecturing at McGill in 2000, Safdie told a full hall at the School of Architecture that "Architecture in the last decade or two has been infected by the deep cynicism that has penetrated the entire creative environment." He continued: "A market economy may produce cheap goods, but it doesn't produce good environments."

IN COMMUNICATIONS AND TELEVISION

In the 1960s, **Harold Greenberg** (1931-1997) was a high school dropout working in his uncle's pawn-shop when he became fascinated with cameras. He bid for and won the right to set up film processing facilities on the site of Expo '67. With capital raised at the World's Fair, he founded Astral Communications and became a major international figure in filmmaking and television. He initiated First Choice and Super Écran on Pay Television, and his company was grossing $300 million a year when he died at age 66.

Harold Greenberg (right) with Senator Leo Kolber and his wife, poet Sandra Kolber.

Also in this era, a young Montreal-born actor was making his mark on pop culture. **William Shatner** (1931-) has had an acting career spanning nearly half a century, but he is best known for his three-year stint (1966-69) as Captain James T. Kirk in the science fiction television series *Star Trek*, and the motion pictures that followed. Shatner graduated from McGill University in 1952 and made his Broadway debut in 1956 in the play "Tamburlaine the Great", followed in 1958 by "The World of Suzie Wong." That performance won him the Tyrone Guthrie Award.

The *Star Trek* series had an immense cult following and the programs were repeated more than three decades after they were first shown. The popularity of Captain Kirk and his crew led to a long series of movies beginning with "Star Trek: The Motion Picture", 1979, followed by "Star Trek II: The Wrath of Khan", 1982; "Star Trek III: The Search for Spock", 1984; "Star Trek IV: The Voyage Home," 1986; "Star Trek V: The Final Frontier," 1989; and "Star Trek VI: The Undiscovered Country," 1991. Two television series followed Star Trek—"T.J. Hooker", 1973-75 and "Rescue 911" 1993-96. But they never achieved the success of *Star Trek*. Shatner began writing science fiction novels called "Tek" in 1989 and by 1994 had published six. They were quite well received by the critics. He acted in and was director of a series of "Tek" television movies.

IN LITERATURE

Nobel laureate **Saul Bellow** was born in Lachine, Quebec, in 1915 of Russian immigrant parents. He lived at 158 8th Avenue until he was three, and from 1918 until 1924, in The Main area at 1092 rue Saint-Dominique, near the Warshaw supermarket. His family moved to Chicago when he was nine, but he remembers the area well. Talking about his childhood in the city, he told an interviewer in 1990, during one of his visits to Montreal: "My life in Canada was partly frontier, partly Polish ghetto, partly the

Middle Ages...I've always been among foreigners and never considered myself a native of anything...I was brought up in a polyglot community by parents who spoke many languages." As a boy, Bellow learned to speak French, Yiddish, and Hebrew on the street. His talent was apparent when he was quite young. "People used to kid me when I was a boy, and they would say, 'Ah yes you're going to have a Nobel Prize one day.'" Bellow studied sociology and anthropology in American universities before launching his career as a novelist. In 1979, he won both the Nobel and Pulitzer Prizes. He is the only writer to have received three National Book Awards. One of Bellow's most acclaimed novels was "Herzog," written in 1964 and incorporating some passages on Quebec. *The New Yorker* magazine described it as "a well-nigh faultless novel" while the *Manchester Guardian* hailed it as "clearly a major work of our time." Other novels included "The Dangling Man," written in 1944, and his first published book, "Mr. Sammler's Planet", 1970, and "Humboldt's Gift", 1975.

He emphasized his Jewishness when talking about his writing. "My first consciousness was that of the cosmos and in that consciousness I was a Jew," he told a San Francisco audience. "Jews stand apart from the prevailing nihilism of the west." Recalling his multilingual childhood, he is sensitive to language. "One's language is a spiritual location. It houses your soul. You can neither lie nor tell the truth in any other language. It is the principle instrument of your own humanity."

He writes the old-fashioned way, preparing his manuscripts in longhand. Then he types the first draft, makes corrections, and retypes. He refuses to use a computer. The city of Lachine renamed its public library "Bibliothèque Municipale Saul Bellow" in 1984, the author's 69th birthday. In 1993, he left Chicago "because so many of my friends had died" and moved to Boston where he taught at Boston University. In 1989, he married for the fifth time and in 1999 fathered a daughter. At the time, Bellow had three adult sons—one aged 56—from previous marriages.

Dr. Lawrence Montague Lande (1906-98), after studying at McGill, Université de Montréal and Grenoble, France, climaxed a career as a writer and collector by donating in the '70s to McGill his immense library, dubbed the "Lawrence Lande Collection of Canadiana." Lande was the first Canadian honoured by the University of San Francisco with its Sir Thomas More Medal for the "significant contributions of a private collector whose book collections have benefited the public."

Dr. Lawrence Lande (Caricature by Lou Seligson, from Canadian Jewish News)

IN BUSINESS

Henry Minzberg (1939-) was recognized by the U.S. Journal of Business Strategy as one of 24 individuals who have "changed the face of business history." Others on the list were Walt Disney, Henry Ford, Bill Gates, and Sony founder Akio Morita. Minzberg was named to the Cleghorn Chair in Management Studies at McGill and taught in Europe.

Czech-born **Harry Halton** was tossing in pain in a hospital bed in the 1970s when his boss dropped by to ask him to accept a new and important assignment at Canadair, the major aircraft manufacturer in Montreal. "I'm too busy dying," Halton told him. However, the mechanical and electrical engineer returned to his offices and continued to design outstanding aircraft for the company, now part of Bombardier. Halton, as Executive Vice-President 1975-1983, was responsible for the design and development of the Challenger business jet. The basic Challenger design has evolved into the series of Canadair regional jets, bringing the company billions of dollars in business over the past 20 years. And the design continues to provide Bombardier with potential sales.

Harry Halton, a key figure in the development of Canadair and its aircraft, including the Challenger luxury business jet.

IN MEDICINE

A number of trailblazing Montreal Jews were breaking new ground in the field of medicine and biotechnology. Montreal-born Professor **Louis Siminovitch** (1920-) became a leading world figure in medical genetics and molecular biology. His work has heightened understanding of genes and had a significant impact on cancer research. He studied at McGill before going to the Institut Pasteur in France on a fellowship.

In 1969, while experimenting in a McGill research laboratory, Professor **Phil Gold** (1936-) discovered a simple blood test to detect bowel cancer, and earned world renown. Gold was born in The Main and attended the legendary Baron Byng High School, and worked as a bottler in Molson's brewery to finance his education at McGill. He has been honoured with a variety of awards including the Canadian Medal in Medicine and the first Terry Fox Medal. He was named Douglass G. Cameron Professor of Medicine at McGill in 1987. He was made a Companion of the Order of Canada in 1986; he is an Officer of l'Ordre national du Québec and member of the Academy of Great Montrealers.

Dr. Phil Gold; he discovered a blood test for identifying the presence of cancer

Dr. **Juda Hirsch Quastel** (1899-1987) was an international figure in medical science. He came to Canada from London in 1947 to become professor of biochemistry at McGill University

THE EYES HAVE IT

It all started when doctors discovered that flyers, during World War Two, had little or no reaction when bits of shattered plexiglass canopies were embedded in their eyes. In time, ophthalmoligists found a technique for using the material in aircraft canopies in the manufacture of an artificial lens for the human eyes. The first successful lens implant operation in Canada was in 1967, and it was performed by Montreal's Dr. Marvin Kwitko. He was on staff at the Jewish General Hospital when he learned of the operation. He flew to Holland to study the technique—and then brought it back to Canada. After many successful implants, Kwitko began to teach at the Jewish General and St. Mary's Hospital. The Montreal course graduated more than 300 ophthalmic surgeons from Canada, the United States and other countries between 1975 and 1985.

In 1979, Kwitko learned about "corneal refractive surgery" from a Russian colleague. The Montreal ophthamologist perfected the technique, enabling short-sighted people to ditch their eyeglasses and contact lenses.

(Kwitko is a great-nephew of the Russian poet, Lieb Kvitko, who was murdered by Stalin in 1952.)

Dr. Marvin Kwitko is presented with the "Order of St. John" by Governor General Romeo Leblanc in 1994 for his work on the rehabilitation of cataract patients.

and director of the McGill-Montreal General Research Institute. Quastel and an associate discovered glucosamine, valuable in scientific efforts to conquer cancer. He taught at University of British Columbia 1966-1983. Quastel is regarded as a founder of modern neurochemistry. He coined the term "phenylketonuria," used in studies of mental defects. He was made a Companion of the Order of Canada in 1970. He received the Royal Society of Canada Flavelle Medal and the Gairdner Foundation International Award in 1974.

While a member of the faculty of the Massachusetts Institute of Technology, **Ronald Melzack** (1929-) and Patrick D. Wall published the internationally hailed theory on pain entitled "gate control." Melzack became the world's greatest authority on pain. His *McGill Pain Questionnaire* created in 1975 is used in clinics around the world.

THE GOLDBLOOM FAMILY

One of Montreal's most distinguished Jewish families is the Goldbooms—Victor, Sheila, Richard and Michael.

Dr. Victor Goldbloom became the province's first Jewish Cabinet minister. In 1966, he left his pediatric medical practice to run in the new, predominantly Jewish, riding of D'Arcy McGee. When Premier Robert Bourassa announced Goldbloom's appointment as the province's first Minister of the Environment in 1970, not a single negative word was said or written in the media—proof that the new Quebec was very different from the 1920s or '30s. Goldbloom was re-elected in 1970, 1973, and 1976. He did yeoman service for the Jewish Community—negotiating a deal whereby Quebec became the only Canadian province to subsidize Jewish education—and for the entire province when he was handed the thankless assignment of bringing the much delayed Montreal Olympics in on time in 1976. In 1979, he left politics and became president and CEO of the Canadian Council of Christians and Jews. In 1991, he was appointed Canada's Commissioner of Official Languages, and in 1999, he became the first Jew to serve as president of an important Roman Catholic charity, the Cardinal Leger Foundation.

Michael Goldbloom, Publisher and President of the Montreal Gazette.

Goldbloom's wife, Sheila, was a McGill University Professor of Social Work and was honoured in 1999 by Jewish Family Services for extraordinary and lengthy service to the agency. Brother Richard became professor of pediatrics at Dalhousie University in Halifax and president of the Atlantic Symphony Orchestra, and son Michael became the influential publisher of the *Montreal Gazette*.

Pierre Elliot Trudeau, Prime Minister (1968-1979), represented the primarily Jewish riding of Mount Royal throughout his political career. In 1965, Trudeau turned up for the Liberal nomination meeting in Mount Royal riding wearing a stylish but totally unsuitable short velvet jacket. His riding advisers hustled him home to change into a suit.

Since the arrival of the Hart family in Trois-Rivières, the cultural contribution of the Jewish community has been an enrichment to Canada, and especially to the province of Quebec. Today it compels recognition in all fields of endeavour: poetry, the novel, theatre, criticism, visual arts, music, medicine, pure and applied sciences, law, civil engineering, architecture... What a long honour list it would take to do justice to each! So outstanding is the Jewish contribution that it is difficult to imagine our society without it.

Pierre Elliot Trudeau, Prime Minister of Canada
in a 1970 letter on the opening of Samuel Bronfman
House, national headquarters for Canadian
Jewish Congress in Montreal.

Author Mordecai Richler, in 1950.
(Canadian Jewish Congress National Archives)

MORDECAI

The Toronto Telegram knew something new in Canadian literature was afoot in 1954 when one of its reviewers wrote about the first novel by a young Montreal author, Mordecai Richler (1931-). "Fresh gust of rage from young Montrealer,"the headline on the article read. The book was "Acrobats," written in Europe by the 23 year old after he had cashed in an insurance policy and sailed to the Old World.

Short of funds and living marginally by writing newspaper and magazine articles, Richler drifted from London to Paris to an island in Spain—searching for the cheapest place to live while he built a reputation. The Telegram declared: "Richler has written a good book. His next book will be better and the after that—perhaps great." The novel received a positive reception in England where it was first published. "Mr. Richler has a fire and frenzy all his own," commented the Spectator. "When they truly take hold of his characters (it) produce(s) a powerful effect."

Richler's biggest break came at age 28 when he wrote "The Apprenticeship of Duddy Kravitz," the first of three novels (the others were "St. Urbain's Horseman" and "Joshua, Then and Now") focussing on memories of life in the old Jewish quarter. His stories of a young man's ruthless bid to make money made many Jews uncomfortable, but the critics hailed his work. And "Duddy" became a movie featuring a disguised Baron Byng High School, Fletcher's Field and Wilensky's sandwich shop.

THE RICHLER FAMILY

Richler was the second son of a scrap-metal dealer and a mother with literary pretensions. He lived at 5257 Saint-Urbain until 1944, when he was 13. At that time his parents separated. He had attended Baron Byng High, and was President of his graduating class in 1948.

He returned to Montreal from England in 1972, stating "coming from Canada, being a writer and Jewish as well, I have impeccable paranoia credentials." He admits he feels "forever rooted in Montreal's St. Urbain Street. That was my time, my place, and I have elected myself to get it right."

The author often outraged members of his own community. On one occasion, when Saidye Bronfman said to him "You've come a long way for a St. Urbain Street boy," Richler retorted rudely "You've come a long way for a bootlegger's wife."

The author departed from his usual caustic comments in a serious moment with the Toronto Star's Tom Harpur. He told the columnist in an interview "In a time when there really is no agreement on values and a collapse of religious values, which certainly created a certain order, or standard, you are obliged to work out your own code of honour and system of beliefs and to lead as honourable a life as possible." He divided his time between a Sherbrooke Street apartment in Montreal and a house in the village of Austin in the Eastern Townships.

His other major books include "Barney's Version," winner of the Giller Prize. His own favorite was "Solomon Gursky Was Here." Robert Fulford of "Saturday Night" was most impressed with "St. Urbain's Horseman" calling it a "tour de force" and the "best Canadian book in a long time." The novel, Fulford wrote, was "the triumphant and miraculous bringing together of all those varied Mordecai Richlers who have so densely populated our literary landscape for so many years."

Mordecai Richler

CHAPTER THIRTY-TWO

EXODUS 401
The Separatist Parti Québécois is Elected;
Thousands of Jews begin an Exodus

Nationalism: a snarl wrapped up in a flag.
        Irving Layton, *The Whole Bloody Bird*, 1969.

*The older man sighed as he heard the election results on television.
The separatist Parti Québécois had been elected to power in
Quebec. It was 1976. The man was a Survivor, and the very word
"nationalism" triggered painful memories for him. (Like tens of
thousands of Montreal Jews he remembered too well the scent of
nationalism across Europe...what "National Socialism", or
Nazism, meant ...And he was scared.) When it was clear that the
Nationalists had won, the man packed his bags and left that same
night.*

TIMELINE—1976-1980
1976. The Communauté Sépharade du Québec (CSQ) is founded.
1976. *Sépharade Festival de Montréal* is created.
1977. *Projet Action Rapprochement* is created to encourage greater understanding between Jews and non-Jews, the French-speaking majority.
1977. Quebec government passes Bill 101, restricting admission to English
language schools.
1977. The Montreal edition of *Canadian Jewish News* is launched with
Community financial assistance.
1978. The Nathan and Maxwell Cummings Golden Age Centre is opened—
one of the most modern facilities of its kind anywhere.
1978. Neighbourhood House becomes the *Centre Communautaire Juif*—
part of the "Y".
1978. The CSQ umbrella organization for francophone agencies becomes a
constituent member organization of Federation.
1979. The *Montreal Holocaust Memorial Centre* is inaugurated at
Cummings House—Canada's first Holocaust museum.
1979. The Golden Age Association and Camp B'nai Brith create a "Senior
Vacation Village" on the grounds of the children's camp.
1980. Jewish Vocational Services establishes Project Retention to assist
recent university graduates in finding positions in Quebec.
1980. Quebec votes No to "sovereignty-association" in a referendum.

By the time the election of the pro-separtist Parti Québécois under René Lévesque won the provincial election in 1976, the Montreal Jewish community had established what was regarded as the best social and community services per size of population of any Jewish community in the world. However, the threat of separation and political turmoil triggered a corporate exodus that exacerbated the decline of Montreal, and began to erode confidence in the future of the Montreal Jewish community. As companies began redirecting their investments and expansion, Toronto became Canada's flagship city, and the premier Jewish community in Canada. The P.Q., once in power, immediately swept aside the Liberal Bill 22 as "inadequate" and introduced Bill 101, a measure designed to put a "French face" on the province in everything from education to signs to communications. The Jewish community, which had identified strongly with the English-speaking community, had to face harsh realities, or leave. The survivor who packed his bags and left the night of the election was the first of tens of thousands to abandon Quebec because of the fallout of political uncertainty—an exodus that continued on and off in the Jewish community for more than two-and-a-half decades.

JEWISH POPULATION DROPS SHARPLY

In 1971, there were 114,000 Jews in Montreal. Ten years later, five years after the P.Q. assumed power, the Jewish population had dropped to 103,000.

But the figures did not tell the whole story by any means. By November of 1978—**only two years after the election of a government committed to taking Quebec out of Canada— 43 per cent of anglophone high school and college graduates of the class of '77 had left the province.** The decline in the number of young people was devastating: the population of Jewish youth, aged 15-24, dropped from 19,995 in 1971 to 14,385 in 1981, and then to 11,705 in 1991. That was a decrease of 9,290, or more than 46%, in 20 years. At the same time, Jews and others were moving their investments and businesses out of Quebec. Some companies, as a precaution, established branches of their offices or factories in other parts of Canada or in nearby locations in the United States.

Head offices, faced with the problem of being legislated to operate nationally or even internationally in French, packed their files and left. Monty Berger, in his book "Lament for a Province", estimates that "in just four years—1977 to 1980—more than 700 companies moved their head offices out of Montreal." One Jewish company reportedly moved the head offices of 23 companies in its portfolio to Calgary.

TORONTO BECOMES LARGEST JEWISH COMMUNITY

After more than two centuries, Montreal's historic reign as the number one Jewish community in Canada was over. **In 1971, Montreal had 4,000 more Jews than Toronto. By 1981, Toronto had 25,000 more**. In less than ten years, Toronto had become the Jewish capital of the country, and the largest city in Canada. Premier Lévesque knew what was going to happen. Five years before his election to office, he had spoken in Toronto about Jews and the Independence movement: "I know that 80-90 per cent of the Jews of Quebec are nervous about the effects of separatism. I know that history shows that a rise of nationalism means Jews get it in the neck. But what can I do about it? I can't change your history. But I know that anti-Semitism is not a significant French-Canadian characteristic."

P.Q. REASONABLE AND FAIR

In power, Lévesque's government was reasonable and fair in its dealings with the Jewish community. The feeling of crisis abated, but the outflow of Jewish people—young and old alike—continued at a lower level. It was not only the threat of separation or language continuing to drive people out; it was the absence of employment opportunities.

Leaders of the community generally were cautious. "My educated guess," suggested Saul Hayes, long-time Executive Vice-President of Canadian Jewish Congress (in 1979), "is that every day, more and more people are coming to the conclusion that many of the excesses that appeared, after the victory of the Parti Québécois, are receding."

Community leaders meet with Premier René Lévesque (right) in 1977. Others in the picture (clockwise from top left) are Ralph Lallouz, representing the Sephardic Jewish Community; Harvey Crestohl, for B'nai Brith; Manuel Weiner, representing the Federation; Joel Pinsky and Alan Rose for Canadian Jewish Congress. (Canadian Jewish Congress National Archives, Montreal)

Hampered by racial-religious distinctions to start with, relations between the French, English and Jews of Montreal are still further complicated by the fact that all three groups suffer from an inferiority complex—the French because they are a minority in Canada, the English because they are a minority in Quebec, and the Jews because they are a minority everywhere.

Gwethalyn Graham, *Earth and High Heaven*, 1944.

PERIOD OF TRANSITION

Dr. Victor Goldbloom, who resigned from the National Assembly in October, 1979, predicted:

"When we have crossed this frightening period of transition and those who are going to go have gone, there will still be a Jewish community here with religious institutions and health and welfare institutions and all the services that a community needs."

Prominent Canadian journalist Peter Desbarats wrote: "The Jews in Quebec have a right to be concerned about nationalist developments in Quebec which would assume a chauvinist character and would create a tolerance for discrimination against non-French groups." Then, he added:

"There are two kinds of Jews in Quebec: the optimists who teach their children French and the pessimists who teach them Hebrew."

"Anglophones are hopelessly out of fashion these days, but ethnics are still quite acceptable—even "in." Unlike Anglos, ethnics are seen as part of the Quebec mosaic: Les communautés culturelles. Moreover, most civil servants are anxious to embrace ethnics—as long as they act cute, wear colourful national costumes and don't demand services or signs in their own language."

From The Anglo Guide to Survival in Quebec.
Josh Freed, Montreal Gazette columnist

LINGUISTICALLY EQUIPPED FOR THE NEW QUEBEC

Members of the Jewish community were the best equipped, linguistically, to deal with the New Quebec. Sixty-one per cent of Montreal Jews were fluent in both English and French. However, the bulk of the community identified with, and felt itself part of, the anglophone community. This was due to a number of factors. For generations immigrant Jewish children attended schools in the English-speaking Protestant School Board, which reluctantly accepted them and eventually accommodated them as their population boomed. In addition, Jews and the Canadian Jewish community have close ties to American Jewish organizations, and in other countries where the common language is English.

The conquest of any nation takes place not on the battlefield, not in business boardrooms, but with the soul of its people and the minds of its leaders.

Peter C. Newman, receiving an Honourary Degree, York University, 1975.

AN ANNIVERSARY

In 1982, when the 150th anniversary of the 1832 Charter of Emancipation was being marked, Herbert Marx rose in the National Assembly to declare: "I have not found a single Quebec law since 1867 that failed to respect the law of 1832, and I have not found a single law in Quebec which discriminated against anyone because of his race or because of his religion."

Furthermore, a year later, at the formal proclamation of the amended and augmented Quebec Charter of Human Rights, Professor Marx added: "Since its adoption, in 1975, our Quebec charter has been the most progressive of all provincial laws in Canada."

Premier Lévesque, responding, told the Assembly, "He who spoke these words this morning was well situated to do so for he is both a jurist and a Jew; that is to say, he is well trained professionally to speak of it, and is shaped by history and by ancestral heritage to be sensitive to these matters."

Between 1981 and 1991, 25,000 Jews had left Quebec for other parts of Canada, the United States, and Israel.

"The Government of Quebec calls upon all the people of Quebec to support its efforts by showing respect for the dignity and rights of every person and by being ceaselessly alert to all manifestations of racism or racial discrimination."
Declaration by the Government of Quebec on Ethnic and Race Relations December 10, 1986.

~

A PASSION FOR LANGUAGE
The Yiddish Language, of course.

If Hebrew was nobler and more dignified—the exterior of the coat—Yiddish was warmer and more comfortable—the lining of the coat.
>   Shemarya Levin, in "Childhood in Exile", 1929

Montreal was the backdrop for the remarkable theatrical career of **Dora Wasserman**, who turned a fledgling local Yiddish theatre into a presence in the city of international rank. Born in Russia in 1919, Wasserman was a graduate of the Moscow Yiddish Art School. During World War II, she met and married a Jewish refugee from Poland. In the wake of the war, they travelled across devastated Europe, and eventually settled in Montreal. She became involved in the activities of the Jewish Public Library, where at that time nearly half the books on the shelves were in Yiddish. She spread her love of Yiddish by reading to children in the library, and she brought familiar tales to life using the children as actors. At a time when most Jews were predicting the demise of Yiddish language and culture, Dora Wasserman

A Montreal Yiddish Theatre performance.
(Saidye Bronfman Centre photograph)

created the **Yiddish Theatre** at the Saidye Bronfman Centre of the Arts, and gathered around her a committed group of actors dedicated to the preservation of the ancient language. More than 30 years later, their children and grandchildren were playing roles in dramas and musicals of a high quality. Many of her performers came out of the Jewish People's and Peretz School system, and its Bialik High School, where Yiddish is part of the languages curriculum. Wasserman created a whole new audience for Yiddish theatre by providing simultaneous translations of the Yiddish projected on a screen above the actors' heads. Suddenly, people with little or no Yiddish could enjoy the performances of old classics and new productions. An upsurge in interest in Yiddish and Jewish culture coincided in the '60s and '70s with the establishment of Jewish studies programs at the university level. At age 70, some 45 years after she left the Soviet Union, Dora Wasserman returned in triumph to Moscow as a guest of the Gorbachov Regime. The 30 Montreal actors gave back to Moscovites Yiddish plays first performed in that city 200 years earlier. The troupe has toured the United States and Israel. In 2000, Dora's daughter Bryna became the Yiddish Theatre's Artistic Director.

There is a very special bond between the performers and most of the audience during the presentation of Yiddish plays and musicals. Yiddish is more than a language. It is a memory... a reminder of the great Jewish communities of eastern Europe, sprawled across a half a dozen countries, annihilated in the Holocaust. The continuity of Yiddish performances is, in a sense, an enduring tribute to the vanished Jews of Eastern Europe, and a commitment to keep that culture alive.

~∼

LEADING THE WAY
"The community is Israel's rampart."
Simeon B. Lakish, "Talmud: Baba Bathra"

Jews form communities wherever they are (not unlike other immigrant groups), and fundamental to the success of their efforts is always the discovery of appropriate leaders. A Montreal couple, Babette and Edward Barkoff, conceived a special award to recognize young leaders, and in 1956, the award became a reality. The Babette and Edward Barkoff Awards were presented for 17 years to 34 men and women in Montreal, and later, scores of North American communities followed their lead.

The idea for the award originated with Barkoff during his attendance at an annual General Assembly of North American Jewish Federations. "I looked around me," he told his wife on his return to Montreal, "and I was one of the youngest leaders there. I decided that we should identify and honour young leaders, and give them, as a prize, a free trip to the next General Assembly."

Winners of the prestigious award were in the spotlight at the annual General Assemblies of the Council of Jewish federations for North America, where the award presentations took place. Therefore, through the years, representatives of close to 800 member federations were witness to the annual ritual. By 1979, eighty American and Canadian communities had taken a leaf from the Barkoff book and instituted similar awards.

Oscar Respitz (centre) is flanked by Babette and Edward Barkoff as he is honoured with the Barkoff Leadership Award.

Every major American Jewish Community—including New York, Boston, Philadelphia, Miami, Chicago and Los Angeles—established their own young leadership awards, and in Canada, Toronto was among the cities instituting this form of recognition.

The award comprised a scroll, but with it came funds, annually, to send the two winners, a man and a woman, to the next General Assembly where they were able to learn about the inner workings of other communities.

These were the Barkoff Award winners:

       1956 - Ruth Goldbloom and Douglas Gross.
       1957 - Sheila Finestone* and Arthur Garmaise.
       1958 - Marilyn Wener and Edward Feigin.
       1959 - Dodo Heppner** and Arthur Roskies.
       1960 - Ruth Nadler and Stanley Hitzig.
       1961 - Faige Gasco and Lionel J. Rubin.
       1962 - Ilse Matalon and Mitchel Garfinkle.
       1963 - Sheila Zittrer and Joel Rottman.
       1964 - Irene Lande and Richard Bornstein.
       1965 - Dorothy Reitman and Hillel Becker**.
       1966 - Bernice Brownstein and Irving J. Halperin**.
       1967 - Anne Nadler and Oscar Respitz, Q.C. ***
       1968 - Maxine Sigman** and Gary Moscowitz.
       1969 - Mitzi Becker and Morton Bessner.
       1970 - Linda Shohet and David Goldenblatt.
       1971 - Rhoda Rappaport and Saul Roseman.
       1972 - Freda Rashkoven and Dr. Jean-Claude Lasry.

  * - became member of parliament and Senator.
 ** - became president of the Federation.
*** - became president of the Jewish Community Foundation.

Eight of the women award-winners assumed top leadership positions in Women's Federation, serving as President, campaign chair or both.

Prime Minister Pierre Elliot Trudeau, who represented the predominantly Jewish riding of Mount Royal in the House of Commons, chats with Saidye Bronfman.
(Canadian Jewish Congress National Archives)

CHAPTER THIRTY-THREE

PROVINCIAL POLITIX
Leading Anglo Robert Libman
and the Fight for Equality

Every dogma has its day, but ideals are eternal.
Israel Zangwill, English author (1864-1926)

As he had received death threats, the young man was flanked by three bodyguards as he pushed his way into the Buffet Crystal, where the Equality Party was holding a victory celebraton. Robert Libman, the young Jewish architect who had formed the party, was still stunned by Equality's victory in four constituencies in the Quebec General election of 1989. In his riding, D'Arcy McGee—which is predominantly Jewish and had never voted anything but Liberal—Libman had been able to defeat that party's candidate, Gary Waxman, by a hefty 6,069-vote margin. Anglophones were fiercely angry at Premier Robert Bourassa's failure to permit English-language signs—an election promise. Consequently, Libman's hastily organized political machine had won a majority of anglophone votes in every constituency in Quebec.

TIMELINE—1981-1995

1981. Quebec bans public signs in English.

1981. The Auxiliary of the Jewish General Hospital launches Hope and Cope, a support program for cancer patients and their families.

1982. Andy Nulman launches Just For Laughs Festival.

1985. The name of the Convalescent Hospital is changed to Jewish Rehabilitation Hospital and its classification changed from long-term to short-term care.

1986. Plans are finalized for relocation and expansion of the Mount Sinai Hospital from Ste. Agathe to Cote St. Luc.

1986. Plans are announced for constructing a new and larger Jewish Nursing Home at a new location west of the Jewish General Hospital.

Election of the independence-minded Parti Québécois in 1976 was followed by the departure for greener pastures of 133,000 anglophones, of whom more than ten per cent were Jewish. Suddenly, the traditional voices of English Quebec were silenced, and into the breach moved concerned Jews. They formed only two per cent of the population of the province, but they moved dramatically and disproportionately into the forefront of the effort to defend English rights. Four of five founders of Alliance Quebec, the English rights group, were Jewish. And a 28-year-old architect left his drafting board and in a few months, without any political background whatsoever, formed a new party and led it to victory in four constituencies and near-victory in five others!

Ever since Premier Jean Lesage and his Liberal party had assumed office in 1960, the province's dominant political parties had marched down the road towards greater autonomy and even outright independence.

Language was at the heart of the confrontation between French- and English-speaking Quebecers. In 1974, Premier Robert Bourassa introduced Bill 22 making French the official language of Quebec. Several protest groups were created in angry reaction.

Former MNA William Shaw formed the "Freedom of Choice Movement" in 1978, signed up 3,000 members, and protested in favour of bilingual signs. But it folded. An outspoken social worker, Carol Zimmerman, drew 5,000 to her "Quebec For All" and staged funeral marches and demonstrated in chains, but it

1986. The Federation Board of Trustees gives high priority to Jewish education, stating "the community should acknowledge the right of each child to a Jewish education."

1987. With a staff of trained volunteers, Jewish Information Referral Service is launched.

1988. Federation launches ProMontreal to encourage and assist young Jewish adults to remain in Montreal.

1991. Plans are announced for a new 160-bed Jewish Hospital of Hope on Victoria Avenue, to replace the 132-bed facility in east-end Montreal.

1993. Concordia University receives a Federal grant of $250,000 to establish a new Chair in Quebec and Canadian Jewish Studies.

1993. CLSC René-Cassin is inaugurated to supplant Jewish Family Services Social Service Centre.

1994. Sylviane Borenstein becomes the first Jewish woman appointed to the Bench of Quebec when she is named to the Superior Court.

1995. A proposal to separate Quebec from Canada is narrowly defeated in a referendum.

too had a short lifespan. Concordia University historian Graeme Decarie was not impressed. "Carol Zimmerman can attract enormous attention and pack halls. You can always get people who are going to turn out and yell." However, she had no understanding of access to money or developing anything resembling a policy.

The most important group to emerge from the language debate was Alliance Quebec, founded in 1982 by half a dozen leaders including Michael Goldbloom, Eric Maldoff and Sheila Finestone. The new organization, attracting an impressive 40,000 members, included veteran Liberal party organizers Sam Berliner and Caspar Bloom. The Federal government provided financial support for the new group and historian Decarie suggested that successful formation was "due largely to political sophistication and basic organizational skills."

Lawyer Maldoff explained the reality of the situation in these words:

"We're up against a government in this province that can, at the drop of a hat, spend millions of dollars to promote its policies, do its research or whatever it wants. And if we're going to meet that challenge...we're going to have to have an infrastructure which can support the services that are necessary."

Colourful exchanges took place between the "independantistes" and the Federalists. PQ cabinet minister Gérald Godin labelled Alliance Quebec "Keystone Cops" and novelist Mordecai Richler dubbed the province's language inspectors "tongue troopers."

D'Arcy McGee riding had been the Jewish power base from its inception in 1966 and, with one exception, remained loyally Liberal. The riding straddles the city of Cote St. Luc and the town of Hampstead, both with large Jewish populations.

Dr. Victor Goldbloom ran sucessfully for the party in 1966 and was re-elected in 1970, 1973 and 1976. In 1968, Goldbloom negotiated an arrangement with the province for subsidization of Jewish schools.

In 1970, he became the first Jew to be named a cabinet minister in the province.

However, when the language legislation was passed, Goldbloom, as a cabinet officer, had two options: support the measure in public or resign.

Goldbloom felt that he could be a more effective representative of his constituents if he remained in cabinet. He faced awkward questioning at public meetings while working, behind the scenes,

Victor Goldbloom, Quebec's first Jewish Cabinet Minister (Canadian Jewish Congress National Archives, Montreal)

for moderation of the province's language policies. In 1976, Goldbloom received a thankless task. Construction of the summer Olympic facilities in Montreal was well behind schedule and the Jewish cabinet minister was assigned the task of ensuring that the Games could start as planned. He was successful and the Olympic buildings were finished on time.

Later in 1976, the hard-line Parti Québécois was elected and scrapped Bill 22, substituting Bill 101 with its harsher restrictions on the use of English. Six years later, Goldbloom commented on how the Jewish community was affected: "Quebec Judaism is flourishing, well-established and in comparison with so many other parts of the world, relatively calm...As Jews, we in Quebec enjoy a very high degree of religious, social and cultural freedom." But by then, Goldbloom had quit provincial politics. He was succeeded as the member for D'Arcy McGee by lawyer and constitutional expert Herbert Marx. He was first elected in 1979 and re-elected in 1981 and 1985. He was named Justice Minister but joined other anglophone Liberal cabinet ministers in resigning when Premier Bourassa—re-elected in 1983—broke his election promise to permit English on outside signs. Herbert Marx is now a Superior Court Justice.

Mr. Justice Herbert Marx. He felt honour-bound to quit the Robert Bourassa Liberal cabinet because he disagreed on legislation limiting English on signs.

In 1989, the Liberal grip on D'Arcy McGee came to an end. The Grits had chosen a bright young lawyer, Gary Waxman, as their standard-bearer. Waxman expected to walk away with the election. But he and the party didn't fully appreciate the anger of anglo Jews. Robert Libman, giving careful consideration to the idea of forming a new political party, took longer and longer lunch hours from his drafting board at Tolchinsky & Goodz. Old hands from the Liberal party, many of them Jewish, joined the ambitious young man. His most difficult job was recruiting likely candidates, and he found the toughest slot to fill was D'Arcy McGee. "It was my mother who first suggested that I consider running in D'Arcy McGee," Libman acknowledges. Goldie Libman had been an enthuiastic supporter of the planned new Equality Party from the moment the idea was presented. She suggested that older voters "would identify me with their many kids or grandchildren who had left the province, and appreciate that I was staying in Quebec to fight for them."

Liberal Gary Waxman, also young and handsome, first realized he had problems when, during election meetings, angry voters attacked the government's language rulings. When the ballots were counted, Libman had defeated Waxman by a large margin. But the Equality party standard-bearer had really defeated the

Liberal party, not Gary Waxman. The Equality party won four seats and placed second in five other ridings. The one-issue party came asunder from squabbling and failed to elect another member. Libman dropped out of the party, commenting, "We tend to be more vicious in our family (i.e. anglophone community) quarrels than in any confrontation with Quebec separatists." Robert Libman offered to run for the Liberals in 1994, but—still licking their wounds from '89—they turned him down. Notary Lawrence Bergman led the constituency back into the Liberal fold and was re-elected in 1998. Libman, having tasted politics, left architecture. In 1998 he was elected Mayor of Cote St. Luc, succeeding Bernard Lang.

An ecstatic Robert Libman at the microphone as he celebrates electoral victories of the Equality Party he started.

Other Jews surfaced to carry on the fight for anglo rights. Lawyer Julius Grey doggedly fought in the courts for individual rights. Businessman Morty Brownstein went as far as the Supreme Court of Canada on the sign dispute but lost. At Alliance Quebec, Hampstead Councillor Anthony Housefather was elected President following a stormy tenure by newspaper columnist William Johnson. Public Relations Executive Howard Galganov whipped up excitement by leading demonstrations against unilingual signs inside stores, where English was permitted. And he won concessions. On radio, Tommy Schnurmacher son of a Rabbi, sniped at the nationalists on his highly-rated talk shows.

Kosher Broadcasting...
(The voice of Anglo Quebec)

No Montreal radio station has featured more Jewish personalities than CJAD. Community surveys indicate that it is the most popular radio station with members of the Jewish community.

In recent years, the important morning talk shows hosts have included two Jewish personalities—Melanie King in the 80s and Tommy Schnurmacher in the 90s and beyond. Both had large listenerships. King's trenchant reporting style and incisive interviews won her a substantial audience before she moved to Australia. Tommy Schnurmacher was a well-known social columnist for the Montreal Gazette for more than 20 years, turning Montreal on its ear with his quick wit and provocative political commentary. In 1996 he was awarded the prestigious Golden Ribbon Award of the Canadian Association of Broadcasters for the depth and humour of his presentations.

Tommy Schnurmacher, son of a rabbi, was one of Montreal radio's most listened-to personalities.

The longest-serving Jewish broadcaster was Rick Leckner, Montreal's foremost traffic reporter. For 31 years, beginning in 1969, Leckner covered the highways and byways of Greater Montreal traffic from a helicopter. On his retirement in 2000, the Gazette reported:

"Leckner had gone beyond simply reporting on traffic tie-ups, accidents and disasters during his career. He's been an advocate for drivers, hounding the authorities over contractors that block the road illegally, safety, the need to build more highways and to simply take delays seriously."

Another influential Jewish voice was CJAD senior newscaster Victor Nerenberg, who presented the morning newscasts from 1981 until 1999, when he experienced health problems. In earlier days, CJAD's most visible news reporter was Sydney Margles, who covered news breaks around the clock, 1954-74. In 1984, Margles became a Vice-President of a branch of CJAD's parent company, Standard Broadcsting.

Many other Jews have made their mark in broadcasting, including CFQR's longtime morning personality, Aaron Rand. He has been a popular performer for a decade and a half. On the sports side, Mitch Melnick and Ted Tevan have scored with more than one station.

MATZOH-GATE

OR, HOW GEFILTE FISH WAS DRAGGED INTO QUEBEC'S LANGUAGE WARS.

The spring of '96 saw a collision between the Provincial Government's Office de la Langue Française—the watchdog organization for the French language—and members of the Jewish community. The dispute, labelled Matzoh-gate, revolved around government insistence that even specialty foods for the eight days of Passover—almost all of which are imported from the United States—must carry bilingual labels. Representatives of l'Office swept through stores carrying kosher-for-Passover food, seizing everything without a French label. That was just about everything. They carted off mounds of Matzohs and gallons of gefilte fish. Importers of the specialty foods say Quebec is too small a market for U.S. maufacturers to re-label their products. None of the Passover products is made in Quebec.

Canadian Jewish Congress intervened between angry importers and determined language inspectors. A compromise was negotiated, giving Jews the right to offer food for that special holiday labeled in English only. Under the arrangement, stores may show Passover products, in English only, up to 40 days before the eight-day holiday, and for 20 days after.

The agreement represented a considerable concession on the part of the provincial authorities. In addition, a spokesperson for l'Office emphasized that the English-only arrangement applies strictly to Passover specialties only. All other kosher foods must be labelled according to the law.

INFLUENCE IN OTTAWA
MONTREAL'S JEWISH PARLIAMENTARIANS

In the 1990s, two men and a woman represented Montreal Jewry in Parliament—-two senators and a Member of Parliament. Human rights activist Irwin Cotler was elected in the Mount Royal Constituency in a 1999 Federal by-election after the sitting member, Sheila Finestone, was named to the Senate. Senator **Ernest Leo Kolber** (1929-) was named to the Senate in 1983. He had been a longtime fundraiser for the Liberal Party. Kolber was founder and later chair of what became one of North America's largest real estate companies, Cadillac Fairview Corporation. The company developed entire downtown blocks in major cities of the United States and Canada. Kolber worked in the Charles Bronfman network of Montreal-based enterprises, including Cemp Investments (Vice-Chairman), Claridge Incorporated (Chairman), The Seagram Company (Director) and E.I. du Pont de Nemours (Director). He remains active with the Bronfman interests in Montreal.

Senator **Sheila Finestone** (1928-) served as a Member of Parliament from 1984-90 and was Secretary of State for Multiculturalism and Status of Women 1993-96. She was the first Jewish woman from Montreal to be named to the cabinet and the first Montreal Jewish woman to be elevated to the Senate. Finestone served the Jewish and general communities in a number of prominent positions. She headed up the Jewish Women's Federation and the Women's Division of Combined Jewish Appeal, and was the first Jewish woman to serve as President of Fédération des Femmes du Québec. The Jewish community honoured her with both the Barkoff Leadership Award and the Bronfman Medal.

Irwin Cotler is an international human rights lawyer and, even as a Member of Parliament, remains active on the world scene. In Ottawa, he became a member of both the Foreign Affairs Committee and the Committee on Justice and Human Rights. In May 2000, Foreign Affairs Minister Lloyd Axworthy appointed

Canada' first Jewish woman Federal Cabinet Minister, Hon. Sheila Finestone (2nd from l), now a Senator, with (l to r) Treasury Board President Hon. Lucienne Robillard, Eleni Bakopanos, Member of Parliament for Ahuntsic, and Professor Irwin Cotler, who succeeded Mrs. Finestone as Member for Mount Royal riding.

him as "Special Advisor" for the International Criminal Court. When Cotler announced he would be a candidate in the by-election in Mount Royal, a constituency that has returned only Liberals since 1940, other would-be nominees cancelled their plans. Although a busy parliamentarian, he continued to serve as Director of McGill's Human Rights Programme and was Chair of InterAmicus, the McGill-based International Human Rights Advocacy Centre. Cotler has immense stature in world affairs. He served as counsel to former prisoners of conscience in the Soviet Union (Andrei Sakharov), South Africa (Nelson Mandela), Latin America (Jacobo Timmerman) and Asia (Muchtar Pakpahan). *Maclean's* called him "Counsel for the Oppressed."

Two Montreal Jews were members of the prestigious Privy Council—Charles Rosner Bronfman and former Cabinet officer Gerry Weiner. At the Provincial level, the community had two members—Lawrence Bergman and Russell Copeman, who had married a Jew and converted.

BRIGHT LIGHTS OF THE '90s

Martin D. Levine (1938-) served as founding director of the McGill Centre for Intelligent Machines 1986-98, developing industrial robots and doing cutting-edge research on making machines intelligent. His centre developed robots ranging in size from miniatures to two storeys in height. Levine used the name "intelligent machines" rather than "robots" because he sees the former title as a "more encompassing connotation. We are interested in seeing whether we can design machines that can interpret, sense their environment, interpret their visual environment." He added: "Machines have been taking over the world for the last two or three hundred years if you look at the progression."

Romanian-born Professor **Ruth Roskies Wisse** (1936-) reluctantly left McGill and her family in 1993 to occupy Harvard University's first Chair in Yiddish. "How can I turn down this opportunity," she told friends. Wisse was one of the founders of the Jewish Studies Program at McGill in 1968. After graduating from McGill, she went to Columbia to study Yiddish—and was the only person in the class! She was one of the first recipients of the Noel Fieldhouse Award for outstanding teaching. The citation for that award read in part:

"Her passionate engagement with literature flashes with intellectual fire, stimulating and constructively provoking her audience as well as intelligently informing and judiciously guiding it."

She joined Professor Harry Bracken in founding Jewish Studies at McGill University which, when she left for her American appointment, had a teaching staff of seven full-time professors and an average enrolment of 400 students. The Harvard appointment underscored her international standing in the field of Yiddish literature. She is an important contributor to *Commentary* magazine and winner of the Manger Prize for Yiddish literature.

Montrealer Prof. Ruth R. Wisse, has occupied Harvard University's first Chair in Yiddish since 1993. (Photo by Jim Gipe)

Eleanor London, Chief Librarian of the Cote St. Luc Public Library from its founding more than 30 years ago, runs one of the finest municipal libraries in Quebec. She directs a staff of more than 60 including 10 master librarians. The Library is located in the geographical centre of Montreal Jewish community.

Sheila Goldbloom concluded a distinguished 28-year career at the McGill School of Social Work (1964-1992), heaped with honours by colleagues. She received the Order of Canada in 1998.

Anne Greenstein (l) has devoted 47 years of her life to teaching art, at the Cummings Jewish Centre for Seniors, assisted for the past 25 years by Dorothy Finkleberg. She has taught thousands of older people and has helped many of them to become recognized artists in their own right. (Photo by Jack Frank)

CHAPTER THIRTY-FOUR

KEEPERS OF THE FLAME
Hassidim, Ultra-Orthodox and Observant Jews

The young man was solemn as he listened to the bearded rabbi counseling him. He had just lost his father and to honour his memory he felt he had to say Kaddish, the mourner's prayer for the dead, but he had struggled to read Hebrew words he had not studied since his Bar-Mitzvah 25 years before. In relearning the prayer and in the comforting world of the synagogue he found a peace he had not known before.

The rabbi, a Lubavitcher Hassid, understood the difficulty of returning to full religious observance. "Let's take it step by step," he said gently. "We call it the Mitzvah route." The young man began attending synagogue and continued after the obligations to his late father were completed.

In the Lubavitcher **shul** *(synagogue), he was surprised at the number of young, successful men and women in attendance. He was grateful for the kindness and understanding the rabbi provided—a spiritual leader almost his own age.*

The most recognizable of Montreal Jews are the **Hassidim**, ('pious ones' in Hebrew), members of Ultra-Orthodox Jewish religious sects. Their distinctive appearance—black broad-brimmed fedoras, black dress-coats, full beards, and side curls—recalls the beginnings of the movement in eighteenth-century Poland. The Hassids of greater Montreal represent ten different courts and ten different approaches to Ultra-Orthodox observance, although many of the Rebbes do not live in Montreal. A court consists of a spiritual leader and his congregation. Seven courts are in the City of Outremont, while the Hassidim of Lubavitch are in Snowdon, Cote St. Luc and Hampstead. The Tasher Hassidim of Boisbriand are located in nearby Ste. Thérèse, Quebec. Each court has a scholarly and often charismatic leader, known as the *Zaddik* (righteous one) or *Rebbe* (teacher). Hassidim stress the joy of being Jewish, and they mark holidays and rites of passage with great celebration, even ecstasy. Hassidim also dedicate themselves to *mitzvot*, deeds of loving-kindness. A number of young people, distanced from regular Judaism, have become attracted to the Hassidic enthusiasm for an Orthodox Jewish life.

A Royal Commission on Bilingualism and Biculturalism in 1970 had this to say about the Jewish mosaic:

> "These Orthodox and Hassidic Jews make up a small percentage of the total Jewish community in Canada and have little connection with other Jewish groups. Even so, their presence has tended to reverse the normal pattern of segregation...Only now, in the latest phase of Jewish life in Canada, do we have what usually comes at the beginning— enclavic groups, intent upon maintaining in unadulterated form their traditional mode of living."

Hassidic Jews in the Outremont area where several courts (groups) reside. (Canadian Jewish News Archives—Howard Kay photo)

The Montreal Jewish community has the highest proportion of orthodoxy of any community in North America. Orthodox Judaism means strict conformity to a Jewish lifestyle according to religious texts. Observant Jews live by 613 commandments or traditions and laws of the Holy Scripture that govern every aspect of daily life, including hygiene, food and its preparation, strict observance of prayer, holidays and the Sabbath. Many devout Jews consider the term "Ultra-Orthodox" somewhat pejorative, and refer to themselves by the Hebrew term *haredim* (meaning Jew) or the Yiddish words *erlicher Yidn* (meaning virtuous Jews).

LIVING HISTORY

The Ultra-Orthodox follow a strict dress code that varies from court to court. In general, Hassidic males from 13 years old wear a small prayer shawl around their body or waist with a number of dangling prayer fringes, or *tzitzis*. The men grow beards and side locks and keep their heads covered at all times with hats or skull-caps. In public, the women wear modest clothing, long sleeves, high necklines, and stockings at all times. With the possible exception of Lubavitcher women, married women wear wigs, kerchiefs, turbans, or hats to cover their heads. A few women shave their heads. In synagogue, men and women sit separately. During celebrations (i.e. weddings), the dinner hall is partitioned, with the men and women celebrating on each side of the barrier in their own way. The Hassidim celebrate their Judaism, and Hassidic parties are ecstatic events with joyous dancing and singing.

Boys and girls are educated in religious segregated schools. There are seven rabbinical schools, colleges, and seminaries in the Greater Montreal area that teach to an Orthodox standard. With the exception of Chabad-Lubavitch, career options are limited to religious study, teaching and small family-owned businesses that serve mainly their own constituents. According to the Survey of the Hassidic and Ultra-Orthodox communities in Outremont and Surrounding Areas (Shahar, Weinfeld & Schnoor, 1997), "work is not valued as a means to develop a career path, or to gain personal satisfaction. Rather it is necessary to provide materially for their family, but (it is) a distraction from the more important duties of religious study and observance." Increasingly however, many Hassidism are becoming computer literate and work as technicians, programmers, etc. Among the most rigid Hassidim, there is high unemployment, especially among the young. The proportion of Jews from Ultra-Orthodox and Hassidic communities living below the poverty line is far higher than the 20 per cent rate for the total Montreal Jewish population. The Federation provides financial aid to Hassidim who are unable to provide for their large families due to death or desertion of the main breadwinner.

FORWARD TO THE 18TH CENTURY

Few Hassidim resided in Montreal before the Second World War, but in the years immediately following the conflict, they began to move to the city in important numbers from Poland, Hungary, Romania, and Czechoslovakia. The first Hassidic leader to settle in the city was the "Tolner Rebbe", who came in 1930 and moved to Israel 25 years later.

The Tasher Rebbe at a simcha. (Mickey Gutstein photo)

The Hassidic movement in Montreal received great impetus in late 1941 when 19 Lubavitch rabbinical students from Warsaw reached the city. As the Germans invaded Poland, the students had fled eastward across the Soviet Union with the co-operation of Japanese diplomats. They reached Shanghai, where they boarded a ship for Canada. In Montreal, the Lubavitchers established their own *shtiblach* (prayer rooms), three *yeshivot* (religious colleges) and began training Orthodox rabbis for Canadian congregations. The mission of these Jews was to reconstruct the religious world they had known in Europe before the war. Another group of religious scholars escaped Poland and found temporary refuge in Japan while they waited for sea passage to Canada.

However, their ship was scheduled to leave on a religious holiday, or *Yom Tov*, and many of the students refused to sail. The Ultra Orthodox Jews who set sail from Tokyo on a High Holiday reached Canada in December 1941, only to learn that Japan had gone to war with the United States. Their colleagues who had stayed behind to wait for another vessel were never heard from again.

POPULATION ESTIMATES

How many Hassidim are there in Montreal? Estimates range from 1,000 families to 1,400! Because of new adherents, mobility and a very high birth rate, their numbers may be much higher. At least 4,000 Hassidim live in the Montreal area, and their numbers are increasing. They have a much higher birth rate than average and families of eight to ten children are common. There is a great deal of intra-city migration between Greater Montreal and New York, where most of the Hassidim are based. With few exceptions, Hassidic marriages are arranged. A 1997 survey of Hassidim and Ultra-Orthodox by the *Coalition of Outremont Hassidic Organizations* estimated a population of 6,250 in the Outremont and surrounding areas alone. Another 1997 population summary estimated that in the ten courts, there were 980 Hassidic families, which could translate into as many as 10,000 individuals. Specifically, the number of families in each group was estimated at:

Lubavitch - 350.	Muncacz - 25.
Satmar - 120.	Pua - 20
Belz - 160.	Klausenberg - 15.
Skver - 60.	Sanzer - 10.
Vishnitz - 60.	Tash - 160.

HISTORY OF THE HASSIDIC MOVEMENT

In the eighteenth century forests of Poland, **Baal Shem Tov** (1700-60) preached a more joyful individualized form of Judaism. The movement was a reaction against authoritarian rationalism. In the gloom of their poverty, many Eastern European Jews enthusiastically began to follow the Baal Shem Tov and the *"tzaddikim"* (righteous men) who became the spiritual leaders of other groups called courts.

For example, the Court of **Chabad-Lubavitch** sprang from the leadership of Rabbi Schneur Zalman of Liaidi. The name comes from an acronym, *Chabad*, from the Hebrew words for wisdom (*chochma*), intelligence (*bina*) and faith (*da'at*). The movement began in the Belorussian town of Lubavitch.

By 1900, there were more than two million Hassidim, mostly in Eastern Europe, but with some representation in New York. By World War II, one-third of Poland's three million Jews were Hassidic—almost all of them were murdered in the *Shoah*. Nonetheless, the movement continued to flourish in New York, Montreal, Jerusalem and London, with numerous Hassidic groups springing up all over the world.

A melaveh malka in honour of Rabbi Shmuel Yankel Kohn of Jerusalem (centre, with white beard) held at the home of a leader of the Vishnitzer Hasidic community. Feldman stands behind Rabbi Kohn. (Mickey Gutstein photo)

LUBAVITCH HASSIDIM

The Lubavitch, the largest group of Hassidim in the city (with more than 3,000 adherents), are different from other ultra-religious communities. While all sects demand strict observance of all religious precepts laid down in the Torah, the Lubavitch sect is the most flexible and modern. Menachem Mendel Schneerson, who assumed the spiritual office in 1950 and was rabbi of the Chabad-Lubavitch for 44 years, led the movement, now headquartered in Crown Heights, Brooklyn, out of its isolation and

Wedding Bells. A Lubavitcher wedding. The bride, in this 1998 ceremony in Montreal, wears the traditional seven veils.

made it a worldwide movement. The rebbe—the eighth since the founder Rebbe Zalman, died in 1994—and Lubavitch leaders decided there would be no successor. A committee of leaders governs the court.

While almost all other Hassidim dress as if they were still living in eighteenth-century Eastern Europe, the Lubavitch are more modern-looking. The men wear black fedoras and black suits, but not exclusively. The women do not shave their heads, and they wear fashionable clothing. They have modern lifestyles with few restrictions on media, communications, and education.

And while the other movements are content to be isolated, self-contained communities, the Chabad-Lubavitch has more than 3,700 teams, generally young couples in their 30s, working in 109 countries to spread the faith. While their goal is to bring lapsed

Jews back to strict orthodoxy, they do not proselytize or recruit aggressively. When Montreal rabbis, who for the most part can speak four languages—English, French, Hebrew and Yiddish—encounter an interested individual, they spend time with them, determining how religious they are and how much Jewish knowledge they have. After that, they patiently encourage the "recruit" through courses and the steps to full religious observance.

While in many ways the Lubavitcher hark back to Judaism's golden days in Eastern Europe, they are, in terms of marketing and communications, very much part of the twenty-first century. The Chabad website is www.chabadonline.com, and the Lubavitch keep in touch with other *Chabadnicks* in the enormous worldwide constituency by every conceivable communications facility. According to American historian Arthur Hertzberg, who at one time was critical of the group, the Chabad-Lubavitch emissaries (known as *schlichim*) are "the most holy group in the Jewish world today."

TASHER HASSIDIM

While the Lubavitcher rebbe led his community toward more openness, the Tash rebbe moved in the opposite direction. Alarmed by the temptations of Montreal in the 1960s, the Tash purchased 130 acres of isolated farmland in the Quebec countryside in order to set up a controlled religious community. In 1963, 18 Tash families settled north of the city in Boisbriand, Quebec. The Tash court, which originates in Hungary, has grown into a self-sufficient community of about 2,500. In addition to the synagogue, they have their own *yeshiva* (religious college), *mikvah* (ritual bathing facility), girls' school, butcher shop, bakery, small shopping centre, and ambulance service.

Communications with the outside world are tightly controlled. Internet, television, radios, and newspapers (with the exception of *approved* religious periodicals) are prohibited. The Federal census recorded the population of the Tash of Boisbriand as 80 in 1961, 120 in 1971, 440 in 1981, and 875 in 1991. Growth came from a high birth rate and the movement of American Hassidim to Canada. Many have lived in Canada for years and have not registered as citizens. The Boisbriand Tasher have recreated in the Montreal area a community similar in religious observance and daily life to that of a pre-World War II Eastern Europe *shtetl*.

Stanley Lewis' "shimmering Hassid", a stonecut print.

Though they disapprove of media, the Tash have had plenty of publicity. In 1995, they broke with the bulk of the Montreal Jewish Community and endorsed the idea of separation from Canada. However, only 250 members of the community took part in the vote. In 1999, the RCMP and Revenue Canada raided the community during an ongoing investigation related to alleged falsification of charitable receipts.

Mother Tongue of Hassidim and Ultra-Orthodox in Outremont area:
Yiddish-51%
English-27.6%
Hungarian-7%
English and Yiddish-6.8%
Hebrew-2.1%
Other-5.5%
Among those born in Canada, 66.7% speak some French.

SATMAR HASSIDIM

The Old Jewish district of Outremont, around Hutchison Street, is home to one of the largest Hassidic sects, the Satmar. On the Sabbath and Jewish festivals, members of Satmar are noticeable in their traditional garb. Bearded males wear fur-trimmed hats, long caftans or gaberdines, and white stockings. In the late 1980s, the Satmar caused a stir in Outremont when they built a synagogue without proper municipal approval. The incident stirred up some opposition to their presence in the suburban city. Projet Outremont was set up to improve relations. The sect's synagogue and community centre is located at 5555 Hutchison, at St. Viateur.

Another population of Ultra-Orthodox Jews, but not Hassidim, lives nearby in the streets between Outremont and Darlington to the West. They belong to the **Ultra-Orthodox Yeshivah community**.

RELIGIOUS PRACTICE IN MONTREAL

The Hassidic and Ultra-Orthodox world is only a part of the Montreal community's expression of religious Judaism. In 2000, Montreal had 66 synagogues—37 Orthodox, 22 Sephardic, five Conservative, one Reform in Westmount, and one Reconstructionist in Hampstead. In addition, there was a Secular Humanist group.

In a "Survey of Jewish life in Montreal" (1997), "three of four Montrealers (did) not attend synagogue on a regular basis." Yet the rate of synagogue participation in Montreal was "significantly higher than in most Jewish centres in North America." Nearly 45 per cent of Jews said they attend synagogue "only on High Holidays" and a few other times. One Jewish person in five went to synagogue only on special occasions, such as weddings and Bar/Bat Mitzvahs. The survey showed that almost two-thirds of Montreal Jews were paying members of a synagogue or temple—with financial support highest among the Orthodox (86.5 per cent). Among traditional Sephardim, 79.2 per cent are synagogue

Montreal City Councillor Saulie Zajdel, longtime municipal leader and member of the city's Executive Committee, and a Hassid.
(The Suburban Photo Archives)

According to an international study in the late 1990s by the United Jewish Communities, Montreal has the highest percentage in North America of Orthodox Jews at 22%, while the average in American communities is 6%. 64% of Montreal Jews belong to a synagogue. The figure for Los Angeles is 26 per cent. 85% of Montreal Jews fast on Yom Kippur, compared to 61% of American Jews. 74% of Jews from Montreal have visited Israel at least once, while the U.S. average is 26%.

The Hillel Foundation was formed to serve the greatly-increased number of Jewish students on campus. A chapel was dedicated in 1946; students in the photo (backs to camera) are left to right Jack Rishikof, Harry Zunenshine, Morrie Neftin and Isaac Reisler.
(Jewish Public Library Archives)

members while 72.5 per cent of Conservative Jews are paying members of a congregation. Formal support is lowest among "Reform/Secular" Jews at 36 per cent. Nevertheless, 85 per cent in 1997 said they fasted on Yom Kippur.

HOLIDAYS AND FOODS

Observant Jews have at least one holiday a week: the Sabbath. "An entire cessation of all the affairs of life on each seventh day is a Jewish institution, and is not prescribed by the laws of any other people," wrote Isaac D'Israeli (father of Benjamin Disraeli) in his "The Genius of Judaism," in 1833. The Jews introduced the idea of the six-day week! Religious Jews honour the Sabbath, doing no work whatsoever from sundown on Friday, until three stars are visible together on Saturday evening. Some consider switching on a light bulb as work, and they turn on necessary lights before sundown. Religious Jews live within walking distance of a synagogue, as operating a motor vehicle during Sabbath is prohibited. Sabbath is spent in prayer, relaxation, social visiting and reading or study. Television, radio, and telephone are not used during this time, except in emergencies.

The traditional foods for the Sabbath are the braided loaf *challah* bread, roast chicken, chicken soup, gefilte fish and wine. *Gefilte fish* is a boiled-fish-and-matzoh-meal-roll served cold with horseradish.

The Hebrew New Year is called **Rosh HaShanah**, a two-day holiday for all Jews except those in the Reform movement, who celebrate one day. As with all Jewish holidays, Rosh HaShanah begins at sundown. The challah served during Rosh HaShanah is round, suggesting the crown of God, and apples are dipped in honey, expressing hope for a sweet and fruitful year.

Rosh HaShanah, and 10 days later, **Yom Kippur,** are known as the Days of Awe. Yom Kippur or The Day of Atonement is a time for fasting and reflection and is considered the holiest day of the year. It is celebrated with a festive meal before sundown. The meal includes lightly seasoned chicken soup, boiled chicken and cooked vegetables—all intended to avoid thirst. Jews abstain from eating until the following day, when the fast is broken with a meal that generally begins with chopped herring, gefilte fish, or pickled fish.

Five days after Yom Kippur comes **Sukkoth**, a celebration of the harvest. Observant Jews eat their meals in a *sukkah;* a hut built in their backyards or on their verandahs with rushes for a roof so the night sky can be seen. It is meant as a reminder of the shelters the Israelites built during 40 years of wandering in the desert. Traditional foods include stuffed cabbage and *kreplach*, pockets of dough stuffed with fruit or vegetables, and dishes made with honey.

Hanukkah is the Festival of Lights, marking the defeat of the Syrians by the Maccabee warriors in 165 B.C.E., when a small cruse of pure oil—normally enough for only one day—burned for eight days in the Temple in Jerusalem. The most popular food for this holiday is the *latke*, potato pancakes fried in oil. (In Israel, they serve jelly doughnuts!) During this holiday, eating foods made of cheese has been customary since the Middle Ages.

Purim is a joyous holiday, commemorating the rescue by Queen Esther of her people in Persia 2,400 years ago. The most popular food is *Hamantaschen*, triangular pastries filled with prunes, cherries, and poppy seeds. The shape of the pastry is a reminder of the three-cornered hat worn by the enemy of the Jews, Haman.

Passover is an eight-day holiday commemorating the exodus of the Israelites from slavery in Egypt. When the Israelites fled, they took with them unleavened bread, or *matzoh*. During the holiday, which commences with two evenings of feasting, called *seders*, different foods are eaten, but no risen bread may be consumed. Kitchens must be scoured for every crumb of bread. Separate sets of dishes are used at this time. As the preparations for this holiday are elaborate and time-consuming, some Jews build a second kitchen.

Shavuot recalls both the giving of the Ten Commandments to the Jewish People at Mount Sinai and acceptance of the Convenant with God. *Blintzes*, cheesecake, and other dairy foods are eaten in accordance with the passage in *Song of Songs* "honey and milk shall be under your tongue." Blintzes may be filled with cheese or meat, and sour cream is eaten with the cheese variety.

Jewish Arbor Day, **Tu BeShevat**, marks the beginning of the spring season in Israel and is celebrated in Canada by eating fruit and vegetables, particularly those mentioned in the Bible— grapes, pomegranates, figs, dates, olives and "bokser", fruit of the carob tree.

Simchat Torah is a celebration of the Torah, the five Books of Moses. When the final chapter of the scroll is unrolled, the reading of the Bible, beginning with Genesis, resumes for another year. While there are no special foods for this occasion, there are many *l'chaims* (toasts to life with whiskey)!

Lawrence Bergman, MNA. He originated the resolution calling for Quebec to hold a Holocaust Memorial Day. It passed the Quebec National Assembly unanimously.

DAYS OF REMEMBRANCE

Jews have added three modern days of commemoration world-wide: **Yom HaZikaron** is a memorial day for those who have fallen defending Israel. **Yom HaAtzma'ut** is a celebration of Israeli independence, during which traditional Israeli foods, such as pita bread, falafel, and hummus, are eaten. **Yom HaShoah** is a memorial day for the Holocaust.

Ten Presidents of Federation and three Executive Directors are among this leadership group, gathered for the author's retirement party in 1989. (l to r-back row) Manuel G. Batshaw****; Manuel Weiner****, Peter Wolkove*, Carl Laxer*, Hillel Becker*, Monty Berger*, Boris G. Levine****, Elaine Goldstein**, Mr. Justice Irving Halperin*, Gordon Brown****, John Fishel****. (l to r, front row) Joe Ain****, Dodo Heppner***, Monroe Abbey*, Joe King, Lavy Becker*, Annette Oliel-Amar**, Ruth Ballon**.

      * - President, Federation.
    ** - President, Women's Federation.
  *** - General Chariman, Combined Jewish Appeal.
**** - Executive Vice-President.

The great secret of Judaism's remarkable survival can be found partly in the fact that Judaism has offered its adherents an entire civilization. It has never been merely another ethnic group. When the religious layer was peeled away, one found beneath it a strong folk tradition with its own institutions, language and culture.

Henry L. Feingold
Zion in America, 1974

CHAPTER THIRTY-FIVE

LEADERSHIP ON THE RAMPARTS
The Jewish Community Today

The Montreal Jewish Community entered the twenty first century grappling with a multitude of problems. Some—including poverty and an aging constituency—are shared with the general population, but others are unique to Montreal Jewry. Numbers tell much of the story.

Between 1971 and 1981, the community declined in strength from 114,220 to 101,365—a loss in a relatively short time of 12,855 individuals, or 11.3%. By the 1991 census, the population had slipped below the 100,000 mark, to 96,710. The June 1996 census projections indicated a further decline to 92,390.

Prof. Jim Torczyner of McGill University disagreed with these figures; he believed that census definitions of "Jewish by religion" and "Jewish by ethnicity" allowed thousands of Jews to slip through the cracks. He felt the actual Jewish population of the city remained at, or above, the 100,000 mark.

Nevertheless, **people continue to leave**. Demographer Jack Jedwab, with a long involvement in Jewish community affairs, saw a continuing outflow. In fact, he predicted that, between 1996 and 2001, Quebec would lose 47,000 people to other provinces. He felt the population loss in that five-year span would be greater than the loss recorded in the 1986-1996 period. People were leaving, in Mr. Jedwab's opinion, because of political uncertainty, high taxation levels and the lure of greater economic opportunities elsewhere in Canada. He could not say, however, how many of the new departures were Jewish.

In the period 1981-1991, meanwhile, the Jewish population of Toronto grew from 123,725 to 151,115, most of it thanks to emigrés from Quebec. (Jews were not allowed to settle in Upper Canada—"Ontario"—until 1803. When Levy Solomon of Montreal applied to purchase land in the Cornwall, Ont., area around 1790, he was informed that "Jews cannot hold land in this province.")

The 1999 Bronfman Medal Winner. Maxine Sigman (r), President of Federation/CJA, 1989-1991, is presented with Montreal Jewry's most prestigious award by Dodo Heppner, Chair of the Medal Selection Committee.

Interestingly, between 1986 and 1991, 1,025 Jews moved to Montreal from other provinces. Some of these arrivals—if not most—were people returning to Montreal. Meanwhile, in Quebec City, where the Beth Israel congregation had been established in 1852, the synagogue was sold in 1990 as the Jewish Community declined from 100 families in the 1950s to about 25.

Studies underscored the discomfort of Jewish people with Quebec nationalism. **Montreal Jews were overwhelmingly and diametrically opposed to the idea of Quebec independence** and even to "sovereignty-association", a proposed linkage between an autonomous Quebec and the rest of Canada.

A Federation/CJA survey in 1997 showed that support for the independence movement was less than 1%—actually nine-tenths of one per cent—among Ashkenazi Jews. Sephardic Jews' support for some sort of sovereignty was slightly higher, but still only 5.7%.

More than the threat of separation drove people, often with great reluctance, to leave Montreal. The economy was negatively affected, and continued to be, by the uncertainty of Quebec's status within Canada. Uncertainty discourages investors. As a result, Quebec has lagged significantly behind Ontario in economic growth. The province has persistently had a higher unemployment rate than the national average.

The Montreal Jewish Community remains the eleventh largest in North America; in 1971, it was seventh.

Montreal Jews were aging. The proportion of the community 65 or older, in 1991, was 22.9% and—almost ten years later—it could be assumed that one Jewish person in four in Montreal was a senior. Across Canada, the percentage of aged Jews was much less: 15.3%; in Ontario, it was even lower across Canada at 13%.

With immigration and birth-rates low, prospects for growth in the Montreal Jewish Community were not encouraging. Most Jews immigrating to Canada, like non-Jewish immigrants, chose to go to Toronto.

Opening the Corridor of History in 1987—marking 70 years of Federation history (l to r) William Gittes, Rosetta Elkin and Munroe Abbey, Q.C.

In 1998, 42% of all immigrants—73,560— settled in Toronto, while only 15% opted for Quebec. (Quebec demographer Jacques Henripin, referring to the "hyper-nationalists", declared that the separatists "are preparing a country for people who aren't there.")

The birth-rate among Montreal Jewry was expected to continue its decline as more and more women entered the work force, families shrank in size and young people chose to marry later.

Divorce rates continued to rise. On the plus side, the intermarriage rates among Montreal Jews were comparatively low.

The Community was well aware of the critical importance of retaining its young people, but numbers were discouragingly low. Only 12.1% of Montreal Jews were aged 15-24—about one in eight—and 25.6% were in the 25-44 age category, or one in four.

The woodworking shop at the Cummings Centre for Jewish Seniors. Older members manufacture children's wood toys and repair furniture for members. (photo by Federation/CJA)

Jews, as an ethnic group, were declining in numbers while others were growing—some very rapidly.

The fastest-growing population segment in Montreal: the Arabs, who increased in number from 24,875 in 1986 to 51,107 in 1991—an awesome growth of 105.5% in only five years. If that trend continues the 2001 census would show there were more Arabs than Jews in the city.

Other large population increases took place among Indians and Pakistanis—up by 43.4% to 27,267, and in the Armenian/Iranian segment, up 36.6% to 21,118.

In the 1986-91 time span, the English community declined by 15.4% to 330,568—a loss of almost 60,000 individuals in five years.

Dr. Frederick H. Lowy, Rector and Vice-Chancellor, Concordia University.

Jews were the best-educated in the Quebec mosaic. 44.9% of the province's Jews had university degrees, compared with 15% in the general Quebec population. The proportion of Ontario Jews with degrees, by contrast, was a remarkable 54.2%; undoubtedly, this high figure was due, in large measure, to the fact that many better-educated Jews from Montreal had moved to Toronto, Ottawa and other Ontario centres.

Jews have the highest household incomes in Montreal. Out of 41,165 households, 10.9%, or 4,500, had incomes greater than $125,000 a year.

Prof. Bernard Shapiro, Principal of McGill University. (His twin brother, Harold, is President of Princeton.)

By comparison, only 2.2% of the general population earned that much. The percentage of Jews in the $70,000-$124,999 bracket was 19.1%, compared with 13.5% among non-Jews.

At the same time, the community still had a poverty problem. **Nearly one Jew in four lived in poverty**: 9,545 households or

23.2% have an income of less than $20,000 annually, compared with 26% in the general population. Most of the poor are aged or single parents.

Higher birth rates among Sephardim and the multilingual (English, Hebrew, French and Yiddish) ultra-religious indicated the community would experience a dramatic change in makeup in only a decade or two.

The level of bilingualism was high—higher than in any other ethnic group. A profile from the 1991 census, in the American Jewish Yearbook of 1995, notes "bilingualism increases with educational level; more than four out of five Montreal Jews in university or having completed a university degree are fluent in both English and French; only half that rate (40%) of Jews without a high school diploma are bilingual."

The start of a Jewish education: youngsters in kindergarten. (Federation/CJA photo)

Finding the human and financial resources to maintain even today's levels of services demanded leadership of extraordinary quality, and some unpredictable positive elements. Fortunately, the roll-call of leaders in the community's first eight generations had been exceptional. They have, in traditional words, led the community "from strength to strength."

Today's communal leaders were well aware of the problems; continuing studies placed the facts—in depth—on their desks. The unanswered question is how effective will their solutions be as the Old Community fades away and a New, smaller Community emerges?

In 1991, Nancy Rosenfeld, then Associate Executive Director of the Federation, offered this assessment on the quality of Jewish life in Montreal:

"All indications from recent attitudinal and behavioural studies conducted across the United States and Canada indicate that Montreal comes out number one in terms of several variables of Jewish quality of life. These include a lower intermarriage rate: 13% versus 30% in the United States; a higher percentage of adults having received a Jewish education: 80% in Montreal versus 70% in the United States; higher contributions to the Annual Federation Campaign: 60% of Montreal Jewish households as opposed to 45% of Jewish American households; and a staggering 71% of Montreal Jews having visited Israel compared to 31% of Jewish Americans."

Lillian Vineberg, first woman chair of the Board of Governors of Concordia University.

This high standard of Jewish quality of life, Ms. Rosenfeld added, "is an important factor to be used in measuring the future of the Quebec Jewish Community."

CARRÉ CUMMINGS SQUARE

In late 1999, one thousand community leaders gathered in the gleaming new "Gelber Conference Centre" as the new "Jewish Community Campus" was dedicated. The $30-million Centre covered six acres, sprawled over four city blocks.

Cutting the ribbon to open the newly expanded Cummings House in 1999. Participating in the ceremony are (l to r) Robert Vineberg, Marilyn Blumer, Deputy Prime Minister Herb Grey, Stanley Plotnick, Premier Lucien Bouchard, Montreal Mayor Pierre Bourque and Danyael Cantor.
Howard Kay Photograph

The investment of a tremendous sum of money in upgrading buildings in the face of so many negative factors—including a constituency declining in numbers and aging— aroused a great deal of discussion.

Marilyn Blumer, who assumed the Federation Presidency in 1999, defended the major expenditure. "That crane," she stated, looking out from her fourth floor office at the newly refurbished Cummings House, "is a symbol. For young people, it is very exciting. It's very encouraging to them."

The most important members of the community, in financial terms, agreed with Federation's assessment; they contributed 75% of the cost of the expansion over and above heavy commitments to the annual Combined Jewish Appeal, which raised a record $35-million in 1999.

Federation President Stanley Plotnick wound up his two-year Presidency, officiating at the inauguration of Cummings Square, with the three levels of Government (participating to the tune of $1.3 million each) represented by Federal Deputy Prime Minister Herb Gray; Quebec's Premier Lucien Bouchard and Montreal Mayor Pierre Bourque.

Premier Bouchard touched a chord when he told the audience:
"The Jewish Community has a rich legacy and the new campus is one of its most eloquent aspects. It is up to us now to make sure this legacy develops, that we deepen our relationship and maintain the ties we have built throughout the years."

The Premier added:
"(The project) is above all a mark of significant solidarity and co-operation that augur well for the future of your community. It provides an example for others, and proves

that, despite the difficulties with which a community may be faced, despite the skepticism that it sometimes combats, even within the community itself, it is still worth making the effort to dream, to hope and to work."

President Stanley Plotnick, before handing the baton of leadership to successor Marilyn Blumer, remarked:
"The mark of successful communities is their ability to evolve as times change and to leave a lasting legacy for future generations."

A JEW AND HIS ZEN

Poet Leonard Cohen during a 1984 visit to his native Montreal.
(Photo by Jean-François Bérubé)

Leonard Cohen (1934-) is arguably Montreal's most famous Jew. In fact, Cohen as poet, song-writer, singer and novelist, is only matched in international celebrity in Montreal by singer Céline Dion. He began writing poetry seriously at age 16 and at McGill University took a course in modern poetry from Louis Dudek, an established poet. Dudek recognized the younger man's talent and when they were walking down a corridor one day, the older man commanded Cohen to kneel before him. Then, Dudek tapped the puzzled student on his shoulder with a rolled-up magazine, dubbing him "poet".

Cohen published his first collection of poems, "Let us Compare Mythologies" in 1956 when he was 21. It was the first title in the McGill Poetry Series. That same year he recorded some of his work for an album entitled "Six Montreal Poets." The young poet's other mentor was the rumpled, more senior (a difference of 22 years) Irving Layton, who came from a poor home, while Leonard Cohen was raised in a Westmount mansion. The poet's father, Nathan B. Cohen, was general manager of a large plant manufacturing men's and boys' clothing. The plant was owned by his grandfather, Lyon Cohen (1868-1937) one of the most important leaders in the community's long history. The artist's family was living at 4028 Vendome, a middle-class area, when he was born, but moved to 599 Belmont Avenue in Westmount shortly thereafter. Leonard Cohen grew up in a world of servants and luxury.

Layton, Cohen and other poets would gather in a corner of Ben's Restaurant in downtown Montreal in an area later called "Poets' Corner," (Le Cour des Poêtes) where signed portraits of A.M. Klein, Layton, Dudek and other poets hung. Additions to the display were only permitted if "The Professor", Layton, informed the Kravitz family it was OK.

At 26, Cohen left home, although he continued to work in the family business for a time, and set up his own apartment on Pine Avenue. He moved out of the city in 1963, but he often returns. He maintains a low-rental, renovated second-floor flat on rue Saint-Dominique. But he travels widely, from Greece to California, where he shaved his head and was a monk in a Zen centre for nearly five years. Cohen shies away from the winters in Canada. "I shouldn't be in Canada at all. Winter is all wrong for me. I belong beside the Mediterranean. My ancestors made a terrible mistake. But I have to keep coming back to Montreal to renew my neurotic affiliations."

The Suzanne in Cohen's famous song-poem "Suzanne" was Suzanne Vaillancourt, wife of Quebec sculptor Armand Vallancourt. But, Cohen added: "We were never lovers, but she gave me Constant Comment tea in a small moment of magic."

Despite his exotic lifestyle, Cohen remains unambiguously Jewish. "As a Jew," said his biographer Stephen Scobie, "Cohen has always been acutely aware of the Holocaust and images of the Nazi genocide permeate and condition his work."

As he approached 70, Cohen said he felt as creative as ever but acknowledged that he worked at a "turtle's pace." "Religion is my favorite hobby," he stated, but remains a practicing Jew even though he studies other beliefs. Typically, visiting Bombay, India, he met with a Hindu guru and then visited the city's oldest synagogue, "Keneseth Eliyahoo." He finished his day attending a reception in a store promoting a new recording.

Cohen is an outspoken separatist: "I've been suggesting Montreal separate from Quebec and Canada. Montreal is a special kind of city-state. We shouldn't tie our destinies to either Quebec or Canada."

> *Ring the bells that still can ring.*
> *Forget your perfect offering.*
> *There is a crack in everything.*
> *That's how the light gets in.*
>
> Leonard Cohen
> From the poem "Anthem" 1992

CHAPTER THIRTY-SIX

THE TEMPER OF THE TIMES
Improvisation in a Troubled Period

This history is being published at a time when Montreal's Jewish Community finds itself journeying into another spell of rough weather. The community, after 240 years of residence, can boast of a splendid network of services open to the entire population. Montreal Jewry's half-dozen hospitals provide a meticulously planned complete range of general and specialized health care. Other agencies care for the aged, the troubled, the poor and the newcomer.

However, community leaders are challenged by the difficulty of maintaining its population when a number of circumstances conspire to drain away some of Montreal's brightest.

The discomfort with what is happening in Quebec does not stem, directly, from the separatist ambitions of the ruling Parti Quebecois government. Provincial governments, of all political stripes, have worked closely and productively with the community. However, from the election of a pro-independence government in 1976, there has been a steady decline in the Jewish population of the city, and that exodus continues.

Imaginative programmes to keep young people home have been introduced but have been only partially successful. Attractive career opportunities are a few hours' drive away, and young people are going where opportunity lies, where taxes are lower and the political situation is stable.

Montreal still is ranked as one of the great Jewish communities of the world and continues to offer a high quality of Jewish life.

However, with the community's population shrunk by more than a third, to 92,000 or fewer, the community will have no option in the near future other than to scale back services in response to the downward trend.

Under study in 2000 were the recommendations of a "Summit Task Force on Service Restructuring," a white paper planning

Members of FederatioNext Leadership for 18-25-year-old volunteers. (Federation/CJA photo)

more streamlined and responsive community services. The study, and Montreal Jews have monitored the community's vital signs for more than 40 years (Manny Weiner set up the Federation Planning Department in the 1960s), indicated with its references to integration and centralization that some organizations likely would be merged with similar agencies. Major shifts were underway as Canadian Jewish Congress Quebec donated its downtown headquarters, Bronfman House, to Concordia University (for its Jewish Studies Department) and two agencies serving seniors—the Golden Age Association and Jewish Support Services for the Elderly—were merged to form the Cummings Jewish Centre for Seniors.

Community leaders will have tough decisions to make as volunteers, associated for much of their adult life with some agencies, will predictably resist change. Federation leaders will have to navigate minefields of resistance to introduce tough priorities and make them stick.

With limited funds, an aging and shrinking community, and government support being reduced, significant change is inevitable.

The community predictably will fracture along a variety of fault-lines. A growing proportion of the community will be Sephardim, although new studies show the new generation is leaning towards the English-speaking portion of the community. Nevertheless, the number and influence of Anglo Jews will decline. The ulra-orthodox component will thrive numerically with its high birth rate, recruitment of new adherents and immigration from the United States, but will continue to remain detached from the organized community.

Furthermore, the community is heavily dependent on donated funds. And there are disquieting indications there will be less in the till as the years roll by. The major bankrollers of the community have been business people, but young Jews are increasingly entering the professions and their gifts are smaller. And few francophone Jews have yet matched the generosity of their anglophone co-religionists.

Much depends on the quality of leadership, lay and professional, of the future. If we can judge by the past, Montreal Jewry's strength has come from generation after generation of exceptional men and women with an extraordinary commitment to their people. The community has prominence and prestige; it is admired by other segments in the community. **And Jews will continue to be pace-setters and innovators in planning and delivering community services.**

Prime Minister Brian Mulroney, a consistently good friend of the Jewish community and of Israel, summarized his feelings about Montreal Jewry, at an Israel Bond Dinner June 5, 1985, in these words:

"Montreal would not be the world-class city it is today without the remarkable contribution of its Jewish citizens to business, to education, to medicine, to science, to law, to all the arts, to religion and politics and sports and—with unfailing generosity—to every good cause this city has known."

This is a community in love with Montreal, concerned about the rights of all its citizens, sensitive to the francophones' feeling of linguistic and cultural vulnerablity and determined to remain viable. The question, answerable only with developments in the next few critical decades, is whether the community will find itself in a setting conducive to renewal or whether the alarming downward trends on the population graph will continue.

Israel day at Cavendish Mall.

As long as the external world agrees that the Jewish people is a unique phenomenon in human history, that its course in history is separate and distinct from all other historical processes, that it is both a stranger and a sojourner at one and the same time—belonging to world civilization and yet distinct from it—that wherever it has gone—whether in agony, in prayer and hope, in tragedy or in creative activity—it has always followed its own way, involved in the paths of history but never swallowed up by them and that this is truly the essence of the Jew.

Yaacov Herzog
Former Israeli Ambassador to Canada
In Montreal, 1971.

APPENDIX 1
Montreal Jews who have received the Order of Canada:

Companions (C.C.)
Charles R. Bronfman
Samuel Bronfman
Phil Gold
Victor Charles Goldbloom

Officers (O.C.)
Leonard Cohen
Irwin Cotler
Pauline Donalda
Louis Dudek
Samuel O. Freedman
Alan B. Gold
H. Carl Goldenberg
Harold Greenberg
Saul Hayes
Naim Kattan
Sheila Golden Kussner
Phyllis B. Lambert
Lawrence Lande
Irving Layton
Frederick Hans Lowy
Ronald Melzack
Henry Mintzberg
Louis Muhlstock
Eva Sophie Prager
George J. Rosengarten
Bernard Shapiro
Samuel Solomon
Sam Steinberg
Arthur M. Vineberg
Leo Yaffe

Member (C.M.)
David J. Azrieli
Samuel Berger
Benjamin Beutel
Gordon Brown
Alexander Brott
Lotte Brott
Morley Mitchell Cohen
Maxwell Cummings
Mitzi Mildred Steinberg Dobrin
Morrie M. Gelfand
Samuel Gesser
Sheila Barshay Goldbloom
Michal Hornstein
Isin Ivanier
Paul Ivanier
Walter Joachim
Sandra Kolber
Jacob M. Lowy
Mildred B. Lande
Richard Gordon Margolese
Sarah Weintraub Paltiel
Arthur P. Pascal
Lazar Peters
Tania Plaw
Isidore C. Pollack
Dorothy Reitman
Alan Henry Rose
Barbara Seal
Ethel Stark
H. Arnold Steinberg
Abraham Stern
Max Stern
Herschel Victor
Dora Wasserman
Ben Weider

APPENDIX 2
Jewish Members of the Ordre National du Quebec

Dr. Andre Aisenstadt, grand officier - 1991
David Azrieli, chevalier - 1999
Manuel G. Batshaw, chevalier - 1995
Alexander Brott, chevalier - 1988
Lotte Brott, chevalier - 1996
Morley Mitchell Cohen, chevalier - 1995
Maxwell Cummings, grand officier - 1990
Alan B. Gold, officier - 1985
Dr. Phil Gold, officier - 1989
Dr. Victor C. Goldbloom, officier - 1991
Harold Greenberg, chevalier - 1992
Michal Hornstein, chevalier - 1993
Otto Joachim, chevalier - 1993
Walter Joachim, chevalier - 1992
Naim Kattan, chevalier - 1990
Sheila G. Kussner, officier - 1999
Phyllis Lambert, chevalier - 1985
Brenda Milner, officier - 1985
David Rome, chevalier - 1987
Phyllis Harriet Godfrey Waxman, chevalier - 1988
Léa Roback, chevalier - 2000
Ben Weider, chevalier - 2000

APPENDIX 3
The Presidents of the Federation of Jewish Philanthropies
Allied Jewish Community Services - Federation/CJA

Federation of Jewish Philanthropies

1917-1920	Maxwell Goldstein, K.C.
1921-1922	Michael Hirsch
1923-1924	Lyon Cohen
1925-1927	Albert Lesser
1928-1930	Joseph Levinson, Sr.
1931-1933	A.H. Jassby
1933-1950	Samuel Bronfman

Federation of Jewish Community Services
(name changed in 1951)

1950-1953	David Kirsch
1953-1956	Phil Garfinkle
1956-1959	Abe Bronfman
1959-1961	Edward Barkoff
1961-1963	Cecil Usher

Allied Jewish Community Services
(name changed in 1965)

1963-1965	Lavy M. Becker
1965-1967	Jacob M. Lowy
1967-1969	Gordon Brown
1969-1970	Boris G. Levine
1970-1973	Monty Berger
1973-1975	Charles R. Bronfman
1975-1977	Joe Ain
1977-1979	Hillel Becker
1979-1981	Irving J. Halperin
1981-1983	Dr. Harvey H. Sigman
1983-1985	Dodo Heppner
1985-1987	Carl Laxer
1987-1989	Peter Wolkove
1989-1991	Maxine Sigman
1991-1993	Harvey Wolfe
1993-1995	Lester Lazarus
1995-1997	Yoine Goldstein

Federation/CJA
(name changed in 1997)

1997-1999	Stanley Plotnick
2000	Marilyn Blumer

APPENDIX 4
Chairs of the Combined Jewish Appeal
(and predecessor Federation fundraising arms)

Year	General Chair	Women's Division
1917	Isaac Friedman	
1918	Maxwell Goldstein	
1919	Joseph Levinson, Sr.	
1920	Samuel Hart	
1921	Sir Mortimer B. Davis	
1922	Edgar Berliner	
1923	Michael Hirsch	
1924	Harry Rother	
1925	Leon H. Fischel	
1926	Leon H. Fischel	
1927	Michael Morris	
1928	Issacher Greenberg	
1929	Clarence Michaels	
1930	J.P. Levee	
1931	Samuel Bronfman	Saidye Bronfman
1932	H.E. Herschorn	Saidye Bronfman
1933	Philip Abbey	Saidye Bronfman
1934	A.L. Mailman	Dorothy Block
1935	Joseph Levinson Jr.	Dorothy Block
1936	Joseph Levinson Jr.	Dorothy Block
1937	S.L. Mendelson	Rosa Singer
1938	Jackson H. Marx	Rosa Singer
1939	Jack A. Klein	Rosa Singer
1940	E.E. Workman	Rhoda Leopold
1941	Allan Bronfman	Rhoda Leopold
1942	Monroe Abbey	Rhoda Leopold
1943	Philip Garfinkle	Rhoda Leopold
1944	William Gittes	Ethel Klein
1945	Edward Barkoff	Ethel Klein
1946	Bernard Marks	Ethel Klein
1947	Joseph Lefcoe	Ethel Klein
1948	Samuel Moscovitch	Celia Isaacs
1949	Walter Friedman	Lillian Jacobs
1950	Irving Riddell	Lillian Jacobs

Year	General Chair	Women's Division
1951	Dr. George J. Strean	Milly Lande
1952	Morris Moscovitch	Milly Lande
1953	J.J. Block	Pauline Coshof
1954	Ben Beutel	Pauline Coshof
1955	J.B. Becker	Ghita Roll
1956	Bernard J. Lande	Ghita Roll
1957	Samuel Samuelson	Bobby Barkoff
1958	Max Pascal	Bobby Barkoff
1959	Percy Caplan	Rhoda Cohen
1960	Arthur Pascal	Rhoda Cohen
1961	Gordon Brown	Lee Gertsman
1962	Jacob M. Lowy	Lee Gertsman
1963	Cecil Pascal	Ruth Nadler
1964	George Scott	Bess Pascal
1965	Henry Blatt	Sheila Finestone
1966	Max Feldman	Irene Lande
1967	Arthur Rudnikoff	Faiga Fisher
1968	Allan Bronfman	Rosetta Elkin
1969	Morley M. Cohen	Phyllis Waxman
1970	Thomas O. Hecht	Dodo Heppner
1971	Joe Ain	Neri Bloomfield
1972	Nathan Scott	Dr. Maxine Sigman
1973	Simon Cobrin	Nettie Weinstein
1974	Saul Tarnofsky	Kappy Flanders
1975	Norman Spector	Irma Polisuk
1976	Jack Zittrer	Leila Paperman
1977	Martin Levine	Anne Nadler
1978	Millie Lande	Marilyn Blumer
1979	Morty Brownstein	Zelda Thow
1980	Syd Glazer	Esther Landsman
1981	Bobby Mayers	Shirley Goldfarb
1982	Ike Wenger	Lois Lieff
1983	Harold Brownstein	Shirley Rabinovitch
1984	Arthur Diamond	Bernice Brownstein
1985	Boris G. Levine	Dorothy Greenbaum
1986	Marvin Corber	Rosalind Goodman
1987	Mickey Rosenthal	Joan Lazarus
1988	Jimmy Raymond	Carole Ann Levine
1989	Eddy Wiltzer	Doris Weiser
1990	Gordy Schwartz	Roslyn Wolfe

Year	General Chair	Women's Division
1991	Sol Polachek	Joyce Tanner
1992	David Vineberg	Rhoda Vineberg
1993	Joe Schaffer	Lily Ivanier
1994	Harvey Levenson	Dale Boidman
1995	Harvey Wolfe	Evie Schachter
1996	Robert Vineberg	Etty Bienstock
1997	Rabbi Sidney Shoham	Alta Levenson
1998	Gary Ulrich	Jewel Lowenstein
1999	Joel King	Harriet Muroff
2000	Steven Reitman	Alice Raby

APPENDIX 5
Federation's Professional leaders:
The Executive Directors and Executive Vice-Presidents

1922-1945	Ernest G.F. Vaz
1946-1954	Donald Hurwitz
1955-1959	Arthur Rosischan
1960-1967	Alvin Bronstein
1968-1980	Manuel G. Batshaw
1980-1985	Emanuel Weiner
1985-1992	John R. Fishel
1992-1997	Steven Drysdale
1997	Danyael Cantor

APPENDIX 6
Constituent Member Organizations
of the Montreal Jewish Federation in the year 2000

Caldwell Residences
Camp B'nai Brith
Communauté sepharade du Québec
Cummings Golden Age Centre
Hillel - Jewish Student Centre
Jewish Education Council
Jewish Family Services of the Baron de Hirsch Institute
Jewish Immigrant Aid Services
Jewish Public Library
Jewish Vocational Services
Montreal Holocaust Memorial Centre
Project Genesis
YM-YWHA Jewish Community Centres of Montreal

Constituent Member Organizations
Medical Services

Sir Mortimer B. Davis Jewish General Hospital
Maimonides Hospital and Geriatric Centre
Miriam Home
Mount Sinai Hospital
Jewish Rehabilitation Hospital
Jewish Nursing Home and Jewish Hospital of Hope

Associated Communal Organizations

Association of Jewish Day Schools
Board of Jewish Ministers
Canada-Israel Committee, Quebec
Canadian Jewish Congress, Quebec Region
Council of Jewish Federations
Jewish Community Foundation
United Israel Appeal of Canada Inc.

APPENDIX 7
Presidents of the Jewish Community Foundation

Arthur Pascal, C.M.
Mildred Lande, C.M.
Barry Clamen, F.C.A.
Sheila Zittrer
Oscar Respitz, Q.C.

L. Michael Blumenstein
Marvin Corber, F.C.A.
Gordon Schwartz
Harvey Levenson
Stanley Hyman

APPENDIX 8
Executive Directors of the Jewish Community Foundation

Harry Berger
Emanuel Weiner
Robert A. Kleinman, F.C.A.

APPENDIX 9
The Bronfman Medal is the highest Jewish community tribute and honours the memory of Samuel Bronfman

1971 Joe Ain
1972 Nathan Scott, Gordon Brown
1973 Moe Levitt
1974 Ben Beutel
1975 Ben Chazanoff, Esther Elkin
1976 Arthur Pascal, Mildred Lande
1977 Joseph Caplan, William Gittes
1978 Michael Greenblatt
1979 Boris G. Levine
1980 Edward Barkoff
1981 Charles R. Bronfman
1982 Sheila Zittrer, Morley Cohen
1983 Maxwell Cummings, Nathan Cummings
1984 Manuel G. Batshaw
1985 Hillel Becker

1986 Morton Brownstein
1987 Thomas O. Hecht
1988 Justice Irving J. Halperin
1989 Dr. Victor Goldbloom
1990 Dodo Heppner
1991 Dr. Harvey Sigman
1992 Marvin Corber
1992 The Hon. Chief Justice Alan B. Gold
1993 Martin Levine
1994 Rosetta Elkin
1995 Sheila Finestone, M.P.
1996 Phyllis Waxman
1997 Harvey Wolfe
1998 Yoine Goldstein
1999 Dr. Maxine Sigman

APPENDIX 10
Chairs - Quebec Region - Canadian Jewish Congress

Munroe Abbey 1949-1953
Lavy Becker 1953-1956
Harold Lande 1956-1962
Leon Kronitz 1962-1968
Nathan Gaisin 1968-1971
Murray Spiegel 1971-1974
Leon Teitelbaum 1974-1977
Melvin Schwartzben 1977-1978

Edward Wolkove 1978-1980
Frank Schlesinger 1980-1983
B.J. Finestone 1983-1986
Morton Bessner 1986-1989
Goldie Hershon 1989-1992
Manuel Schachter 1992-1998
Dorothy Howard 1998

APPENDIX 11
Montreal Jewish winners of the Governor General's Literary Awards

1948 - A.M. Klein: *The Rocking Chair and Other Poems* - Poetry
1956 - Adele Wiseman: *The Sacrifice* - Fiction
1959 - Irving Layton: *A Red Carpet for the Sun* - Poetry
1968 - Mordecai Richler: *Cocksure* and *Hunting Tigers Under Glass* - Fiction and Essays
1968 - Leonard Cohen: *Selected Poems 1956-1968*
1971 - Mordecai Richler: *St. Urbain's Horseman* - Fiction

APPENDIX 12
Jewish Members of Parliament

GEORGES-ÉTIENNE-CARTIER RIDING
1917 - Samuel William Jacobs - Liberal
1925 - Samuel William Jacobs - Liberal

CARTIER RIDING
1925 - Samuel William Jacobs - Liberal
1926 - Samuel William Jacobs - Liberal
1930 - Samuel William Jacobs - Liberal
1935 - Samuel William Jacobs - Liberal
1940 - Peter Bercovitch - Liberal
1943 - Fred Rose - Labour-Progressive
1945 - Fred Rose - Labour-Progressive
1949 - Maurice Hartt - Liberal
1953 - Leon David Crestohl - Liberal
1957 - Leon David Crestohl - Liberal
1958 - Leon David Crestohl - Liberal
1962 - Leon David Crestohl - Liberal
1963 - Milton L. Klein - Liberal
1965 - Milton L. Klein - Liberal

LAURIER RIDING
1979 - David Berger - Liberal
1980 - David Berger - Liberal
1984 - David Berger - Liberal

ST. HENRI-WESTMOUNT RIDING
1988 - David Berger - Liberal
1993 - David Berger - Liberal

MOUNT ROYAL RIDING
1984 - Sheila Finestone - Liberal
1988 - Sheila Finestone - Liberal
1993 - Sheila Finestone - Liberal
1999 - Irwin Cotler - Liberal

PIERREFONDS-DOLLARD RIDING
1988 - Gerry Weiner Progressive Conservative

BROSSARD-LAPRAIRIE RIDING
1997 - Jacques Saada - Liberal

LAVAL-OUEST RIDING
1997 - Raymonde Folco - Liberal

APPENDIX 13
The suburban Montreal Jewish Mayors

Côte St. Luc: Sam Moscovitch, 1963-1976
Bernard Lang, 1976-1998
Robert Libman, 1998

Dollard-des-Ormeaux: Gerald Weiner, 1982-1984

Hampstead: Irving Adessky, 1974

Town of Mount Royal: Harry Schwartz, 1994-1999

APPENDIX 14
Montreal Jewish Aldermen and City Councillors

1849 - 1852	Samuel Benjamin		1957 - 1962	Harry H. Kliger
1912 - 1918	Abraham Blumenthal		1960 - 1982	Abraham Cohen
1914 - 1931	Louis Rubenstein		1960 - 1970	Gerald N.F. Charness
1918 - 1924	Lyon W. Jacobs		1970 - 1974	Hyman Brock
1924 - 1926	Julius Levine		1970 - 1974	Sydney Wise
1926 - 1940	Joseph Schubert		1974 - 1994	Michael Feinstat
1930 - 1960	Max Seigler		1974 - 1990	Arnold Bennett
1931 - 1934	Bernard Schwartz		1978 - 1982	Manuel Feldman
1940 - 1942	Michael Rubenstein		1978 - 1982	Sid Stevens
1940 - 1957	William Victor Victor		1982 - 1986	Sam Berliner
1944 - 1960	Harry Kolber		1982 - 1994	Abe Limonchik
1947 - 1957	Louis Bass		1982 - 1998	Sam Boskey
1950 - 1954	Harry Binder		1982	Marvin Rotrand
1954 - 1978	Nat Aranoff		1986	Saulie S. Zajdel
1957 - 1960	Harry Dubrovsky		1994	Michael Applebaum
1957 - 1960	Mrs. Saul Hayes		1998	Gerry Weiner
1957 - 1960	Moe Shalinsky			
1957 - 1960	Oscar Hyman Singer			
1957 - 1962	Harold H. Cummings			

APPENDIX 15
The Jewish population of Metropolitan Montreal (by religion)

1901- 6,975	1961- 102,724
1911- 28,838	1971- 109,480
1921- 45,845	1981- 101,365
1931- 58,032	1991- 96,155
1941- 63,937	1996- 89,905*
1951- 80,829	*Jews by ethnicity

APPENDIX 16
Montreal Jewish members of the Quebec Legislative Assembly or National Assembly (Years Elected)

D'Arcy McGee:	Victor Charles Goldbloom	1966
		1970
		1973
		1976
	Herbert Marx	1979
		1981
		1985
	Robert Libman	1989
	Lawrence Bergman	1994
		1998
Montreal-Saint-Laurent:	Joseph Cohen	1927
		1931
		1935
Montreal-Saint-Louis:	Peter Bercovitch	1916
		1919
		1923
		1927
		1931
		1935
		1936
	Louis Fitch	1938
	Maurice Hartt	1939
		1944
	Harry Blank	1960
		1962
Notre-Dame-de-Grâce:	Russell Copeman	1994
		1998
Saint-Louis:	Harry Blank	1966
		1970
		1973
		1976
		1981
Trois-Rivieres	Ezekiel Hart	1807*
		1808*

* Not permitted to take his seat

BIBLIOGRAPHY

A partial list of the books, booklets and manuscripts consulted in the preparation of this history includes:

ABELLA, Irving and TROPER, Harold - *None is too Many* - 1982.
ABELLA, Irving - *Coat of Many Colours* - 1990.
ABBOTT, Elizabeth, Editor-in-chief - *Chronicle of Canada* - 1990.
ADAIR, John - *Founding Fathers* - 1982.
ARNOLD, I.N. - *Life of Benedict Arnold* - 1880.
AUSUBEL, Nathan - *Pictorial History of the Jewish People* - 1953.
AVAKUMONIC, Ivan - *The Communist Party in Canada* - 1975.

BAIN, James - *Travels and Adventures in Canada and the Indian Territories* - 1969.
BELKIN, Simon - *Through Narrow Gates* - 1966.
BELL, Andrew - *History of Canada* - 1862.
BELL, Don - *Saturday Night at the Bagel Factory* - 1972.
BELLIN, Mildred Grosberg - *The Jewish Cook Book* - 1958.
BERTON, Pierre - *The Great Depression, 1929-1939* - 1990.
BIRD, Harrison - *Attack on Quebec* - 1968.
BISHOP, Arthur - *Courage in the Air* - 1992.
BORTHWICK, Rev. J. Douglas - *History of Montreal* - 1891.
BOWMAN, Bob - *Dateline: Canada* - 1967.
BOYARSKY, Abraham and SARNA, Lazar - *Canadian Yiddish Writings* - 1976.
BRADLEY, A.G. - *Lord Dorchester* - 1911.
BREWER, Rev. E. Cobham - *Historic Notebook* - 1899.
BROTMAN, Ruth C. - *Pauline Donalda* - 1975.
BROWN, Michael - *Jew or Juif* - 1986.
BRYM, Robert J., SHAFFIR, William and WEINFELD, Morton, Editors - *The Jews in Canada* - 1993.

CAPLAN, Usher - *Like One That Dreamed; a Portrait of A.M. Klein* - 1982.
CARRIGAN, D. Owen - *Crime and Punishment in Canada, A History* - 1991.
CHARBONNEAU, Jean-Pierre - *The Canadian Connection* - 1976.
CHODOS, Robert and HAMOVITCH, Eric - *Quebec and the American Dream* - 1991.
CLARK, Gerald - *Montreal, the New Cité* - 1982.
CLARK, Gerald - *For Good Measure; The Sam Steinberg Story* - 1986.
CLEMENT, W.H.P. - *The History of the Dominion of Canada* - 1897.
CLOWES, William Laird - *The Royal Navy: A History* - 1898.
CODMAN, John - *Arnold's Expedition to Quebec* - 1902.
COHEN, Dr. Zvi, Editor - *Canadian Jewry* - 1933.
COLOMBO, John Robert - *Canadian Literary Landmarks* - 1984.
COMAY, Joan - *Who's Who in Jewish History* - 1974.
CONRON, Brandon, SYLVESTRE, Guy and KLINCK, Carl F., Co-Editors - *Canadian Writers* - 1966.
COOPER, John Irwin - *Montreal, a Brief History* - 1969.
COWAN, Dors and WEBER, Ken - *Portraits of Our People* - 1983.

DALY, Charles P. - *The Settlement of the Jews in North America* - 1893.
DALY, Patrick - *Journal of the Siege and Blockade of Quebec* - 1775-76.
DAVIES, Raymond A. - *A Printed Jewish Canadiana, 1865-1900* - 1955.
DELISLE, Esther - *The Traitor and the Jew* - 1993.
DELISLE, Esther - *Myths, Memory and Lies* - 1998.
DIMONT, Max I. - *Jews, God and History* - 1962.
DOIGE, Thomas - *Alphabetical List of Merchants, Traders and Housekeepers* - 1819.
DONALDSON, Gordon - *Battle for a Continent: Quebec 1759* - 1973.
DOUGHT, A. and PARMALEE, G.W. - *The Siege of Quebec and the Battle of the Plains of Abraham* - 1901.

DOUGLAS, Tamsin and LAZAR, Barry - *The Guide to Ethnic Montreal* - 1992.
DOUVILLE, Raymond - *Aaron Hart* - 1944.
DRAKE, Samuel G. - *The Founders of New England* - 1860.
DRIEDGER, Leo - *The Canadian Ethnic Mosaic* - 1978.
DUBRO, James - *Mob Rule* - 1985.
DUROCHER, Rene, LINTEAU, Paul-André and ROBERT, Jean-Claude - *Quebec A History* - 1867-1929.

EBAN, Abba - *Heritage: Civilization of the Jews* - 1984.
EDWARDS, Peter - *Blood Brothers* - 1990.
ELEAZOR, Daniel J. - *Community and Polity* - 1976.
ENGLISH, John - *Shadow of Heaven* - 1989.
ETZIONY, M.B. - *History of the Montreal Clinical Society* - 1963.
EVERETT, Allen S. - *Moses Hazen and the Canadian Refugees in the American Revolution* - 1976.

FEINGOLD, Henry L. - *Zion in America* - 1974.
FIGLER, Bernard - *Sam Jacobs: Member of Parliament* - 1959.
FIGLER, Bernard and ROME, David - *Hannaniah Meir Caiserman, A Biography* - 1962.
FISCHEL, Jack and PINSKER, Sanford - *Jewish American History and Culture* - 1992.
FLEMING, Thomas - *1776; Year of Illusions* - 1975.
FOGG, Walter - *One Thousand Sayings of History* - 1929.
FRANCIS, Daniel - *National Dreams; Myth, Memory and Canadian History* - 1997.
FREGAULT, Guy - *Canada: The War of the Conquest* - 1969.

GARRATY, John A. - *The Great Depression* - 1986.
GEDDES, Gary and BRUCE, Phyllis - *15 Canadian Poets* - 1970.
GIBBON, John Murray - *Canadian Mosaic* - 1938.
GIBBON, John Murray - *Our Old Montreal* - 1947.
GILBERT, Sir Martin - *Jewish History Atlas* - 1978.
GILBERT, Sir Martin - *A History of the Twentieth Century, Vol. One: 1900-1933* - 1997.
GRAHAM, Gwenthalyn - *Earth and High Heaven* - 1944.
GRANT, W.L., Editor-in-chief - *The Makers of Canada Series* - 1926.
GUBBAY, Aline - *A Street Called The Main* - 1989.

HAMILTON, Robert M. and SHIELDS, Dorothy - *Canadian Quotations and Phrases* - 1979.
HANNON, Leslie - *Redcoats and Loyalists: 1760/1815* - 1978.
HART, Arthur D. Editor - *Jews in Canada* - 1926.
HATCH, Robert McConnell - *Thrust for Canada* - 1979.
HERTZ, Rabbi Joseph Herman - *A Book of Jewish Thoughts* - 1937.
HERTZBERG, Arthur - *The Jews in America* - 1995.
HOWE, Irving and GREENBERG, Eliezer - *A Treasury of Yiddish Poetry* - 1969.
HOWE, Irving and LIBO, Ken - *How We Lived* - 1979.
HUTCHISON, Bruce - *The Struggle for the Border* - 1955.

JEFFERYS, C.W. - *The Picture Gallery of Canadian History* - 1945.
JENKINS, Kathleen - *Montreal: Island City of the St. Lawrence* - 1966.
JOHNSON, Kirk, and WIDGINGTON, David - *Montreal Up Close* - 1998.
JOSEPH, Anne - *Heritage of a Patriarch* - 1995.

KILBOURN, William - *Religion in Canada* - 1968.
KING, Joe - *Samuel Bronfman; A Biographical Tribute* - 1971.
KING, Joe - *Six Decades* - 1977.
KING, Joe - *The Batshaw Era* - 1980.
KING, Joe - *Three Score and Five* - 1982.
KING, Joe - *Mr. Profile* - 1993.
KINGSFORD, William - *The History of Canada* - 1894.
KIRKPATRICK, D.L., Editor - *Contemporary Novelists* - 1986.
KLEIN, A.M. - *The Second Scroll* - 1951.

KNIGHT, Dr. Bryan M. and ALKALLAY, Rachel - *Voices of Canadian Jews* - 1988.

LANCTOT, Gustave - *Canada and the American Revolution* - 1967.
LANGLAIS, Jacques and ROME, David - *Jews and French Quebecers* - 1991.
LAPPIN, Ben - *The Redeemed Children* - 1963.
LEACOCK, Stephen - *Montreal* - 1942.
LEGGET, Robert F. - *Railroads of Canada* - 1973.
LEWIS, William A. - *The Blue Book of Canadian Business* - 1997.
LIGHTBALL, W.D. - *Montreal after 250 Years* - 1892.
LINDSAY, J.O., Editor - *The New Cambridge Modern History* - 1957.
LONN, George - *Canadian Profiles* - 1965.
LOW, Charles Rathbone - *Her Majesty's Navy* - 1888.
LOWER, Arthur R.M. - *Canadians in the Making* - 1958.
LYMAN, Darryl - *Great Jewish Families* - 1997.

MARCUS, Jacob R. - *Early American Jewry* - 1951.
MARKS, Gil - *The World of Jewish Cooking* - 1996.
MARRUS, Michael R. - *Mr. Sam; the Life and Times of Samuel Bronfman* - 1991.
MARTZ, Fradie - *Open Your Hearts* - 1996.
MCNAUGHT, Kenneth - *The Pelican History of Canada* - 1976.
MIKA, Nick and Helma - *Railways of Canada* - 1978.
MIQULON, Dale - *Society and Conquest: Social Change in French Canada, 1700-1850* - 1977.
MORGAN, Edmund S. - *Puritan Family* - 1944.
MORGAN, Henry J. - *Sketches of Celebrated Canadians* - 1862.

NATHAN, Joan - *Jewish Cooking in America* - 1994.
NEWMAN, Peter C. - *Titans* - 1998.
NOLAN, Brian - *King's War* - 1988.

ORKIN, Sarah F. - *Roots and Recollections* - 1995.

PALMER, Dave Richard and STRYKER, James W. - *Early American Wars and Military Institutions* - 1986.
PARIS, Erna - *Jews. An Account of their experience in Canada* - 1985.
PARKER, Gilbert and BRYAN, Claude G. - *Old Quebec* - 1904.
PATERSON, T.W. - *Canadian Battles and Massacres* - 1977.
PERCIVAL, W.P. - *The Lure of Montreal* - 1964.
PREVOST, Robert - *Montreal, A History* - 1993.

RABINOWICZ, Harry M. - *Hasidism; the Movement and Its Masters* - 1988.
RADDALL, Thomas H. - *The Path of Destiny* - 1957.
RANDALL, William Stere - *Benedict Arnold - Patriot and Traitor* - 1990.
REZNICK, Samuel - *Unrecognized Patriots. The Jews in the American Revolution* - 1975.
RHINEWINE, A. - *Looking Back A Century* - 1932.
RICHARDSON, Bill - *Scorned and Beloved* - 1997.
RISCHIN, Moses - *The Jews of North America* - 1987.
ROBERTS, Kenneth - *March to Quebec* - 1938.
ROBINSON, Ira and BUTOVSKY, Mervin - *Renewing Our Days* - 1995.
ROGERS, Francis M. - *Americans of Portuguese Descent* - 1974.
ROME, David - *On Our Forerunners - At Work* - 1978.
ROSEN, Claudia - *The Book of Jewish Food* - 1996.
ROSENBERG, Louis - *Chronology of Canadian Jewish History* - 1959.
ROSTEN, Leo - *Hooray for Yiddish* - 1982.

SACHER, Howard M. - *A History of the Jews of America* - 1992.
SACK, Benjamin G. - *History of the Jews in Canada* - 1965.
SACK, B.G. - *Canadan Jews - Early in This Century* - 1975.
SHARP, Rosalie; ABELLA, Irving and GOODMAN, Edwin - *Growing Up Jewish* - 1997.

SHERMAN, C. Bezalel - *The Jew Within American Society* - 1960.
SINCLAIR, Gerri and WOLFE, Morris - *The Spice Box* - 1981.
SKELTON, Oscar D. - *The Railway Builders* - 1916.
SLOAN, Irving J. - *Jews in America; 1621-1970* - 1971.
SMITH, H. Murray - *Footprints in Time* - 1962.
SMITH, Janet Adam - *John Buchan, A Biography* - 1965.
SMITH, Donald E., Editor-in-Chief - *The New Larned History* - 1894.
SMITH, Justin H. - *Arnold's March from Cambridge to Quebec* - 1903.
SMITH, Justin H. - *Our Struggle for a 14th Colony* - 1907.
SMITH, Mackay L. - *Jews of Montreal and their Judaisms* - 1997.
SMITH, William - *History of Canada* - 1815.
SMOLLETT, T. - *The History of England* - 1823.
STANLEY, George F. - *New France; The Last Phase, 1744-1760* - 1967.
STANLEY, G.F.G. - *Canada Invaded 1775-1776* - 1973.

TRUDEL, Marcel - *La Revolution Américaine* - 1949.
TULCHINSKY, Gerald - *Branching Out* - 1998.
TZUK, Yogev - *History of the Jews in Canada* - 1993.

WADE, Mason - *The French Canadians 1760-1967* - 1975.
WAXMAN, Chaim I. - *America's Jews in Transition* - 1983.
WEINFELD, M, SHAFFIR, W., and COTLER, I. - *The Canadian Jewish Mosaic* - 1981.
WEINTRAUB, William - *City Unique* - 1996.
WHITTON, F.E. - *Wolfe and North America* - 1929.
WILLCOX, William B., Editor - *The Papers of Benjamin Franklin* - 1775-1776.
WILLIAMS, Basil - *The Life of William Pitt* - 1914.
WILLIAMS, Henry Smith - *The Historian's History of the World* - 1908.
WINBOLT, S.E. - *American Independence and the French Revolution* - 1912.
WINSOR, Justin - *History of America* - 1887.
WOOD, William, Editor-in-chief - *The Storied Province of Quebec* - 1932.
WOODSWORTH, J.S. - *Strangers Within Our Gates* - 1909.
WRIGHT, Robert - *The Life of General James Wolfe* - 1864.
WRONG, George M. - *Canada and the American Revolution* - 1924.

Dictionaries, Directories, Encyclopediae and Studies

Calvert, Brigadier Michael - *A Dictionary of Battles 1715-1815* - 1979.
Canadian Anecdotes, edited by Douglas Fetherling - 1988.
The Canadian Encyclopedia - James H. Marsh, Editor-in-chief - 1999.
Canadian Global Almanac 2000 - Susan Girvan, Editor-in-chief.
Canadian Jewish Congress - *Canadian Jews in World War Two* - 1947-48.
Canadian Jewish Congress Archives - *Our Forerunners at Work* - compiled by David Rome.
Canadian Jewish Congress Archives - *On the Early Harts* - compiled by David Rome.
Canadian Parliamentary Anecdotes, edited by Marc Bosc - 1988.
Canadian Parliamentary Guide - Kathryn O'Handley and Caroline Sunderland, Editors - 1997.
Canadian Political Anecdotes, Edited by Jack McLeod - 1988.
Colombo, John Robert - *The Dictionary of Canadian Quotations* - 1991.
Concise Dictionary of Biography - edited by Sir Leslie Stephen and Sir Sidney Lee - 1965.
Dictionary of Canadian Biography - Frances G. Halpenny, General Editor - all volumes to 1900.
Encyclopedia Americana - 1972.
Encyclopedia Canadiana - 1963.
Encyclopedia of Canada - 1936.
Encyclopedia of the American Revolution by Mark Mayo Boatner III - 1966.
Encyclopédie du Québec - Louis Landry - 1973.
Federation/CJA - *Jewish Populations in Geographic Areas* - 1995.
Garraty, John A. and Carnes, Mark C., General Editors - *American National Biography* - 1999.

Gottesman Eli - *Who's Who in Canadian Jewry* - 1965.
Harbottle, Thomas Benfield - *Dictionary of Battles* - 1904.
The Hutchison Encyclopedia 1995, Michael Upshall, Editorial Director.
The International Directory of Company Histories, edited by Lisa Mirabile - 1990.
The Jewish Information Source Book, edited by Ronald H. Isaacs - 1972.
Jewish Women in America, edited by Paula E. Hyman and Deborah Dash Moore - 1997.
Jonson, Allen and Malone, Dumas - *Dictionary of American Biography* - 1960.
Lee, Sidney - *Dictionary of National Biography* - 1897.
Magocsi, Paul Robert, Editor - *Encyclopedia of Canada's Peoples* - 1999.
Mirror Guide to Montreal, edited by Annarosa Sabbadini - 1994.
The Montreal Jewish Directory, Editor Harriet Safran, 2000.
The New Dictionary of Thoughts, compiled by Tryon Edwards - 1961.
Notes on The Canadian Family Tree - Federal Department of Citizenship and Immigration - 1960.
The Northclffe Collection - *Canada Public Archives* - 1926.
Prominent People of the Province of Quebec - the Biographical Society of Canada - 1923-1924.
Quebec Directory for 1851.
Rare and Unusual Canadiana - *Lawrence Lande Foundation* - 1971.
Roberts, Sir Charles G.D. and Tunnell, Arthur L. - *The Canadian Who's Who* - 1936-37.
Segal, Igal, Editor-in-chief - *Who's Who in World Jewry* - 1981.
Seidel, Judith - *The Development and Social Adjustment of the Jewish Community in Montreal* - 1936.
Shahar, Charles - *The Sephardic Community* - 1995.
Shahar, Charles - *A Survey of Jewish Life in Montreal* - 1996.
Shahar, Charles - *Sepharade 2000* - 2000.
Shahar, Charles; Weinfeld, Morton and Schnoor, Randal F. - *Survey of the Hassidic and Ultra-Orthodox, Outremont* - 1997.
Shahar, Charles and Schnoor, Randal F. - *A Survey of Jewish Life in Montreal, Part II* - 1997.
Seidel, Judith - *The Development and Social Adjustment of the Jewish Community in Montreal* - 1939.
Shamir, Ilana and Shavit, Shlomo - *Encyclopedia of Jewish History* - 1986.
The Standard Jewish Encyclopedia, Cecil Roth, Editor-in-chief - 1966.
Stephen, Leslie and Lee, Sidney - *Dictionary of National Biography* - 1897.
Sourcebook of Canadian History - 1959.
Summers, Jack L. and Chartrand, Rene - *Military Uniforms in Canada 1665-1970* - 1984.
Thenstrom, Stephan - *Harvard Encyclopedia of American Ethnic Groups* - 1832.
The Universal Jewish Encyclopedia, Louis Rittenberg, Executive Editor - 1942.
University of Victoria - *Creative Canada* - 1972.
Wallace, W. Stewart - *The MacMillan Dictionary of Canadian Biography* - 1945 and 1978 editions.
Wigoder, Geoffrey - *Dictionary of Jewish Biography* - 1991.
Wigoder, Geoffrey - *New Encyclopedia of Zionism and Israel* - 1994.

Periodicals consulted include The Beaver, Canadian Jewish News, Canadian History Review, Canadian Jewish Times, The Suburban, The Gazette, The Globe and Mail, Montreal Star, Modern Judaism, The National Post, New York Times, Saturday Night, Canadian News Facts, The Canadian Annual Review of Politics and Public Affairs, The Jerusalem Post, History Today, The Jewish Journal of Sociology, Horizon Canada, Currents, Maclean's magazine, Outlook and the Journal of Canadian Studies.

INDEX

Joe King; A Biography

Joe King is a Toronto-born journalist and broadcaster. He began his career with The Canadian Press News Agency and ultimately served as Senior News Editor of Broadcast News, its radio division.

He served in the Royal Canadian Air Force in World War II, attaining the rank of pilot officer.

After the war, he pioneered in television news and public affairs broadcasting and in 1960 participated in the founding of CJCH-TV, the CTV television station in Halifax, N.S. He was named Vice-President, News and Public Affairs. His major awards earned in Halifax included the Liberty Television News Documentary Award (for a documentary on Adolf Eichman) and a Gold "D" from Dalhousie University.

In 1966, King began working with CFCF-TV, CFCF-Radio and CFQR-FM in news and public affairs, winning two radio documentary awards from the Radio and Television News Directors Association (for "Cry Of A Child" and "Vimy Ridge").

During this period, he journeyed to the Middle East to survey Israel in the immediate aftermath of the Six Day War (he was sniped at in occupied Syrian terrain), the first of nineteen visits to that region.

In 1969, he joined the staff of the Montreal Jewish Federation as Director of Communications, a position he held for 20 years.

King retired in 1989 but shortly thereafter became Executive Director of Canadian Friends of Tel Aviv University, for six years.

In 1998, he became involved in the formation of the Montreal Jewish Publication Society and is executive-secretary of that body.

King has been active in the arts throughout his adult life and is President-Emeritus of the Montreal Print Collectors Society.

He is married, to Shandle Lipkus, and they have two sons, one daughter, and four grandchildren.

Selected publications and Videos by Joe King bearing on the history of the Montreal Jewish Community:

- A Biographical Tribute to Samuel Bronfman, 1971.

- "Six Decades", the first 60 years of the Montreal Federation, 1977.

- "Six Decades", television documentary produced in cooperation with CFCF-TV, 1977.

- "The Batshaw Era", the distinguished professional leadership of the Community by Manuel G. Batshaw, 1978.

- "Three Score and Five", printed community history, 1982.

- "The First Two Centuries", a history of Montreal Jewry produced in cooperation with CBC-TV, 1982.

- "Three Score and Ten", an updated Federation history, 1987.

- "The First 75 Years", a history of the Jewish People's and Peretz Schools, produced in printed form and as a documentary. 1988.

- "Hillel 1944-1989, A History", produced in print form and as a documentary. 1989

Selected other productions by Joe King:

- "Cosmonaut and Capitalist", a television documentary with the first man in space, Yuri Gagarin. 1962.

- "After The Storm." a large screen documentary on Israel after the Six Day War 1967.

- "Destiny Canada", a 50-program series on Canada's future, produced in cooperation with McGill University and broadcast over CFQR-FM. 1970.

- "Background To Conflict," a booklet on the facts behind the continuing confrontation in the Mideast, 1975.

- "The Right To Freedom," an audio and audiovisual presentation on the suppression of freedom in the Soviet Union, premiered at the Universite de Montreal, 1977.

- "Breakdown", a 62-program series on social distress in Montreal, brodcast over CFQR-FM, Montreal, 1980-81.

- "Hunt and Kill", a 30-minute television documentary on NATO submarine strategies, broadcast over the CTV network. 1982.